PENGUIN BOOKS

THE EASTERN FRONT 1914–1917

Norman Stone is Professor of International Relations at Bilkent University, Ankara. For the period 1984–97 he was Professor of Modern History at the University of Oxford. Professor Stone's numerous publications include *Europe Transformed 1878–1919* (1983), *The Other Russia* (1990) and *The Russian Chronicles* (1990).

The Eastern Front 1914–1917 won the Wolfson Prize for History in 1976.

NORMAN STONE

THE EASTERN FRONT 1914–1917

PENGUIN BOOKS

PENGUIN BOOKS

Published by the Penguin Group
Penguin Books Ltd, 27 Wrights Lane, London w8 5TZ, England
Penguin Putnam Inc., 375 Hudson Street, New York, New York 10014, USA
Penguin Books Australia Ltd, Ringwood, Victoria, Australia
Penguin Books Canada Ltd, 10 Alcorn Avenue, Toronto, Ontario, Canada M4V 3B2
Penguin Books India (P) Ltd, 11, Community Centre, Panchsheel Park, New Delhi – 110 017, India
Penguin Books (NZ) Ltd, Private Bag 102902, NSMC, Auckland, New Zealand
Penguin Books (South Africa) (Pty) Ltd, 5 Watkins Street, Denver Ext 4, Johannesburg 2094, South Africa

Penguin Books Ltd, Registered Offices: Harmondsworth, Middlesex, England

First published by Hodder & Stoughton 1975
Published in Penguin Books 1998
5

Copyright © Norman Stone, 1975
Introduction to the Penguin edition copyright © Norman Stone, 1998
All rights reserved

Printed in Great Britain by Antony Rowe Ltd, Chippenham, Wiltshire

For J. H. Plumb

Contents

Maps

The maps are based on those reproduced in *The History of the First World War* published by Purnell for B.P.C. Publishing Ltd.

Author's Note

A 'common-sense' system of transliteration from Cyrillic script has been used throughout. I have used the English 'y' as a consonant, and left 'i' to cover both Russian vowels approximating to it. I have omitted apostrophes signifying soft or hard signs. 'Kh' and 'zh' signify, as usual, 'ch' in 'loch' and 'j' in 'jardin'.

I have tried to be consistent as regards place-names that have changed several times in the course of this century, but it is difficult. My own inclination is to call every town by its modern name, but sometimes this becomes strikingly anachronistic (e.g. 'Olsztyn' for 'Allenstein' in East Prussia) and I have sometimes made concessions from my own rule.

Introduction to the Penguin Edition

When it came out in 1975, this book was something of a pioneer. In the West, there had been, in the sixties, a huge wave of interest in the First World War (my own interest in it was sparked off partly when I found Churchill's *World Crisis* in the school library, and particularly when, in 1958, I read Leon Wolff's *In Flanders Fields*). But from the Soviet Union, not much came out. Every belligerent country, including shattered Turkey, produced lengthy official histories and the archives were remarkably well-ordered to produce them. However, there was nothing comparable from the Soviet Union, the military archives of which remained, mainly, sealed. Of course the whole subject was vast and very difficult—even the Germans had not completed their official history by the end of the Second World War—and it cannot have helped that some qualified military historians were purged by Stalin in the thirties. Whatever you said about the Tsarist Russian army might give you trouble. If you wrote in a positive, patriotic way about it, you might offend against the Communist orthodoxy, by which everything Tsarist was condemned. If, on the other hand, you concentrated on the negative side, you could offend against the nationalist line which emerged with Stalin and which flourished under Brezhnev. Even the obvious sources were quite difficult to obtain; I was told, some years later, that *The Eastern Front* was listed in an East German catalogue, but could not be read without permission. Alexandr Solzhenitsyn had great difficulty in assembling various books and articles for the enormous, semi-demi-fictional account of the First World War and the Revolution, *The Red Wheel*, that he was planning, because the subject was still, in the seventies, taboo. Nowadays, we might of course expect a proper history of the First World War from Russia's new historians, but in present circumstances they all have other things to do. So, for the moment, my own book is still a filler of the gap.

When I wrote it, in the later sixties and early seventies, I could not have obtained access to Russian archives. However, there was a great deal in the West. The Hoover Institution in Stanford, California, collected documents from the Russian emigration; its founder, the later President Hoover, had been in Russia after the Civil War to organize famine-relief and he collected documents in return for food—some of the documents very revealing indeed. In Paris, the *Bibliothèque de documentation internationale contemporaine* had a vast amount, and at home in England I found a remarkable number of books, whether in Cambridge University Library, where Professor Elizabeth Hill had built up astonishing reserves, or the British Museum and that enduringly splendid institution, the Imperial War Museum. I could also use the records of British and French observers, some of whom wrote with great talent, and of course there were the archives of the Austro-Hungarian army, in Vienna, where I had spent three years. These archives survived remarkably well, and like other British historians, I had been given a privileged run of them by a very friendly and helpful staff. The German side of things could be studied from printed sources only, although, as it turns out, quite a number of the documents on which the German official history was to be based were taken to Moscow after capture in 1945. I shall be interested to see whether my accounts of some of the battles—sometimes 'hunches'—stand up. I was flattered to discover that the most up-to-date account on the side of the Central Powers, Manfred Rauchensteiner's *Der Tod des Doppeladlers* (1993), bears out what I said about the calamitous miscalculations made over mobilization in 1914.

As *The Eastern Front* moved on, it became much more of a Russian than an Austro-Hungarian or German book. Its focus had originally been on the battlefields, and reconstructing events there was laborious enough, but quite quickly I became interested in the functioning of the army as an institution, and especially in the Russian economy at war. In the sixties, historians were interested in 'modernization and so, disastrously, were English and Scottish local authorities and architects, who tore apart our Victorian cities in order to create what they hoped would be little Chicagos. The American, Walt Rostow, had produced the fashionable optimistic American book of the decade when he published his book about industrial 'take-off' saying that places became modern when they were able to save ten per cent of their national incomes, and as an undergraduate at Gonville and Caius College, Cambridge, taught by the legendary Neil McKendrick, I had become aware of the importance of industrial revolutions in general. There was a Russian equivalent, of a lurid kind.

Moving into the history of Russia, I had inevitably become involved

in the business of Stalin's alleged modernization of a backward country. After all, he defeated the Germans, whereas the last Tsar had been
defeated by them. In the early days of working on *The Eastern Front*, I
had come under the influence of E. H. Carr, the historian of the
Bolshevik Revolution, and he had no time at all for Tsarist Russia, a
backward place, he said, filled with feckless peasants. Stalin imposed
Five Year Plans, dragooned the peasants into industry, starving or
imprisoning millions of them in the process. 'Was Stalin necessary?'
was a question that, in those days, historians seriously asked. Carr
clearly thought so.

How backward was Tsarist Russia in 1914? There could be no
better test of this than the First World War itself—as Orwell said, war
is a try-your-strength machine, and only muscles get the jack-pot.
Early on, on the basis of Tsarist generals' memoirs, or even just of
Stalinist economic histories, I had picked up the standard version, that
the Russian economy was too feeble to produce war-material in
adequate quantities. This view of things was quite widespread, and it
had been taken up by both Lloyd George and Churchill, who wanted
to divert British troops from the charnel-house of the western front
into more promising campaigns elsewhere to help the Russians.

In fact, when I reached the Hoover Institution, I discovered
accounts there of what had really happened as to the supply of war-
material, and it was not what I had expected at all. The wherewithal
for a proper war-economy was in fact there, and, by September 1915,
war-goods were being produced in quantities that were at least
respectable. In the mean time, there had been what I now recognize
as a very Russian story—of mistrust, of the wrong people in charge, of
bizarre rivalries, of paralyzing secretiveness. Especially, the bureaucrats
did not trust the industrialists, and supposed that, given state money,
they would just make a mess of things and levant with the proceeds.
Then, when matters did improve, artillerists did not co-operate with
each other or with the infantry. Of course, in terms of the figures for
the condition of the Russian economy in 1914, we have known, now,
for generations that, in the years before 1914, it was booming. That,
in my opinion, was really what made the German government ready
for war in 1914: if it had waited until 1917, then Russia would indeed
have been too strong to be overthrown by a German army that also
had France to deal with. Converting the new industrial strength into
a war-effort was very difficult, but the industrial strength was there.
E. H. Carr did not like this, and I escaped from his influence, which
was not in any event a benign one.

The 'backwardness' had less to do with economic power than with its utilization, and, here, the nature of the Tsarist military organization was of the greatest importance. William Fuller's *Civil-Military Conflict in Imperial Russia 1881–1914* (Princeton 1985) covers this in much greater detail than I could command, and bears out much of what my 'hunch' told me.

My account of the Russian shell-crisis seems to be on the right lines, but in an important matter I may have erred. Soviet historians were a great deal more prolific on economic and social matters than on military ones, and they were no friends to the private industrialists who were engaged on war-work. Until we have studies properly based on the archives of the War Ministry, or, if they survive, those of the factories themselves, we shall not know how effective private producers were. My own account needs correction through two books—Lewis H. Siegelbaum's *The Politics of Industrial Mobilization in Russia 1914–1917. A Study of the War-Industries Committees* (London 1983) and Peter Gatrell's *Tsarist Russian Economy 1851–1917* (London 1986) which is partly based on his own studies of archives in the Soviet Union on precisely this subject. The Institute of History in Moscow also published a four-volume record of the *Osoboye Coveshchaniye po oborone gosudarstva 1915–1918 gg.* (Moscow 1975–1980) and the British dimension of the whole story is ably described in Keith Neilson's *Strategy and Supply* (London, 1984).

By the end of 1916, the military events of the Eastern Front had petered out, and I should have needed a whole new book to do justice to the Revolution that followed. My final chapter was therefore just an essay on 1917, where I suggested that 'modernization' was going on, under war-time disguise, and that our old friend, the Russian peasant, had got in the way, preventing adequate supplies of food from reaching the cities and thereby provoking revolution. Part of this is fair enough, I think: it is right to call attention to inflation as a factor in the Revolution, and it is right to show how the Tsarist government lost control of its finances. However, it now seems clear that the Russian peasantry were not at all as backward as legend has it. On this, there are some important books. Heinz-Dietrich Löwe's *Die Lage der Bauern in Russland* (Munich 1983) shows that, in point of fact, they ate rather better than the West German population of 1952, and Lars T. Lih's *Bread and Authority in Russia 1914–1921* (Berkeley, California 1990) has a far more knowledgeable story than my own, which was still quite heavily based on the prejudices of E. H. Carr, not a respecter of peasants. Under the benign influence of Teodor Shanin, whose *Awkward Class*, about the peasants, had come out in 1972, I had begun to understand something of Russian agriculture, but the tendency to blame 'the peasants' nevertheless makes too much of a showing in this book. Solzhenitsyn in *The Red Wheel* approaches the problem of food-shortages in a quite different way, showing how they generated anti-Tsarist myths and legendry. Saint Petersburg faced far, far worse shortages in 1942, but never rebelled. Why?

There is one great omission in this book, which, I hope, later generations will make good: the common soldier. Apart from an aside or two, this was not a subject with which I felt at all familiar. Nowadays, partly because of the great wave of sixties interest in the First World War, the study of soldiers' letters, and of military morale in general, is rather well-advanced, and my old Cambridge colleague, Hew Strachan, is shortly to produce a two-volume history of the First World War which promises to deal with this question at serious length. How did the ordinary soldiers and the junior officers stand the horrors of the Western or Italian fronts? How did their Russian equivalents respond to those of the Eastern front, and what exactly occurred in the summer and autumn of 1917, when the force, somehow, just seized up? Orlando Figes's *A People's Tragedy* (1997) and Richard Pipes's *Russian Revolution* (1990) have dealt with this, in different ways, but until we have a proper investigation of the archives, assuming that they still have the material, we cannot be sure as to what happened. Armies do not usually mutiny, and junior officers usually have close relations with their men, as was shown when, in defeat, the German army had to evacuate France and Belgium. Why, and in what sense, the Russian army mutinied as it did in 1917 is still something of a mystery. I hope that, at some stage, we are going to have a proper, authoritative history of it all from Moscow.

I should like to record some debts of gratitude. Michael Sissons gave me an enormous boost, both when he suggested this book thirty-three years ago, when I was still a student, and put up with its decade-long gestation. I was delighted to take up the offer, from him and from Simon Winder, of Penguin, that we should reissue the book. I have also had much support from Dr Ali Dogramaci, the Rector of Bilkent University at Ankara, who invited me to help establish a Turkish–Russian Institute, for which we have high hopes. I should like to thank Bahadir Koc, a virtuoso of the Internet, for finding out new publications, and to Mr Alkan Kizildel, an amateur military historian of that old and admirable school, for identifying questionable assertions as to weaponry, and misprints which had escaped my own scrutiny.

Bilkent University, Ankara
April 1997

Introduction

Winston Churchill wrote a book about the eastern front of the First World War. He dedicated it to the Tsarist army, and titled it 'The Unknown War'. His book is a brilliant piece of narrative, bringing out the drama of this front to the full. But the events of this front are still 'unknown', for this part of the First World War received much less coverage in English or French than even the Balkan or Mesopotamian fronts. It did receive coverage in German, but very often these works present a purely German view of the Russo-German war, and the bias has been transferred to well-known English works, such as those of Liddell Hart. Churchill's own book was based on a very narrow range of sources, most of them German, even though his 'feel' for the subject allowed him to make much more of these sources than a lesser writer would have done. There has been little in western languages since then, although Soviet and émigré writers produced a substantial number of studies of the front that might have permitted more authoritative western-language presentation of the battles of this front. There is no official Soviet history of the army's performance in the First World War; and until there is, much that happened must remain unclear. None the less, it is possible to arrive at a basic narrative of events, and to make some effort at explaining them, especially when comparison can be made of the various Russian, German and Austro-Hungarian sources.

My first aim, in writing this book, has therefore been a relatively straight-forward one: to fill a gap in the military history of the First World War. It was often said that Germany could have won the war, if she had pursued a full-scale offensive against Russia in 1915, as Ludendorff wanted, instead of the partial schemes that Falkenhayn preferred. But I do not believe that Ludendorff's bold schemes for eliminating Russia in 1915 would have worked; and indeed, the effects of the various episodes in Ludendorff's personal *Drang nach Osten*—Tannenberg, the Winter Battle in Masuria, Kovno—seem to me to have been over-rated. On the contrary, it was Falkenhayn's policy of limit, attrition that probably offered the Germans a better way forward, if he had been allowed to stick to it. Ludendorff would merely have led them into yet more square miles of marsh and steppe, for it was not at all as easy to overthrow the Russian army as Ludendorff maintained. Deaths, for instance, formed a higher percentage of German casualties in the east than in the west,* until the end of 1916; and until the turn of 1916–17, the Russian army had even captured a greater number of German prisoners (and of course a very much greater number of prisoners altogether, in view of the Austro-Hungarian army's weakness) than the British and French combined. The idea that Germany had limitless possibilities in the east was a legend, however powerful its influence on Nazi thinking thereafter.

At the same time, there was an equally powerful legend on the allies' side: that Russia, had she received proper help from her western allies, could have contributed decisively to an overthrow of the German Empire quite early in the war. Lloyd George wrote forcefully in maintenance of this view; 'half the shells and one-fifth the guns . . . wasted' in the great western offensives could, he alleged, have contributed decisively to Russia's performance. I am not so sure. In 1915, the Russian army certainly suffered from material shortages, but the allies could hardly make them up, because they had material shortages of their own; and in any case, to assume that guns and shell would have made any greater difference to the east than they did to the west was to mistake the importance of mere quantity. My study of the engagements of 1915 showed that shell-shortage was very often used as an excuse for blundering and disorganisation that were much more important, in causing Russia's defeats of that year, than mere shortage of material. In any case, by 1916, the Russian's own output of war-goods had reached generally satisfactory dimensions. On 1st January 1917, Russian superiority on the eastern front was in some ways comparable with the western Powers' superiority eighteen months later in France. It would have taken much more than despatch of guns and shell to the eastern front to cause the defeat of Germany there.

This was a discovery that came as a surprise to me, since I had always assumed, following Golovin and others, that the Russian army had lost battles because of crippling material shortages; and I had gone on, as other writers have done, to assume that this was an inevitable consequence of the economic backwardness of the Tsarist State. But when I consulted the figures for Russia's output of war-goods, I soon found that the short-

---

* Reichskriegsministerium: *Sanitätsbericht über das Deutsche Heer im Weltkrieg* vol. 2 (Berlin 1935) p. 2 and 'Tafel' 5.

ages had been exaggerated, and sometimes invented after the event. It is not really accurate to say, for instance, that the Russian army was not ready for war, and that it plunged in before it was ready, in order to save the French. At the time, commanders asserted they were ready even four days before the army crossed the German border. But what they understood as readiness, was of course woefully at odds with war-time reality. They had had no idea what to expect. But 'unreadiness' was discovered subsequent to the battles, and was at bottom a hard-luck story. In 1914–1915, lack of war-goods was not a comment on Russia's economic backwardness, but rather on the slowness with which her régime reacted to the needs of war. The politicians and the generals used shell-shortage as a 'political' football against the government and the war ministry, and their tales of shell-shortage were therefore treated with scepticism; the artillerymen wrote off infantrymen as stupid and alarmist; and, when the government did decide to do anything, it turned to foreign producers who failed to deliver on time. But once the government made up its quarrel with industrialists, the country proved able to produce war-goods in fair quantity. By 1916, it could produce aircraft, guns, gas-masks, hand-grenades, wireless-sets and the rest—if not in immense quantities, as in the Second World War, at least in quantities sufficient to win the war in the east if other things had been equal. By September 1916, for instance, Russia could produce 4,500,000 shells per month. This compares with German output of seven million, Austro-Hungarian of one million; and since the bulk of this quantity went elsewhere—to the western or Italian fronts—there was not much truth in the assertion that Russia lost the war because of crippling material weaknesses.

It was the country's inability to make use of its economic weight that began to interest me, rather than the backwardness of which many writers had spoken. I began to examine the army's structure, and again discovered some surprises. The army, as it grew before 1914, split, roughly between a patrician wing, of which Grand Duke Nicholas, Inspector-General of Cavalry, and commander-in-chief in wartime, was the head, and a praetorian one, dominated by the war minister Sukhomlinov. I had always read accounts that made out Sukhomlinov to be bungling, corrupt: he was detested by 'liberal' Russia on both counts, and was imprisoned after the March Revolution. But, much to my surprise, the evidence as I saw it showed that Sukhomlinov, and not his enemies, was the real reformer. His enemies, though eventually coming to power in the war-years, were much less 'technocratic' in their approach than they claimed to be. They resisted essential reforms before 1914 and their old-fashioned attitudes did much to reduce the army's effectiveness in the war-years. No system of tactics emerged to combat the shell-shortage of 1915; and the disasters of that year also owed much to the commanders' wholly mistaken belief in fortresses. Moreover, the division of the army between patricians and praetorians even affected strategy, for it added a dimension to the usual rivalries and battles of competence that prevented emergence of coherent plans, with corresponding movement of reserves. The structure of the army, as shown in tactics, conscription, transport-organisation, strategy, relationship of infantry to artillery and the rest, all of which I have tried to investigate, displayed that the country's great weak point was not, properly-speaking, economic, but more administrative. I have tried to account for this, as far as evidence allows, at least in the armed forces' case.

This book proved difficult to conclude. The fighting stopped in January 1917, except for a few episodes; and yet it was in 1917 that all of the problems that I had seen came to a head. To narrate the year 1917 would have made this book intolerably long, and I should have gone far beyond my original strategic brief. What particularly interested me was why the country, the war-economy of which was successful as never before, should have gone through vast social change even though, with the German enemy at the gates, there was ostensibly every argument for retaining an unbroken front at home, at least for the duration. My last chapter is an effort to explain this. I have seen the First World War, not as the vast run-down of most accounts, but as a crisis of growth: a modernisation crisis in thin disguise. It was much more successful than is generally allowed. It failed, I think, against the bottle-neck of peasant agriculture. Inflation had accompanied the country's economic growth in the First World War; and it was inflation that, in the end, caused Russia's food-suppliers to withhold their produce at a critical time. A book that began with battle-fields thus ends with discussion of war-economy, inflation, revolution in the towns and the countryside. This was the pattern of the First World War itself, and I have tried to record its course in eastern Europe as best I can.

In the course of writing this book, I have had a great deal of support and encouragement. I should particularly like to thank the staffs of the *Bibliothèque de documentation internationale contemporaine* in Paris, and of the Hoover Institution in Stanford, California, where the bulk of my work on Russia was done. The *Kriegsarchiv* in Vienna has also been, for many years, a second home for me, and I am always grateful, particularly to Dr. Kurt Peball, Herr Leopold Moser and Frau Professor Christina von Fabrizii, to whose interest and support I owe so much. Academic colleagues have given me stimulation and encouragement. Professors Marc Ferro and Teodor Shanin have taught me a dimension of Russian history that I should not have found by myself: they bear some of the responsibility for my last chapter, however much they might wish to repudiate it. I am also grateful to Mr. Raymond Carr, Mr. Peter Gatrell, Professor Israel Getzler, Professor F. H. Hinsley, Professor Michael Howard, Mr. Dominic Lieven, Mr. Donald Tyerman, Mr. David Warnes, Mr. Andrew Wheatcroft, Mr. H. T. Willetts—to whom I owe two very stimulating discussions in St. Antony's, Oxford—and Professor S. R. Williamson for their willingness to submit to bombardment. It is, finally, a pleasure for me to record my debt of gratitude, collectively to the Faculty of History at Cambridge, to my colleagues—and particularly Mr. D. J. V. Fisher—in Jesus College, to whose kindness and tolerance I owe so much, and to Madame Andrée Aubry, for her generous hospitality throughout the writing of this book.

Norman Stone
Jesus College, Cambridge

4th October 1974

CHAPTER ONE

The Army and the State in Tsarist Russia

In 1906 the Tsarist empire seemed to be on its last legs. It had just been defeated in war with Japan; and a series of internal disturbances had almost swept Tsar Nicholas II from his throne. Now, the empire had barely recovered. Its finances were in disrepair, being dependent on French loans that were given tardily, and on insulting terms. The army was in confusion, and even some of the Imperial Guard units were openly seditious. The navy had been shattered: the Pacific Fleet sunk at harbour in Port Arthur, and the Baltic Fleet, after a blundering Odyssey to the Far East, defeated in battle in the Straits of Tsushima. Fifteen capital ships and fifty-four other vessels had been sunk: losses calculated, with a maniacal accuracy as characteristic of the Tsarist bureaucracy as the sinkings themselves, at 255,888,951 roubles.[1] In the land campaigns in Manchuria, there had been a similar epic of incompetence. Infantry, artillery, cavalry had each gone its separate way. Supplies had broken down—even three years later, soldiers still did not have iron rations. Yet the generals were at a loss to explain what had happened. Kuropatkin, for instance, had recognised that charging Cossacks had been defeated by small bodies of Japanese infantry, but instead of seeing that this was an inevitable consequence of changes in infantry fire-power, he supposed that it had happened because the Cossasks had been cowardly; he ordered their carbines to be removed, so that henceforth they would have to rely on sabres.[2] General bewilderment was such that it took the authorities years to produce an official history of the war, and it was produced, in the end, only for form's sake.

But this defeat, though humiliating, was salutary: it showed even the most convinced conservatives that the system must be changed. There came a series of reforms in the army, and in the State as a whole. An effort was made to enlist middle-class Russia for the régime: the old system of autocracy was modified, with the creation of a parliament, the Duma, and a form of cabinet government, with a functioning Prime Minister and a Council of Ministers less dependent than before on the whims of the Tsar and his wife. Certain liberties were guaranteed, though grudgingly: freedom of speech and assembly made their first appearance in Russia, and so did trade unions. Restrictions that tied the peasant to the land were lifted; and there was even a gesture towards emancipation of the Jews. It seemed, for a time, as if the energies of Russia were at last to be tapped, if only for the benefit of a régime that was almost universally detested.

These political reforms coincided with a period of unexampled economic growth. After 1906, the country moved out of the depression that had bankrupted much of its industry at the turn of the century. Years of government railway-construction and foreign investment began to pay off, as new markets, new sources of raw-materials and labour, could be tapped. A series of good harvests, combined with high prices for grain—Russia's principal export—gave prosperity to the country as a whole. The war with Japan itself had a salutary effect, since it forced the government, usually painfully orthodox in its application of deflationary policies, to spend money: 2,500 million roubles beyond ordinary outgoings, which gave a much-needed fillip to consumption in Russia. The new prosperity even enabled Russia to reduce her dependence on foreign capital. Foreigners lent much the same—indeed rather more—in terms of quantity, but their share of Russia's capital formation declined from one half in 1904-5 to one eighth just before the First World War, and the direction of their lending also altered significantly, from government bonds to growth-related stocks in banking, commerce, industry. The government's revenue reflected the country's rising prosperity, since it almost doubled between 1900 and 1913-14, when it reached 3,500 million roubles.

Russia's armed forces profited from this, since a regular third of government revenue was devoted to defence; and by 1914, her recovery from the disaster of 1906 was, as the German General Staff noted with alarm, complete. The army contained 114½ infantry divisions to Germany's 96, and contained 6,720 mobile guns to the Germans' 6,004. Strategic railway-building was such that by 1917 Russia would be able to send nearly a hundred divisions for war with the Central Powers within eighteen days of mobilisation—only three days behind Germany in overall readiness. Similarly, Russia became, once more, an important naval Power. In 1907-8 she had spent £9,000,000 on her navy, to the Germans' £14,000,000; but by 1913-14 she was spending £24,000,000 to the Germans' £23,000,000. Plans were going ahead for seizure by naval coup of Constantinople and the Straits, and a naval convention with Great Britain allowed for co-operation in the Baltic against Germany. It was small wonder that Germans took fright in 1914 at the size of Russian power to come.

But, to overcome economic straits was one thing; to overcome the social and administrative heritage of backwardness, quite another, since the days of backwardness had created mental attitudes less easy to eradicate than backwardness itself. Whether the régime could survive into the twentieth century depended on its making its institutions fit modern requirements; and this was a problem that the armed forced experienced just as much as did Russia as a whole. As the European arms-race went ahead, armies became much larger, and the pace of technological change increase. Training had to go beyond the acrobatic drilling of the past, for the men had to be given essential skills, as their weapons grew more complex. The composition of officers' corps had to change: courage had to make way for trigonometry, the horse for the internal combustion-engine. Modernisation altered the terms of military relationships: it altered the rôles of cavalry, artillery, fortresses, infantry, and sometimes abolished their rôle. To make the necessary changes, and to plan for war in accordance with them, armies needed a central planning body, the dictates of which might over-ride the vested interests of the past. A General Staff was needed—a corps of officers specially trained, in an academy and by experience, not so much to lead troops as to study war in its higher aspects.

The need for a General Staff had been clear in Russia before 1905, but fulfilment of it had been resisted. Administration, rather than policy, dominated Russia, and power tended to go to bureaucrats capable of working the system rather than visionaries who wanted to replace it. There was a General Staff Academy, but it produced too few graduates, and these few were in any case needed, with the overall inadequacy of the officers' corps, to command troops rather than to do staff-work. Even in the war of 1914–17, chiefs of staff were simply deputy-commanders, and sometimes effective commanders, rather than experts in staff-work. The Inspectors-General in charge of separate arms—infantry, cavalry, engineering-troops or artillery—were usually Grand Dukes, and they resented any attempt on the part of General Staff officers to dictate to them; while regimental commanders, and the heads of the dozen military districts into which the country was divided regarded the General Staff as simply remote and interfering. Accordingly, the General Staff had a very limited rôle before 1905; the war minister was head of the army, and the staff ('*Glavny Shtab*' as it was then called) was only one department among several others. It was supposed to be the nucleus of the field headquarters of wartime, and contained a number of sections. One of these, equivalent in scale to the topographical section, was known as 'General Staff', but it was small and its functions were not defined.[3]

Theorists felt that Russia's defeat in the war with Japan had come from

lack of a proper General Staff, a muscle to move the army's administrative fat. In 1905-6 a series of reports by influential generals convinced
the Tsar that change must come; and, with the rise of the Duma, creation
of a functioning General Staff acquired more importance still. Now,
the war minister was answerable to the Duma. If power could be given
to a new Chief of the General Staff, answerable directly to the Tsar, then
the Duma's sphere of interference would be restricted to war ministry
matters, administrative routine. The General Staff became independent
of the war ministry, and its chief could appeal directly to the Tsar. Its
dictates were supposed to cover artillery, training, fortresses, railways,
planning for war, engineering-troops. The war ministry was left with
routine work, executing these dictates; and the old *Glavny Shtab* was now
confined to promotions, military prisons, statistics, the affairs of Turkestan. Grand Ducal Inspectors-General similarly remained in existence,
but there was always conflict between them and the General Staff. A
statute of 1907 failed to clarify the position; but as the General Staff
understood the matter, Inspectors-General had the task of keeping material
in good shape, and little more. The new chief of the General Staff was
named as F. F. Palitsyn, who had studied German military institutions
for many years. The new system was crowned by a Council of State
Defence, which assembled the Prime Minister, the war minister, the
chief of the General Staff, their naval equivalents, and the Inspectors-
General. Usually, the body was chaired by Grand Duke Nicholas, Inspector-General of Cavalry, and its terms of reference were simply the
whole field of defence.

Two factors, in the main, prevented this system from becoming the
permanency it was supposed to be: the vastness of the administrative
task, which made it difficult for any central body to exert its will; and
the division of the officers' class, which left General Staff officers talking
mainly to themselves. In the long run, the second of these mattered
more, for it complicated administrative business—battles of competence
and the rest—to an overwhelming extent. The Russian army was not,
like western European armies at the time, largely dominated by upper-
class figures. Russia was a poor country, without that plethora of jobs
in the economy that attracted the socially-mobile in more advanced
countries. As in the Hispanic world, church and army in Russia offered
roads for social advancement that were not so much needed in other
countries: the army was a vehicle for social mobility, and not, as in
Germany, a refuge from it. Ambitious peasants needed the army; and
the army needed ambitious peasants, because it could not otherwise
find officers. Attempts had been made in the past to confine officers-
posts to upper-class men, but they had always broken down. The

State could not afford to pay officers very much. In Russia, a lieutenant-colonel received a quarter of the salary of a German one, a Russian captain, 1,128 marks to the German's 2,851. Russian officers usually travelled third-class on the railways, until in the 1880s the ministry of transport agreed to let officers with third-class tickets travel second-class. In the 1870s, despite efforts to make the officers' corps more 'bourgeois' in recruitment, a third of the 17,000 army officers had not passed through primary school; and between 1900 and 1914, almost two-fifths of officers between the ranks of subaltern and colonel were of peasant or lower-middle-class origin.[4] A great many more were only one generation removed from such origins: usually, men (such as Denikin, Kornilov of Alexeyev) whose fathers had climbed from serfdom to an officer's post, after serving for twenty-five years in the ranks and passing a simple examination in the military institutes, scripture, and letters. This element was reinforced by a further 'hereditary' one—foreigners, · and their descendants, who had made a military career in Russia, and who counted almost as personal legionaries of the Tsar. Germans, usually from the Baltic coast, were the strongest element here, and had supplied a third of the generals in the middle nineteenth century. Even in 1914, foreign names—though the bearers were now, normally, Russian—were much in evidence in high places. Of sixteen men commanding armies in the war-months of 1914, seven had German names, one a Dutch name, and one—Radko-Dmitriev—had even been Bulgarian minister to Saint Petersburg until 1914. Seven had Russian names, but two of them were by origin Poles. The officers' corps was thus a mixed bag. The Tsar thereby lessened the chances of a military coup in the Hispanic style, and at the same time gave himself a populist argument of some force. The régime might be autocratic: but it was a system in which men of low social origins could find a place. Although upper-class Russians dominated some parts of the army—notably, the cavalry[5]—they were by no means the dominant element in it, as a whole. By 1902, 23·2 per cent of the graduates of the *yunkerskiye uchilishcha* producing most of the new infantry officers were of peasant origin, and further 20·2 per cent lower-middle-class, and two-fifths gentry—at that, landless.

There was a contest between patrician and praetorian in the army, as elsewhere in the Tsarist State, and the Tsar preserved his freedom of action by balancing between them. Tsarist Russia was not so uncomplicatedly a 'gentry-bourgeois State' as has sometimes been suggested. On the contrary, gentry figures provided much of the active opposition. Their economic basis had been weakened by emancipation of the serfs, and loss of two-thirds of their lands. Some found a way forward in the bureaucracy, or the *zemstva*; some stayed on their lands, and tried without much success, to make a go of them; some went into active opposition to a State now, seemingly, leaving them little place. A large number of liberals and revolutionaries came from their ranks—a tradition promoted by the Decembrists in 1825, and continued, in one form or another into the ranks of the Bolsheviks, of whose leaders at least Lenin and Chicherin could lay some claim to patrician status. It was useful to the State, in these circumstances, to recruit peasants whom it could then release against their masters; and such ex-peasants were frequently encountered in the army and the police, as Count Tolstoy discovered when the police raided his house, on suspicion that literacy was practised there.

There was a carapace of Tsarist functionaries, men who served for uncomplicated motives of patriotism and self-advancement, who managed the armed forces before 1905; members of military families on the one side (Skalons, Dragomirovs), Germans who owed their all to the Tsar, on the other (Rödiger, Evert, Plehve). The Tsar relied again and again on such men, despite their often very great age, and made Vannovski, octogenarian war minister, minister of education in 1902. When the younger officers campaigned for a General Staff, what they had in mind was the destruction of these old men and their system, which 1905 was supposed to have discredited. The demand for an all-powerful General Staff came unmistakably from the patrician wing of the army. Only gentry or bourgeois figures could pay the costs of the General Staff Academy, the products of which were overwhelmingly upper-class. In 1883, of 122 men accepted, fifty-eight were from Saint Petersburg, and most of the rest from Warsaw or Moscow; later on, almost ninety per cent of the intake was of middle- or upper-class origin. When an independent General Staff was instituted, it occurred quite fittingly with the emergence of the Duma: General Staff officers and parliamentary liberals often were brothers or cousins. There were Trubetskoys, Struves, von Anreps, Golovins, Zvegintsevs, Moeller-Zakomelskis in the General Staff as much as on the benches of the Duma's 'Progressive Bloc'. No doubt these men would have inaugurated 'the career open to talent' in the army. But they interpreted 'talent' in their own sense,[6] and their interpretation certainly did not include many of the officers who had found their way through the old system. Not surprisingly, the General Staff officers, whose writ was supposed to run throughout the army, encountered much opposition from the old praetorian guard.

Besides, although these officers were self-pronounced technocrats, they had a way of falling into pure traditionalism. Full of bright ideas as they were, they were not sure which ones to apply. The lessons of the Russo-Japanese war were not very clear. The naval authorities, for instance, had appreciated that the shell they used was unsuitable, but they

did not know with which type to replace it, and therefore went on
supplying the same shell for the next three years. Artillery and infantry,
in particular, disagreed as to the lessons of modern war, each accusing
the other of high-handed behaviour. Infantrymen complained that
gunners had let them down in refusing to 'waste' precious shell on infantry
tasks; artillerists complained that infantrymen were illiterate, that, for
instance, General Dragomirov had threatened to court-martial any
gunner who used the maximum range of his gun. A similar quarrel
opened up on the subject of Russia's many fortresses. Some officers
read the example of Port Arthur to mean that all fortresses were so
vulnerable to heavy artillery as to make their maintenance a waste of
time; others read it to mean that fortresses should be greatly strengthened
to enable them to withstand heavy guns. The shadow of redundancy
fell still more heavily on cavalry, and was still more vehemently denied,
although infantry weapons could now fire so far and so fast as to knock
out charging horesemen quickly enough.

Artillery,[7] like cavalry, formed a strong centre of reaction. The artillerists despised infantrymen, and resented attempts to subject them to
infantry orders. By 1906, it had become clear that the old eight-gun
battery was unnecessarily large. The quick-firing revolution in gunnery
had given a six-gun and even a four-gun battery (as in the French army)
as much effective fire-power as the old eight-gun affair. The artillerists
agreed, with reluctance, that this was the case, but said they had no
money to create smaller batteries, and the larger ones were still in existence in 1914. The truth of this matter was that eight-gun batteries
were commanded by senior officers, where a six-gun one would be
commanded by a captain. Promotions and pensions were at stake, and the
Artillery Committee accordingly found excellent reasons for doing its
senior officers a good turn. On the other side, they indulged a mania
for heavy artillery, to be placed in fortresses and not in the field, that
cost the army a great deal more: in 1906, for instance, they presented
a bill of over 700 million roubles for fortress-guns, as against one of
112,900,00 for field artillery.[8] They also pronounced against high-
trajectory field artillery, such as the Germans had, on the grounds that
it was a 'coward's weapon'. The infantry should charge field-fortifications,
and not expect gunners to lob shells behind them when they had so
many important tasks in hand. Palitsyn and his colleagues adopted,
though platonically, the infantry standpoint in these matters, but against
the united resistance of the Artillery Department, and the Inspector-
General of Artillery, he could not prevail. A General Staff representative
was duly sent to sit on the Artillery Committee, chief executive body
of the Department, but the Inspector-General and the Artillery chiefs

(Kuzmin-Karavayev, Smyslovski and Dimsha) deliberately made their discussions highly technical, until the representative faded away. In 1907, a statute was produced, governing the relationship of infantry and artillery, but it was so ambiguously-worded that no-one knew what to do. In some units, artillerymen went their own way. In others, infantry captains were allowed to give orders to single batteries. The wrangles within the army reached the Council for State Defence, and the General Staff was speedily discredited in ministers' eyes. After three years of independent General Staff, there was almost no progress to show.

The system came to grief in 1908, after wrangling between military and naval leaders. Progressive ministers wanted a navy. Navies acquired colonies, trade. They stimulated important industries. They also gave some freedom of choice in foreign policy, unlike armies, which simply made an accumulation of weight on the border and hence reduced rather than expanded a country's options. Naval authorities sometimes had an air of administrative competence that impressed civilians, who found army men depressingly innumerate. The Tsar wished to promote a Russian navy, and in doing so had support from the Duma. This was expensive: a single Dreadnought cost forty million roubles. The army leaders protested that their own force mattered much more, and was being starved of resources. In the end, the Council of State Defence became unworkable. The army leaders combined to resist naval demands, but could not agree among themselves as to what should be done with the resources thus saved—Grand Duke Sergey Mikhailovitch, Inspector-General of Artillery, naturally had fortresses and heavy guns in mind; Grand Duke Nicholas was an unrepentant cavalryman; Palitsyn inclined to the infantry cause, though, like the bulk of General Staff officers, he would never promote the cause of lower-class infantry officers at the expense of his class-associates in the artillery and cavalry. The Tsar had to step in to arrange finance behind Grand Duke Nicholas's back. In the autumn of 1908, the Council of State Defence in effect ceased to function. The Tsar dismissed Palitsyn, and Grand Duke Nicholas reverted to his post as Inspector-General of cavalry, and commander of the Saint Petersburg military district.[9]

Meanwhile, the Tsar had recourse to his carapace of elderly servants. To succeed Palitsyn, he appointed V. A. Sukhomlinov, commander of the Kiev military district, a man connected with the old establishment of Skalons, Dragomirovs, Korffs, Vannovskis. He counted as a conservative, and as such was thought to have sabotaged the General Staff's attempts to reform infantry in the various military districts. His was none the less the name associated with the progress made by the Russian army between 1908 and the war.[10]

Sukhomlinov has had an extremely bad press. He was held up as a by-word for corruption and incompetence. The Duma hated him, because of his unrepentantly autocratic attitude. In June 1915 he was dismissed, and arrested. The government imprisoned him in the Petro-pavlovski fortress on suspicion of corruption, and his management of the war ministry was subjected to a 'high commission of investigation'. The Provisional Government also imprisoned him, and it was, strangely, the Bolsheviks who let him go. He also made innumerable enemies in the army, and a flavour of this enmity comes through the various works of General Golovin, who works a denunciation of him into all of his books. Sukhomlinov, as a sort of uniformed Rasputin, belongs to the demonology of 1917. But the case against him is far from watertight. He was part of the old army establishment, and as such had strong links with the army's praetorian wing. In effect, he supported the infantry interest against artillerists, cavalrymen, fortress-officers; and, once he had taken control of the General Staff, he made it work, sometimes despite itself, in ways of which Palitsyn himself would have approved, but which he had never been able to entertain. The difficulty for Sukhom-linov was that the bulk of upper-class officers was unsympathetic to him: high aristocrats, installed in cavalry regiments, regarded his chief assistant, Danilov, as 'an agrarian revolutionary' because he pruned the privileges of the Guard Corps; the supports of Grand Duke Nicholas and Palitsyn hated him because he had excluded them from office; gradually, too, he acquired enemies in the Artillery Department and among the Inspectors-General, whose functions the Sukhomlinovite General Staff began to usurp. Sukhomlinov replied by promoting lower-class officers to posts that would have been closed to them in Palitsyn's day, and he developed a whole clique, throughout the army. It was always said by artillerists, for instance, that Sukhomlinov really wanted to introduce a six-gun rather than an eight-gun battery because it would allow him to create new officers' posts for his own lower-class clients.[11] On the other hand, Sukhomlinov himself would never promote lower-class men too far in the army. Two-fifths of officers below the rank of colonel might be of lower-class origin; but only a small fraction of the generals were of this origin, and Sukhomlinov would have been dismissed if he had tried to extend that fraction.

His position was therefore always fragile, and to survive, and push through his reforms, Sukhomlinov needed control of the promotions-machinery. This was not easy, since the 'Higher Attestations Committee' that dealt with senior promotions was controlled to a large extent by upper-class enemies of Sukhomlinov; and in any case, few of Sukhom-linov's clients would, in the circumstances of Tsarist Russia, have made general's rank. But promotions lower down could be strongly influenced by Sukhomlinov. He appreciated this at once. Promotions were a matter for the *Glavny Shtab*, along with other routine affairs which the General Staff had decided to leave alone, and the *Glavny Shtab* itself was a department of the war ministry. Sukhomlinov decided that the way to real power lay through the war ministry, and not the General Staff, despite its formal superiority, because the former could more easily *control* both jobs and money. In Palitsyn's day, the war ministry had not exerted itself: it was in the charge of Rödiger, a pedant preoccupied with routine work. Sukhomlinov profited from confused conditions within the war ministry. Polivanov, Rödiger's deputy, intrigued to overthrow Rödiger, and perhaps supplied 'inside' material to the Duma opposition to enable it to attack him. Rödiger's response was so discreditably confused that the Tsar decided to remove him. But, knowing of Polivanov's contacts with the opposition, he decided to appoint Sukhomlinov instead to the vacant post; and Sukhomlinov then announced that the old system, by which the war ministry was superior to the General Staff, suited Russian conditions better. Henceforth, the General Staff became a department of the war ministry, along with other departments (artillery, engineer-troops etc.); while Sukhomlinov seized control of the promotions-machinery.[12]

To prevent the emergence of opposition to him, Sukhomlinov turned the formal position of chief of the General Staff into an empty one, by the simple device of arranging for a constant turnover of occupants: Myshlayevski, dismissed after a year; Gerngross, a nonentity who presently died; Zhilinski, packed off two years later to command the Warsaw military district; the clerk, Yanushkevitch. There were thus as many chiefs of the General Staff in the last seven years before 1914 as Germany had had in the previous century. In the same way, Sukhomlinov ran a regiment of rats against his highly-placed enemies at court, in the government and the Duma. His agents, among them Myasoyedov, spied on the officers' corps while ostensibly working for counter-intelligence; a clutch of gendarmes in the capital also served Sukhomlinov's cause—Voyeykov, commandant of the Palace Guard, who marketed a Russian version of *Perrier*, called *Kuvaka*, had himself appointed 'Inspector-in-Chief of the Physical Condition of the Populations and Peoples of the Russian Empire', and discovered that improvement of this condition required consumption of *Kuvaka*; the manager of Grand Duke Nicholas's headquarters canteen, Bayrashev, also a marketer of *Kuvaka;* the unspeakable Kurlovs and von Kottens of the Police Department; the Austrian profiteer Altschiller, to whom Sukhomlinov gave signed, blank letters that could be used for testimonials. To combat the Duma, Sukhomlinov also employed his own client journalists: Prince Meshcherski, with his anti-semitic *Grazhdanin;* Rzhevski, who 'ghosted' Sukhomlinov's newspaper-articles (including a famous one of 1914 announcing Russia's readiness for war); Prince Andronikov, who combined in familiar pattern profiteering, snobbery, high-church views and pederasty. All of these supported Sukhomlinov, informing him of currents of opposition, whether in the officers' corps, the Duma, the government or the court, and received in return advance information enabling them to profit—in Andronikov's case, for instance, Sukhomlinov told him which pieces of land the army would try to buy, so that Andronikov could buy them first and then sell at a profit; while Sukhomlinov himself appears to have made handsome profits from inside dealings on the Stock Exchange. The system, overall, was protected against Sukhomlinov's highly-placed enemies by astute use of the promotions-machine. Grand Duke Nicholas and his cohort of cavalrymen were confined to the military districts; Palitsyn inspected the fortresses of the Caucasus; all manner of their lower henchmen found themselves howling with frustration in some distant regimental command, while Sukhomlinov filled important posts with faceless technicians such as Shuvayev or Vernander, or dim-witted characters of the old establishment—the aged Evert, or the ex-peasants Kondratiev, head of the *Glavny Shtab*, or Ivanov, chief of the Kiev military district. The lower posts of the General Staff itself were invaded by men of simple origins, though the structure of the Russian empire being as it was, there were always strict limits to their numbers.[13]

The officers' corps split between *Sukhomlinovtsy* and their enemies; and it was this that accounted for the peculiar pattern of wartime Russian command-posts. When war broke out, power slipped from the administrators to the commanders, in other words from Sukhomlinov's war ministry to Grand Duke Nicholas's General Headquarters (*Stavka*). The two machines then fought as to which of their nominees should be appointed; and, quite often, appointment of one side's nominee to one command would be cancelled out by the appointment of the other side's nominee to be his chief of staff, and then reinforced by appointment of the first side's man to the third most senior post, that of Quarter-Master-General. It was common for commanders not to talk either to their own chiefs of staff, or to a neighbouring army commander, but to have excellent relations with their Quarter-Master-General. Rennenkampf in East Prussia was an aristocratic cavalryman, who refused to have any dealings with his chief of staff, Mileant, but developed good relations with his Quarter-Master-General, Bayov; Ruzski, commanding III Army against the Austrians, was a stout Sukhomlinovite, who quarrelled with his chief of staff, Dragomirov, but greatly favoured his Quarter-

Master-General, Bonch-Bruyevitch. *Stavka*, or the war ministry, seized
any opportunity to discredit the other side's men, but, if dismissed, they
would then usually be caught in the safety-net of their own side, and
appointed to some other command. Quite often, men would be dismissed
from a divisional command for supposed incompetence, and would
then be appointed to command an army corps; or they would be dismissed from a post of chief of staff, and reappear commanding a division,
even an army. The careers of Bezobrazov, Tsurikov, Zuyev, Kurlov,
Dragomirov and even Ruzski illustrated this process, and it was not one
that helped the army towards a coherent strategy.[14]

It was also a split that went beyond 1917. Of course the pattern was
never simple, and there were changes of side as even stout *Sukhomlinovtsy*
tacked to join the powerful *Stavka* group. But study of those Tsarist
officers who went into the Red Army shows a remarkable connection
with the old *Sukhomlinovtsy*. Unpretentious technicians of modest
origins, younger officers impatient with the trumpetings of the cavalry—
General Staff establishment, found their way into the Red Army, while
cavalrymen and the more old-fashioned type of artillerists made for the
White Army. Ushakov and Rattel, transport-officers in *Stavka* itself, went
Red, while their senior, Ronzhin, emigrated; the Red Army's artillery was
run by technicians promoted by Sukhomlinov in the teeth of Artillery
Department resistance—Barsukov, Kirey, Ipatiev; and the list even of army
and corps commanders of Tsarist days who went into the Red Army is
surprisingly long, including Bonch-Bruyevitch, Gutor, Balanin, Kamenev,
all of them Sukhomlinovite rather than Grand Ducal appointments.

The impression that Sukhomlinov, and not his enemies, was the real
promoter of a modern cause is strongly confirmed by the story of his
army reforms. Despite their technocratic trumpetings, Sukhomlinov's
enemies were deeply traditionalist, and their obstruction of reform—in
cavalry, artillery, reserve-formations, fortresses and, in the end, planning
as well—had much to do with the army's failure to develop its organisation
as, increasingly, its economic means would have permitted. The increase
in government revenue left a financial latitude for reform that had not
been known before. Between 1909 and 1913, some 3,000 million roubles
were found for the army, 1,000 million for the navy—together, a third
of government revenue. Ordinary defence-expenditure rose as follows:

TABLE 1: ORDINARY DEFENCE-EXPENDITURE, 1909–1913: (million
roubles, rounded)[15]

	1909–10	1910–11	1911–12	1912–13	1913–14
Army:	473	484	498	528	581
Navy:	92	113	121	176	245

At the same time, a series of capital grants ('extraordinary expenditure') were made to both army and navy, in three stages: the 'little programme' of 1908-9, the 'reorganisation' of 1910, and the 'Great programme' of 1914. The first two supplied defence with 700 million roubles before 1914, of which army and navy took roughly half each. The third programme catered for an increase in recurrent expenditure of 140 million roubles p.a. for the army, and a capital grant of 432 millions, payable over three years; the navy had had its equivalent in 1913, 800 million roubles being earmarked for naval expenditure, mainly for the Black Sea Fleet. By 1913-14, the Russian army was receiving more money than the German: by the German official historians' calculation, 1,577 million marks to 1,496 million, though no doubt it remained true that the Germans got more for each mark they spent. The pointers for the future were unmistakable.

Sukhomlinov was widely accused of mismanaging his resources. It happened quite frequently that both the army and the navy would ask the Duma for large sums, only to explain, to investigating members, that a substantial part of previous credits had remained unused. There was, of course, a good deal of mismanagement. The naval authorities blundered between the Baltic and the Black Sea, ending up with two half-navies; and the army leaders, as befitted the confused relations of war ministry, Artillery Department, General Staff and the rest, also failed to plan their spending properly. But these confusions concealed what was really a basic problem of development-economics. Guns and ships could not be constructed until a great deal of primary investment had been made, and money devoted by the Duma to ship-building would often end up in endless projects for dredgers, ice-breakers, navigational-schools, light-houses and site-surveying. In 1906 even the Kronstadt naval base was lit by kerosine-lamp, and water-supplies arrived in horse-carts.[16] Similarly, again a reflection of Russian backwardness, simple matters of supply cost the Russian army more than other armies. A Russian sack cost sixty-five kopecks; a British one, thirty-five; Russian boots cost eight roubles and forty kopecks the pair, American ones, even in the depreciating currency of 1915, six roubles.[17] Finally, there was a severe difficulty, in so far as Russian factories were often new, of untried capacity, such that the placing of army and navy contracts was sometimes a lengthy business. In finance, Sukhomlinov's administration fell victim to development-economics rather than to corruption, or mismanagement.

It was the obstacles to reform, rather than financial mismanagement, that counted for more in holding the army back. In 1909, following Russia's humiliation in the Bosnian crisis—and, no doubt, also as a response to the victory of the naval leaders a few months before—Sukhomlinov produced a list of desirable reforms. They were intended to strengthen the infantry, the field army as a whole, and the fate of these reforms showed how far the supposed 'technocrats', the Palitsyns and Golovins, Shcherbachevs and Alexeyevs, were prepared to resist change. Sukhomlinov proposed the creation, for instance, of real reserve-divisions, so as to increase the number of field-divisions in wartime. As in France or Germany, peacetime units would have a special group attached to them ('secret cadre') which would, in wartime, be detached, and used to form the nucleus of a further unit, the numbers of which would mainly come from reservists. A peacetime battery consisted of eight officers, 201 men, and in wartime, two officers and forty-six men would be detached from it to form another battery, the bulk of the personnel of which would be made up of reservists called up for wartime service. In infantry divisions, much the same would happen. Each German regular peacetime division contained a supernumerary nucleus of a further wartime brigade, such that the twenty-six German regular corps could form twenty-six reserve divisions in wartime. The drawback was of course that the bulk of the personnel of these reserve-divisions was of lesser quality, since only ten per cent of the force would be made up of serving soldiers, the rest of reservists who might have forgotten a good part of their training. But, if the army was to be able to field a large number of divisions in wartime, without having the expense of maintaining them in peacetime, the system was a good one. Sukhomlinov introduced it into Russia, creating thirty-five second-line divisions for the seventy first-line ones. The generals in the field responded by failing to use these divisions, and the artillerists did their best to see that guns were not 'wasted' on them.[18]

Sukhomlinov also ran into trouble for suggesting that the bulk of Russia's fortresses should be scrapped. In the later nineteenth century, a system of fortresses had been created, to offset the likelihood of speedier German mobilisation. Novogeorgievsk and Ivangorod stood on the Vistula; Osowiec, Grodno and Kovno on the river-barriers of northern Poland. The war-plan developed around these fortresses, the one conditioning the other. But development of artillery and railways made them redundant. Even the stoutest places could be reduced by heavy artillery, as 1914 showed. But in any case, it did not need very heavy artillery to reduce Russia's fortresses, for they were already out-of-date in 1900. The Novogeorgievsk forts had been built to keep the artillery of the 1880s out of range of the central part of the fortress, i.e. were usually eight kilometres distant from it. Now, even a field gun could fire that distance. The forts were usually of brick, not concrete. Kovno had

become little more than a museum, its central 'place d'armes' being, as
Palitsyn said, 'a sort of yard through which people drive their cattle to
market'. Ivangorod's foundations had been continually weakened by the
Vistula floodings, and even the vegetation had not been cleared, so that
an attacker could move up unseen. Schwarz, who commanded it in
1914, said: 'standing on the parapet, I could not even see the glacis.'
There were ostensibly good arguments for building these places up,
rather than letting them run down. But it was Sukhomlinov, who said
that they should be scrapped, whose judgment was borne out by events.
All fortresses in the First World War, unless in special circumstances,
collapsed in a matter of days. The French defence of Verdun was, sensibly,
conducted from trenches, and not from concrete traps such as Douaumont
or Vaux. But Sukhomlinov's opponents were aghast, and said that the
fortresses should be built up, not razed. They presented huge bills for
this—in 1908, 800 million roubles, or roughly what the Black Sea Fleet
was to get six years later; and the artillerists indulged their mania for
fortress artillery at the expense of heavy field artillery, since they demanded nearly 5,000 modern heavy guns for the fortresses, while leaving
the field army with less than 500. Sukhomlinov's proposal to raze fortresses encountered heavy, and in the end successful, resistance. Local
engineer-officers simply disregarded their instructions—even, in the case
of Ivangorod, finding the engaging pretext that to raze the fortress would
cost as much as to build it up. Chieftains in the military districts, particularly Alexeyev in Kiev and Klyuev in Warsaw, protested; Duma opinion
was stirred up, and government ministers were also lobbied; the cause of
fortresses was taken up by Sukhomlinov's own deputy, Polivanov, no
doubt as a way of discrediting Sukhomlinov. By 1912, the programme of
fortress-razing had to be abandoned.[19]

The retention of these fortresses gave a decisive, and fatal, twist to
the development of Russian artillery. Its resources were swallowed,
partly by the navy, but particularly by the demands of fortresses, in
which investment was a largely self-generating affair since, once the
first step had been taken, the rest had to follow. Russia's lack of heavy
field guns was later read as a sign of economic backwardness. In reality,
it only showed that Russia lacked artillerists prepared to cater for infantry
needs, and a General Staff capable of dictating to technique-proud
specialists. Slavering at the mouth, the Artillery Department chased after
larger and larger calibres for their fortresses, and subjected all the rest to
this insatiable 'manie du grandiose'. In the plans for extra expenditure
in 1908, they were prepared to spend over 700 million roubles on fortress
artillery, 112 million on the rest. In 1910, they planned for 620 extra
fortress-guns, 240 heavy field guns; with the 'Great Programme' of

1913-14, fortresses were supposed to have a further 516 heavy howitzers, while the heavy field artillery took only 228 more guns. In 1914, the fortresses contained 2,813 modern guns, and were due to have, by 1920, 4,998 to supplement the 3,000 older ones; but the field army had only 240 heavy howitzers and cannon. When the time came for these fortress-guns to prove their worth—in the summer of 1915—Sukhomlinov, who had been laughed at for his ignorance, was proved overwhelmingly right. Warsaw, Novogeorgievsk, Kovno, Grodno, Osowiec, Brest-Litovsk collapsed in a matter of days, or were voluntarily evacuated. In most of them, the Germans captured thousands of guns and millions of shells. On the other hand, the field army, suffering from lack of mobile heavy field artillery, could only retreat. The Department's concern for heavy fortress-guns affected ordinary artillery adversely, because of the resources that it swallowed. In the 'Great Programme', for instance, the Department proposed to spend 209 million roubles of the 400 million it was due to receive on fortress artillery. Not enough was left, therefore, for development of high-trajectory field artillery—the light howitzer, of which the German army made impressive use, and which was particularly useful in trench warfare. Similarly, there was still not enough money to convert Russian batteries to the more flexible six-gun type, and most batteries continued to waste their fire-power in eight-gun batteries until the summer of 1915. The shell-reserve, too, suffered from the artillerists' concern elsewhere. It was built up to 1,000 rounds per gun, where the French reserve was 2,000 and the German, 3,000; besides, nothing of significance was undertaken to provide for increased shell-output once war came. There was talk, correspondence. But none of it had the slightest urgency. Sukhomlinov, himself knew, of course, that much more shell would be needed. He also suspected that high-trajectory field artillery and six-gun batteries would be more important than fortress artillery. But he could not dictate to the powerful men in the Artillery Department, among them Grand Duke Sergey Mikhailovitch, and his reforms stopped short there.[20]

His proposals on fortresses also broke down because they offended against the orthodoxies of planning. The fortresses were thought to be essential, because of Russian backwardness, for all planning had been dominated, in the later nineteenth century, by considerations of extreme prudence. German mobilisation was more rapid than Russian, because of German railway-building, and the Germans would be ready within a fortnight, whereas the Russians would take at least six weeks. Moreover, the Russian strategic position was poor, because Poland jutted out, vulnerable to a pincer-movement, between the Central Powers' territory. Russian railways were poor, with irregularities even within single main lines: for instance, the Moscow-Kazan line could take forty trains in a day, but its Arapovo-Ryazan section, only twenty-one, and bottlenecks of this type immobilised much of the scarce rolling-stock. The field-kitchens at Smolensk and Vyazma could manage only 35,000 hot meals in a day; the signalling-capacity in important junctions such as Minsk and Bialystok was low, and trains could therefore be exposed to German bombing as the sidings jammed; at Trawniki, where troops would be unloaded for the Austro-Hungarian front, twenty trains could arrive in a day, but, for lack of long platforms, only ten of them could be unloaded. Not surprisingly Obruchev, chief of staff in the 1890s, felt that 'until we have built up our railways, there is no plan that can guarantee success.'

Despite talk to the French of an offensive, Russian planning remained very defensive. Poland west of the Vistula was to be altogether evacuated, and the great concentrations of troops were far from the border—in 1890, 207 battalions on the Niemen, 324 on the middle Vistula, 284 on the Galician border, 188 in reserve around Brest-Litovsk. In 1906, by the provisions of 'Plan No. 18, restored', the groupings were much the same, based on the fortresses: thirteen divisions on the Baltic coast, eleven and a half on the Niemen, thirty-four on the middle Vistula, fifteen on the Galician border and six in reserve. This plan seemed to guarantee safety against a pincer-movement from northern and southern Poland; it also gave the Russian army a chance to strike either at Germany, or at Austria-Hungary, since the bulk of forces was gathered in the middle. But, to attack, the Russian army would need at least six weeks, if not two months. By 1909, this delay seemed to be inadmissible; in any case, the Bosnian crisis revealed Russo-German hostility as nothing else had done.

In 1910 Sukhomlinov and Danilov re-wrote the plan. No. 19 was a radical change. They felt that, to save the French from isolation in the first weeks of war, Russia must mount an attack. But to attack from the centre would be dangerous, as the flanks would be threatened both from Galicia and from East Prussia. One of these bastions must be 'taken out'. There was little sense in 'taking out' the Austro-Hungarian one, for Austria-Hungary would not influence the first period of the war. An attack on East Prussia was indicated; and because it was a salient, it could be attacked from two sides, south and east. A fairly accurate picture of German intentions meanwhile developed: it was thought, by the French and Russians, that the Germans would leave between sixteen and twenty-five divisions in the east, and would concentrate their forces in the west where 'the great battles will probably take place, in the first two weeks, in Luxembourg, Belgium and Lorraine'. It was clear that a Russian offensive would do much to help divert German troops from the west, and with Plan No. 19, a serious offensive was to be made. However, knowing that East Prussia would make for severe tactical difficulties, Danilov prepared to allot to this province four armies, with nineteen out of twenty-eight army corps. The other nine would contain whatever the Austrians decided to send against Russia. In the circumstances, it was not worth while to waste money on the upkeep of fortresses, and Danilov proposed that they should be razed. For the full programme, he received Sukhomlinov's support.[21]

But there was an immediate outcry, the more so as important interests had not been consulted. All of Sukhomlinov's enemies in the army and the Duma united to save the fortresses; and the Grand Duke's men in the Warsaw and Kiev military districts were also mobilised to denounce the plan, which they would have to execute. Some people, among them Stogov, of the General Staff, thought that the French would certainly be defeated within three months. Russia would then have to fight Germany alone, and she might do better, in the early period, to knock out Austria-Hungary and thus secure a free hand for the later Russo-German war. Austria-Hungary's 'multifarious army would not survive the blow' since 'it is to be assumed that, if Russia wins, the Slavs will gravitate towards her'.[22] Moreover, the East Prussian offensive, launched by four armies, would always suffer from a weak flank to the south, and a rapid Austro-Hungarian thrust could penetrate this flank and disrupt progress in East Prussia. 'Studies' of this possibility displayed that Austro-Hungarian troops could reach far into Volhynia by the twentieth day of mobilisation, and could capture even Brest-Litovsk not long afterwards. These notions, though sometimes reciprocated in the Austro-Hungarian General Staff, were pure fantasy. By the twentieth day of mobilisation, the Austro-Hungarian armies were still a long way south of their own border, and although there was an Austro-Hungarian cavalry raid on the fifteenth day, it had difficulty penetrating the cordon of gendarmerie. Just the same, Klyuev in Warsaw and Alexeyev in Kiev mobilised General Staff opinion against Danilov. Conferences of the chiefs of staff of the military districts were held, and demands were raised for a re-shaping of the plan, to allow for action against Austria-Hungary. In the meantime political events had produced Austro-Russian, rather than Russo-German, crises, and the planners now felt that they should cater for an Austro-Russian war. Accordingly, in May 1912, Plan No. 19 'altered' came into existence. In theory, there were two variants: Plan G, for the case that Germany attacked Russia, and Plan A, for the case that Germany attacked France. Only the latter one was real, as everyone knew. It provided for a concentration of Russian troops not against Germany, but against Austria-Hungary. Twenty-nine and a half infantry divisions were left for the German front, forty-six and a half for the Austro-Hungarian, and, in the event, rather more. Danilov's East Prussian offensive was retained, but, missing two of the armies meant for it, was bound to be weaker than was safe. The fortresses were also kept up, and thenceforth planning and fortresses kept each other pinioned in a deadly embrace.

Faulty planning had much more to do with the initial Russian disasters than material weakness, or the supposed unreadiness of 1914. A compromise had been established between Danilov's ideas and Alexeyev's, and neither East Prussia nor Galicia really received enough strength. The counter-part of the quarrel, in England, of 'westerners' and 'easterners' was, in Russia, between 'northerners' and 'southerners'. These latter represented the traditional cause, of Pan-Slavism, Constantinople, the Balkans, whereas Sukhomlinov's men appreciated that the real danger, now, was Germany, and that it would be grotesque for Russia to begin a European war with an offensive against an enemy that did not matter very much. The weight of pre-war investment in fortresses—and of course in planning too, for the making of a plan was an arduous affair, not to be repeated too often—naturally swung things towards the traditionalists; and the political crisis of 1912–13 confirmed the trend. The whole planning-machine ceased to act on the logic of the situation, but became a kind of delayed-action seismograph, recording the diplomatic tremors of months before. By 1912, the Russian army was already fatally split between the northern operation and the southern one. Links between them were tenuous. In recognition of this, two separate army group commands, the 'fronts', were to be established in wartime. This was not an appreciation that affairs of command had become so complex that not only army commands, but also army group ones, were needed to administer the land forces; it was rather a perception that the army had to be divided between irreconcilable tasks. The construction of these separate groups was, as events were to show, an almost insuperable hindrance to the evolution of coherent strategy. It was not Danilov's plan that illustrated the weakness of the Russian army's command structure, but rather the upsetting of his plan.

With the 'Great Programme', deliberated throughout 1913 and becoming law in June 1914, the Russian army ostensibly became a European super-power, in conformity with the economic growth that Russia had experienced since 1906. The annual recruit-contingent was raised to 585,000, for three-year service, such that the peacetime army alone would reach almost two million men—three times as large as Germany's. Infantry divisions would rise to 122½ (from 114½), to Germany's 96, and there would be 8,358 field guns to Germany's 6,004. Each division would have twelve howitzers in place of six (fifty-two German regular divisions had eighteen), and would have four heavy field guns to the German regular division's eight. Six-gun batteries would also, at last, be introduced, and the artillery was to have an extra 5,000 officers and 30,000 men.[23] Railway-improvements were also proposed, to help with mobilisation. But beneath this weight, there was not much muscle. The Tsarist régime could profit, outwardly, from economic progress; but the structure of the army, if anything, suffered from economic progress, which left so much money available for the wrong choices that so many of the army's functionaries unerringly made. There were now guns, railways, trained men in plenty. But commanders neglected their reserve-divisions, preferred to place guns in fortresses, and set up a plan for war that did not exploit strategic railways particularly; besides, the continuing belief in cavalry's efficacy meant that railways that might have sent infantrymen speedily to the front were loaded, instead, with horses and fodder for them. The sacrifice of locomotives to horses was a suitable way for this army to enter the war in 1914.

CHAPTER TWO

The Military Imperative, July 1914

Russian preparations for war alarmed the Germans more and more, and news of the 'Great Programme' deprived them of their senses. It was the last straw in an atmosphere of unprecedented international tension. Berlin felt itself to be encircled by powerful and unscrupulous enemies. In France, there had been a 'national re-awakening', which produced the nationalist Poincaré as President, and a new army law re-introducing three-year military service. The British, far from being frightened out of hostility to a Germany possessed of a large battle-fleet, were also unmistakably likely to join battle against Germany in a European war. True, some German statesmen hoped otherwise. But German soldiers had no illusions, and their plans allowed for the landing of a British expeditionary force in France.[1] Italy, too, had changed from warm alliance to open unreliability; and in 1913, Balkan conditions caused a similar change in the attitude of Romania. In such a situation, the Russian threat to Germany seemed more dangerous than anything else, and German statesmen began to foresee a day when Russian troops, in the name of Pan-Slavism, caused a destruction of the Habsburg Monarchy, and the creation of a Russian empire reaching as far as Stettin and Trieste. Moltke, chief of the German General Staff, wrote in February 1914 that 'Russia's preparedness for war has made gigantic progress since the Russo-Japanese war, and is now much greater than ever in the past'.[2]

In Europe at the time, there were widespread ideas that the German army was the most powerful in Europe, a vast war-machine of unconquerable strength. It was certainly a machine of considerable efficiency, as the campaigns of 1914–18 were to show. But it was not nearly as strong as foreigners feared, and as the Kaiser suggested. On the contrary, German generals felt very weak when they contemplated the forces of other generals.[3] The army had fewer battalions than the French army (1,191 to 1,210), and in 1914 fewer guns than the Russian army (6,004 to 6,700), to the 1,876 battalions of which it was also, of course,

inferior. It was also inferior to the French army in technical equipment of
many kinds—lorries and cars for one.

The Germans were incontestably superior to their enemies only in
one area—high-trajectory artillery—and even here their superiority was
much over-rated.[4] They had appreciated before their enemies that this
type of artillery, with a high-explosive rather than shrapnel munition,
would be of importance in the war to come. A field-cannon, which still
made up the overwhelming majority of every army's guns, fired fast,
far and straight; it could be used to break up mass infantry-attacks.
High-trajectory weapons were slower, and their range was less. But they
could reach behind enemy fortifications, such as earth-parapets, that
were inaccessible to field-cannon. The war to come would, of course,
be a war in which field-fortification played a preponderant part, and the
Germans were first off the mark in developing field-mortars—their
regular divisions had eighteen such weapons to fifty-four field-cannon,
whereas the Russian army, in 1914, had only six per division (and forty-
eight field-cannon). Plans to counter this were made by the French and
Russians, but the Germans went ahead to equip their reserve-divisions
as well with field-mortars. Moreover, in heavy field artillery, the Germans acquired some superiority. The *schwere Artillerie des Feldheeres* in
1914 contained 575 heavy guns, cannon and howitzers, whereas the
French army had 180, the Russian army 240. Borrowings from the
Austrians of 300 mm. howitzers gave the Germans a greater margin
of superiority. But neither advantage was very great. The 'monster
artillery' with which the Germans are thought to have 'shattered' their
way through Belgium was a legend. They possessed in all, for instance,
only three 420 mm. Krupp heavy cannon, although, as the war progressed, many more of these were produced. There was certainly no
reason, in German field-mortars or heavy artillery, for Moltke to forget
his fears, especially when he recognised other armies' intention to close
the gap.

In any case, the German superiority in both areas came not from
supposedly unconquerable industrial might, but from the accident of the
campaigns, that Germany would have some besieging to do, and the
other Powers would not. The German plan involved attack on French
and Belgian fortresses, whereas in French and Russian plans, besieging
fortresses played almost no rôle at all. The artillery of the two sides
simply reflected this difference. A further accident came to Germany's
aid: she had a greater proportion of her army's resources free for development of artillery than the other Powers had.[5] This happened for reasons
that, far from contenting German generals, frightened most of them out
of their wits. In any army, the mere supply, transport, administration of

hundreds of thousands of men came by a long way first in the army expense-sheets. In the Russian army of 1913-14, though no doubt it was an extreme case, 'intendantstvo'—food, fodder, clothing—took 450 millions out of 580.[6] But there were strict limits, for reasons to be explained below, to the number of conscripts that the German army was allowed to take in in any year: generally, 250,000, to the Russian army's 450,000 (and in 1914, 585,000), whereas the armies' budgets were roughly equal. The financial resources freed by the restriction of recruiting could be passed to artillery and technical services, and could of course also be used to maintain a higher proportion of long-serving soldiers and N.C.O.s, as distinct from conscripts, than was true of other armies. All in all, German artillery owed its superiority to accidents, sometimes unwelcome to the generals, and not to a mighty industrial machine.

The factor that most worried German generals in the period 1912-1914 was the restriction on recruiting.[7] Although Prussia had been a pioneer of universal military service, her successors had let the practice lapse, although the principle still held good. The army authorities were not allowed to take in more men, in a year, than the *Reichstag* would allow them; and the *Reichstag* was not very accommodating. The mass-parties—socialists and clericals—were overtly hostile to an army that they regarded as an upper-class preserve, and a constant menace to mass-parties. Even the middle-classes, though they might frequently give their souls to the army, were reluctant to give it their money as well. In any case, less obvious factors counted against significant increase of recruit-contingents. The German navy was first of these. It demanded a growing share of the defence-budget, and left no room for expansion of the army's expenses on supply. In the Tirpitz years, the German recruit-contingent barely expanded at all, although the population rose by ten million, and although there was now much less emigration than before. But the army leaders themselves sometimes feared mass-conscription. It would mean extending the officers' corps, to cater for the large numbers of men to be taken in; and extension of the officers' corps could only mean including elements that traditional minded Prussians, fighting the class-war, did not think suitable. Reserve-officers who were men from nowhere, perhaps even Jews, would not combat 'the social peril' as effectively as a homogeneously Junker officers' corps. The Prussian War Ministry, in the years before 1914, itself offered stout resistance to any application of real universal conscription. Consequently, the military burden on the German people was inferior to that laid on the French people, whose military leaders suffered from few such inhibitions, who, indeed, were concerned to extract the last ounce of military potential from the French people so as to counter-act the faster-growing German population. In Germany, liability to service ended at forty-five; in France, at forty-eight. In Germany, not fifty per cent of the liable young men were conscripted and trained; in France, eighty-five per cent—that is, all but the physically disabled. In 1914, there were five million Germans trained for war, and of military age, and five million untrained. In France, there were five million trained, and one million untrained; and the French army in the west, together with small Belgian and British contingents, actually contained more men than the German army, although the difference in population, especially near the younger end, was considerable—there were almost two young Germans to a young Frenchman. The French army of 1914 represented a tenth of the French population, the German army one-twentieth of the German population. Certainly, a change was rail-roaded through the *Reichstag* in 1913, but since it was followed by the Russian 'Great Programme', its effects were not great. It was not surprising that the German military urged war before it was too late, for, with the military law of 1913, and the cumbersome wealth-tax that had paid for it, they thought that they had reached the limit of their resources: better war with Russia than with the *Reichstag*.

This calculation was given a further support by news of Russian strategic railway-construction.[8] The German war-plan had been more or less forced by the facts of the situation, in which Russia and France were allied against Germany. The German army contained ninety-six divisions —fifty-two first-line, with eighty guns each, twenty-five second-line, with thirty-six guns each, and the equivalent of nineteen third-line, with at best twenty-four guns each. The French army contained forty-six first-line and thirty-seven second-line divisions, with, on average, forty guns each. The Russian army had 114½ divisions, with fifty-four guns each or, if army heavy artillery is included, fifty-six or fifty-seven. Once the Russian army had been mobilised, Germany would stand little chance of winning. Her only chance was to knock out France before the Russian army had begun its march to the west; then she could, at leisure, turn about to face Russia. Count Schlieffen had arranged for this: seven-eighths of the German army to proceed against France, via Belgium, in the first week of war. It was not thought that any other plan offered Germany the chance of success. Defensive action on the two fronts could only lead to a long throttling of Germany.

An essential part of the Schlieffen Plan was therefore the calculation that Russian mobilisation would be slow. This was true enough in the 1890s and 1900s. Not even 200 trains could move daily to the western borders, against the 650 that Germany could pass over the Cologne bridges alone; and there would be problems in transferring rolling-stock from Central Russia to the western border on mobilisation. The want of rolling-stock and railway-mileage was complemented by a multitude of technical problems, as Russian railways were built cheaply, without that wealth of equipment that western railways had—signal-boxes at frequent intervals, watering and coaling capacity, skilled technicians in plenty. In consequence, Russian planning itself developed with extreme caution as its guiding-light—troops drawn up in lumps, far from the German border, and large, defensive installations being erected. It would take these forces at least six weeks to be ready for action, and even then they would be unable to move fast. Schlieffen felt that the dozen divisions, many of them second- or third-line, that he proposed to leave for the defence of East Prussia would suffice in the first six weeks or so, while the rest defeated France. It was an opinion that many Russian soldiers shared.

The rise of Russian strategic railways struck this entire edifice at its base. Commercial development alone required increases in Russian rolling-stock and railway-mileage which, in 1914, was greater than Germany's. The Germans could make 250,000 railway-waggons free for mobilisation; the Russians, now, 214,000. By 1910, Russian mobilisation could proceed at the rate of 250 trains per day; by 1914, 360; while by 1917, Danilov planned to have 560 trains rolling to the west every day. In August 1914, Russia mobilised under the prescriptions of the old plan, No. 19 'altered', dating from the period 1910–12. Mobilisation took thirty days for the 744 battalions and 621 cavalry squadrons involved, but was over for two-thirds of them by the eighteenth day of mobilisation. With Plan No. 20, due to take effect in September 1914, and still more with Plan No. 21, to take effect in 1917, mobilisation was to be completely over by the eighteenth day—only three days later than the termination of German mobilisation in the west. Meanwhile, from 1912 onwards, there was a series of preparatory measures. Two-fifths of the army was permanently stationed in Poland, thus reducing the railways' carrying-task. A legal 'period of preparation for war' was introduced in February 1912, permitting measures of preparation, in advance of formal mobilisation, at the discretion of the war ministry—for instance, call-up of the three youngest classes of the reserve in areas threatened by enemy action (e.g. Poland west of the Vistula). These measures, put into effect from 26th July onwards, allowed Germans to suggest that Russia had 'secretly mobilised', although in reality the Germans were told what was going on. Finally, to offset the period when a new intake of conscripts would be at their least ready—the first six months of their service—the oldest class was to be kept under arms for a further half-year, such that in the winter, the Russian army would even in peacetime have two million men, as much as the German war-time army. In 1913–14, further measures of strategic railway-building were announced. The French government would guarantee railway-loans placed in France, of 500 million francs per annum, and French generals made suggestions as to the lines Russia should construct or double-track, so as to make her mobilisation quicker; French pressure even led to a Russian project, given some effect in 1914, for the assembly of an invasion-force in Poland west of the Vistula, an area hitherto judged too vulnerable to be occupied, and therefore left empty of railways. In the 'Great Programme' of 1914-17, nearly 150 million roubles, out of 700 millions ear-marked for military purposes, were to go on strategic railways. The Germans were already alarmed that Russian mobilisation had speeded up as much as it had. By 1917, they recognised, it would be almost as fast as their own. Russians would be in Berlin before Germans were in Paris.

Both Moltke in Berlin and Conrad in Vienna felt that 1914 was the last chance. After that, the Central Powers, losing allies, structurally unable to exploit their own peoples, and indeed, in the Austro-Hungarian case, unable to count even on basic loyalty, would have no hope of winning the war that, with every political crisis in Europe, seemed to come nearer. The generals pressed for war, in Moltke's case from March onwards. The statesmen's attitude was more complicated, since Bethmann Hollweg hoped to find some device for bringing about British neutrality, and since other German statesmen had hopes of invoking the conservative cause of alliance with Russia. But the statesmen, too, increasingly sympathised with the generals' statements. An accident, the murder of Archduke Franz Ferdinand by Serb terrorists, acted as catalyst, at the end of June 1914. The Central Powers would provoke a quarrel with Russia, by threatening her client, Serbia, with political extinction, ostensibly as a punishment for Serbian government complicity in the assassination of the Archduke. Bethmann Hollweg explained on 8th July that if Russia went to war to protect Serbia, better then than later; if she did not go to war, it would be because the French had let her down, so that she would come round once more to the German side. He explained to Lichnowsky, ambassador in London, that 'not only the extremists, but even level-headed politicians are worried at the increases in Russian strength, and the imminence of Russian attack', and Jagow, for the Foreign Office, echoed this with the remark that if war had to come, then in view of Russia's attitude, it would be better then than later.[9]

An ultimatum was served on Serbia, and was duly refused on 25th July. The Austrians declared war on her three days later. There was some indecision in Russia. Sazonov, foreign minister, felt that Austria should be threatened, but not Germany; consequently, the army was asked to mobilise only those corps ear-marked for the Austrian front. But, increasingly, most people suspected that Germany was behind Austria; and in any case the soldiers had good technical arguments for rejecting partial mobilisation. It was all or nothing; and by 31st July Russia had decided on general mobilisation. This broke down the last barriers in Germany, where Bethmann Hollweg had begun to have second thoughts. The Schlieffen Plan demanded that there should be at least three clear weeks when the German army, untroubled by Russian invasion, could defeat France. As soon as the first Russian reservist pulled on his boots, the alarm bells would ring in Germany, for by 1914 the timetable of the Schlieffen Plan had already become uncomfortably tight, and loss even of a day's preparation might be disastrous for Germany. Accordingly, the Germans mobilised as well; declared war on Russia when she failed to demobilise; and began to effect the Schlieffen Plan with a fabricated declaration of war on France. The railway, chief production of nine-teenth-century civilisation, had proved to be chief agent in its destruction.[10]

CHAPTER THREE

The Opening Round: East Prussia

Panic and desperation had prompted the German generals' behaviour in July. But their mood came from factors that the First World War showed to be unreal. Schlieffen had suffered from visions of a two-pronged invasion of Germany, from France and Russia, and his famous Plan seemed to be the only possible way of countering this threat. But the war showed, first, that armies' mobility on the offensive was so limited as to reduce much of the danger, and second that defensive fire-power was so powerful that even a superiority of three to one did not suffice to overcome it. There was, in other words, every chance for a defensive operation. After September 1914, this became clear to all sides, though it came as a great surprise.

However, in August, the first month of the war, things went much as men had imagined they would before the war. There were great offensives: the Schlieffen Plan set the bulk of Moltke's army marching through Belgium into the French flank; Plan XVII set most of Joffre's army attacking German positions in Alsace and Lorraine; Plan No. 19 set two Russian armies against East Prussia, and four others against Austrian Galicia; the Austro-Hungarian army also attacked both Serbia and Russia. On all of the fronts, there were great strategic manoeuvres, bringing the Germans far into France, the Russians far into Austria; in East Prussia, there was a great encounter between the German VIII Army and the two Russian armies, in which troops marched and counter-marched much as men had expected them to, until one of the Russian armies was resoundingly defeated in the battle of Tannenberg (25th–30th August), and the other expelled from East Prussia in the battle of the Masurian Lakes (7th–14th September). It was only after the first month that the real character of the war became apparent. Troops, particularly in the west, came to appreciate the possibilities open to defensive action, and offensive manoeuvre did not really return to the western battlefields until 1918.

August 1914 was thus an anomalous month. It reflected, not wartime realities, but pre-war illusions. Commanders on both sides deliberately neglected the possibilities of the defensive, both strategic and tactical. Instead of waiting to be attacked, they themselves attacked, and thus allowed their men to be decimated before they had a chance to prove their worth in defensive action. The doctrine of out-and-out offensive dictated their conduct. This was, in part, because military historians and General Staff theorists alleged that the offensive 'corresponds to the national character'. More prosaically, it reflected disbelief in the men. Commanders felt in their hearts that it took ten years to make a real soldier. Since the turn of the century, they had been allowed to take conscripts only for three active years, and even then a large number of conscripts had had to be released after two years, because the army could not afford their upkeep. Moreover, the number of conscripts had risen to such a point that there was only one officer for thirty men, one N.C.O. for ten men; and both officers and N.C.O.s were sometimes of uncertain quality. Army leaders concluded that the men could be taught nothing complicated. Tactical training was therefore limited; complicated manoeuvres were ruled out. The Russian General Staff Academy taught only two manoeuvres after 1912—forward and back—and the men's tactical formations were also constructed on an understanding that nothing fancy should be attempted, or the men would end up as a panic-stricken mob milling around the field. The men were simply gathered in thick masses, and set to charge the enemy line, regardless of their vulnerability to artillery. Similarly, the bulk of each army's artillery was laid in following assumptions of high-speed, open-country, mass-warfare, and therefore became almost obsolete when trench-warfare began. August 1914 took its own peculiar course, unlike any other month of the Great War, because all of the European armies tacitly agreed to treat it as a museum-piece of nineteenth-century warfare rather than an expression of the new possibilities open to twentieth-century soldiers. The men paid heavily for this. Deaths were greater in that month than at any later time—in the Austro-Hungarian army, they made up 15 per cent of casualties in 1914, as against 7.5 per cent in 1916.[1]

Franco-Russian General Staff agreements had been built on an assumption that the outcome of the war would be decided within six weeks. The French expected German attack, and were also virtually certain that it would infringe Belgian neutrality. Between sixteen and twenty-five German divisions were (with exaggeration) expected in the east. Russia must therefore mobilise fast, and attack the Germans' eastern forces, in order to divert some of the western ones from the French. There had always been rather empty undertakings to the effect that 800,000 Russians would take the field against Germany three weeks after mobilisation was

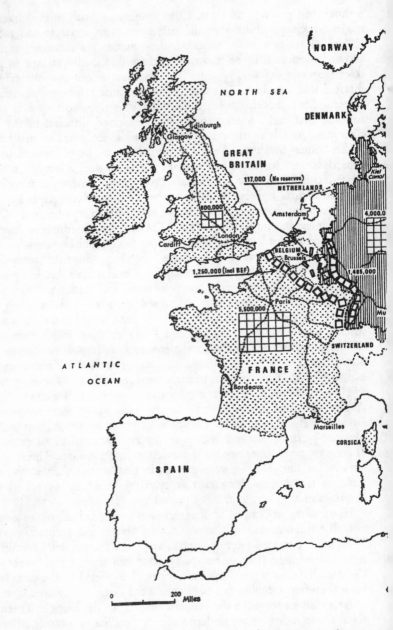

The line-up for war, 191

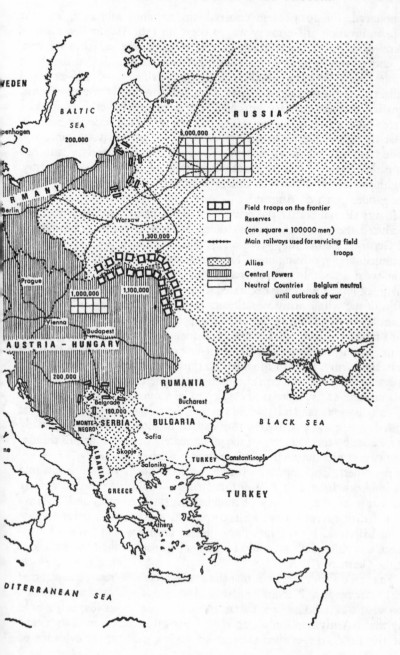

announced. By 1914, these undertakings acquired substance, and the Russian invasion of Germany was to begin on 15th August. Two armies were set to invade East Prussia—I, under Rennenkampf, from the east, II, under Samsonov, from the south. Later on, it was alleged that these armies' early crossing of the border was evidence of self-sacrificial gallantry on the Russian side. In reality, it showed only common sense. Ignatiev, Russian military attaché in Paris, reported that French losses were very high—in some regiments, fifty per cent—and added 'it becomes clear that the outcome of the war will depend on what we can do to deflect German troops against us'. The French had themselves launched an early offensive; and Yanushkevitch, chief of staff of the field army, told his troops to begin their offensive 'by virtue of the same inter-allied obligations', on 15th August.[2]

It was also said, after the event, that the Russian I and II armies had sacrificed themselves in France's cause, rushing to begin their invasion of Germany before they were ready, and suffering from shell-shortage, confused supply, missing units. This was a confusion of thought. Mobilisation went smoothly enough, according to Dobrorolski, who was in charge of it (and who was decorated for his work). In the first place, two-fifths of the whole army was already concentrated in the west in peacetime; the anticipatory measures of the 'preparatory period' were useful; and only two-fifths of the 5,000,000 men serving in the army when mobilisation came were due for front-line service, hardly more than the peacetime army. Russian mobilisation thus needed only 4,000 transports, as against the 7,000 of German mobilisation. There were 744 battalions of infantry and 621 squadrons of cavalry to be moved, and by the 20th day of mobilisation, 544 and 361 had reached their de-training points, by the 27th day, 644 and 453. By the 18th day, 63 infantry divisions were ready for action, by the 29th, 73½ of the 98 ultimately designed for this theatre. The two armies due to invade East Prussia were in fact ready before any of the others. Zhilinski, who commanded the north-western front, told Yanushkevitch on 10th August that I Army would be completely ready for action by the 12th day of mobilisation (11th August) and II Army even earlier, except for one of its corps, 6th, which had to arrive on foot from Bialystok. By the 12th day, the two armies would have 208 battalions and 228 squadrons ready for action (against less than 100 battalions in the German VIII Army).[3]

The real difficulty was not that the armies were not 'ready'; it was that they were ready as Zhilinski understood it—that is, gloriously unprepared for what was to come. It is characteristic that one writer (Savant) should say that I Army had 'only' 420 rounds per gun when it took the field.[4] At the time, the artillerists regarded such a quantity as evidence of unparalleled generosity on their part. After a year of fighting in the Russo-Japanese War, each gun in the I Manchurian Army had used just over 1,000 rounds, while each gun in the other two Manchurian Armies had used respectively 708 and 944. No-one imagined that I Army in East Prussia could possibly use more than a few hundred rounds per gun in the course of a few days' action, and would have cashiered any gunner who suggested anything different. As it was, the experts arranged for shell to be supplied with what they themselves saw as crazy prodigality. On the 12th day of mobilisation, I Army's guns had 785 rounds apiece, 11 Army's, 737.[5] The staff of the Warsaw military district reckoned that, by the 10th day of mobilisation, II Army would have enough shell for a long engagement. Similar smugness was expressed, with equal inappropriateness, in other matters. The staff of II Army arranged for 10,415 hospital-beds to be prepared, assuming a ten-day occupation by patients.[6] This, too, was thought to be munificent. In practice, just as shell was fired off at rates no-one had thought possible, so casualties were vast, from the outset, and II Army's hospital-places barely sufficed for the cases of syphilis. But all of this unreadiness was discovered subsequent to defeat. At the time, judging from a collection of documents assembled by editors sympathetic to tales of unreadiness, there was only one complaint: the Kexholm Guard Regiment, made up of Latvians with small feet, complained that Russian-issue boots were too big.[7] 'Unreadiness', like 'Russia sacrificing herself to save France', was at bottom a hard-luck story.

A lot more than 'unreadiness' was wrong with the army's behaviour in this period of the war. In the first place, there was a wholly mistaken reliance on cavalry. Promises to invade Germany by the 15th day of mobilisation, and German fears of such an invasion, were really concerned with cavalry—a wave of Huns would sweep into *deutsches Kulturland*. I and II Armies had nine cavalry divisions between them, and each infantry division also had its cavalry units. A great deal was sacrificed to make these cavalry units effective. Mobilisation would probably have gone faster if there had been less cavalry to shift. A disproportionate amount of rolling-stock went into its transporting and supplying; about the same number of trains (forty) for a cavalry division with 4,000 men and twelve guns as for an infantry division with 16,000 and fifty-four. Maintenance of these divisions was also a great burden for already strained railway-systems. A horse needed twelve pounds of grain every day, even for a few hours' work, and transporting of grain was usually the largest item in railway-supply—the British, for instance, using more tonnage to ship horses and fodder to the western front than was sunk by German submarines. Cavalry retarded armies' mobility, as much as it promoted mobility.

In any case, an initial surprise for Russian generals was that their cavalry in the field was ineffective. 4,000 men wandering around a wide area, barely in touch with each other or their commanders, could not achieve very much. The information sent back by them was inaccurate and late. In action, they could quite easily be knocked out by well-handled infantry units. In the old days, even a foolishly-led Light Brigade could at least charge artillery batteries with some hope of reaching them, since guns could not fire either with much accuracy or at a great range. Now, infantry rifles alone could fire up to fifteen rounds in a minute, at a range of 800 metres; enough to defeat a charging horse. There were sporadic cavalry engagements in East Prussia after 15th August, but they usually ended in a bloody withdrawal of the cavalrymen. Elderly cavalrymen, who had looked forward to the crowning achievement in a life of boots-and-saddles, broke down in bewilderment. The cavalry commander of I Army, the aged Khan of Nakhichevan, was the nearest that the Russian army came to a Hun. He was found in a tent, within a few miles of the border, weeping, out of touch with his troops, and suffering so badly from piles that he could not get on his horse at all.[8]

Of course, to be fair, there was maybe not much else that commanders could do but rely on cavalry. It was one of the conundrums of the First World War that there was not much alternative to the horse. The internal combustion-engine was, through no fault of the generals, in a primitive state. Even the German army had only eighty-three lorries, and most of these broke down while crossing the Ardennes. The Russian army requisitioned 3,000 private automobiles, but had to leave most of them rusting in the Semenovski Platz in Saint Petersburg for lack of maintenance and fuel.[9] In any case, horses, in the muddy conditions of the eastern front, were often more useful than lorries and, for that matter, tanks. The authorities overdid their reliance on cavalry, but that reliance was not as witless as it later appeared to be. In general, the First World War was marked by an extreme, and extraordinary, dichotomy between weight and mobility, the two vital principles of warfare. Armies had been able to benefit from the economic strides of the nineteenth century, but not yet from those of the twentieth. Agriculture and railways had developed far enough for the supply and maintenance of millions of men to become possible: the Great Powers conscripted between twelve and fifteen million men each between 1914 and 1918. The front-line strengths of the Powers usually reached two million without much effort. But, though these could be given lavish armament and supply, there was not much to make them mobile once they got beyond railheads. There was, in other words, a twentieth-century delivery-system, but a nineteenth-century warhead. In the Russian army, for instance, communications were primitive. The Russian II Army had twenty-five telephones, a few morse-coding machines, and one Hughes apparatus, a primitive tele-printer capable of discharging 1,200 words per hour, which broke down and forced the commander to move around on horseback to find out what was going on.[10] The Germans themselves had only forty wireless-stations for their whole armed forces; the Russians had even fewer, and in any case men did not know how to use them. Corps lost each other's codes, and had to broadcast *en clair*, to the Germans' satisfaction. Similarly, for its 150,000 men II Army had ten automobiles, and four defective motor-cycles. It also had forty-two aeroplanes, but most of them were grounded from one mechanical fault or other.[11] All in all, the Russian invasion of East Prussia was bound to be slow, moving at the pace of a marching man and a plodding horse. If troops could manage even ten miles in a day, they expected and perhaps deserved congratulation.

But these inevitable consequences of the age were made much more serious for the Russian army because of its peculiar structure. The civil war that had gone on within the army before 1914 resulted in absence of a real plan for war: troops were frittered away between different operations, since there was no single authority to impose its will on the army. More-over, when war broke out, that single authority did not emerge even when an ostensible supreme command (*Stavka*) was appointed. *Stavka*, in the early phase of the war, was a helpless victim of circumstances. The pre-war conflicts between soldiers who wanted to concentrate against Germany, and soldiers who wanted to concentrate against Austria-Hungary, had not been resolved. Instead, the army was split into two groups, and set to conduct separate operations. There were two separate 'fronts' or army groups: the north-western front, under Zhilinski, with three armies, to face Germany, and the south-western front, under Ivanov and Alexeyev, to face Austria-Hungary, with four armies. The construction of these separate groups was not undertaken because army leaders recognised that strategic handling of large armies needed army groups. Rather, it followed from men's recognition that compromise was impossible; better have two different operations. Real power was held by the separate army groups, and not by *Stavka*.

The supreme command itself was botched together at the last moment. Sukhomlinov, as war minister, had been expected to assume the supreme command. But he calculated that *Stavka* would remain powerless—as indeed, in a short war, would have been the case—and no doubt also foresaw defeats, in the first period of the war, because of Germany's rapid mobilisation. With a show of patriotic endeavour, he offered the post to the Tsar.[12] The Tsar calculated much as Sukhomlinov did. There was need of 'a great poster' to fill the post; and on 2nd August, it was offered to Grand Duke Nicholas, who had been expecting only the command of VI Army, along the Baltic coast. He knew neither the plans nor his subordinates. Yanushkevitch, translated from his post in Saint Petersburg to be chief of staff to the new commander-in-chief, went to see him at his estate. The other officers met him only at field-headquarters in Baranovitchi. *Stavka* itself was scraped together at the last moment. Yanushkevitch, the ostensible chief of staff, was a figurehead—chosen in the usual Sukhomlinov way to prevent anyone dangerous from taking over the job, and surviving in it from sheer force of characterlessness. The real force in *Stavka* was Danilov, who, despite his title ('Quarter-Master-General') was effective director of military operations. It was characteristic that Danilov took over the only suitable building in Baranovitchi, with his staff of fifteen officers, while Yanushkevitch had part of a railway-carriage, and a single adjutant. The Grand Duke himself was still more of a figurehead than Yanushkevitch. He entertained foreign military representatives, signed orders, and surrounded himself with aristocratic aides-de-camp, among them his brothers (whom he referred to as 'my sleeping-pills'). In important matters, he was silent: at a conference of the front-commands late in September, for instance, he stayed in a different room from the generals 'so as not to get in their way'. Foreigners were quite impressed with him, and his men are also supposed to have had much affection for him—though, since they saw him only once, this is difficult to account for. A few other officers were tacked on to make up numbers—Ronzhin was named as head of field transport, while Kondzerovski, who had been secretary of the 'attestation commission', dealing with senior promotions, was told at the last moment to join *Stavka* as adjutant-general (*dezhurny general*). He and Ronzhin shared a carriage, and neither had any staff to speak of. If *Stavka* had been a real supreme command, these conditions would of course have been laughably inadequate. But it was a mere shadow; and the number of officers, though far too small to discharge the duties of a supreme command, was also large enough in comparison with the officers' conception of their duties. None of them seem to have had much difficulty in composing voluminous diaries, or in writing long, daily letters to their wives; they spent long hours at the table—Kondzerovski having arranged for meals to be prepared 'by the Tatar K. with one of the best restaurant-cars in Russia, and a full complement of well-trained personnel'. Ronzhin made a collection of the Grand Duke's cigar-bands; Kondzerovski was always busy with the intrigues of senior promotions-matters; Yanushkevitch developed his taste for pornography.*13

Baranovitchi was chosen as headquarters town because of the universal idea that headquarters would have to be mobile. It lay on railway-lines to north and south, east and west, and *Stavka* put up with the various discomforts in the name of mobility. In much the same way Kondzerovski bought himself binoculars, a revolver, a saddle, a map-frame and a cloak. His only visit to the front occurred in fact by the *Stavka* Rolls, the driver of which had to lend him gloves. There was not even, in the first weeks, any convenient way of communicating with the front commands. Six men operated a morse-coding machine (capable of 600 words per hour) until the end of September, when some mechanics arrived from Minsk, at the behest of the ministry of posts and telegraphs, to instal links to Rovno and Cholm; even in October, the Council of Ministers were being asked for 161,000 roubles to help equip *Stavka* with the required cable. Baranovitchi, though not much more than a collection of huts and railway-carriages, became headquarters of the Russian army for the next year of war. But in August 1914, no-one imagined that the war would last for very long, or what it would be like.

In these circumstances, *Stavka* was in no position to enforce a plan, even if it had had one. It took over the compromise-arrangements haggled over between Danilov and Alexeyev, with a supporting-chorus of Postovski, Klyuev, Dragomirov and the rest, between 1910 and 1914. In theory, the front against Germany should have been considered the main one, since the war would be decided only by Franco-Russian victory over Germany. But various modifications had been made to this, and in 1912 the plan was changed: twenty-nine and a half infantry divisions against Germany, forty-six and a half against Austria-Hungary. In this way, the army was set two different operations, and there was little contact between the two army groups leading them. Even so, there seemed to be sufficient strength on the north-western front, for intelligence established, quite early on, that there were at most four German corps and some reserve divisions

---

*To start with, the atmosphere was quite different. As in all European armies, it was one of uplift. Officers in *Stavka* did without drink; women were forbidden in the staff compound; religious services were held every day. In the same style, Conrad von Hötzendorf, on the Austro-Hungarian side, slept on straw in the Zasanie barracks in Przemyśl; Hindenburg, on the German side, promised to write to his wife every day—all of it no doubt evidence as to how widespread was the supposition that this would be a short war. The strain of lengthening war soon told, however. By the end of 1914, wine was being served to *Stavka*, and vodka to senior officers. The Grand Duke told *Stavka's* chaplain to have the choir sing pieces from *Prince Igor* instead of Masses. What happened as regards women is not documented. Hindenburg managed to write about 1,500 letters to his wife in the war. The Austrians solved their problem by moving to comfortable villas in Moravia, and having their wives live there—although that was not enough for Conrad, who continued to write long, though not daily letters to other men's wives.[14]

in East Prussia: enough for the nine corps of I and II Armies to deal with. Zhilinski was told to invade East Prussia.

In reality, the plan to invade East Prussia needed more force than it was given. Ostensibly, the province was a good target for attack, since Russian armies could be launched from two directions, south and east. But the province was also well-set for defensive action by the Germans. It had lakes, forests, small hills and defiles, which gave excellent cover for defenders and severe obstacles for attackers. The railway-links on the Russian side were poor, on the German side sufficient for a flexible defence. When the two Russian groups came across the border, they would, just at the point where they would be most tired from marching, become separated by about a week's march by the line of lakes known as the *Angerapp-Stellung*, difficult to force without powerful siege-artillery. The two groups would have to move north and west of this position, exposing their outer flanks to attack, in the one case from the fortress of Königsberg, in the other from that of Thorn. It would be possible for the Germans to attack one group, relatively free of worry for the other, provided they used their communications properly. The Russians appreciated this; and Joffre regarded East Prussia as 'an ambush'. In reality, the plan made sense only if there were two whole armies protecting the outer flanks of the main ones—which Danilov had intended in the first place. But the structure of the army told against him, and only two armies plunged ahead into East Prussia.[15]

Stavka weakened this plan still more, because it thought up a third operation. The East Prussian route was not, after all, the shortest road to Berlin, and the French had quite often wondered why Russians neglected to make their most obvious manoeuvre—an attack from the Polish plains. Attack from west of Warsaw, direct towards Berlin, would strike the Germans hardest, and just before the war French representatives were keen on urging it. Russian confidence grew as railways were improved in this region—as a precaution against German invasion, this had been neglected before 1912. In 1914, Yanushkevitch decided that armies would be sent to the Warsaw region as a prelude to invasion of Germany by this most direct route. On 7th August he told the front commands that a new army, IX, would be set up here, and as new army corps arrived from the interior, they would form a further army, X, also to be assembled near Warsaw, for invasion 'in depth' of Germany. As things turned out, this plan was not put into effect, at least for the moment. But its existence meant that the East Prussian operation was weakened, and a third operation mounted instead.[16]

It was later said, notably by Golovin, the best-known writer on the subject, that the Russian invaders of East Prussia had been considerably inferior to the Germans, each of whose divisions was said to be worth one-and-a-half Russian divisions. There was not much truth in this. The Russian army ought to have been able to send overwhelming forces against Germany—it had sixty-seven first-line and thirty-one second-line infantry divisions, with thirty-seven and a half cavalry divisions and 5,800 guns against thirteen German infantry divisions (half of them second-line) and one German cavalry division in East Prussia, and some forty Austro-Hungarian infantry divisions in Galicia. Subtractions for the Austro-Hungarian front and for the new IX Army reduced the forces at the disposal of Zhilinski, commanding the front against Germany. Even so, there was a respectable superiority on the Russian side; the north-western front commanded twenty-nine and a half infantry divisions, the German VIII Army in East Prussia only thirteen.[17]

On the field, this superiority was whittled down. In the first place, the Russian commanders had little faith in their own second-line troops, whose divisions had more than two-thirds of their complement made up of reservists, not serving soldiers. The training of these reservists was thought to be too primitive for them to count as first-line soldiers, and the first-line elements in such divisions were alleged to be overwhelmed by the poor material surrounding them. I Army went to war with six and a half infantry divisions; but there were six more second-line divisions in its rear, disingenuously said 'not to have taken part in initial operations'[18]—in other words, left kicking their heels in Grodno and Kovno. Similarly, the various fortresses of the area were thought to require large garrisons—Novogeorgievsk in particular—and the field army lost many men and guns in an unnecessary attempt to hold these various artillery-museums. All this was in strict contrast to German behaviour: the Germans used their second-line and even third-line troops to the full, and ruthlessly stripped their fortresses (Königsberg, Graudenz, Posen) of mobile guns. Of their thirteen divisions, only six were first-line and four second-line; the other three were a composite of four Landwehr brigades (made up of men in their late thirties and early forties) and two garrison, Landsturm brigades, containing in some cases men who had not been trained at all; moreover the seven non-first-line divisions were actually weaker in artillery than average Russian divisions, although, in the legendry of the time, this was not given prominence. The forces that actually reached the field in East Prussia were therefore less unevenly-matched than they might have been; and it is certainly true that, for the circumstances of East Prussia, the Russian army would have needed a more comfortable superiority. As things were, the German VIII Army contained thirteen infantry divisions, one cavalry division and 774 guns,

Tannenber

Mallwischken
Pillkallen
Wladislawow
R. Szeszuppe
Stallüponen
Preny
mbinnen
kehmen
Olita
Tollmingkehmen
Kalwaria
RSSIAN FIRST ARMY (nenkampf)
Goldap
R. Niemen
Suwalki
R U S S I A
Marggrabowa
Widminnen
Augustow
Lyck
RUSSIAN TENTH ARMY (Pflug)
Grajewo
R. Lyck
Biala
III SIBERIAN CORPS
Osowiec
POLAND

0   20
                          Miles

German Eighth Army
Russian Armies
Withdrawals of Russian Second Army
Front line between Germans & Russian Second Army
                                        Aug 22
                                        Aug 21
Front line between Germans & Russian First Army
                                        Sept 6
                                        Sept 10
—x—x—x—   Sept 12
Command boundary between Russian First & Tenth Armies
Roads

usually in batteries of six—in all, 158 battalions and seventy-eight cavalry squadrons. The Russian I Army had six and a half infantry and five and a half cavalry divisions, or 104 battalions and 124 squadrons, with 492 guns, usually in batteries of eight; the Russian II Army had fourteen and a half infantry and four cavalry divisions, or 304 battalions and 111 squadrons, with 1,160 guns. But, after an exercise in the non-bringing of troops to the decisive point that out-did the finest exploits of the Austro-Russians at Austerlitz, II Army was reduced to nine and a half infantry divisions, three cavalry divisions or 188 battalions, seventy-two squadrons and 738 guns; and it was this force that fought Tannenberg. The Tsarist army was not crippled by its inferiority in artillery or men; it was crippled by its inability to use its superiority.

The affairs of the north-western front were also bedevilled by an element of mistrust among senior officers that, in this first, confused, phase of the war mattered more than it did later. The leading personnel had been chosen from different cliques of the army—friends and enemies of Sukhomlinov, plebeian infantrymen on the one side, aristocratic cavalrymen on the other. Lord and peasant stared resentfully at each other across the staff-maps. As Grand Duke Nicholas's *Stavka* came into existence, it could insist on key appointments, to cancel those made by the War Ministry. Zhilinski, commanding the front against Germany, was a Sukhomlinovite; but Rennenkampf, commanding I Army, was a notorious enemy. Samsonov, commanding II Army, was a Sukhomlinovite appointment, but their chiefs of staff, Mileant and Postovski, reversed the pattern—Rennenkampf communicated with Mileant only in writing throughout the East Prussian campaign, and refused to act on information given first to Mileant. For IX Army command in Warsaw, Sukhomlinov had named 'the coarse Siberian', Lechitski; Grand Duke Nicholas appointed as chief of staff one of his favourites, the 'gentleman', Guliewicz, an aristocratic Pole. The two men ended by addressing not a word to each other, after Lechitski refused permission for Madame Guliewicz to live in headquarters.[19] Communications, particularly between Zhilinski and Rennenkampf, were confused to the point where Zhilinski, nominally commander of the front, sometimes barely knew what was happening. The communications from I Army were so insultingly laconic and infrequent that Zhilinski, had to ask *Stavka* to intervene. Five messages were sent to Rennenkampf, and an adjutant of the Grand Duke himself—Kochubey—to remind him that he should let his seniors know what the army was doing.[20] In reality, the front command was almost as much of an illusion as was *Stavka* itself. The armies were merely allotted their forces and told to get on with their jobs. There was no real command-structure, merely a continual jostling between and within the great command-groups, as men strove to defend their spheres of competence, or in Zhilinski's case, incompetence.

The Russian I Army was set to march west into East Prussia, while II Army came up from the south. In theory, this would catch the German defenders in a 'pincer-movement': the Germans' flanks would be rolled up on either side of the *Angerapp-Stellung*, and they would be forced to retreat. This was a reasonable plan, but it depended on co-operation of the two armies involved. They would be separated by at least sixty miles as they encountered the main German positions, and an agile defence could attack first one, then the other. The Russian planners had been aware of this. But they chose inadequate methods of coping with the problem. They decided that the greatest danger would be an attack on the western flank of II Army—which could also affect the formation of the new IX Army near Warsaw. It was decided, therefore, to leave one corps of II Army virtually at a standstill, guarding this flank, and other troops—second-line divisions and cavalry—were given much the same task. In the same way, I Army worried about its open flank on the Baltic: maybe the Germans would organise a descent on the coast. A further group was detached as 'Riga-Schaulen group' to guard against this. Finally, to ensure that the inner flanks of I and II Armies kept together, one corps of II Army was kept between the two armies, and another pushed some way to the east, where it would be less effective. In this way, it was the Russians and not the Germans, who suffered from excessive concentration on their flanks. This reflected old-fashioned views of warfare. In earlier days, to have an enemy on the strategic flank was to risk all manner of tactical disadvantages—the enemy cavalry could cut communications with ease. Now, with cavalry so greatly reduced in serviceability, this danger was not so great. None the less, Zhilinski behaved as if the flanks were all-important. As a result, the attacking group of I Army was reduced to six and a half infantry divisions, that of II army to nine and a half; and the two groups would be at least six days' march apart. Both were inferior to the German VIII Army, which would therefore have a chance to knock out first one, then the other. Tannenberg did not illustrate Russia's economic backwardness. It merely proved that armies will lose battles if they are led badly enough.

The German VIII Army more or less had its plan laid out for it. One of the Russian armies must be held by a weak screen, and the rest of the Germans' forces sent against the other army. It was not clear, to begin with, which of the two armies must be attacked; it would depend on circumstances. There would be some advantage in attacking the Russian II Army from the west—here there were good railways. But the tactical circumstances decided against this plan. The Russian I Army crossed the border on 15th August, from the east; II Army, struggling up from the south, reached the border only five days later, and did not make serious contact with German troops until 22nd August. Moreover, almost as soon as I Army crossed the border, it was engaged by German troops. The German VIII Army suffered from something of the same general problems as the Russians did. But it was much smaller than Zhilinski's forces, more easily-controlled and supplied, and in the present case it had sense almost imposed on it by the nature of its task. Just the same, there was a problem with rebellious subordinates—in this case General von François, commander of 1. Corps, who arrogantly decided that he alone knew East Prussia, that the Russians could be defeated before they had even crossed the border. He engaged the Russians, to mutual bewilderment, in a set of flanking operations just after they came over the border. Both sides acquired a first experience of the deadly effect of enfilading gunnery; but nothing was decided. The German commander, Prittwitz, saw at least that large Russian forces were coming from the east, and he elected to attack these before those coming from the south could enter the battle. Tactically, he acquired a favourable position, since, as the Russians moved forward, they would have to divide their forces as they encountered the great heath of the river Rominte, and would perhaps leave their northern flank open.

Prittwitz let the Russian I Army advance, and attacked it on 20th August with nine divisions—half as much again as Rennenkampf deployed. He led off with a tactical success. The Russian northern group expected cavalry—of which there was a considerable quantity—at least to provide advance warning of any German movement. The cavalry failed to give this warning. In consequence, two German first-line divisions were able to march through woods, in the night of 19th-20th August, and fall on the unsuspecting Russian northern group—parts of which fled as far as Kovno, bearing regimental flags. François, commanding the German forces here, started off in pursuit, but then encountered a problem that came up subsequently, in greatly magnified form. Attackers might win a considerable tactical success; but they would be unable to follow it up, because cavalry was ineffective and supply-problems intervened. In this case, François's two divisions were held up by the afternoon of 20th August, and François appealed to the rest of VIII Army to help him. But the German commanders to the south did not have the advantage of surprise that François had had. On the contrary, they had to launch expected, frontal attacks against an enemy that had begun to dig trenches of a sort. Mackensen, commanding the central corps of the army, lost 8,000 men in an hour or two, was then attacked in flank, and was rescued only with difficulty when the flanking Russian group was

itself taken in flank by a German division to the south. By the evening of
20th August, it was clear that Prittwitz's attack had gone wrong; Gumbinnen was a clear Russian victory. Prittwitz panicked, for he knew that not
only had he been beaten in the Gumbinnen battles, but also that there
was a new Russian army approaching from the south. He might not even
have time to retreat. He telephoned the German high command and told
them that he must retreat as far as the lower Vistula, leaving East Prussia
altogether; even the river could not be held, 'it can be waded across
everywhere'. All this was an exaggeration: the Germans had not been
badly defeated, and could in any case recover quickly enough. The
corps commanders themselves soon recovered their nerves as they noted
Russian failure to pursue. Moltke, in the west, was struck by the indecision and panic of Prittwitz, and decided to have him removed. He
selected as successor, Hindenburg, and chose as Hindenburg's chief of
staff one of the best technical experts of the German army, Ludendorff.
These arrived to take command on 23rd August—Prittwitz learning of
his dismissal, characteristically, only when his transport-chief reported
that arrangements had been made for a special train carrying his
successor.

When Ludendorff arrived, Prittwitz's staff had already recovered.
Clearly, it would now not be possible to attack the Russian I Army—
the attack would be expected, and in any case would be threatened from
the south by three and a half Russian corps, of II Army. The obvious
manoeuvre was to attack the left wing of II Army, an attack that could
be carried out without fear for the rear, and the very scheme that
Russians and Germans alike had foreseen before the war. Arrangements
were therefore made to take one corps out of the Gumbinnen positions,
by rail, together with some of the *Landwehr*, and collect them on the
southern borders of East Prussia, where they could attack II Army's left
flank. Ludendorff sanctioned this idea. In his memoirs, he also asserts
that he had the idea of taking the right wing of the Russian II Army as
well—the other two corps from the Gumbinnen positions to march
south-west, against this right wing, the manoeuvre eventually made, to
decisive effect. But it is doubtful if Ludendorff saw this far ahead. A more
difficult problem was simply to withdraw these two corps from their
exposed positions, to the north-east of a Russian army. The railways
were already taken up with the evacuation of one army corps, to the left
of II Army. The other two corps would simply have to march south-
west to join up with German troops facing II Army. If they encountered
Russian troops, there would be a battle, but one at least quite close to the
concentration-areas of other German troops. Ludendorff was merely
keeping his options open, and was not to tell in advance on 24th August,

what series of miracles would give him a victory as great as Tannenberg. By 25th August he had laid out his forces: François, with two first-line divisions and some territorials, to attack the left wing of II Army; 20. Corps, with a Reserve division and some *Landwehr*, to hold the centre of II Army and engage its attention; 1st Reserve Corps and 17. Corps to march south-west towards this new battle area; and the entire Russian I Army to be held off by a cavalry division and a territorial brigade, with, in the north, the fortress of Königsberg and in the centre that of Lötzen.[21]

What followed depended to a large degree on the activity, or lack of activity, on the part of the Russian I Army; II Army was not given the help it needed. In the first place, Zhilinski, who was theoretically responsible for the armies' co-operation, did little. By nature, he was extremely prudent—just after Gumbinnen, for instance, ordering a guard to be maintained for Grodno,[22] far in the rear. He mistrusted such information as he received, and received nothing from *Stavka* to elucidate matters. I Army seemed to have enough to do. It would have to deal with the fortress of Königsberg, which now lay on its northern flank. Not until 23rd August was the Germans' withdrawal noted, and even then both Zhilinski and Rennenkampf thought two of the German corps had retired towards Königsberg—the prudent, textbook behaviour to be expected from Russian generals. Organising the siege of Königsberg was difficult enough, and was thought to need 'five to seven infantry divisions', or three-quarters of the army's infantry, as well as siege-artillery that had to be dragged forward.[23] I Army had in any case suffered from the fighting since it crossed the border on 15th August—3. Corps had lost over 6,000 men, and shell-supply was in disorder. The force had undoubtedly won a victory, and Rennenkampf supposed he had done his work. On 26th August, orders were issued for the siege of Königsberg; the advance over the Angerapp lines went very slowly, with cavalry performing its rôle, as usual, with painful inadequacy. Everyone supposed that the real task was now II Army's: it must cut off the German's retreat to the lower Vistula. Only on 27th August did the attack on II Army's left begin to affect calculations; only on the 28th was there an order for I Army to help II, even then countermanded. In effect, the Germans would have until 30th August at least in order to concentrate all their forces against the Russian II Army.[24]

Given that II Army advanced steadily into the ring Ludendorff was setting up, a great victory was set up for him. Ill-luck and misjudgment thwarted the operations of Samsonov, commanding this army. He was told that the Germans were retreating, that II Army must cut them off; and his forces were directed even further from I Army than before—

something of a gap opening between his right and his centre. On his left was 1. Corps, forbidden until 27th August to go over the border. Supply and communications were in disorder. A new supply-system had been introduced just before the war, giving a front supply-chief full powers, in place of the army ones; and no-one knew how to work this system. Even in Bialystok, bread had been lacking, and the habit of allotting the same supply-route to different corps meant that one corps would receive too much, and another not nearly enough. For 25th August, commanders appealed for a day's rest, which Zhilinski forbade, but which they no doubt took. Communications, too, were in disorder. Telegrams to the army command went to the Warsaw post-office, and from there went in bundles, by car, to Samsonov's headquarters.[25] On the right, 6. Corps manoeuvred along sixty kilometres of front, receiving messages in a code unknown to it. Yet Samsonov was not too perturbed. He was told on 25th August that two German corps had retired into Königsberg; for 24th August he was also told by Zhilinski that there were 'only insignificant forces' in front of him. In any case, his centre, as it came over the border, had already done quite well against these forces, taking seven guns in one frontier-battle.[26] Samsonov therefore pushed forward the two-and-a-half corps of his centre, expecting 1. Corps on his left to be sufficient guard, and 6. Corps on his right to be free from all danger.

The problem became all the greater since there were delays in German action. François, who was supposed to attack the Russian left wing, refused to move on 25th August—his group had just arrived by train, after severe fighting, and its guns had not come in. On 26th August, François again prevaricated, received a visit from Ludendorff, and attacked feebly, with endless deliberation. Ludendorff was annoyed; but François's delays, accidental as they were, in practice lent a dimension of success to Ludendorff's scheme that its author had not imagined—for Samsonov, unperturbed for his left, pushed on his centre all the more. Even in the morning of 27th, François's attack met with difficulties on the southern wing. But his two first-line divisions on that day attacked the right wing of the Russian 1. Corps, which had been told not to cross the border, and, in the area of attack, was particularly thin. François broke through between it and the left-hand group of the centre, nearly 200 German guns being opposed by only fifty; and by the end of 27th August, François had entered the frontier-town of Soldau, through which led one of the vital lines of retreat of Samsonov's central group. He had snapped the link between left and centre; but this, with the state of communications in Samsonov's army, was appreciated hardly at all. Artamonov, commander of 1. Corps, stood bravely with his men in the front trenches, and thought he had already done his duty, and at least saved himself.

The delay in François's attack had allowed Samsonov's centre to move forward, through country that gave little visibility to commanders. From 26th August two corps and a division moved forward against the Germans' central group. They began to win some successes, on the river Drewenz and south of Allenstein, and gained misleading confidence in consequence—again, despite Ludendorff's wishes. A series of flanking operations, in which the greater weight of the Russians told, began to go badly for the Germans; and even the intervention of a fresh *Landwehr* group (Goltz) brought little relief. On 28th August there was even 'a major success'[27] for the Russians at Waplitz, where they almost destroyed a German division, incontinently attacking. Ludendorff benefited from this, in the long run, because the Russian centre group persisted in its course; but he did not see it, and ordered François on the 28th to send back a division to help the threatened centre. Whether because he knew what was happening, whether because of some natural disinclination to obey the plebeian Ludendorff by sending first-class Prussian troops to the help of some third-rate *Landsturm* unit, François closed his eyes and continued his advance east of Soldau, thus arriving far into the rear of the Russian central group, much of which could not now retreat. Early on 29th August, François's cavalry units entered Willenberg, on the road east of Soldau, and there encountered units of a German corps that had marched from the north-east, Mackensen's 17. Corps: Samsonov was surrounded.

This, too, had been achieved partly by accident. Ludendorff had told the corps remaining in the Gumbinnen positions to march south-west as fast as they could. Probably he merely hoped they would come to the help of his centre, but he maybe had more ambitious ideas. On 26th August these two encountered the right-hand corps of Samsonov's army[28]—the two divisions of 6. Corps (Blagoveshchenski). No-one had told Blagoveshchenski that there was any danger—on the contrary, both corps were thought to be in Königsberg. Blagoveshchenski's front was too long, his task not at all clear. His two divisions were separated, one of them under a veteran of Plevna; and even the divisional reserves had lost touch with their command. News did reach the Russians that there were troops marching south-west—aircraft had noted this. But the movement was thought to be of Russian troops, certainly not four German divisions, two of them first-line.[29] As a final twist, the Germans' intervention, despite great superiority, was not even particularly crushing: they were tired, the first-line troops had lost heavily at Gumbinnen, and the second-line forces were insufficiently-trained; moreover, neither corps commander (Mackensen and Below) had much idea of what was happening. There was a series of actions, the greatest of them on 26th August against one of the Russian divisions, the flank of which was on a lake, and enfiladed by powerful artillery from the other shore. Its troops suffered forty per cent casualties, a third of the guns were lost, and the divisional command was in such disorder that even its report of events could not be written until a week later. The two Russian divisions retired in disorder towards the south. But they had not lost so heavily for men to believe that they had been attacked by overwhelming forces. Samsonov assumed that the matter originated in Blagoveshchenski's misdoings, not in a German threat of any significance. Such news as reached him merely prompted him to push forward the centre.

In this way, two German corps found themselves well into the right flank of Samsonov's army. Accident again made this more effective than it might have been. The two corps commanders quarrelled about what to do next—each prompting the other to stay put, in order that he could use the convenient road towards Allenstein and safety. Ludendorff intervened on 27th August to tell Below, commanding the less reliable force, that he should use the road and come to the help of the German centre, around Allenstein; Mackensen was to follow. There were delays in executing this order, and in the mean time Ludendorff woke up to reality—with François well into the Russian left, Mackensen was well-placed to close the circle from their right. On the 28th Mackensen was told to move west rather than north-west, and in so doing he met up with François's units in Willenberg. The other German corps moved towards Allenstein, and forced the Russian centre there to turn about, its guns now facing north-west and east.

Samsonov's situation, which even at midday on 27th had seemed bright, had now become hopeless. His left wing and his right wing had been thrust away from the central body, and there was no way of getting orders through to them, since the Germans had, by 29th August, closed the roads leading to the south. The centre of his army had been involved in a complicated series of flanking manoeuvres, some of them misleadingly successful. But the arrival of a German corps in the rear, near Allenstein, now blocked even roads to the east. No doubt a command that functioned properly could have found some way out—the German cordon was thin enough. But there were over 100,000 men in this pocket, insufficiently in touch with each other, badly-supplied, and in an area that their commanders did not know. In the broken country, some units had already disintegrated, without fighting at all. There were merely confused reports of German troops blocking the passages to the south. In any case, roads to the south were few: one, through the Kurken defile, would have to be used by two corps, and already it was under German artillery-fire: and since it was only 500 yards wide, to use it would be calamitous. Tired and bewildered, the Russian soldiers began to surrender on 29th August— a whole series of captures, in which German battalions received the surrender of Russian brigades. Only ten thousand men escaped; Ludendorff, who had expected only thirty thousand prisoners, had to report nearly 100,000. Samsonov himself rode off towards Willenberg with his chief of staff, a Cossack guard, one map and a compass for the entire group. He is said to have shot himself. As a final act, the corps of the left and right—1. and 6.—stumbled forward, under Zhilinski's prodding, on 29th August. They caused panic in the German cordon, and then prudently retired. Rennenkampf, further off still, ordered his cavalry forward on Allenstein, and then told it to stop. Confusion was such that Zhilinski himself failed to appreciate what had happened until 2nd September.[30]

Tannenberg—which, on rather dubious grounds, gave its name to the battle—was the most spectacular victory of the war, and generated a propaganda-myth for years to come. East Prussia had been defended, seemingly against overwhelming odds; 100,000 men and nearly 400 guns were captured. In practice, the victory was overrated at the time: the Russians recovered, and invaded East Prussia again a few weeks later. But what was dangerous to the Germans was the myth that Tannenberg launched. Men supposed—and the version produced by Ludendorff, later, buttressed their supposition—that Hindenburg and Ludendorff had made a brilliant strategic manoeuvre, leading to a new Cannae. There was something in this, but it was distorted by exaggeration. The transfer of troops to Samsonov's left was arranged before Ludendorff arrived, and formed part of a sensible scheme foreseen some years before—a coup against the Russian left by troops that also had a good line of retreat if things went wrong. Even this developed as well as it did largely because François disobeyed Ludendorff's instructions. The manoeuvre that brought two German corps into Samsonov's right flank was certainly Ludendorff's; but that, too, was calculated as a form of retreat, and only chance and delay turned it into the coup against Samsonov's right flank of the type eventually attained. In a sense, the vital part of this battle was the expensive and protracted fighting of the central groups—frontal engagements that were far from being in the Germans' favour—for this pinned the two corps of Samsonov's centre to the point of immobility. But the essential features were on Samsonov's side—confused command, disorderly supply, above all a completely mistaken picture of the Germans' dispositions. The Germans won because they were defenders, on whom sense was almost imposed by the lay-out of the land and the railways, and the nature of the task. Tannenberg none the less launched a myth of the brilliant strategic coup, a perpetuation of the Napoleonic myth in eastern Europe which, in the circumstances of 1914–1918, was dangerous enough. It was common sense, discipline, de-centralisation that won Tannenberg; just the same, Ludendorff discovered from it that he had military genius, and found a large number of Germans to agree with him.

The realities of 1914 caught up with Ludendorff almost at once, when he turned against the Russian I Army. On 31st August the remnant of II Army had retired over the border. This left I Army extended between Königsberg and the Angerapp line, its left wing isolated in a region of lakes and forest in the south-eastern corner of the province. Rennenkampf had now called in further troops, making some twelve divisions; and the new X Army was to be assembled in the south-eastern corner of East Prussia to make the flank safer. Ludendorff had also received reinforcements—in the last days of Prittwitz's command, the panic he divulged had led to his being sent two first-line army corps from the western front (11. and Guard Reserve) with a cavalry division—a withdrawal of troops from France that did something to halt the German invasion and thus justified the Russian offensive of August. Now, VIII Army contained eighteen and a half infantry divisions and two cavalry divisions, most of which Ludendorff was prepared to concentrate against the Russian I Army.

He hoped for another Tannenberg—a strong group (again under François) would move against the isolated Russian left; it would then move into the rear of the centre groups, and Ludendorff hoped for mass-surrenders, as before. He performed a commendable effort of concentration—of the 232 battalions and 1,212 guns in East Prussia, 184 and 1,074 were used for this operation: the rest were strung out along the southern borders against the chance of a Russian attack there. The Russian I Army had 228 battalions and 924 guns, but scattered along the front, and much of it concentrated on the northern side—on the left there was a second-line division, some cavalry, a few battalions of the new X Army, supported to the north by three second-line divisions weak in artillery. Once more, the Germans were led into a tactical success by Russian blundering. Some Russians did foresee Ludendorff's action against I Army's left—Oranovski, chief of staff to Zhilinski, asked Rennenkampf how he would face this extremely probable enveloping manoeuvre'.[31] But Zhilinski was worried that a retreat by Rennenkampf would allow the Germans to pursue II Army—which had been told to go back as far as Warsaw, even to destroy the bridges there.[32] In any case, the new X Army would do something for the open flank. Meanwhile, Rennenkampf made free an army corps and sent it marching south; he also pulled back his forward troops a few miles. Quite mysteriously, he and other commanders seem to have expected that there would be a German attack from Königsberg—an illusion that Ludendorff, through false messages, fostered. There were worries, but they fell through the complicated structure of Russian command; and no-one foresaw that Ludendorff would act with speed.

In practice, the German VIII Army was re-assembled after Tannenberg with much efficiency,[33] and an attacking group of three divisions was drawn up against the Russian left. The other corps were placed on lines to the north. François led off on 7th September—with sixteen battalions and thirty guns against him, he attacked with forty and two hundred. The weak, second-line troops against him scattered; they appealed to elements of the newly-arriving X Army, a few battalions near the rail-heads. But Brinken, the local corps commander, did not want to split his force, and his army commander—Pflug—was anxious not to have his new force scattered before it even arrived. Both men failed to respond, and François's group, by 9th September, moved north to cut off some of the Russian troops before Lötzen—taking sixty guns from them.

But this tactical success ended German victories, and the engagement—the battle of the Masurian Lakes—formed an accurate model of operations to come in the east. Ludendorff urged on François, and set his other corps to attack. But François's cavalry turned out to be almost as ineffective as Russian cavalry had been before: it could be held up even by retreating troops. The frontal attacks of German corps to the north were, almost uniformly, a failure—although, again true to pattern, they often began with minor tactical successes that egged commanders into trying again and again to break through the Russian lines. Moreover, with his left wing turned, Rennenkampf did not make the mistake into which Samsonov had been led: he gave orders for retreat in time. His front had been transformed into a semi-circle, and he could bring troops more rapidly from the north than the Germans, who had to go round the semi-circle, were able to do; and the retreat, in general, was skilfully managed. By 13th September, the Russian I Army had once more crossed the border, to safety. Ludendorff grumbled—François should have made a greater effort. But François could have done little more: he suffered from supply-problems, fatigue, increasing Russian resistance as reserves came in, all problems that tactically successful troops often encountered. These problems came up still more after 13th September, as the Germans moved into Russian territory. By 20th September they were meeting serious tactical reverses; by 25th September, the two Russian armies organised a counter-offensive that drove back the Germans to their frontier, in the end even as far as the Angerapp lines. VIII Army had captured 30,000 prisoners—almost all of them as a result of François's initial tactical success on 7th and 8th September. But it had also lost heavily—100,000 men, of 250,000—and the battle of the Masurian lakes ended with a complicated stalemate. Unnoticed at the time, this formed the pattern of battles in the east for the following year of war.

CHAPTER FOUR

The Opening Round: Galicia

The German VIII Army in East Prussia had won, at least partly because sense had been imposed on it. The army was small enough to be controlled. The invasion-routes, the lines of retreat, and the possible areas of riposte had been clearly marked-out; there was a railway-system that allowed transport at least of François's corps; and in any case there were seven other armies in the west to pick up the pieces if things went wrong. The Austro-Hungarian army in Galicia did not have these advantages. The theatre of operations was the sprawling, flat land of southern Poland, with neither railway-lines nor roads prominent—hundreds of featureless miles, dominated either by dust or by mud. Neither Russians nor Austrians had their plans made for them.

On the Austrian side, men felt—characteristically—that something must be done, but they did not perceive quite what might be done. They knew that Austria-Hungary must do something to take the load from Germany's shoulders when war broke out. The Austro-Hungarian General Staff agreed that, in the event of two-front war, Germany's most sensible course would be to concentrate against France in the first round; consequently, Austria-Hungary would have to undertake a large part of the work in the east, until German troops could come from France. There were plans for an offensive against Russia, in which the German VIII Army might co-operate. Two factors spoke for this offensive: first, the exposed nature of the Russian position in Poland, which jutted out between the two Central Powers, and where large numbers of Russian troops might be surrounded, and second, the calculation that Russian mobilisation would be slow, slow enough, in the first period, to offset any numerical inferiority of the Central Powers in the longer term. Formally, the Austro-Hungarian plan before 1914 was therefore for a full-scale offensive against Russia; formally, too, there was an undertaking on the Germans' part that VIII Army would, if possible, contribute a parallel offensive from East Prussia. The Austro-Hungarian chief of staff, Conrad von Hötzendorf, dreamt of expelling the Russians from Poland,

and was confident enough, when war broke out, to appoint an Austro-Hungarian governor of Warsaw.

But in Vienna there was always a large gap—perhaps larger than anywhere else—between ideals and reality. The Austro-Hungary army was not strong enough for the rôle cast for it by Conrad. It had steadily declined in relative weight. In the 1880s, Austro-Hungarian planners had supposed that their thirty-two infantry divisions would have to encounter twenty-nine Russian ones. The proportions then changed, and by 1914 the Austro-Hungarians could foresee that about fifty Russian divisions would be mustered against their own forty. The Habsburg Monarchy could not stand the strain of an arms-race; more and more, it became a system of institutionalised escapism, and the chief benefit that it conferred on its subjects was to exempt them from reality.[1] Universal military liability was never seriously asserted: the Hungarians would not give money for it, the military authorities themselves shrank from its consequences, and the people very often expressed their view of it by the simplest method—running away, as Hitler did. Formally, universal conscription was introduced in 1868, but money and will were so far lacking that only about one in five of the liable young men ever reached the colours, the rest being exempted under one heading or other, even sometimes by lot-drawing. Even that fifth frequently did not have to serve the full three years prescribed by law, for many were 'sent on permanent leave' after two years. The army became so limited in size that many units were amalgamated—resulting in the curious, though not unique, twist that the Austro-Hungarian field army of 1914 contained fewer infantry battalions than the army that had been defeated in 1866, despite a population-increase, since then, of nearly twenty millions.[2] After 1906, there were attempts at reform. But they simply broke into the never-never world of Habsburg politics: Hungarian obstruction, threats of abdication, followed more prosaically by jugglings of half-percentages and promises of petty payments to nationalist blackmailers, until a few coppers rattled through the machine to reward the soldiers for trying. As war approached, the Austro-Hungarian army was less and less capable of sustaining it.

The chief problem was that Austria-Hungary, too, would have to face a two-front war, with means even less adequate than Germany's.[3] Her forty-eight infantry divisions must take on not only the fifty that Russia could send against them, but also the eleven infantry divisions of the Serbian army. The Serbian problem was difficult to deal with. If Austria-Hungary tried to defeat Serbia in the first period of the war, she would have to assemble some twenty divisions, to be occupied no doubt for a month. This would leave less than thirty for the Russian front—not enough to take advantage even of the very first period of the war, when Russian mobilisation had not yet told to its full extent. It might be better to leave a minimal defensive force against Serbia, and concentrate the rest against Russia, and this, formally, was the Austro-Hungarian plan for war: seven divisions against Serbia, the rest for Russia. In the early period of war, these latter would have superiority—enough at any rate to hold the Russians off while Germany defeated the French. Moltke approved of these plans, and promised support from East Prussia.

These plans took account of everything, except the facts. War was not at all likely to begin with a joint Russo-Serbian declaration of war. On the contrary, it was much more likely that Austria-Hungary would first go to war with Serbia, and that Russia would intervene only later on Serbia's side. If it came to an Austro-Serbian war, then a substantial part of the Austro-Hungarian army would have to go south—about twenty divisions were foreseen—while the rest of the army was not mobilised. If Russia then came into the war, the rest of the army would indeed be mobilised, but, with less than thirty divisions, it would not suffice for the great offensive that Conrad had promised Moltke. Troops would have to be brought back from Serbia. But two things counted against this: first, the relative poverty of the railway-links between south and north-east, second the inadvisability of suspending a campaign against Serbia in the middle. Before 1914, men did not make up their minds as to how this case—which Conrad none the less described to Moltke as 'the most difficult, but also the most probable'—might be dealt with. Formally, there was an undertaking that all would be subordinated to the offensive against Russia, but within the General Staff there were serious misgivings. It might look, at the least, peculiar for a Great Power to begin a European war with an extra-tour in the Balkans; but maybe the discrepancy between Austrian means and Austrian pretensions left little choice. Certainly, by the spring of 1914, Conrad was clearly a prey to doubt. Despite his protestations to the Germans, his staff was busied with means by which the forces against Serbia could be strengthened at the expense of those against Russia; and in March, Conrad sketched a deployment-plan for the troops in Galicia that could only mean almost complete abandonment of any schemes for offensive action there. Instead of drawing the troops up in the north-eastern part of Galicia, close to the border with Russia, he suggested unloading them far to the south, on the rivers San and Dniester. This occurred in response to alarms (well-founded) as to the speed of Russian mobilisation and the size of the Russian forces. But characteristically Conrad shrank from formal alteration of the plan, such that the great offensive against Russia was still its main object. Before 1914, the Austro-Hungarian General Staff had thus, in effect, failed to decide which of the two fronts would be treated as more important. This was to happen as circumstances dictated.

Guaranteeing this flexibility on the ground was difficult, for the railway-technicians had to work out ways by which parts of the army could be treated separately, once mobilisation began. The greater part of the army ('A-Staffel') would obviously have to be reserved for the Russian front, whether or no war broke out with Russia, and a lesser part, *Minimalgruppe Balkan*, would have to be reserved for Serbia, whether for offensive or defensive purposes. The third part of the army (the twelve divisions of 'B-Staffel') would be directed against Serbia or Russia as circumstances dictated. If Serbia alone went to war, it would go south; if Russia and Serbia jointly intervened, it would probably go north-east, but even for this case Conrad seems to have wanted flexibility. The railway-planners were told to work out a method by which the mobilisation of these various groups could proceed separately. They found an obvious one: the troops of 'A-Staffel' should be sent first to Galicia, those of 'B-Staffel' only afterwards, so that people would have a chance to make up their minds what was to be done with them. The result was a serious delay in the mobilisation-programme against Russia. Although good railways stood at the disposal of the troops of 'B-Staffel', they would not, even at the best of times, be able to reach Galicia until the period between the 21st and 25th days of mobilisation, whereas the others would be there a week before. Still, this method seemed to make it possible for 'B-Staffel' to make an independent movement, if this appeared to be necessary, without disrupting the mobilisation against Russia or Serbia; and the railway-planners were pleased with their performance. 'B-Staffel' could either go south against Serbia, or be pulled out of a Serbian campaign, or be sent direct to Galicia, and the necessary flexibility had thus been attained.

When war began there was a great muddle on the Austro-Hungarian side; and it was not much cleared up by the explanations that were offered, which were, first, that there had been no muddle at all and then that it was the Germans' fault. On 25th July the Serbians rejected the Austro-Hungarian ultimatum, and Austria-Hungary mobilised half of her army, declaring war on 28th. The seven corps of 'B-Staffel' and the Balkan group were to move south; a further one was also mobilised, although it was part of the Galician group, and the railway-planners were told to send it to the Balkans, although Conrad told everyone that it had been mobilised only as protection against Italy, or perhaps revolt in Bohemia. According to Conrad, the bulk of this force was due to be turned against Russia if she intervened. But he could hardly divert troops from the Serbian theatre merely because Russia threatened to intervene;

and, according to him, it was not until the very end of the month that Russia's intention of intervening became clear. Late in the evening of 31st July, accordingly, Conrad tried—by his own account—to turn the bulk of his southern forces against Russia. But he was told by his chief railway-expert, Straub, that this could not be done. So many troop-transports had already left for the Serbian theatre that to turn them about would cause chaos, in the middle of mobilisation against Russia. There was nothing for it but to have these troops (by now, more or less identical with II Army) continue their journey to Serbia. They could de-train there, and be transported back to the north-east, for their Russian campaign, once the lines there had been cleared, i.e. after completion of the mobilisa-tion of the rest of the army against Russia. Conrad had, in other words, lost his chance to send 'B-Staffel' direct to Galicia because the Germans had failed to extract 'clarity' about the attitude of Russia before these troops had begun their journey south.

Conrad goes on to state that, even with this Balkan trip, the troops of II Army arrived hardly a moment later in Galicia than they would have done had they gone there directly; indeed, this was the railway-experts' reason for allowing the Army to make its peregrinations in the first place. This was, odd as it may appear, true enough. According to the mobilisa-tion-programme, the troops of 'B-Staffel' were supposed to follow those of 'A-Staffel' to Galicia. These latter were mobilised only in response to Russian mobilisation, on 31st July, and, if the railway-programme were adhered to, they were due to arrive in Galicia between the 15th and 20th days, the 'B-Staffel' troops only in the course of the next four or five days. The 'B-Staffel' troops would therefore have to wait in any event before going to Galicia, and it was, from the railwaymen's viewpoint, more or less unimportant whether they spent their waiting-time in barracks or in trains and tents on the Serbian border. Had it not been for activities on the part of the local Balkan commander, Potiorek, most of 'B-Staffel' would in fact have arrived in Galicia on schedule, though only because that schedule was in any case preposterously long.

However, Conrad's own explanation was a dangerously misleading one, for it did not reveal the real causes of the initial disaster that Austria-Hungary met. There was, in the first place, something unreal in Conrad's constant asseveration that he did not know what Russia's attitude would be, at least until 31st July. On the contrary, Russia made her attitude plain enough from the beginning. Even before the ultimatum had been pre-sented, she warned that she could not be indifferent to the fate of Serbia. On 25th July, the Council of Ministers instructed the war minister to proceed with 'the period preparatory to war', and over the next few days a stream of reports from consuls and businessmen reached Vienna to the effect that substantial troop-movements were taking place within Russia. On 28th July the Russians announced that they would mobilise partially against Austria-Hungary; there was talk of general mobilisation a day later; and on 29th July Conrad himself drafted a document, for presentation to the Emperor Franz Joseph, to the effect that European war was imminent. He himself says in his memoirs that '31st July brought clarity' to Russia's attitude—not, in other words, 31st July, on which day Russian, German and Austro-Hungarian general mobilisation was formally announced to the world. Russia's attitude was really quite clear all along, and Krobatin, the Austro-Hungarian war minister, announced as much when he remarked to the Council of Ministers later on that 'no-one was ever really under any illusion as to the likelihood of Russian intervention'. Whether Conrad thought it likely or not, he behaved at least fool-hardily in arranging for the transport of 'B-Staffel' against Serbia until 31st July.

The documents make plain what Conrad and his apologists concealed: that Conrad had in effect decided to pursue his war with Serbia despite the obviousness of Russian intervention; and this had much more to do with the initial disaster than any difficulties with the railways. The diary of his chief railway-expert, Straub, makes plain what happened. On 30th July, Conrad told him that, with Russian intervention round the corner, he would have to mobilise the rest of the army, 'A-Staffel', to go to Galicia. According to the plan, 'B-Staffel' should also go to Galicia to meet Russian intervention. But Conrad said he wanted it to go on to Serbia, and asked Straub if he could arrange for simultaneous movement of 'A-Staffel' to Galicia and of 'B-Staffel' to Serbia. Straub said that this would be extraordinarily difficult, for 'none of the prepared variants covered this new case'. Success could not be guaranteed, but he would do his best. However, to enable him to do his best, he would have to have a few days' grace before the mobilisation of 'A-Staffel' began. Mobilisation against Russia was proclaimed on 31st July. But, to give Straub his few days' grace, 'the first day of mobilisation' was named as 4th August. What this meant in practice was that not a man would have to report to the colours before 5th August, since the first day of mobilisation was given to the men to arrange their own affairs.[4] A grotesque situation resulted. Many men were full of patriotic zeal, and reported at once to their units, instead of waiting until 5th August. They were told to go away again—not the last dampener to patriotic emotion that Austrian soldiers were to receive. Meanwhile, Straub used his few days' grace to develop a new programme, permitting separate despatch of 'A-Staffel' and 'B-Staffel'. Conrad held to this programme although news built up throughout 30th and 31st July of an impending European war, and he did not learn until late in the evening of 31st July that, independent of his will, technical railway factors had now intervened to make any further change impossible. While still in the belief that the programme could be changed, and while knowing all of the factors that could make change desirable (Russian and German mobilisation having been proclaimed at noon) Conrad persisted in sending orders to the units of 'B-Staffel' that their mobilisation was to go on as it had been begun, and added for the benefit of II Army Command in Budapest that 'for all troops mobilised before 28th July the instructions of the war ministry and the General Staff will, despite the intervention of Russia, remain in force'. In other words, the despatch of II Army against Serbia had nothing very much to do with railway-necessities; indeed, the railwaymen had protested against it. It was Conrad's own strategy that dictated its course.

In the early evening of 31st July Conrad seems to have had second thoughts. On the face of things, it was absurd for Austria-Hungary to begin European war by launching half of her army against an insignificant Balkan state. Moltke, when he heard of the plan, protested energetically. A series of messages came from Berlin—Moltke, several times; Bethmann Hollweg; Jagow; and finally the German Kaiser himself, in a telegram to Franz Joseph, saying 'in this gigantic struggle it is vital for Austria not to split her forces by going against Serbia'. Within the Monarchy, there were also alarms. Tisza, the powerful Prime Minister of Hungary, had been told on 28th July by his representative in Vienna what Conrad's plan was: to ignore Russia and strike down Serbia 'with rapid blows'. He saw through the technical obfuscation with which Conrad decked out his plan,[5] and protested that, if too few troops were placed against Russia, there could be a defeat that would attract a Romanian declaration of war. He tried to persuade Conrad to send another two corps against Russia. These pressures brought Conrad round. After receiving the text of the Kaiser's telegram, he telephoned Straub, summoned him back to the office, and asked him how he would react, 'if the prevailing Balkan mobilisation were to be transformed into a Russian one', in other words, if 'B-Staffel' were to go after all to Galicia.

Straub was aghast. He had been told the day before to improvise a plan, despite his own protests, by which precisely this was not to happen. The orders had been sent out; any countermanding of them would swamp the telegraph-lines, and in any case the troops had begun to move against Serbia—by the late evening of 31st July, 132 troop-trains. To stop this movement now, Straub said, would mean 'a mess ... chaos on the railway-lines for which I can take no responsibility'. There was no way of improvising yet again movement, direct, of the transported parts of II Army to Galicia, as some officers suggested. Of course, the trains that had left could simply be directed back to their depots. But this was not done for revealing reasons—'We feared moral, political and disciplinary damage; the men's confidence in their leaders' professional competence would have suffered'.[6] Indeed it would, if troop-trains that had left, Prague, Leitmeritz, Budapest a few days before, to flowers and bands, steamed back again in the middle of mobilisation. The satirical journals of Prague and Budapest would have had a field-day; the old saying, '*L'Autriche est toujours en retard d'une armée, d'une année et d'une idée*' being once more triumphantly borne out. But in any case, as Straub and his assistants pointed out, even if this were done it would not advance by a minute the time of II Army's arrival in Galicia. The mobilisation-schedules had been so arranged that the corps of II Army would, as 'echelon B', take the railways to Galicia only after all the other corps had gone to the Russian front. Even if the trains were now taken back, these troops would simply have to kick their heels in the depots of Prague and Budapest. It would simplify the railwaymen's problem, they said, if these heels were kicked on the Danube instead. On 1st August Conrad therefore decreed that II Army, with a few omissions, should go first to the Balkans, wait there for ten days, and start back to Galicia when 'A-Staffel' had already finished its deployment to the north-east—i.e. around 18th August. As a consolation, the corps might be used 'for demonstrative purposes' in the south against the Serbians, over the river. Embarrassment was such that the Balkan commander, Potiorek, was told nothing of all this until 6th August. With justice, he recorded: 'How the supreme command could arrive at such a radical change in its decisions is a mystery to me. It reveals much as to the functioning of the machine.'

Conrad hints, in his memoirs—and other writers have gone further—that the railway-technicians behaved incompetently. This was unfair: the railway-technicians had simply behaved according to a plan that Conrad had prescribed for them. II Army did, in fact arrive in Galicia on schedule—about the 24th day of mobilisation—although with a few exceptions that had nothing to do with the technicians. On the other hand, the technicians failed in so far as they did not respond to the crisis with any imagination. A more rapid despatch of II Army could, probably, have been attained. But the technicians behaved with incurable routine-mindedness, impenetrable smugness. They exaggerated the difficulties of their task—made out, for instance, that they had over 11,000 transports to cater for, where the true figure for the Russian front was less than 2,000, the technicians having increased it by including return of empty trains from Galicia and small-scale suburban movements in Lwów, Cracow and elsewhere. In the same way, they demanded great reserves of rolling-stock which were never used—suspending the country's commercial life for three or four weeks just the same. They acted according to out-of-date ideas of what the railways could do. No military train had more than fifty carriages, the lines' capacity being supposedly capable of only this. In practice, the great *Nordbahn* from Vienna to the north and Cracow usually took a hundred-waggon trains. The military failed to use with any intensity the line between Budapest and Przemyśl, supposing it to be a poor, mountain railway, not a double-tracked line capable of taking quite fast and heavy trains on most sections. On the contrary, the technicians behaved as if the railways of the Monarchy were primitive affairs, mismanaged by civilians who needed a dose of military efficiency. They behaved with a crazy caution that ruled out improvisation. In order to preserve 'a uniform pattern' in the movement of mobilisation-trains, all of these were told to go at 'maximum parallel graphic'— meaning the maximum speed of the slowest train on the worst line, with only minor variations. The average speed of Austro-Hungarian mobilis-ation-trains was therefore less than that of a bicycle. Moreover, troop-trains were arbitrarily halted for six hours every day for 'feeding-pauses', despite their having field-kitchens with them in the trains. Since stations with the necessary equipment did not regularly occur on the lines, this meant that troops would travel for hours without being fed, then to be given two square meals, more or less in succession, in the middle of the night. Journeys lasted for an astonishing time. III Army command, for instance, left Bratislava at 6 a.m. on 5th August, and arrived in Sambor at the same hour on 10th August—a performance of which a healthy walker would have been capable. IV Army Command took forty hours travelling between Vienna and the San—three times as long as usual.[7] Yet all this was maintained with a contempt for civilians and a stupefying assertion of the superior virtues of the military. The railway-technicians often talked of their great clockwork; but it was a machine that owed something to the cuckoo.

Just the same, the blame for difficulties in mobilisation lies mainly with Conrad. He had sanctioned the original plan, by which the corps of II Army were scheduled to arrive in Galicia only by the 24th day of mobilis-ation. It was he, also, who sanctioned the change of plan, by which these corps were told to go south. The most important effect of this was not the delay in going north again; it was rather that, to let the movement to the south go on, the first day of the general mobilisation, of the rest of the army corps, against Russia, had been postponed to 4th August. This meant that the 24th day of mobilisation, on which the corps of II Army were supposed to arrive in Galicia, would not be until 28th August—indeed, before 11th August there seems to have been astonishingly little movement at all on the lines to Galicia. The main forces for Galicia would not be able to collect before the 15th–19th days of mobilisation—now, between 19th and 23rd August. IV Army, for instance, had collected fifty-seven battalions and thirty-nine batteries on 13th August, and its full force—120 battalions and sixty-three batteries—only by 23rd August. This was a peculiar method of exploiting the supposedly slow mobilisation of the Russian army. Besides, the troops of II Army were not able, after all, to leave entirely as scheduled. The Balkan commander, Potiorek, had decided to attack Serbia, and began—with Conrad's support—in mid-August. The offensive came across difficult country in the western part of Serbia; the Austrians were inexperienced, out-numbered; the Serbians knew the country well and had a row of victories behind them. The Austrians advanced confidently, regarding the Serbs much as the British regarded the Turks later on, as upstart monkeys who needed to be taught a lesson in western warfare. Putnik, the Serbian commander, behaved sensibly—letting the Austrians advance some way until they were beset by supply problems, then attacking their flank, and driving them back to the border. Potiorek turned to II Army, the divisions of which were strung out along the rivers to the north. Conrad gave him one of its corps—8.—and allowed a second—4.—to be dragged into the Balkan action. In this way, only two of II Army's corps left as intended for Galicia, beginning on 18th August; one corps did not go at all; and the other, 4., left only beginning on 24th August, ran into difficulties on the Hungarian railways, and reached Galicia only in the first week of September.

Only two of II Army's corps arrived, even by 28th August, in Galicia. But there were further delays in the assembly of the other three armies. Conrad had decreed that their troops should be unloaded at stations on the San and Dniester—clearly intending a purely defensive action, while the other armies defeated Serbia. On 31st July, he returned to his old plan, of attacking from Galicia. But the unloading-points could not, now, be altered. The original unloading-points for IV Army had been Lwów, Gliniany and other stations quite close to the Russian border. They had been altered to become Jaroslau, Przemyśl, and stations on the river San. The army's forces had been supposed to reach these advanced unloading-points between the 12th and 18th days of mobilisation. Instead, these days found them far to the rear. 2. Corps's three divisions, for instance, arrived on 12th, 16th, and 20th August at Jaroslau on the San, not at Zolkiew, near Lwów; 6. Corps unloaded two divisions at Przemyśl, not Lwów, on 17th August, and another on 20th August. In the same way, the corps of III Army were unloaded at Stryj and Sambor, on the Dniester —even in some cases at Chyrów, far in the rear, and Varannó, on the Hungarian side of the Carpathians. Since Conrad had now returned to his scheme of an attack from Galicia, these troops were set to march forward, up to a hundred miles that they could quite easily have covered by rail. Far from taking advantage of Russian unreadiness, the Austrians fought the opening battles some way inside their own territory; and the full-scale engagements in Galicia did not even begin until long after decisive events were under way on the French and East Prussian fronts.

The army's deployment did not offer much promise of success. Supply-lines functioned inefficiently: the station-master at Podborze in Austrian Silesia broke down, reversed all his signals, held up eight troop trains for several hours, and shot himself in the subsequent investigation. Austro-Hungarian infantry tended to fire at Austro-Hungarian aircraft, such that IV Army had to issue an order, several times repeated, that no aircraft should be fired on—three Austro-Hungarian planes having been already shot down by the army. Staff-work was not efficient, the telephones at times close to breakdown from the volume of talk, de-coding of important messages, even in army headquarters, sometimes taking fifteen hours.[8] There were actions on the frontier, to which commanders reacted with exaggeration—expecting their men to die a hero's death for the sake of some customs-post or other. In this first period, the major activity was an Austro-Hungarian cavalry raid—ten divisions, drawn up in a semi-circle, riding off into the unknown. There were engagements, of a romantic, old-fashioned sort: the largest of them on 20th August at Jaroslawice, where two cavalry divisions wheeled around and sabred each other, the commanders having tacitly agreed to behave as if the twentieth century had not happened. This went on until a Russian infantry unit arrived to spoil the performance. In any case, the Austrians could not ride far, because they had insisted on using a saddle that only well-prepared horses could use. It was designed to give the rider a fine seat on parade, but, with the requisitioned horses, turned out to rub the skin from their backs in hot weather. Many Austrian cavalrymen arrived back on foot, leading their mounts. In any case, the supplying of these horses soon broke down. 'By the third week of August, almost half of the horses were out of action, and the other half very nearly so'.[9] The main effect of these cavalry battles was to draw in infantry units that would best have been spared for more serious business.

From the beginning, the Austro-Hungarian forces in Galicia were bedevilled, not only by delays, but also by a fundamental uncertainty as to what they were meant to achieve. They were supposed to attack. But attack from the semi-circle of Galicia was difficult—if Conrad attacked on the western side, his eastern flank would be increasingly bared; yet if the attack went to the east, it would run into all manner of difficulties. Railways were few; roads, on the Russian side, few; the Germans far away; the attackers maybe exposed to some Russian stroke against their communications to the west. In July 1914, Conrad opted for the western attack. His I and IV Armies, drawn up east of Cracow and on the San, were not too far from the Russian border, concentrated before the other armies, and could move north against a flank with German troops not too distant. This was a good enough plan. Conrad did not, however, allot enough force for it. In the first place, because of subtractions to the Balkan front, thirty-seven, and not forty, infantry divisions would now assemble in Galicia; and some of these would arrive only late—four only by 28th August, two others only by 4th September, at that, at stations some way behind the front line. Up to 28th August, Conrad had, in effect, only thirty-one infantry divisions in the area, although *Landsturm* formations could, despite their weakness, at least swell the numbers involved. Moreover, the concentration was not great enough for Conrad's purposes. I Army, in the west, had three army corps; IV Army, to its right, had three, to which a fourth was attached from the Balkans[10]— these two to form the attacking force, going north. The eastern side was protected by III Army, marching forward to Lwów, and the nucleus of II Army, collecting on the Dniester (at Stanislav). Together, they had, at the outset, four corps, to which two were to come from the Balkans. Conrad later made out, again, that technical, railway-factors had deter-mined this, since the corps could only be delivered to the front in this way. But there was not much in this explanation. The deployment reflected Conrad's irresolution, not 'railway-necessities'. The difficulty was that, as the Austro-Hungarian attack developed to the north, its eastern flank would be increasingly bared. Coverage for that flank would be essential for the attack to succeed. Yet troops were not sufficient to achieve both coverage for the flank and sufficient strength for the front of attack. Conrad compromised—gave troops that were not sufficient for coverage, but that also weakened too far the front of attack. Having gone this far, Conrad found that III and II Armies, on the defensive, eastern side, had four army corps, with another due to come in. To leave them far to the rear was thought to be impossible. They too must march forward to engage the Russians. On 18th August these corps were marched forward to Lwów and towns to the south-east of it: taking, inevitably, up to eight days in covering seventy miles or so. Conrad told them to wage 'an active defensive'—they could not do nothing, but quite what they were to do remained imprecise. Brudermann, commanding III Army, was full of fight. He would advance boldly against the Russians in eastern Galicia. Conrad let him do so, subsequently blaming him for disobedience. Indeed, he later made out that intelligence-services had failed to reveal the true strength of Russian forces in this area. There was, again, nothing substantial in this explanation—the intelligence-maps of IV Army showed,

on 10th August, six Russian corps (7. to 12. inclusive) at Kazatin, Zhmer-
inka and Dubno; on 13th August the maps showed, rightly, 21. Corps as
well; and by 14th August the Austrian high command was already report-
ing to its liaison officer with the Germans in East Prussia a commendably
accurate picture of Russian deployment—at Dubno, the Russian 11.
Corps; over the eastern Galician border, 'certainly' 7. 8. and 12. Corps and
'probably' 9. 10. and 21.[11] The only corps missed out was 24. which arrived
from Bessarabia only some time later. In this way, Austro-Hungarian
intelligence itself showed that the four corps of Brudermann's group
would be taking on seven Russian corps, a force double their size. Moreover, instead of waiting—as the German VIII Army did in East Prussia—
Brudermann's group was advancing into the path of these Russian forces,
many of the divisions already exhausted by various peregrinations before
they even joined battle.

This had been allowed by Conrad for the sake of his attack to the
north. His I and IV Armies were ready before III, and advanced towards
the border from 19th August. Confidence seems to have been astonishingly high. A governor-general of Warsaw—Count Collard—was
appointed; IV Army command issued instructions for severe treatment of
the Russian population, excepting Jews; a warning was even issued to the
troops that cholera had broken out 'in distant parts of Russia',[12] and
troops must therefore do without alcohol, which would weaken resistance
to the disease. The German VIII Army was also asked to co-operate, by
launching an attack on the northern flank of the Polish salient over the
Narev—an attack that, in Prittwitz's circumstances, could only be lunatic,
but regarded by Conrad—or so he later alleged—as an indispensable part of
his plan.

At least for the attack on I and IV Armies, Conrad was running into
roughly equal forces, such that tactical factors might give him some
chance of success. In practice, Russian miscalculations gave him a rather
better chance in this than perhaps he deserved. The Russians performed
almost in reverse what Conrad had done—running head-on into his
attack on the northern side, failing at the outset to use their superiority on
the eastern side. No one man had dominated planning on the Russian side
as Conrad had dominated it on the Austrian. The armies in Galicia adopted
in essence two plans—one by Alexeyev, for a stroke against the Austrian
railways leading to Cracow, and one by the General Staff, under Danilov,
for an attack along the Carpathians from the eastern border of Galicia.
These plans had been originally based on a supposition, at the time
correct, that the Austro-Hungarian armies would be concentrated in
north-eastern and eastern Galicia. Alexeyev's attack would cut their
communications; Danilov's would bind them in eastern Galicia, and

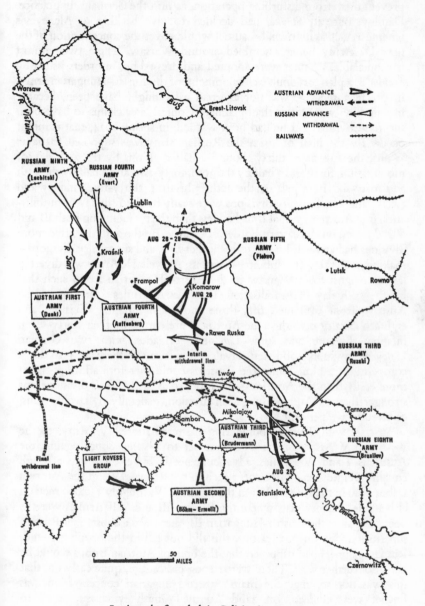

Lwów—the first clash in Galicia, August 1914.

prevent them from disturbing operations against the Germans. In practice, Danilov, once in *Stavka*, had decided to give backing to Alexeyev's scheme as well as his own, because it would cover the concentration of the new IX Army being assembled around Warsaw. These two, almost irreconcilable, schemes were adopted and dressed up, in orders issued by *Stavka*, as a plan for 'double envelopment' of the Austro-Hungarian army. In practice, the risk was not as great as it might have been, because mobilisation went faster than planned. Conrad later claims to have been surprised by this; but he had been warned, in spring 1914, that it might occur. By the plan of 1912, the Russian army was supposed to have, against the Austrians, thirty-six and a half divisions by the 25th day of mobilisation, forty and a half by the 30th, forty-two and a half by the 35th and forty-six and a half by the 40th.[13] In 1914, thirty-five infantry and twelve and a half cavalry divisions were ready by the 18th day of mobilisation (the Austrians at that time had less than thirty) including both III and VIII Armies, on the eastern border of Galicia. By the 25th day, five more divisions had arrived; by the 30th another five, and six cavalry divisions— making in all forty-five infantry divisions. As well, IX Army was diverted late in August from Warsaw to the Austro-Hungarian front, such that by the 30th day of mobilisation, the Russian armies operating on the Austrian front contained fifty-three and a half infantry divisions and eighteen cavalry divisions; the Austrians presenting by then thirty-seven infantry divisions and some *Landsturm* brigades, with two German *Landwehr* divisions, and ten cavalry divisions. If there was to be a competition in blundering, the Russians could therefore afford it much more easily than the Austrians—the more so as each of their divisions was stronger than an Austro-Hungarian division, generally by twelve guns, or twenty-five per cent.

To start with, Russian blundering mattered more. IV Army, to the west, and V Army on its left, were set to advance south against the Austrians' I and IV Armies, advancing north. Here, there was a rough equality of numbers—three corps each in the Russian IV and the Austrian I, four each in the Russian V and the Austrian IV, roughly 350,000 men on either side. Further east, where the Russian III and VIII Armies were to operate against the Austro-Hungarian III, there was a substantial Russian superiority. For various reasons, this did not tell in the opening round. Russian planners had supposed that the bulk of Austrian troops would be here, not further west. There were strong indications, quite early on, that this was not so, that the main Austro-Hungarian concentration was further west; indeed, on 22nd August Yanushkevitch suggested to Alexeyev that this was the case, that the attack of his IV and V Armies 'no longer corresponds to circumstances', and that III and VIII Armies should move forward more quickly. The next day he said 'the Austrians may have collected troops further west than we have so far supposed'[14]—characteristically adding that he had no proposals to make. But it was one thing for *Stavka*, even Ivanov and Alexeyev, commanding the army group, to come to recognitions of this kind; it was a different matter altogether for the army commanders on the spot. There were, at the time, only nine Austrian divisions in the path of the twenty-two of the Russian III and VIII Armies; but Ruzski, commanding III Army, behaved with the utmost caution. He acted as if old suppositions held good—that the Austrians would concentrate thirty divisions in eastern Galicia by the 15th day of mobilisation. He kept his four corps bunched together by Beresteczko, announced that VIII Army was not ready for battle, advanced even on Russian territory at a rate of five miles a day, and crossed the border only on 20–21st August. As in East Prussia, staff-work was inadequately done. In Cholm, headquarters of the army group, Ivanov and Alexeyev quarrelled as to who should open telegrams first; two copies of each were prepared, for commander and chief of staff; each then wrote different orders in consequence. In III Army command, matters were strained between Ruzski, a Sukhomlinovite, and his chief of staff Dragomirov, who also quarrelled with the operations-chief, Bonch-Bruyevitch. Not until 26th August did the considerable Russian superiority on this side become effective, even then only because Brudermann advanced into it, and it was less effective, on 26th August, than it could have been.

This subtraction of strength on the eastern side allowed Conrad to hope for victory on the northern one. Here there was, in Conrad's words, 'a happy beginning'. The three corps of the Russian IV Army advanced onto Austrian territory. Their cavalry-screen failed to reconnoitre; the army's passage was obscured by woods, hills, and marshy country; one of its corps, 14., was stretched out over twenty miles. Its two divisions ran, in a tactically disadvantageous way, into five Austrian divisions of I Army, lost liaison with Russian groups further west, and on 23rd August one of the divisions lost half of its strength. Disorderly attempts were made to restore the position, a further division receiving contradictory orders from different corps commands, losing 1,500 men in one regiment, 900 in another. The Austrians took first the eastern flank, then the western flank, of the Russian IV Army, and by 25th August, having lost 6,000 men as prisoners and twenty-eight guns, the army retired to the Kraśnik positions south of Lublin. This gave misplaced confidence to Conrad. More importantly, it caused trouble among the Russian commanders. IV Army commander, Salza, and a corps commander, Geysmans, complained at the behaviour of 14. corps commander, Voyshin-Murdas-Zhilinski, whom Yanushkevitch dismissed. Ivanov intervened to dismiss Salza and Geysmans for daring to complain about Voyshin. General Evert was summoned from Siberia to take over IV Army; Voyshin was given Geysmans's corps—by no means the last time such phenomena occurred. In the confusions, Ivanov supposed that he would have to fall back a long way, ordering IV Army to protect 'the sector Drogiczyn—Brest-Litovsk'. He also demanded from *Stavka* that the new IX Army should be used on the Austro-Hungarian front. *Stavka* felt there was an emergency, that Austrian cavalry could even ride up to raid the rear of the north-western front; IX Army was therefore diverted against the Austrians—in succession the Guard Corps, 18th Corps, 3rd Caucasus Corps as well as three reserve divisions and more cavalry. These were due to arrive by the end of August. In the mean time, a series of flanking operations pushed the Russians back towards Lublin, and the railheads at which these new troops could arrive. Now, the natural forces of 1914-18 began to tell. The Austrians outran their supply-lines, could not bring in reserves as quickly as the Russians, exhausted themselves in marching, and fought a purely frontal battle. By 1st September, they had fifteen and a half infantry and four cavalry divisions in the area; the Russians, with their new forces, having twenty-six and a half infantry and nine and a half cavalry divisions.[15]

Both sides looked to armies further east—the Russian IV appealing to its neighbour, V (Plehve), with four corps, and the Austrian I appealing in turn to IV (Auffenberg), also with four corps. Plehve was 'to collect his corps and strike against the flank and rear of the enemy attacking IV Army'. These corps were strung out on a long front, moving south across Russian territory. They were to be diverted towards the south-west, with poor liaison to either side, and a gap of thirty miles to one neighbour, fifty miles to the other. As they moved south-west, they collided with Austro-Hungarian corps moving due north, of a strength the Russians had not been led to expect: 144 battalions and 526 guns on the Russian side, 156 and 470 on the Austro-Hungarian. Neither commander quite appreciated the extent of the flanking manoeuvres being carried out. On 26th August, there was a first collision: a Russian corps, marching south-west, brushed past an Austrian one marching north, and suffered from Austrian artillery; one of its divisions had marched for several days, had only four-fifths of its strength, and 120 rounds per gun. It retired in bewilderment and the left wing of the Austrian IV Army advanced to Zamość, between the two Russian armies, on 27th August. But further east it was the Russians who had the advantage. Their two central corps came up against Austro-Hungarian flanks; on 27th August an Austro-Hungarian cavalry division, acting with more bravura than sense, was broken up and fled to the south. In the night of 27th–28th August, the same fate overtook an isolated infantry division (near Laszczów) which lost almost all of its guns and 4,000 men as prisoners. In the centre, near the town of Komarów, a 'soldiers' battle' developed, frontal attacks being exchanged.

These engagements pinned the two central corps of Plehve's army. His right-hand group had also been forced back—divided, now, between IV and V Armies, tired and confused to the point of losing the cross-roads at Krasnostaw and allowing the left-hand Austro-Hungarian corps to threaten Plehve's centre. No doubt the reinforcements due to arrive from IX Army in this area would help; but in the meantime the Russian situation would be difficult. It was further endangered by events on the other flank, to the east. This flank was 'in the air'—unconnected with III Army, operating some way to the east under Ruzski's prudent control. It contained one corps, the commander of which had been given control of the two central corps, and spent his time with them; its chief of staff, Stremoukhov, had no plan and no way of communicating it, had he had one. The divisions marched south-west. The Austrian commander recognised this: that if he attacked them in flank, he would be able to surround Plehve's forces. He asked Conrad for permission to use the left-hand corps of the Austrian III Army, which was then thirty miles away. Conrad knew that safety in the east might depend on this corps's remaining under III Army command. But Auffenberg's entreaties swung him the other way: he sanctioned use of this corps, 14., under Archduke Joseph Ferdinand, by Auffenberg. The corps moved towards the Russian left on 28th August, and on the 29th and 30th did well against disorganised Russian divisions—taking a third of their troops prisoner, and sixty guns. This brought the right of Auffenberg's army far into the rear of the two central corps of Plehve's—separated only by two days' march from the left of the army, near Zamość. An encirclement of the Russian V Army seemed possible. But Plehve did not behave as Samsonov had done—advancing into an enemy ring. On the contrary, he gave orders for retreat. In any case the Austrians did not act with Prussian resolution. The two flanking groups did not appreciate what they had achieved, and were tired. The left-hand group, under Archduke Peter Ferdinand, dimly appreciated the strength of Russian reinforcements building up to its left; the right-hand one, under his brother Joseph Ferdinand, noted Cossack divisions in the great spaces to the east. Neither dared move too far forward. On 30th and 31st August first one, then the other, pulled back; and the central corps of Plehve's army withdrew to the north. This battle—Zamość–Komarów—was an Austrian victory. IV Army took 20,000 prisoners and nearly 100 guns; Plehve's army had lost forty per cent of its complement. Auffenberg and Soós, his chief of staff, said they had won a great victory; there must now be a pursuit into Russian Poland. For the moment, Ivanov and Alexeyev almost agreed with this.[16]

In response to the increasingly menacing news from the northern sector, Ivanov and Alexeyev spurred on their III and VIII Armies, to advance with all speed from eastern Galicia. They were to move north-west, to the direct help of Plehve. But Ruzski behaved with almost psychotic prudence.[17] His army had crossed the border on 20th–21st August, and moved slowly forward thereafter, expecting that most Austrian troops would be concentrated against it. Indeed, the close concentration and slow advance of these four corps were such that Brudermann felt he had only 'an isolated corps' to deal with, advancing ahead of the main Russian force; with Conrad's encouragement, he marched his troops against it. East and south-east of Lwów, there was, between 26th and 28th August, a first collision, on the river Zlóta Lipa. It was a disaster for the Austrians. With 91 battalions and 300 guns to 192 and 685, they advanced in close order, down hills and across rivers, against the four Russian corps. The break-down of their attacks was followed by Russian counter-attacks, and losses of up to two-thirds in many of Brudermann's eight divisions. Many of the Austrians fled in panic as far back as Lwów; and III Army could not restore the situation easily, since its left-hand corps, the Archduke's 14., had already been detached to help IV Army.

A swift follow-up by Ruzski would have helped Plehve at once, and Ivanov ordered him again and again to swing III Army to the north-west. Ruzski would not do this—his right-hand corps delayed, to Plehve inexplicably, and the other three did not much better, since Ruzski had exaggerated the strength of the Austrians who had attacked him, and even managed to congratulate his own commanders on 'a fine defensive success'. He did not even notice the Austro-Hungarian retreat until 28th August, worried endlessly for his southern flank, and was maybe more concerned to capture Lwów than to help Plehve. Ivanov protested; but as Golovin said, he was like a pianist with a badly-tuned instrument—never knowing quite what sound would result when he touched a chord. Ruzski's headquarters, as Ivanov and later commanders discovered, had a habit of making everything sound like a dirge. The Austrian III Army was able to withdraw in some order, to the river Gnila Lipa. Here it received reinforcements from the Balkans, while the command of II Army arrived to take over the southern sector of the line. By 30th August the Austrians, here, had increased to fourteen infantry divisions and 828 guns—though still facing a considerable superiority—twenty-two infantry divisions and 1,304 guns. Brudermann had told Conrad that he had had to face greatly superior numbers—at least 400,000 men. But since the Russians did not follow up, Conrad disbelieved him. The commander of II Army was told to attack the Russians; and on 29th–30th August, on the Gnila Lipa, there was a repeat performance of the Zlóta Lipa action—tired Austro-Hungarian troops stumbling forward with inadequate artillery preparation against an enemy nearly double their numbers. There was a further disaster, and this time it reached such dimensions—20,000 men and seventy guns captured—that even Conrad could judge he was facing an immeasurably superior enemy. On the other hand, on 30th August, he believed he had won a great victory on the northern side. He decided that he must let the Russian III and VIII Armies advance, if necessary as far as Lwów, and then turn his IV Army from the north, into their open flank.

This decision belongs, as the Austro-Hungarian official historians said, 'to the most finely-balanced of the world war'. In real terms, it was almost lunatic. IV Army had been exhausted by a fortnight's marching and heavy fighting. III Army had been badly beaten already. But Conrad was not a man to take such things into account. He had learned that VIII Army in East Prussia had won a great victory; he must emulate the feat, perhaps exploit it for his own ends. III and II Armies would retire west of Lwów to a good line on the river Wereszyca, and when the Russians had followed, IV Army would intervene on their flank, by marching south-east across Rawa Ruska. Orders for this went out on 1st September. Meanwhile, Ruzski advanced towards Lwów, spent two days reconnoitring its empty and ancient forts, and finally made a ceremonial entry on 3rd September. Now, belatedly, he responded to suggestions that he might help V Army; the incessant proddings of Ivanov were reinforced by religious literature from *Stavka*, which made Ruzski transport one of his corps to his northern flank, and orientate the march of III Army towards the north-west. In this way, he met head-on the Austrian IV Army, marching south-east. These troops were exhausted, and had suffered heavy loss; they could no longer be moved around in Conrad's fashion like so many coloured pins on a staff-map. After a few tactical successes of no great importance, they became locked west of Lwów in a frontal battle of no issue. By a curious twist, the out-flanking effect sought by Conrad was to some extent achieved further south, by III, and particularly by II Army—now reinforced by 4. Corps from the Balkans. Between 7th and 9th September the Austrians here won some considerable tactical successes, which encouraged Conrad to go on trying up to the last moment.

In the event, he had to retreat. Now, on the eastern side, he had built up at least equality of forces with the Russian III and VIII Armies. But he had done so, inevitably, at the expense of his northern side. His I Army had arrived before Lublin by 1st September, but it had to face a constant inflow of Russian reserves, as IX Army arrived to buttress this front. IV Army alone rose from six and a half to fourteen divisions, facing the

Austrians' thirteen; and the only fresh force on which the Austrians could count was a weak German *Landwehr* Corps which had just marched 200 miles from Silesia, had only eight machine-guns, one aeroplane, no field-kitchens. The Austrians had now 558 guns, the Russians 900. As new Russian troops arrived, they pressed the Austrians back towards Kraśnik, with a series of embarrassments on the flanks. Worse still, the Russian V Army—reported to have been destroyed—recovered quickly enough, and sent two further corps against the Austrian northern side. Against them, the Austrian IV Army had left a single corps, such that, on this northern side, there were twenty-six and a half Russian divisions to fifteen and a half Austrian ones; and the other two corps of the reviving V Army moved into the rear of Auffenberg's forces attacking III Army at Rawa Ruska. The northern side began to crumble. To defend Auffenberg's rear, there was only one corps—again, Archduke Joseph Ferdinand's. It had lost all but 10,000 of its 50,000 men, and was rudely pushed aside by the reviving Russian divisions—one regiment, with Franz Ferdinand's military secretary at its head, being cut to pieces in a marsh. Further west, I Army's front also collapsed. At Sukhodoly, an Austrian corps lost two-thirds of its guns and men as it stood up to the attack of three Russian corps. On the left, the Russians attacked along the Vistula, and broke up the Germans' *Landwehrkorps* on 8th September, which lost 8,000 men and fell back over the Vistula. By 9th September, the Russians were threatening Conrad's western communications, his line of retreat towards the Germans.

Conrad appealed to the Germans for help. He was told that, for the moment, nothing could be done—the Kaiser remarking, 'You surely can't ask any more of VIII Army than it has already achieved'. Stubbornly, he urged the troops of III and II Armies into a further attack over the Wereszyca—even, uniquely, turning up himself, with the nominal commander-in-chief, Archduke Friedrich, to watch the armies' doings. By 11th September, with Russian cavalry raiding even the headquarters of his divisions, Conrad elected to retreat. The retreat itself was extremely disorderly. Nothing had been prepared in anticipation of it—it was thought that preparations for retreat would demoralise the troops still attacking on the eastern side. Consequently, the few roads were taken up with two-way traffic—men and guns moving west, hospital-carts and munitions-carts moving up to the front. A steady downpour went on, turning the roads into marshes. Inside the San fortress of Przemyśl, narrow streets were blocked by military carts, standing axle-to-axle. The only thing that saved Conrad from even greater collapse was the sluggardly Russian advance. Ivanov took the view that 'the Austrians' retreat will secure for our army the chance of an essential break in operations'. Rest-days were lavishly distributed. Ruzski ordered fortification of

Lwów. Cavalry, unfamiliar with the terrain, caused some panic in the Austro-Hungarian baggage-trains, but was less effective in this than men had hoped. With some speed, Conrad withdrew his stricken armies to the San, then to the rivers east of Cracow—the Dunajec and Biala, which were reached in mid-September. Both armies were exhausted. The Austro-Hungarians had suffered casualties of nearly fifty per cent—400,000, of which the Russians took 100,000, with 300 guns; the Russians had lost 250,000 men, 40,000 as prisoners, with 100 guns. Conrad could now only wait for German help; and the two operations of August–September 1914 now came together in their consequences, if not their course, as Ludendorff himself arrived to discuss matters.

CHAPTER FIVE

The First War-Winter, 1914-1915

By mid-September, the pattern of the war had been set up. The Germans had fought their way into France, but stand-still had followed; the Russians had been defeated by the Germans; the Austro-Hungarians by the Russians. Thereafter, the western Powers and the Germans sought to break the dead-lock in the west; the Germans had continually to help their ally; and the Russians sought to reverse the verdict of Tannenberg. In the latter part of September, too, the tactical pattern of the war was laid down. In the west, troops began to dig trenches, at first, sketchy and primitive ditches, and later on interlocking systems of some complexity. They did this because of a sudden discovery that soil proved to be the best defence against enemy artillery. Concrete fortresses offered it a target that was too obvious, whereas trenches in the earth were not vulnerable except to very well-aimed shells; even then, if the trenches were well-constructed, they could hold out against even heavy shell. Dug-outs with a ceiling ten metres thick were invulnerable to heavy shell, and if the ceiling were reinforced with concrete, it need even be only three metres thick. Of course, trench-warfare was a static form of defence, which had made it impossible in previous ages. But now, the attack itself was semi-static, since cavalry had become ineffective, and the internal combustion-engine was barely developed. To the generals' bewilderment, a line of trenches began to snake across France and Flanders, and both sides found their attacks slackening and failing against this seemingly 'unsoldierly' defence.

The war in eastern Europe continued, however, to be one of manoeuvre. One essential reason for this was, paradoxically, that communications were more primitive than in the west, so that reserves could not be rushed in to fill a gap as quickly as in France. When Ludendorff broke through the British army in March 1918, fourteen French infantry divisions were moved to fill the gap by 1st April, within ten days of the break-through—indeed, within three days of it there had arrived five by rail, three by bus and one by lorry.[1] By contrast, it took the Russians in October 1914 a month to transport eighteen divisions from east of

Cracow to south of Warsaw. Moreover, the eastern front was much less thickly-filled with infantry divisions than the western one, despite the obviously greater resources of man-power of Russia and even of the Habsburg Monarchy. Conscription, for reasons to be explained in Chapter 10, was a more haphazard business than in France. There were severe limits to the supply-capacity of the Russian army. Consequently, the Russian field army was not more than a fraction of the available man-power, and was indeed, for most of the time in the first year-and-a-half of war, only marginally superior to the field armies of the Central Powers. By October 1914, there were ninety-eight Russian infantry divisions serving against the Central Powers, but sixteen of them were in VI and VII Armies, guarding the Baltic and Black Sea coasts. In the same period, the Central Powers had between seventy and eighty divisions of infantry. By January 1915, for the start of the Central Powers' offensive, there were seventy-nine Austro-German infantry divisions, and fifteen and a half cavalry ones, to eighty-three Russian infantry and twenty-five cavalry divisions. By May 1915, the Central Powers were actually superior in number—109½ infantry divisions to just over 100, the Russian forces having in the mean time devoted thirteen and a half infantry and nine cavalry divisions to their Caucasus front against Turkey. It was only in mid-1916 that the Russians built up a comfortable superiority in man-power, with 150 infantry divisions to the Central Powers' 100. On the western front, there were always at least as many divisions as on the eastern front, and usually more. In 1914–15, the Germans deployed 100 infantry divisions in the west, the Entente 110; and thereafter the Entente's strength rose as new British divisions were gradually fielded. By February 1916, at the start of the Verdun offensive, there were 120 German divisions in the west, forty-seven and a half in the east; they faced 105 French, forty British, five Belgian divisions. By mid-1917, the forces west and east were roughly similar. In the west, 2,219 Entente battalions faced 1,314 German ones; in the east, 2,403 Russo-Romanian battalions faced 1,528 of the Central Powers. In terms of artillery, there were always of course many more guns in the west than in the east, a superiority still more important if shell-weight is counted. By the end of 1916, each side in the east had some 8,000 guns, but in the west, there were 18,000 allied guns to 11,000 German.[2] Yet the western front was not much over half the length of the eastern one which, imposed on a map of western Europe, would have stretched roughly from Rotterdam to Valencia, and, after Romanian intervention, to Algeria. It was calculated that one and a half German divisions occupied in the east space that would have absorbed five divisions in the west; the Austrians similarly calculated that they had one rifle for every two metres of front in the east, whereas they had three rifles for every metre on their Italian front. Of course, differences in tactics and handling of troops overall also counted. But the essential reasons for the eastern front's remaining for so long a place of manoeuvre, not of *Stellungskrieg*, were the lower defensive fire-power and the lesser mobility of reserves than in the west. Finally, the Germans' more rapid overcoming of problems of rifle and shell-supply put the Russians at a disadvantage in defensive warfare that was to be particularly important in the early summer of 1915. This point is more fully discussed in Chapter 7.

Moreover, the Russian army was at a great disadvantage in a war of manoeuvre because of the structure of command in the army, its division into often hostile 'fronts' or army groups. Hence, manoeuvring on the Russian side consisted of a series of blundering and ill-co-ordinated responses to misunderstood crises. There had always been difficulty in combining the requirements of the two separate 'fronts', against Germany and Austria-Hungary. The staff of the Warsaw Military District had naturally wished to devote as much as possible against Germany, that of the Kiev Military District against Austria-Hungary. Because the General Staff's own position had been so vulnerable before 1914, there was—except briefly, in 1910—no way by which it could impose its view on these separate planning agencies. In recognition of this, the two agencies were allowed to plan virtually independently, and two separate commands were set up in wartime. They fought, virtually, separate wars. The high command, *Stavka*, was botched together at the last moment, and was regarded with suspicion in so far as it was regarded at all. In reality *Stavka* existed mainly to co-ordinate the army's movements with the French; and for the first weeks of war it lacked even proper communications with the separate fronts.

In theory, of course, *Stavka* could control things because it controlled reserves: it could determine where newly-arrived units should go. But by early October, virtually all of the divisions had arrived at the front, and what remained did not give the high command very much influence. The two 'fronts' were independent in all but name, and controlled huge areas of Russia, in their rear-areas, as well as large quantities of rolling-stock and railway-line. Naturally, *Stavka* might determine strategic priorities, and decide that this action of this front was to be preferred to that action, proposed by the other front. In this case, resources would have to be transferred to the main front. But, for a variety of reasons, transfer of these resources was difficult, even impossible. Since the fronts controlled their own transport and reserves, their commands could obstruct *Stavka* easily enough. If Ruzski's front against Germany won priority, when Ivanov and Alexeyev felt that they should have it, they would find endless ways of preventing any re-settlement of resources. The movement of reserves was slow; and there was certainly no transfer of troops from East Prussia to Galicia or vice-versa to match the shuttling of German troops between west and east. This was subsequently blamed on railways; but strategic disagreements had at least as much to do with it. In reality, the only way by which a front could be made to co-operate was to give it responsibility for the operation, even where that front's command had opposed the operation in the first instance. In other words, the only way to get anything done was for *Stavka* to cease functioning. Inflexibility of reserves and confusions of command therefore marked the first few months of the war on the Russian side; nor was this problem ever successfully overcome. Ancient truths of Russian administration were thereby illustrated: centralisation brought inefficiency, de-centralisation brought anarchy.

In mid-September, there was already a crisis between the two fronts.[3] Ivanov and Alexeyev were determined to push on against the retreating Austro-Hungarian army. They would invest the great fortress of Przemyśl, on the San, would capture Cracow and maybe Budapest as well. On the other side, the armies of the north-western front, against Germany, were retreating. Ruzski, who—after a typical episode*—had replaced Zhilinski in mid-September, suffered from visions of a German advance against Warsaw, and sometimes even talked as if the Germans, after their great successes in East Prussia, could go on to Moscow or Saint Petersburg. The only way to stop this was to withdraw the stricken I, II and X Armies a long way back, he thought—at least to the Niemen, where the fortress of Kovno would protect them. Warsaw might have to be abandoned; and the forts and bridges there were blown up (the first of three separate occasions). At best, Novogeorgievsk, an ostensibly impregnable fortress down-river from Warsaw, should be retained. This set of circumstances brought the two fronts into unwilling contact. Ivanov and Alexeyev would not go forward to Cracow if their northern flank, in the Vistula plains, had been bared by retreats of the type adumbrated by Ruzski. If the north-western front pulled right back, there was nothing to stop the Germans from advancing into these plains and cutting the communications of the south-western front; already there were signs

---

*Zhilinski blamed Rennenkampf for not helping Samsonov, and then for running away during the battle of the Masurian Lakes. Rumours were also put about that Rennenkampf had been profiteering in matters of army supply, and a commission was set up to examine them. Rennenkampf mobilised the cavalry mafia in his defence, sent coded telegrams to friends at court (Orlov) and Zhilinski then found that he was being blamed for what had happened. The Grand Duke sent a telegram to the Tsar, saying that Zhilinski had panicked. Zhilinski was thereupon dismissed, Rennenkampf confirmed in office. But the Sukhomlinov system saved Zhilinski, who re-appeared—to the Allies considerable bewilderment—as Russian representative at Chantilly.

of German activity here. If Ruzski retired, then Ivanov and Alexeyev would also have to go back—they threatened to give up even Lwów, a proposal that put Grand Duke Nicholas 'into indescribable fright'. Conferences between *Stavka*, Ruzski and Ivanov produced no decision. Ruzski would agree, under pressure, to postpone his retreat; would return to his headquarters and decide that it should be carried out after all.

Events produced the decision that the commanders were unable to produce. In the first place, the expected German stroke against Warsaw or Kovno did not take place, or rather, was frustrated at the outset. The Germans crossed the East Prussian border, in the hope of great victories, and were simply stopped before they got very far—supply-problems, exhaustion, inferior numbers, unfamiliar terrain all counting. By 25th September, the Russian X Army was able to stage a counter-offensive that pushed the Germans back to their borders. In Galicia, it was the other way about. The Austro-Hungarian retreat went on over the San. Russian forces followed. There too supply-problems became insuperable; the fortress of Przemyśl[4] at least in theory was an obstacle, and no advance to Cracow could be made until it had fallen. Russian forces inched forward through the Galician mud. Finally, there came news that the Germans were arriving in force north of Cracow. On 18th September, Ludendorff saw Conrad. Ludendorff had been told that 'direct assistance to the Austrians is now politically essential'. It also made military sense. If the Russians came forward to Cracow, then their northern flank, in the Vistula plains, would be open. Consequently, Ludendorff prepared to assemble a new German force, IX Army, to be commanded by Hindenburg and himself. By 22nd September its vanguards had arrived north of Cracow. Ivanov could not go on against Cracow: he would have to meet this new threat, four corps and a cavalry division.

This gave *Stavka* a chance to smuggle in its old scheme, invasion of Germany from the central part of the front, the plains west of the Vistula. Ivanov would have to send troops to this theatre in any event, to match the arrival of Germans. One of Ruzski's armies would have to remain west of Warsaw, such that a considerable force would be assembled in the middle. Towards the end of September, Ivanov agreed to send substantial forces to this theatre—'not less than ten army corps, and better still, three armies'. Ruzski would contribute another army (II) and in this way, at least sixteen army corps would take on the Austro-Hungarians' and Germans' seven. Joffre took the chance to air his favourite idea, an offensive into Silesia or Poznania. Yanushkevitch therefore ordered 'preparation of an offensive, of the greatest possible weight, with a view to deep invasion of Germany, proceeding from the middle Vistula to the upper Oder'. To make sure that Ivanov behaved properly, he was given charge of this operation, II Army being put under his command. Ruzski was of course annoyed. He felt that such operations could only succeed if their northern flank—East Prussia—were securely held. He preferred to develop plans for a new offensive against East Prussia, and refused to part with troops or supplies if this offensive were thereby endangered. In this way, two operations were once more conducted, with little contact between the two, and as well there were engagements of lesser importance in Galicia. Twenty-five divisions, generally, were pinned down in a set of operations in East Prussia, which eventually succeeded in pushing the Germans back to the Angerapp lines. Another thirty were pinned down in Galicia, along the Carpathians and on the San. The supposedly decisive central offensive received barely more than thirty divisions, and supply problems meant that these were less effective than they could have been. The only way to make either front collaborate properly in the offensive was to give it responsibility. Thus Ivanov was, first given control of all four armies. Then Ruzski failed to make II Army as strong as he could have done, and also failed to supply it as he was supposed to. Ruzski was then given control of it, and the operation thus acquired two commanders. The invasion of Germany, not surprisingly, failed to get off the ground.

The events of October were confused and bewildering—a situation not helped by Ludendorff's subsequent construing of these events as a great German victory. The German corps pushed forward from their railheads north of Cracow, expecting to find a Russian flank. Instead, they found an empty space. From 24th September, Ivanov withdrew his forces west of the San, and set them marching back along the eastern banks of the Vistula. Once they came to safe crossing-points, such as Ivangorod, they would muster on the western banks, in preparation for the invasion. This movement took a great deal of time: for over three weeks, some thirty divisions were more or less subtracted from the battle-field while they took up positions elsewhere. The Central Powers were free to manoeuvre at will: Conrad followed the Russian retreat as far as the San, and Ludendorff pushed his troops, with an Austro-Hungarian corps, towards the Vistula. Both represented these advances as a victory. In reality, the only serious engagement, between 11th September, when the Austro-Hungarian retreat began, and 11th October, when the first real action opened on the Vistula, was a minor affair, at Opatów, in the Vistula plains. The Russians left a cavalry screen west of the Vistula. A mixed group of infantry and cavalry under Mannerheim ignored its orders to retreat. Early in October, a German and an Austro-Hungarian corps collided with this force. The Russian cavalry decided not to risk battle after all, and withdrew—incidentally breaking the only convenient bridge under the weight of its horse-guns, and not informing the infantry brigadier, whose flank it was supposed to protect. In the outcome, the infantry brigade could not get its guns out, and also lost half of its men as prisoners. After that, the Germans arrived on the western bank of the Vistula, and indulged in desultory bombardment of such targets as they could find. Ludendorff wondered what to do. He decided that the Russians must have decided to give up the Vistula plains, and for want of anything better, sent three of his corps under Mackensen towards Warsaw. Conrad, on his side, thought that recapture of Lwów was first priority, and told his troops to cross the San. Only two corps and some cavalry remained at the join of the two armies' fronts, opposite the fortress of Ivangorod.[5]

Ivanov could not take much profit from this. His troops' movement along the eastern bank of the Vistula suffered from one delay after another. They marched over a hundred miles in a downpour, on bad roads swamped in mud. Of the three armies involved—IV, V and IX—V was in the worst position. It could not feed its horses because hay did not arrive. The horses dropped. Shell-boxes had to be left behind, along with bridging equipment needed for the crossings to come. Even the railway-journeys that could be made once the forces came to usable railheads were difficult: one of the lines, through Ivangorod, came under German bombardment. Moreover, when V Army reached its stations to the south-east of Warsaw, it became dependent on Ruzski's front for supplies, although receiving orders from Ivanov. It did not get priority from Ruzski, such that V Army was more or less out of action for a month. The other two armies arrived by 8th October, strung out along ninety miles of river, with only two crossing-points, at Ivangorod and Novo-Alexandriya. II Army assembled in Warsaw, also dependent on Ruzski for its supplies, and also left in the lurch. Its commander, Scheidemann, was mesmerised by reports that Ludendorff was attacking Warsaw, and his staff wrestled with problems of logistics as the army became an almost unmanageable mob in the Polish capital. On 11th October, after much prodding from *Stavka*, Ivanov told IV, IX and V Armies to cross the Vistula. IV and IX Armies, at Ivangorod and on the river to the south, attempted to cross, but were pinned by German and Austro-Hungarian bombardment to small bridgeheads, in which they lost heavily. V Army had no bridges, and its troops had to cross by raft or barge, through machine-gun fire. Pontoon equipment did arrive some days later, and a bridge was thrown up. Then the Vistula rose, and carried off the bridge, which floated downstream to the suburbs of Warsaw, where it came to rest. The army staff 'forgot' what it had done with the field-mortars; and all manner of other equipment lay strewn around the roads to the south, such that the army really depended on supplies from Warsaw, itself in a state of seemingly inextricable confusion. By mid-month, the Russians' attempts to cross the Vistula had all broken down.[6]

The Central Powers did not do much better. Ludendorff had sent a strong group against Warsaw. It had not much difficulty in following the Russians' advanced-groups' retreat into the city, and by mid-October there was talk of a German occupation of Warsaw. But Ludendorff appreciated that his flank on the Vistula was weak, and he was also told that there were about nine Russian divisions in Warsaw to his five. Prudently, on 18th October, he decided not to risk anything, and secretly ordered retreat, to begin on 20th October. Conrad on his side was less prudent. He set his armies to cross the San. Their attempts to do so broke down again and again, for much the same reasons as Russian attempts to cross the Vistula had broken down. Further south, there was nothing but an indecisive imbroglio in the Carpathians. Conrad produced a fancy scheme. He would, as Ludendorff demanded, send troops (his I Army) to help hold the line opposite Ivangorod. These troops, and the German corps on their left, would withdraw; the Russians would cross; and then the Austro-Hungarian group would counter-attack, when the Russians were only half-across. By 22nd October three separate operations were thus planned. Ivanov wanted to set IV and IX Armies across the Vistula, at Ivangorod and Novo-Alexandriya. Conrad was prepared to meet them with his supposed flank-attack: Ludendorff meanwhile would retreat from Warsaw. Matters on the Russian side now became still more disjointed because Ruzski was put in charge, first of II and then also of V Army, because this was the only way by which they could rely on his support. As it happened, the Austro-Hungarians were sharply defeated opposite Ivangorod. They allowed the Russians to cross, but their own flank-attack was not successful, and in any case they could not interfere with the crossing of all the Russian divisions hitherto penned in on the wrong bank of the Vistula. On 22nd October there were ten divisions to the Austro-Hungarians' and Germans' eight; on 26th October, thirteen to eight. The Austro-Hungarian I Army was itself taken in flank, lost 40,000 men and withdrew to the south-west.* At the same time, Ludendorff retreated as he had planned. By the end of October, the Central

---

*There is a famous story concerning this retreat, told by Hoffmann. A German communications corporal overheard a message from one Austrian unit to another, to the effect that the Austrians were to retreat, but not to tell their German neighbours that they were doing so. It turns out that this was bungling, rather than bad faith. The Austrians meant to retire on 27th October, but did so, from force of circumstances, on 26th. Their links to the neighbouring German unit was poor, and they informed the German corps beyond it what was to happen. The chief of staff of this corps asked them

Powers had retired almost to where they had started from a month before.

The Russian armies had clearly had the best of this fighting, whatever Ludendorff subsequently claimed. The Germans' attack in central Poland had encountered nothing substantial; their attacks on Warsaw and Ivangorod had failed; and now they were retreating towards the south-west. The Austrians had failed to break out across the San and made progress only in the scarcely-defended Bukovina, far to the south-east. As Russian forces advanced on the north bank of the Vistula, the Austrians were forced to retire south of it, abandoning the San, and allowing the fortress of Przemyśl to be once more shut in, with a garrison of 120,000 men. They fell back towards the Dunajec-Biala positions in early November, covering Cracow, and the Russian III Army duly followed.

Had the Russian command-system been functioning with anything like adequacy, this might have been a dangerous moment for Ludendorff and Conrad. But the two fronts were divided: the south-western one naturally gravitated towards the south-west, the north-western one, when Ruzski allowed it to gravitate anywhere at all, to the north-west. The armies in central Poland were divided now, for reasons of supply, between the two commands. Ivanov tended to draw IX Army, the southernmost one, into his battles with the Austrians, whose resistance, on the San, turned out to be stronger than expected. Consequently, its neighbour to the north, IV Army, was perpetually confused as regards its southern flank. On the other side, Ruzski was preoccupied with East Prussia and even, grotesquely, felt that there should be a strong flank-guard against a German breakthrough from there towards Warsaw—mistaking a German *Landsturm* brigade at Thorn for an army corps. This was a thesis that *Stavka* itself endorsed: 'The Grand Duke insistently expresses himself on the indispensability of securing success in East Prussia and on the San, without which there can be no proper safety for our operation in the plains of the Vistula'. A new I Army was therefore placed to guard II's right and X's left. There were nine army corps in II and V Armies, and these were placed across the open western flank of the Germans, with four army corps. But V Army was held up for the sake of the flank of II, II was held up because Ruzski expected German resistance where there was to be none, and supply-problems completed

---

to delay informing their neighbouring corps, which was then fighting successfully. The Austrians then consulted higher quarters, the conversation no doubt overheard by Hoffmann's corporal. In the event, the Austrian liaison officer, at some risk to himself, hurried to inform the corps concerned that retreat was imminent. The affair was thoroughly investigated by an Austrian communications-officer involved: O. Wolf-Schneider-Arno: 'Der Gefreite des Generals Hoffmann' in a *Sonderdruck* of the *Oesterreichische Wehrzeitung*, Folgen 43–46, of November 1924. The original documents of I Army (Fasz. 140) confirm Wolf's account, not Hoffmann's.

the picture. All commands now vacillated between the needs of front and flank; and *Stavka* itself behaved like 'a weather-cock'—telling Ruzski on the one side to pursue the Germans towards the south-west 'with iron energy', on the other that 'the next step in securing further advance must be to press the enemy in East Prussia and on the San'. Early in November, contradictory instructions were issued four times, Ivanov remarked that 'frankly speaking, it is impossible to detect in *Stavka's* instructions either an exact task or a fixed objective'. Russian soldiers stumbled bewilderedly through empty Polish territory, supplied, in IV Army, by biscuit brought along by staff-cars. Not until 12th November was the shell-dotation per gun brought up even to ninety rounds; and the railways were not brought back into service until mid-November. The wounded were taken back, first to Warsaw, where they lay on straw in long lines along the station-platforms, and then to Petrograd or Moscow, where they were also unloaded onto straw, on station platforms—this time, perhaps, with the amelioration of being tended by a Grand Duchess. *Stavka*, aware of these problems, and knowing, too, the division of the fronts regarding the directions of advance, decided to call a halt. The invasion of Germany was not to begin until 11th November; meanwhile, to make sure it was co-ordinated, Ruzski was put in charge of IV Army as well as II and V. This meant that Ivanov and Alexeyev would continue their private battle with the Austrians—though without IV Army, the help of which could have been decisive.

Meanwhile, the Germans were supposed to be passively waiting on the borders to the west. It was thought that they would defend Silesia. Ludendorff had a different idea. He disliked having to co-operate with the Austrians, would be happier further north; he was also, by the hour, in receipt of Russian wireless-messages, now ably decoded. He appreciated the delays on the Russian side; knew that his own troops could be transported by rail. He transported most of IX Army in five days to Toruń, from where it could move south-east, into the flank of the Russian II Army, as it moved west to invade Germany. In the former positions north of Cracow, he agreed to leave the *Landwehrkorps* and the Guard Reserve Corps; to these, the Austrians added five divisions, taken as II Army from their troops in the Carpathians. These troops were sufficient to hold the Russian IV Army, while the Austrians held the attention of IX, III and VIII to the south.

Two manoeuvres were being planned—an advance by the Russian II and V Armies towards Germany, which Ludendorff proposed to counter by a great flank-attack on II Army. By attacking south-east from Toruń, he did find the weakest point in the Russian line. Most of the Russian divisions in central Poland had already been committed to the

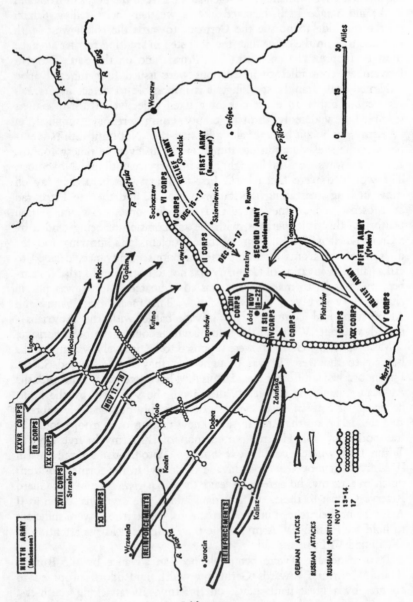

Łódź, 1914.

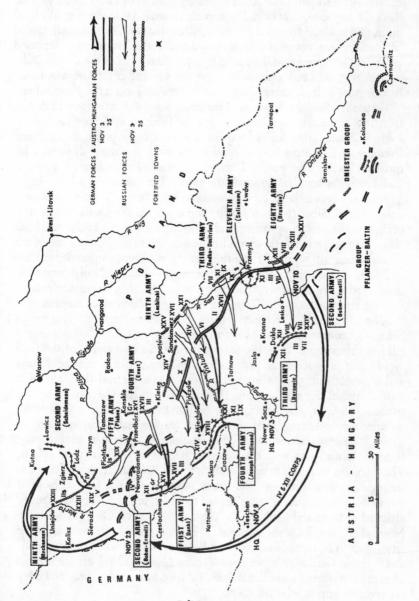

Galicia, 1914–15.

invasion of Germany, and could not easily react to this new threat to their flank. In any case, *Stavka* did not guess at what Ludendorff could have done, and told the front on 9th November that the Germans maintained 'at least five-six corps at Czestochowa and Kalisz'—a message repeated three days later, and four days later by a personal letter of the Grand Duke to Ruzski. *Stavka* still, essentially, took this view after the German attack had begun—indeed, three days after its opening on 11th November.[7]

Tactically, too, the Russians were unprepared for what was to come. II Army expected, legitimately, that its flank would be guarded by I Army. But I Army had a long front to control, opposite the southern frontiers of East Prussia, and it was too weak to cover all areas adequately. Ruzski also prodded its commander, Rennenkampf, towards East Prussia rather than towards the south. The corps on its left wing— 5. Siberian—was isolated on the southern bank of the Vistula, its nearest neighbour (6. Siberian Corps) being some way to the north; the nearest bridge was fifty miles upstream, and although a makeshift bridge was built closer than this, it broke down under the weight of heavy guns. One of the divisions was still supplied from the fortress of Novogeorgievsk; another had no technical equipment, and the corps as a whole had only thirty-five small spades per company. The commander, Sidorin, responded fitfully to these circumstances—half-digging first one position, then another.

When, on 11th November, three German corps with five times Sidorin's artillery attacked, his force inevitably collapsed—his artillery (all but fifteen guns) typically saving itself while two-thirds of the men were made prisoners. The rest of the corps went back along the Vistula and a gap of thirty miles opened between the river and the right of II Army. Ruzski did not see this. He still thought the Germans were far to the south-west, and, having little faith in the second-line troops under Sidorin, ascribed their defeat to at most two German divisions, making a feint. The only response, both on his and *Stavka's* part, was to encourage II Army to hurry up with the invasion of Germany, V Army to help it. The Germans had only fifteen divisions to the Russians' twenty-four, but strategically their situation was much superior. Of the five corps of II Army, four were already some way to the west; and the fifth was already attacked in front and flank by the German IX Army. On 14th and 15th November, the Russians suffered a further tactical reverse of some seriousness. The right-hand corps of II Army was almost overwhelmed; and a single German reserve corps (under Morgen) held off the attacks of such reinforcements as the Russian I Army had managed to send over the river to help 5. Siberian corps.

Only on 15th November did the Russian commanders appreciate quite what had happened. II and V Armies prudently decided not to go on with the invasion; instead, they swung about, to go back east on their supply-centre, the large town of Lódz. They performed something of a miracle, marching almost without stopping for two days and more, and reached Lódz before the Germans, marching south-east, could do so. When the first German troops arrived, they found seven Russian corps on the perimeter of Lódz—a manoeuvre that, in the end, saved the battle for the Russians. For the moment, none of the Russian senior commanders appreciated the virtuosity of II Army's performance. *Stavka* announced to Ruzski its 'extreme irritation at some of your senior commanders' dispositions'; of the retreat, Ruzski complained, 'Everything has followed from this blunder. The details are not worth going into, they're too depressing'. Both *Stavka* and Ruzski wanted a concentric attack—the troops brought over the Vistula by I Army, the troops in Lódz, and the corps of II Army that had been defeated in detail a few days before. These orders sometimes did not reach the army commanders, who in any case were hardly in any position to execute them. By 18th November they were content merely to hold Lódz against Germans, rapidly arriving. Ludendorff as often before and later imagined he had won a great strategic success, instead of a good tactical one. He thought the Russian armies were now retreating to the Vistula, and sent his men against Lódz in the hope of cutting the Russians off before they could accomplish their retreat. In practice, he was running into a trap. II and V Armies were not only defending Lódz, they were better able to do so than the Germans to attack it, for it was their supply-centre. They also out-numbered the Germans—on the western sector, thirty-six battalions and 240 guns to sixty-four and 210, on the northern sector thirty-six and 240 to seventy and 170, in a terrain greatly favouring the defender. By 22nd November, many German units had run out of munitions—one corps having only seventy rounds left per battery of six guns. German attacks slackened, failed.

Only in one area, east of the town, was there still a gap in the defence. A German reserve corps and a Guard division—thirty battalions and 140 guns—had reached it before the retreating Russians could; following Ludendorff's instructions, they moved south-east to cut off a Russian retreat they supposed to be occurring. On the Russian side, not much, initially, could be done. In Lódz the defenders were held along the city perimeter. Further north, I Army command was still sorting out the troops hit first at Wroclawek, on 11th–13th November, and then at Kutno on 14th–15th November; a thin German cordon sufficed, for the moment, to contain most of I Army and even to drive it back. In the circumstances, there was nothing substantial in the path of the three German divisions. They went on to the south, then turned west towards Lódz. Here they met Russian troops hurriedly sent to the city's eastern side, and although they were only twenty miles from the German western wing, the three divisions were held, by 21st November. Their situation was dangerous— they could not break out to the west, south or east; and their passage to the north might be blocked by a reviving Russian I Army. By the 22nd Russian troops did indeed take Brzeziny, on the road to safety in the north. What followed was an illustration of the superior quality of German reserve divisions, for a force of lesser quality would simply have been taken prisoner—indeed, Danilov ordered trains brought up to take the expected 50,000 prisoners back to Russia.

But Scheffer, commanding the German reserve corps, kept his force together. Cavalry to the south and east co-operated with him, covering the retreat; Scheffer himself stayed awake for seventy-two hours to organise retreat along poor, icy roads as his battalions and batteries withdrew, in the night of 22nd–23rd November. The retreat succeeded. On the western side, the Lódz defenders were too exhausted to react with any speed. On the southern side, German cavalry put up a considerable performance, and the Russian commander there, far from pressing the retreating Germans, even demanded congratulations and promotion for his fine defensive performance. To the east, Russian cavalry seems to have supposed, from the numbers of prisoners accompanying Scheffer on the march, that the Germans were much stronger—the prisoners having been assumed to be German soldiers. On the northern side there was a remarkable piece of muddle. I Army had organised a force of one and a half infantry-divisions (second-line) and two cavalry divisions, collectively known as 'Lowicz detachment'. It marched south-west towards Lódz. But it did so reluctantly. Rennenkampf had conceived his task as being essentially defensive, protection of Warsaw. Ruzski, even more bemused, changed from irrelevant bellicosities to craven defensiveness overnight, and *Stavka* was powerless to put across its occasional intimations of reality. The German force east of Lódz was put at three corps by a British military observer attached to the Lowicz detachment. Its commander, Slyusarenko, advanced five miles towards Lódz and then retired. Rennenkampf sent a different commander, Shuvalov; Ruzski sent another one, Vasiliev, who won. By 23rd November the force arrived in Scheffer's rear. But one division went to the west, and became confused among the defenders of Lódz. The other dug in along a railway-embankment. At dawn on 24th November, the German Guard division brushed past a weak force on Scheffer's left, and re-took Brzeziny. More significantly, the two reserve divisions under Scheffer's control managed to break through the defenders of the railway-embankment—although these two divisions were second-line ones and, at that, troops that had been marching and fighting for a considerable time. The Russian divisional commander, Gennings, suffered nervous collapse, and only 1,600 of his men were collected by the Lowicz detachment. In this way, the three German divisions were able to retire to the north-west and to link up with the rest of IX Army. They brought back 16,000 prisoners. As a final touch to this epic of inappropriateness on the Russian side, the commander of 2. Corps, to the north, announced that Scheffer's group was attacking him, and demanded help from Gennings.[9]

The affairs of Ruzski's command had now reached a pitch of confusion that seemed to demand retreat from the exposed positions of his armies around Lódz. II and V Armies had lost, between them, 100,000 men. Hospitals in Lódz, built for 5,000 men, were taking ten times as much. Rifles were running short—or rather, would have done had the troops not been reduced, in many cases, to a third of their complement. The shell-reserve was low—only 384 rounds per gun—and because communications were disordered, batteries at the front had considerably less than this. Even boots were running short, and Ruzski claimed that, where he needed half a million pairs, his reserve consisted of less than 40,000.[10] It was at least clear that the invasion of Germany could not occur. Ruzski had concluded from the events of Lódz that no advance towards Germany could be made so long as the flank was unsecured—in other words, the armies must be prepared for an offensive against East Prussia. Until this could happen, there was no sense in holding exposed positions in Central Poland—better to retire to the line of the Vistula. In the meantime, the Germans were once more threatening the Lódz positions. Ludendorff managed to persuade highly-placed Germans that Lódz had been a great strategic victory, not a complicated draw with tactical advantages on the German side. He bludgeoned Falkenhayn, Moltke's successor as effective German commander-in-chief, into sending further troops—four corps under Linsingen, Fabeck, Beseler and Gerok. Falkenhayn had grumbled that transfer of troops to the east was dangerous; the war could only be won by attacking the British, 'with whom the enemy coalition stands or falls'; 'in the last analysis' defeat on the Marne was to be explained by 'weakening of the western armies for the sake of the *Ostheer*'. But German defeats in Flanders removed some of the force of these arguments, and reinforcements went east by early December. Ludendorff planned another offensive in central Poland. In the circumstances, Ruzski was still more adamant on retreat than before—although initial German attacks, launched frontally by the new corps, made little headway.

There was another strategic wrangle: If Ruzski wanted to go back, Ivanov and Alexeyev wanted to go forward. The two fronts had to act jointly, for Ivanov could not advance in western Galicia without security on his northern flank, which only Ruzski could give; and that security could be obtained only if Ruzski stayed further forward than he intended. Ivanov made out that a final defeat of Austria-Hungary could be obtained. In November, he had worsted the Austrians in the Carpathians; he had advanced towards Cracow; and an Austro-Hungarian attack north of Cracow had broken down in unusually lamentable circumstances. Now, IX and IV Armies fought a frontal battle against mixed Austro-German forces north of Cracow, while the Russian III Army advanced steadily against Cracow from the east. He expected it to fall, and appointed Laiming, commander of Brest-Litovsk, to take charge of the siege. He summoned troops from the Carpathians to help out. If Ruzski went back, the Germans would threaten his northern flank; therefore Ruzski must stay where he was. Ruzski would not. A conference at Siedlce, his head-quarters, failed to settle anything. In the event, enemy action settled things for him. German pressure led to a withdrawal from Lódz, early in December. In any case, the Austrians recovered. They sent troops south of Cracow, attacked the open flank of the Russian III Army, and Ivanov's commander there mismanaged his reserves—one corps spending valuable time going back and forth over the Vistula. In the Carpathians, Russian withdrawals gave the Austrians superiority of numbers; and in these mountains, where flanking-operations could be conducted with relative ease, the Russian corps commander (Lesh) suffered one embarrassment after another. The emergence of Austro-Hungarian troops from the Carpathians threatened Ivanov's southern flank, while Ruzski's with-drawal in central Poland threatened his northern one. Ivanov withdrew towards the San, although Austrian pursuit was ineffective, such that, by the end of December, the forces were established on the Dunajec-Biala lines and in the central Carpathians.[11] Action in central Poland was similarly indecisive. The Germans launched a series of frontal offensives against the lines to which Ruzski had withdrawn, on the rivers Bzura and Rawka. They were an almost complete failure, in which IX Army lost 100,000 men. Some of the new corps, already hard-hit from the fighting in Flanders, were reduced to a few thousand rifles; munitions ran down, to the point where each gun could spend virtually only ten rounds daily. Ludendorff's staff confessed, 'It has to be said that the Russians have the advantage of the defensive, where they have always been good, and at that have a prepared field-position between the Vistula and the Pilica.' Trenches were dug on both sides in central Poland, and by the end of the year a decision seemed as far-off as before.

Both sides never the less felt that some decision must be made. Already, there were alarms that neutral states would intervene—Romania, Bulgaria, above all, Italy. The diplomatic equivalent of cavalry was a belief that the intervention of small states mattered—thus, for instance, George Clerk of the British Foreign Office: 'If Bulgaria and Romania can be got in now it is the beginning of the end of the war',[12] as if, in this battle of the Great Powers, a few ill-armed peasant divisions would make much difference either way. There was already talk of an Anglo-French expedition against Turkey, designed, in part, to bring in Greece and other Balkan states. Perhaps a resolute 'push' on the Russian side would be needed as well. On the other side, Conrad and Falkenhayn debated on how best to counter the threat of small states' intervention, particularly, of course, Italian intervention. For the moment, events themselves did not push either side firmly towards one course of action, and there was much wrangling. Falkenhayn argued that the best course of action would be an assemblage of troops in the west: if France were beaten, the whole problem would cease to exist. Failing this, an expedition could be made against the Balkans. Conrad disliked this. He could not spare the troops, and in any case, after a further débâcle in December, felt that much more force would be needed than Falkenhayn offered. He believed that the neutrals would be deterred from intervening only if the Central Powers won a decisive success on the Russian Front. He was seriously alarmed for Przemyśl, the great fortress on the San, now blockaded by a Russian army. Its garrison of 120,000 men could not hold out longer than spring, as their supplies would not last longer—had even been depleted in October to maintain the troops that had relieved the fortress. The fall of Przemyśl must be averted; and an offensive must therefore be made from the Carpathians. Falkenhayn disliked this scheme. He disliked still more a scheme of Ludendorff's for a renewed offensive in the north. Germany had formed four new army corps, and Ludendorff wanted them for the eastern front. At the turn of the year, the Germans were more divided than before; but the politicians' intervention proved decisive. Falkenhayn had failed to supply victory in France, and politicians felt that his policies should be abandoned.

His position was turned by Conrad and Ludendorff. Conrad made out, early in January, that his Carpathian position was going wrong; Ludendorff offered him two and a half infantry divisions and a cavalry division; Conrad then announced that he would use these for an offensive; Falkenhayn could do nothing against this, since the movement of reserves in the east was a matter for Ludendorff. But Conrad's Carpathian offensive did not make much sense on its own; it would have to be supported by a parallel offensive, taking the other Russian flank in East Prussia—a point that Ludendorff did not fail to make. Yet that could not be staged without the four new corps. Falkenhayn gave way, by mid-January.[13] Conrad

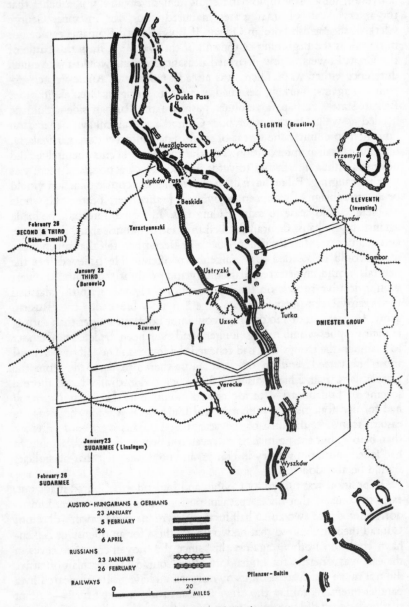

AUSTRO-HUNGARIANS & GERMANS
23 JANUARY
5 FEBRUARY
26
6 APRIL

RUSSIANS
23 JANUARY
26 FEBRUARY

RAILWAYS

0   20
                         MILES

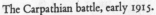

The Carpathian battle, early 1915.

and Ludendorff had mystified him with the virtuosity of their interpretations—Austria-Hungary so weak as to need help; Austria-Hungary
strong enough to make an offensive; the Austro-Hungarian offensive
too weak to be left on its own; an East Prussian offensive thus emerging
from these constructions—and Falkenhayn's internal position was too
unstable for much resistance to be made. In this way, the Central Powers
were to be engaged in two offensives, for which they had not the strength.
Conrad planned to use the German troops—joined with an equal number
of Austrians to become *deutsche Südarmee*—in the middle Carpathians,
with Austro-Hungarian armies to left and right, to re-take Przemyśl.
Ludendorff would launch a parallel attack with VIII Army and the four
new corps (X Army) from the Angerapp lines in East Prussia. Falkenhayn
had faith in neither—particularly the Austro-Hungarian offensive. He
complained to Conrad that the terrain and time of year were alike extremely unsuitable. He received a message to mind his own business,
'to rely on my personal knowledge of the area'. The most that Falkenhayn
could do was to attempt to saddle Ludendorff with responsibility,
gazetting him as chief of staff to *Südarmee*. Ludendorff's swollen reputation should be drowned in the Carpathian snows. At this, Hindenburg,
at Ludendorff's dictation, sent a letter offering to resign; and Falkenhayn
drew back. It was, in the event, one of Falkenhayn's protégés, Linsingen,
with Stolzmann as chief of staff, who took over *Südarmee*.

Similar confusions existed on the Russian side, the two fronts drawing
apart. Ivanov and Alexeyev made out, as before, that decisive action on
their front could produce a collapse of Austria, particularly of Hungary—
'she is ready to make a separate peace'. The Balkan states and Italy would
be impressed; Przemyśl would fall. Ruzski and *Stavka* disagreed with
this. In mid-January, Danilov and Ruzski between them, in secret,
concocted a memorandum, arguing that the only place for an offensive
was East Prussia. It was the Germans' flanking-position in East Prussia
that had made invasion of Germany impossible late in 1914—an analysis
to which there was much foundation—and 'You get the idea that energetic pressure here could throw the Germans back'.[14] An attack on the
southern border of East Prussia ought to be made, by a new Army (XII);
troops could be drawn into this from other parts of the front. There was
certainly no sense in attacking again in central Poland, with what the
Grand Duke described as '*toutes les horreurs*' of German fortifications. An
attack in the Carpathians would meet obstacles of climate and terrain.
East Prussia was therefore indicated. This was not an analysis that the
south-western command accepted. They first wanted troops for an
offensive; then, as German troops arrived in the Carpathians, for a
defensive action. They would not give up a man, insisted, on the contrary,

that they should be given troops. By 26th January Danilov had been persuaded to send them a corps from Ruzski's front. At the same time, Ruzski went ahead with plans for his new offensive: the Guard and 4. Siberian Corps were due to arrive, and corps re-constituted after Tannenberg (13. and 15.) together with corps taken from X and I Armies could make up a substantial XII Army, to gather on the southern borders of East Prussia. In theory, this made a substantial force. But the Russians had divided themselves between two different operations, and were therefore unable to bring decisive force to either. Ivanov controlled, in the Carpathians, twenty-nine divisions, to which another two were attached when the fresh corps arrived. In the central plains of the Vistula, he had eighteen divisions (IV and IX Armies). Ruzski maintained seventeen and a half divisions in East Prussia, reduced to fifteen and a half when 22. Corps went off to the south-western front, and twenty-three and a half divisions (of I, II and V Armies) on the Bzura-Rawka positions and north of the lower Vistula. The Central Powers had eighty-three divisions to the Russians' ninety-nine (with four to come); forty-one German and forty-two Austro-Hungarian. For the offensive to succeed, the entire Russian superiority should have been concentrated against East Prussia. But the demands of Ivanov made certain that this would not happen, and although, as Danilov had said, the shell-reserve per gun now reached over 450 rounds, and although the intake of new manpower was secured by entry of the 1914 class of recruits, these advantages were thrown away.

The campaign of 1915 opened with a characteristic episode. Ludendorff decided that there should be another attempt in the central plains of the Vistula; at the end of January IX Army attacked, near Bolimów, using gas: its first appearance in the war. The attack went wrong—gas blew back on the Germans, and the cold weather ensured that it would in any case be ineffective. The Germans were sensible enough to break off their attack when it failed. The Russians counter-attacked—using eleven divisions, under a single corps commander, the cavalryman Gurko. Command failed to keep in touch with troops; there was no coherent plan, little training, only a mad persistence. 40,000 men were knocked out in three days. Characteristically, failure was ascribed to the wrong reasons. The inappropriateness of the season, the lack of planning, the crazy over-loading of a single corps command—none was noted. Instead, Ruzski told Smirnov, the aged commander of II Army: 'Victory on your front cannot fail, as you have eleven divisions on a front of only ten kilometres'. This was, in a sense, the very reason for failure— German artillery could concentrate on a very small area, enfilading it on one side. But Ruzski blamed 'lack of resolution', and Russian troops were driven again and again into much the same pattern of attack—failures being blamed, first on cowardice, and then on lack of shell.[15]

In the main offensives, it was the Austrians who were first off the mark, with forty-one divisions to thirty-one infantry and eleven cavalry divisions, on 23rd January. An Austro-Hungarian army was to seize the passes of the western Carpathians, *Südarmee* those of the centre, and further east, in the flatter area of the Bukovina, a further Austro-Hungarian group was to seize the Russian flank. The offensive maybe looked sensible on a map. On the ground, it was—in the words of Austrian official historians whose kindness to Conrad amounts to considerable distortion—'a cruel folly'. Mountains had to be scaled in mid-winter; supply-lines were either an ice-rink or a marsh, depending on freeze or thaw; clouds hung low, and obscured the visibility of artillery-targets; shells either bounced off ice or were smothered in mud; whole bivouacs would be found frozen to death in the morning.[16] Rifles had to be held over a fire before they could be used; yet even the thick mountain-forests were of no great help for fuel, since there was no way of transporting logs out of these primaeval forests. The task was altogether a grotesquely inappropriate one, but Conrad's staff, comfortably installed in their villas in Teschen, with their wives in attendance, waved protests aside, even when they came from the reliable Boroević, commanding III Army. For better or worse, they had tied their strategy to a fortress, and like Haig at Passchendaele could see no other way of proceeding.

The offensive opened on 23rd January, Boroević taking the Uzsok Pass. On 26th, *Südarmee* also attacked, and went forward at a rate of perhaps a hundred yards a day. By the end of the month, it had taken a line south of passes it had been expected to take on the first day; and the arrival of a fresh Russian corps from Ruzski's front held the line. Further east, the Austro-Hungarian attack did better, in flatter country where only Cossack groups offered resistance, and the river Dniester was reached on this side by mid-February. With this, the Austro-Hungarian offensive collapsed. It was followed, early in February, by a Russian offensive, against the western side. The Russians were closer to supply-lines than the Austrians; the Austrians had been exhausted by their own offensive; their positions in the valleys were often broken through, such that Austrian defenders on the mountains surrendered. There were persistent rumours, too, that the Slav soldiers of Austria-Hungary were giving in too easily—rumours perhaps exaggerated, for their own purposes, by both sides. By 5th February the western wing had fallen back over the railway centre of Mezölaborcz, through which ran an essential supply-line to the exiguous salient originally won by the offensive of 23rd January. Four divisions, counting ten thousand men altogether, were spread out over twenty miles. Then the Russians ran into much the same problems as had bedevilled the Austrian offensive.

Conrad was now desperate to relieve Przemyśl, and could only repeat his offensive, for Kusmanek, commanding the garrison, said he would be starved out by mid-March. Twenty divisions were assembled on Boroević's front for a new attack, but many of them existed only on paper. In any case, Boroević complained, and had half of the front taken from him, and given to another army commander, Böhm-Ermolli, who could be trusted to be more sparing with recognition of reality. In the mountains, things went much as before. Böhm-Ermolli's counter-offensive opened on 17th February, but no-one noticed. Ice and snow condemned the troops to passivity, only the guns firing ineffectually at Russian lines. Throughout the latter part of February, troops were driven into piecemeal attacks that won at best a few hundred yards of snow. The main group of Böhm-Ermolli's force—50,000 men under another general for whom Conrad had a mysterious fondness, Tersztyánszky—sank in a week to 10,000 men—bewildered, frozen, often not understanding what their officers were saying. Kralowetz, chief of staff to one of the army corps, later wrote that the Russians' counter-attacks succeeded because they encountered 'men already cut to pieces and defenceless . . . Every day hundreds froze to death; the wounded who could not drag themselves off were bound to die; riding became impossible; and there was no combating the apathy and indifference that gripped the men'. Some 800,000 men are said to have disappeared from the army's fighting strength during the Carpathian operation—three-quarters of them from sickness. This was eight times the number of men supposed to be saved in Przemyśl. The Austro-Hungarian peoples paid heavily for Conrad's inability to confess error.

Nothing, now, could save Przemyśl. Conrad's adjutant confessed: 'There is nothing more the troops can do'.[17] Falkenhayn would not send reinforcements—merely remarking that he had always predicted failure. Ludendorff had nothing to spare. Success in the Bukovina was too limited, too remote, to affect the issue. By mid-March, the Przemyśl garrison elected to surrender—making an attempt at a sortie that one British observer described as 'a burlesque'.* On 22nd March, Kusmanek

---

*The 'heroic defence of Przemyśl' had of course been a stock theme of propaganda. But the defenders had, in reality, very little to do but wait, since the Russians had little heavy artillery to knock down the defences, and could not manoeuvre such heavy guns as they had. The garrison was not impressive. A British observer thought the men looked 'half-starved'; 'a more hopeless, dejected crowd I have never seen', whereas 'the officers were immaculately dressed and wore a prosperous and well-fed look and, according to the inhabitants, had lived in every luxury including female society of the most aggressive type'.[18]

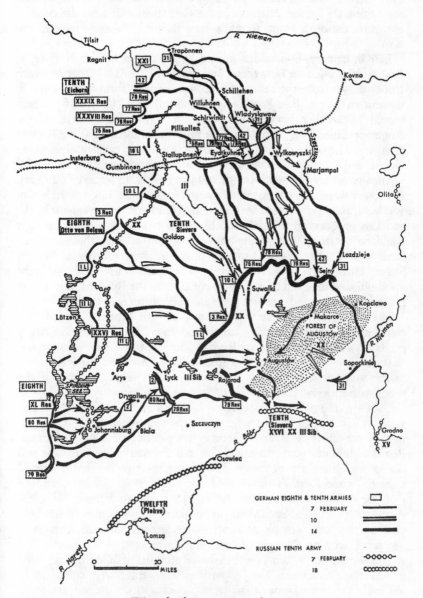

Winter battle in Masuria, early 1915.

surrendered, with a garrison of 120,000 men. The way was now open for a full-scale Russian offensive in the Carpathians; and the direction of events on the other front, Ruzski's, now inclined *Stavka* to take up this plan.

Late in January, Ludendorff moved his headquarters to Insterburg, in East Prussia. The four new corps, and those of VIII Army, together with troops drawn from the central front, were now to form two armies, in the eastern part of East Prussia—X (Eichhorn) and VIII (Below). There would be another 'pincer-movement'—X Army from north of the Angerapp Lines, VIII Army from south of them, directed at the Russian X Army. The Germans had fifteen infantry and two cavalry divisions to eleven and two and some artillery superiority—seventy-seven light, twenty-two heavy batteries to 154 and forty-eight. In terms of numbers, the forces were roughly equal, at about 150,000 men. Ludendorff's plan was bold, and in reality not very sensible. Weather counted against it, the attackers on occasion running into blizzards. No doubt a tactical success could be obtained. But as the two armies moved east, their southern flank would be lengthened, and on this there were substantial Russian forces, capable of acting offensively. But Ludendorff underrated the possibilities of this, and imagined he could force the Russians to evacuate Poland—Germans and Austrians pressing them from each flank.

The offensive got off to a good start, on 7th February. It led to a considerable tactical success—largely because the Russian X Army produced a repetition of earlier Russian patterns. In the first place, it was strategically isolated. *Stavka* and Ruzski were busy forming XII Army, to the south-west—six corps, to advance in mid-February against the southern frontier of East Prussia. Only two of its corps were in line, the rest not arriving till some time later—4. Siberian Corps and the Guard at Warsaw, 15. Corps at Gomel, 20. Corps still attached to X Army. Intelligence did as usual report German troop-movements in East Prussia. But the rumours were dismissed: on 6th February, Danilov was still saying that 'they are probably distributing their forces in the central theatre'; while Ruzski's director of operations, Bonch-Bruyevitch, felt that 'they will not dare to attempt anything in East Prussia, with XII Army on their flank'. Such alarms as occurred merely prompted acceleration of this new army's concentration. Consequently, X Army was neglected, with no strategic reserve ready to assist it.

This would not, maybe, have mattered so much if X Army had been in reasonable condition. The proportions on its front were considerably less in the Germans' favour than were proportions on the western front in the Allies' favour; and yet the Allies generally failed to secure tactical victories of any scale, because German defences were sensibly-arranged.

A suitable method of defence could, in 1915, cancel out even three-fold superiority in guns, and more in numbers. But X Army did not have a sensible method. It had been disheartened by activities since August 1914—a lion-hearted crossing and re-crossing of the border, at much expense. Commanders had, seemingly, learned little—had even, in the case of Pflug,[19] been dismissed for attempting to apply such lessons as had been absorbed. The trench-system was primitive—at best a thin, interrupted, ditch, Over half of the divisions were second-line ones, containing only a tenth of their numbers from first-line troops; and since, in the Russian army, artillery commanders regarded such divisions as barely worth saving, there was always a tendency for guns to be saved at the expense of men. Moreover, the positions had been changed, on the right, shortly before. Following skirmishes further north, the right of the army had been pushed forward; and the expected co-operation of X Army with the offensive of XII had led to an over-extension of the front-line—on the right, to the edges of the Lasdehnen forest, where German troop-movements were effectively concealed. That two of the three divisions on the right had been told to garrison Kovno in case of emergency, did not lend X Army greater weight; while, to hold the newly-extended line, the commander—Sievers—had had to commit virtually all of his reserves to the front line. He warned Ruzski early in February: 'Nothing can prevent X Army from being exposed to the same fate as I Army in September 1914.'[20] These fears were waved aside: XII Army would solve everything. Yepanchin, commanding the right, was similarly told not to bother commanders with his tales of woe.

The position worsened in the first two days of the offensive, because weather-conditions delayed the German attack, in its full weight; the German movements could be dismissed as 'isolated groups' such that the attackers gained much advantage from Russian commanders' failure to respond. The whole of VIII Army, attacking on 7th February, was dismissed as 'a small German detachment'. This army encountered, first, a relatively isolated second-line division, that regarded its main task as the protection of the fortress of Osowiec, to the south; the German attack was thought to be an attack on this, not on X Army's flank. Most of this division disintegrated, though it lost only eight of its fifty guns. By 10th February, VIII Army had advanced some way into the left flank of the Russian X Army. Thereafter, a soldiers' battle developed, as the Germans split their forces between attacks to south and east—both sets, in the event, held. The true tactical success came with the northern part of Ludendorff's 'pincer-movement'. On 9th February the full weight of this was felt, initially by two cavalry divisions on the extreme right. These broke up, 'disappearing from the horizon'. The three second-line divisions did not much better—suddenly struck, in frozen bivouacs. Yepanchin thought that an attack was being launched on Kovno, which he had been told to protect; and he led his men there, himself allegedly at their head. His divisions, unused to action, disintegrated—again, typically, losing only 17 of 150 guns, as artillery left the 'cattle' in the lurch. By 11th February, the Russian right had disintegrated, and German troops were stretched across the centre of X Army—by mid-February arriving in the rear of this centre, which contained three corps, one of which was engaged with VIII Army.

The central one of these three corps—20. (Bulgakov)—was to be surrounded. X Army command should have ordered retreat in time, but it did not know what was happening. Only on 14th February did Yepanchin announce himself from Kovno, wondering what had happened to his division. Until then, the whole of the German X Army was thought to be 'about a corps'. Yepanchin's feebleness was considered responsible for what had happened. In any case, since Ruzski felt that the main German blow was that of VIII Army, towards Osowiec, on 11th February he ordered XII Army to prepare for a counter-offensive with this in mind. The central corps of X Army were told not to retreat, in case they endangered the new manoeuvre. Only on 14th February was a retreat begun—the southernmost corps occupying one road, the northernmost one the other, so that the central one had to stand and fight. By the time it could withdraw, German troops had already penetrated the forests of Augustów in its rear, and controlled the roads. Conditions were such that the Russian groups that did escape were unaware of 20. Corps's fate, and so did little to help. Four German corps gathered in a circle around Bulgakov's group, and between 16th and 21st February it was pressed closer and closer—in the end, two divisional staffs being forced to use the same forester's hut. From battle-casualties and stragglers, regiments ran down to a few hundreds, instead of three thousand men—in the case of 105th Orenburg regiment, to less than a hundred. On 21st February Bulgakov surrendered, with 12,000 men, most of them wounded. This was given out by Ludendorff as a new Tannenberg, and so it appears in his memoirs. There was talk of 100,000 prisoners; in practice, the figure was 56,000 for losses of all types in the Russian X Army, although since most of 20. Corps's guns were lost, the Germans took 185 guns.[21] German losses have not been revealed.

This was a tactical success like many others in the First World War—barren of strategic consequence. It led the Germans to extend their flank into Russian territory; yet there could be no advance to the east without security towards the south, and much of VIII Army had to be diverted into besieging the fortress of Osowiec (from mid-February to early

March). This failed: Osowiec was well-defended, and enjoyed a position of some strength, commanding the few ways across marshes of the Bobr. It provided an object-lesson in the proper rôle of fortresses in the First World War: its various works were not strong and the defenders could not, therefore, have many illusions—they were almost forced to a flexible defence based on field-positions, and the Germans, despite an expenditure of shell calculated to be 250,000, failed to make progress.[22] Further west, there were German attacks from East Prussia against the newly-forming XII Army. On 24th February a well-executed manoeuvre against the town of Przasnysz resulted in capture of 30,000 Russians; but an equally-well executed manoeuvre on the Russian side resulted in capture of 30,000 Germans a week later, with sixty guns. Early in March, the pressure of XII and X Armies resulted in a German withdrawal to the frontiers. Tactical successes had balanced each other out, and Ludendorff, with forty-two and a half divisions to sixty-four, decided to abandon further schemes. At bottom, Falkenhayn had been right: the winter offensives had been foolhardy.

The Russian offensives had also failed to produce much result. Grand Duke Nicholas opposed any further attack on East Prussia 'where we should simply be exposed to the East Prussian railway-network'. Ruzski was told to take up a good defensive position. He protested, but received word that the Grand Duke's 'will' was 'unflinching'. What this meant was that Ivanov and *Stavka* had now taken up a different scheme—a renewed Carpathian offensive. If Ruzski were to be pushed onto the defensive, it would be sensible for him to abandon the more exposed parts of the Russian line in the central theatre. But the Grand Duke would not have this, because it could weaken the south-western position. Ruzski was left holding a front longer than needed, and his troops were committed to it such that few reserves could be created. When *Stavka* elected to launch a further Carpathian attack, Ruzski's nerve cracked: he resigned, alleging 'extreme exhaustion, brought on by general weakening of the organism'. Alexeyev—supposed by the Grand Duke to be more sympathetic to *Stavka's* plans—took his place, towards the end of March.

By then, various factors arose to require a Carpathian offensive, to knock out Austria-Hungary.[23] First, there was the simple failure to produce 'decision' on the German front. There was also the prospect of an Anglo-French coup against the Dardanelles, an opening-up of the Balkan theatre and the intervention of Italy. It was clear that Russia's political and military interests 'powerfully demanded' concentration against Austria-Hungary: Russians, rather than Italians, or French clients such as the Romanians, should take Budapest. Moreover, this was the Russians' only way of helping the western Powers in the eastern Mediter-

ranean. The Russian front against Turkey was far to the east, in the
Caucasus, and although, here, the Russian army generally had the better
part, supply-difficulties prevented any deep penetration of Turkish
territory. In any case, most people, German and Russian, assumed that
the Dardanelles would be opened up by the British—the Russian Council
of Ministers, for instance, ordering coal from England on the supposition
that it could be transported through the Dardanelles.[24]

Ivanov was therefore instructed, just before the fall of Przemyśl, to
complete the ruin of Austria-Hungary. But, typically, he was not given
enough force for this. Two-thirds of the Russian army remained frozen
on the other front. Alexeyev, far from sympathising with Ivanov, as
before, now adopted in redoubled form the policies of Ruzski, and
resisted suggestions that he should part with troops. A second-line
division was at last extracted from him; and he promised, also, 3. Caucasus
Corps—although it took a month to arrive, even then requiring a 'categorical order'. Ivanov thus had barely over thirty divisions for his Carpathian offensive. To make up, he took troops from his own sector of the
central theatre; but, because of a need to impress Romania, they were
sent, together with others, to the remote, sometimes inaccessible Bukovina,
and spent the next month in forming a new, IX, Army. The troops of
February were reinforced, in the Carpathians, only by three second-line
divisions, drawn from the former blockading army at Przemyśl; otherwise, III Army could only weaken its right wing, on the Dunajec-Biala
positions near Cracow, in order to create sufficient force, for the attack
of its left wing in the mountains.

The Carpathian operation went on in much the same conditions as
before—'a labyrinth of mountains', with periods of thaw more frequent
now, than before. The Russian forces were hardly stronger than the
Austro-Hungarian ones, at least in terms of divisions. In terms of morale,
there was, however, a great difference. In its March offensive, the Austrian
II Army had lost heavily—52,000 men in the week preceding Ivanov's
attack, 17,000 of them from frost-bite. *Südarmee* had lost two-thirds of its
strength. The Austrian III Army, to the west, had also been hard-hit.
Windischgrätz, Austrian liaison officer with German troops, said that 10.
Corps was 'no good at all'; in II Army 'the mood is very bad'; in Teschen,
Conrad's headquarters, the mood was 'below zero. The chief never stops
grumbling'.[25] Russian attacks came in a series of short jabs through the
valleys, broken off for lack of force after they had won initial successes.
This, in mountain-conditions, was an excellent way of proceeding, for
the Russians completely confused Austrian reserves without, themselves,
running into insuperable supply-difficulties. Yet the Austrian commanders could not afford the general retreat that might have saved things:

once they lost the mountains, they thought, they would be pushed back on Budapest. Their armies stayed in the mountains, losing thousands of prisoners. An attack on III Army produced crisis; appeals went from Conrad to Ludendorff and Falkenhayn; by 6th April a new German force—*Beskidenkorps*, under Marwitz—was made up of troops from Ludendorff's front and *Südarmee* (two and a half divisions). Its intervention, together with the problems of supply brought by the Russians' advance, brought the Carpathian offensive to a halt. On 10th April, Ivanov stopped it, explaining: high losses, exhaustion, thawing of the roads that produced impassability, and snow had brought things to a halt; even the most essential supplies could be brought up 'only with the greatest difficulty'. He also complained, not wrongly, that inactivity on the rest of the front had allowed the Germans to send in reserves. Even so, the operation should be renewed. More troops must come; and the new IX Army, assembling on the Dniester, would bring decisive results. In this way, mid-April found the south-western command in a mood to capture Budapest.

CHAPTER SIX

The Austro-Hungarian Emergency

In January 1915 Ludendorff had told Falkenhayn, 'Austria's emergency is our great incalculable'; and by spring, with the fall of Przemyśl, the Habsburg Monarchy appeared to have reached the limit of its endurance. The Austro-Hungarian army was small, badly-armed, badly-led; the Carpathian front brought an uninterrupted tale of woe. Cramon, German liaison officer, reported to Falkenhayn that the Austrians were 'exhausted, rotten'. II Army had lost two-thirds of its men; 'then there is the business of the unreliability of some nationalities'. It became more and more difficult for the army leaders to count on Czech or Ruthene troops in battle against Russia. Slav troops ran through their commanders' hands and, after the Carpathian campaign, it became clear that the Austro-Hungarian army could only survive with German help. The *Beskidenkorps* of early April could only be a stop-gap, for the imminence of Italian entry into the war would make the Habsburg Monarchy's military position impossible.

The weakness of Austria-Hungary was no great surprise to anyone, but it ought not to have reached such dimensions: Austria-Hungary contained over fifty million inhabitants, and her war-industry, with Skoda and Steyr, should have been able to produce a more respectable war-effort. To start with, too, there was not even such sign of dissidence on the part of potentially rebellious peoples, such as the Czechs: rather the contrary. But the Habsburg Monarchy had become incapable of harnessing its peoples' energies. A hopeless muddle was made of conscription. Before the war, not more than a fifth of the liable young men were ever conscripted, and less than a fifth received full training, because there was no money to keep more than that, and because the army leaders shrank from the creative effort of turning hundreds of thousands of peasant youths, with fifteen different languages, into serious soldiers. In 1914, 3,500,000 men were called up—virtually the whole of the trained reserve, and a section of the untrained territorial army. Losses knocked out a substantial proportion of these—to the end of 1914, 1,250,000, and a further 800,000 to March 1915. Services in the rear took up the activities of most of the rest, and in the early months of 1915 Austria-Hungary was really relying on the 1914 class of conscripts, together with some untrained territorials. The army at the front therefore ran down—not much above 250,000 in December 1914, and not 500,000 in April 1915. Anticipated conscription of the class of 1915, and hasty conscription of classes of territorial troops, made up some of the gap, but in spring 1915 there was a severe man-power crisis.[1]

In matters of war-economy, too, there was a crisis, owing mainly to slipshod pre-war arrangements, No provision had been made for a war lasting more than a few weeks, and manufacture of munitions was woe-fully low. When the Allies set up their blockade, the foreign trade on which the authorities had calculated naturally came to an end. But the authorities had little idea as to what might take its place, and went on counting on the Germans' sending them what they needed—although of course the Germans needed every scrap of shell they produced. Austrian production had even been cut back, because of cartel-agreements with German firms. In this way, prices would rise, and the Austrian firms would profit because they held shares in the German ones. Moreover, it was difficult for the Austrians to produce munitions by mass-production, because a large part of their artillery was old-fashioned. The army against Russia had had less than 2,000 guns to the Russians' 3,000; even so, there were forty-five different types of gun, each needing different munitions; and a further problem was that many guns were made of bronze which, though much less efficient than steel, lasted longer and therefore suited the exiguous pre-war army budgets. The authorities blundered about in a fog: imagining at one moment that they could modernise the whole of their artillery at a stroke, and then finding that their resources had to be frittered away on endless separate artillery and munitions-programmes. The tone of their summaries of their own activities is one of unshakable self-satisfaction. Just the same, their performance was woeful—116,000 rounds produced in the whole of December 1914, as against a minimal demand of 240,000 per week. Austrian shell-output never reached more than one million rounds per month, even in 1916, when the Germans produced seven million, and even the Russians more than four. However, low shell-output was made at least supportable, because the out-put of artillery, for allied reasons, remained low also. The artillery section of the Vienna war ministry was the most characteristically Viennese of them all: more and more complicated, for less and less return. Problems of labour and raw materials were serious, as in other countries, but the authorities, lacking the pressure of an energetic régime demanding results, whatever the cost in orthodoxy, behaved in their pre-war fashion, and failed to cut corners. The army lost 1,000 guns in the first six months of war—excluding those of Przemyśl—and had 278 replacements.[2]

The chief difficulty of administration was that nothing could ever be really centralised. In theory, the Common Council of Ministers was the central authority, containing the Prime Ministers of Austria and Hungary, and the three common ministers—War, Finance, Foreign Affairs. But real authority had slipped to the two separate Austrian and Hungarian governments, and the only way of making sure that even correct information reached the Council of Ministers was to invite separate cabinet ministers to attend its deliberations—a procedure that increased the body far beyond manageable size, the more so as there was, in Austria-Hungary, an indirect relationship between power and garrulity. The Council met infrequently in the course of the war—about forty times—and the efforts of the new Emperor, Karl, to breathe some life into it led to complaints that men were wasting their time in useless chatter.[3] In reality, Habsburg administration suffered from a degree of fragmentation that makes even its records difficult to deal with, since at all levels the centres of decision were not well mapped-out.*

One centre of decision was, however, very well-established: Budapest. Fanaticism and racketeering distinguished the Hungarian war-effort. Most war-goods were produced in Vienna and Bohemia, the largest industrial region of the Monarchy. The inhabitants of these were dependent on Hungarian food. Hungarian producers took advantage of scarcities to increase their prices, allegedly to combat the fall of exports, and forbade imports that might have lowered prices. A concurrent fall in the prosperity of the Austrian towns meant real hardship for the populace, but protests met a barrage of obstruction from the Hungarians: the figures must be wrong; it was only natural for farmers to profit in wartime; in any case, it was really Hungary that was fighting the war. This last point was best-developed, as usual, by Tisza, the Hungarian Prime Minister: 'Unless one is quite blinded by prejudice, it is impossible not to see from the experience of this war that not only the natural energies of the Hungarian race, but also the strong structure of the Hungarian national state form the greatest force in the Monarchy, the stoutest pillar of its European position'.[4] That they were all so well-fed no doubt helped. Hungarian land-owners went on to complain that they were lacking labour, and, by an ingenious trick, made the army auth-

---

*The Monarchy's servants even began to lose their grasp of ceremonial, unthinkable in Franz Joseph's day. At Karl's coronation in Budapest, there was a revealing scene. A representative of the magnates made a long and emotional speech. Karl's attention wandered, and as a result he missed his cue for the response, until Tisza, with exquisite symbolism, gave him a nudge.

orities, at their own expense, commandeer troops to help with the Hungarian harvest. Throughout the summer months of 1915, there were never less than half a million soldiers thus occupied.[5] Austrian functionaries were dazzled by such virtuosity in egoism; and to any grumble, the Hungarian government could always stir up a display of chauvinist antics on the part of its own opposition, so as to convince the Austrians how moderate the Hungarian government was being. It was a simple enough construction: the Austrian army might mis-use Hungarian peasants, so long as Hungarian land-lords could misuse Austrian towns. Heavy doses of Hungarian chauvinism could anaesthetise at least the Hungarian victims of it all.

The Czechs could be forgiven for concluding that, whatever Austria had achieved against the Turks, she had failed to save western civilisation from the Hungarians. A combination of nationalist and social restiveness, on the one side, and military mismanagement, on the other, led to the Slav troops' becoming increasingly less reliable. The structure of the army broke down. It had always been supra-national, and professional officers made an effort to learn the languages of their men (Conrad himself, for instance, spoke seven languages). Recruits were expected to learn only a few hundred German words—the 'language of service'—so that they would know what was meant when 'sights', 'barrel', 'sabre' and the rest came up; and for other purposes, the language of the men was used, even if, as happened, a single regiment had three different languages. 1914 changed this. The professional officers were speedily wiped out, victims of their own virtues. The new officers were men of a different stamp—products of the middle-classes of Prague, Budapest, Vienna or Cracow, who had neither the will nor the chance to learn their men's languages. In any case, most officers' posts went to Germans or Hungarians, and Czech or Slovene reserve-officers frequently found their accents mimicked and their cultures mocked by arrogant sprigs of the German or Hungarian universities. The language-problem became ungovernable, in time; there was even a Slovak regiment commanded in English, since the men—with a view to emigration—had learned it, and the officers spoke it from their high-school days. Behind the Carpathian disasters, there was a real collapse of the structure of the Austro-Hungarian army. Men froze, resented injustices at home, did not know what their officers were saying, had not much artillery to help them in the field, and sometimes understood Russian better than any other language.

Desertion began. It would no doubt be wrong to conclude that this was a consequence of initial disloyalty on the part of the Slavs, although this was subsequently asserted by both sides—military leaders, to show that desertion was a consequence of politicians' blundering, Czech apologists, to explain that the Habsburg Monarchy was a tyrannical place, and that revolt was just round the corner. In reality, the peoples' enthusiasm for the Monarchy, when war broke out, took the authorities themselves by surprise. IV Army command reported of its journey through Bohemia in August 1914 that 'the behaviour of the populace, of all nationalities, was the best conceivable throughout our journey. Patriotic feeling was everywhere in evidence, and at the larger stations the troops were given bread, tea, cigarettes etc. by women of all classes'.[6] Men of all nationalities hoped—in accordance with official pronouncements—that now at last they would be regarded as equals by the German and Hungarian establishment, not just as tolerable minorities. But 'equality before supreme sacrifice' had a way of becoming equality before supreme incompetence. Czech soldiers, largely urban, literate and questioning, were bewildered at the army's treatment of them as half-witted peasants; at the other end of the scale, Ruthene peasants resented having to fight Russians whose language they understood and whose religion they shared. Red Prague produced a series of incidents, stimulated in particular by grain-shortages, and feelings ran high in the army as well. The high command overreacted. Its own displays at the front were not such as to foster notions of military efficiency; but if Conrad could not defeat the Russians, at least he could make short work of the Bohemian bureaucracy. The army interfered more and more in its affairs, and cramped, blundering army officers ruined the Habsburg Monarchy's hitherto, in the main, deserved reputation for fairness of treatment. The *Kriegsüberwachungsamt* was established to control 'disloyal' elements, and there following a uniquely Austrian combination of tyranny and comedy. Czech washerwomen were imprisoned because they threw notes over the barbed-wire of Russian prisoner-of-war camps, 'for the purposes of initiating a carnal relationship';[7] shop-keepers were molested because they had failed to put up enough flags to celebrate the re-capture of Przemyśl; schoolboys were arrested for hiding their patriotic double-eagle badge behind their lapel;[8] school-teachers were inspected to make sure that they had their charges sing four verses of the *Gott Erhalte* every morning—a huge machinery that would have been much better-employed against Hungarian land-lords.

The disaffection that all of this brought about was not confined to the civilian population. The army could not be isolated. No doubt, if the officers had been Czech or Ruthene, Czech and Ruthene troops would have fought better. But the structure of the army was against this. Two-thirds of the officers were German, most of the rest Hungarian; and a Ruthene who became an officer almost ceased, by definition, to be a

Ruthene. Furthermore, the army was not ruthlessly tyrannical, in the Prussian style. The Austrians did not have the Prussian knack of making anybody and everybody fight for Prussia, by virtue of a ruthless authoritarianism. By 1917 it had become clear that the Czechs would fight in the Russian army, or under German command; but they were quite ineffective, at least on the eastern front, under Austrian command. By the spring of 1915, tales of Czech desertion had become quite frequent, and although many or them were without substance—there was never, for instance, any case of a Czech unit's marching over to the Russian lines, flags flying and music playing—there could be no doubting that Czechs were unwilling soldiers, and that Romanians and Ruthenes were not far behind them.[9] More serious than formal desertion to the Russians was these soldiers' unwillingness to take risks even in their own defence. By spring 1915, the Austrian army seemed to be on the verge of disintegration, and the process could seemingly only be halted if the Germans intervened.

The threat of Italian intervention against the Habsburg Monarchy made German help all the more urgent. When war began, Italy had declared neutrality, but as Austrian defeat succeeded Austrian defeat, the temptation to her to come into the war, and seize Austrian territory, was very strong. Moreover, if she stayed out, the Russians and their south Slav allies might re-make Central Europe without reference to an Italy that coveted much of the Adriatic coast. Finally, when the western Powers attacked Turkey, it opened up huge possibilities for partition of the Turkish Empire, which would naturally be closed to Italy if she failed to participate in the war at the right time. The matter was dragged out, partly to increase the terms Italy would get from the Entente, partly from domestic disputes, since the socialists and clericals were, on the whole, against joining in the war, but a coup d'état, with semi-Fascist methods, finally prompted Italian intervention on 23rd May.

Falkenhayn had always been reluctant to help the Austrians. Both he and Conrad thought that Italian intervention, especially if, as both felt likely, it came together with Romanian intervention, would mean the end of the war—the Italian army in Zagreb within three weeks, in Vienna in six. They disagreed altogether as to what should be done.[10] Conrad wanted the Germans to send troops, to brow-beat the Italians. Falkenhayn thought that he could not spare them, and that Austria should concede bits of land the Italians coveted—they could, after all, be taken back at the end of a victorious war. Conrad replied that this would only whet Italian appetites still more, and the government shrank from the extreme unpopularity that such cessions would have involved in the Germanic heartland of the Monarchy. Perhaps a generous offer would have taken the wind from Italian interventionists' sails; perhaps it would merely have made them increase their demands. At all events, Vienna conceded ungenerously and slowly; and Falkenhayn would not send support to Austria-Hungary for her eastern front in case it stiffened her will not to give way to Italy. By March, the Austrians were exasperated, and they hit upon the one argument that a weak ally always has against a stronger. If the Germans withheld support, then they would collapse. There were persistent rumours that Austria-Hungary would make a separate peace;[11] Conrad—usually the soul of honour—complained to Bolfras, Franz Joseph's military secretary, that the Germans were 'unscrupulous, brutally selfish' and added, 'We can always threaten a separate peace with Russia, as a counter-weight'. On 1st April he told Falkenhayn that he would rather lose Galicia, in separate peace with Russia, than Trieste to Italy.

Falkenhayn's position was difficult. If he sent help to the Austrians, they might turn round and refuse to concede anything to Italy; if he failed to send help, they would disintegrate. Gradually, as the Carpathian disasters went ahead, he came round to Conrad's plan of limited attack on the Russian front. Characteristically, he proceeded with extreme stealth: for he had little faith in Austrian generals, and none at all in their ability to keep secrets. As early as 31st March he commissioned Groener to study the railways of Silesia and western Galicia; on 5th April, ostensibly as a private gesture, Cramon, the German liaison officer, asked the Austro-Hungarian railway-chief, Straub, what railway-facilities would exist south of Cracow for transport of German troops.[12] But it was not until 13th April that Falkenhayn officially asked for the Kaiser's permission to go ahead with an offensive in the east. After some discussion with the chiefs of the western front, eight divisions were made free for an offensive in the east, to be commanded by Mackensen, with Seeckt as his chief of staff. After some futile warring over prestige-questions, Mackensen's force was established as XI Army, and Mackensen, while commanding the Austro-Hungarian IV Army, himself took orders from the Austro-Hungarian high command, 'after due consultation' with the German one. This, to make sure that consultation went on. was moved from its western headquarters in Mézières to new ones in the east, in Pless, only a few hours' journey from Austrian headquarters in Teschen.

Afterwards, a quarrel developed as to whether Conrad or Falkenhayn had first put forward the scheme for an offensive in western Galicia, south of Cracow. But it was not a very original scheme. An attack from south of Cracow could proceed along the northern slopes of the Carpathians, dislodging Russian troops in the mountains, until the river San was reached. Conrad had attempted the operation in March, when his

IV Army had failed to break-through to relieve Przemyśl. Falkenhayn had certainly been first to propose the operation as a joint offensive, and, as Conrad later said, the whole thing had been dependent on his willingness to supply German troops. Both men had in mind a limited success: maybe the Russians would be forced back to the San, and the Austrians' position in the Carpathians would correspondingly be easier, so that they could, if need be, divert troops to the south if Italy intervened or a Balkan campaign—which Falkenhayn always sought—became necessary. Troops were moved between 21st April and the end of the month to the Austrian lines south of Cracow.

The Central Powers' May offensive attained much greater results than Ludendorff's and Conrad's enterprises in February, although the forces allotted were not greatly different. It was partly a matter of weather: by 2nd May, when Mackensen's attack began, the roads were everywhere passable, which had not been the case in February. It was partly a matter of Russian weakness in matériel, though this—certainly for the initial break-through—was exaggerated. The factor that lent Falkenhayn's May offensive such dimensions of success was above all strategic. The Russian III Army, defending the front south of Cracow and in the western Carpathians, was strategically isolated and lacked reserves, because of the quarrelling seemingly endemic to *Stavka* and the two front commands.

This isolation ought not to have happened, since the army was in the central part of the Russian front and theoretically could call on help from armies to north and south. In Ludendorff's February offensive, X Army had been isolated, to some extent, in terms of ground: other troops were some way off. On the other hand, the German advance against X Army was always weakened because its flank was extended, with in particular the Russian XII Army in position to strike that flank. In May, the Russian III Army did not have these advantages. *Stavka* had first decided on an East Prussian offensive, in the first three months of the year. Then it had gone for a Carpathian offensive, in April, and proposed, now, to carry it into May. A new Army, called IX, was to be assembled in the Bukovina, in the end with six army corps, withdrawn mainly from the central theatre. XI Army went from the blockade of Pszemyśl into the Carpathians, joining VIII. III Army itself had been obliged to take over a substantial part of the Carpathian front, and the gaze of its commander, Radko-Dmitriev, was fixed there. This part of his long front contained five of the seven corps staffs, and all but five and a half of the eighteen and a half infantry divisions he commanded. The need to build up a substantial force for the renewed Carpathian offensive also meant that there were few disposable reserves for III Army's western front. This, in the first instance, was a consequence of *Stavka's* decision to pursue a Carpathian offensive. More profoundly, it was a consequence of the abdication of *Stavka's* responsibilities between two front commanders, north-western and south-western. The north-western front was now relatively inactive. Yet it had fifty-seven and a half infantry divisions, soon to be fifty-nine and a half, against the south-western front's forty-one. *Stavka* did ask Alexeyev to part with some of these, and met obstruction after obstruction: the front was too long; it lacked 300,000 men; the Germans were going to attack; the railways were too occupied with current business; there should be an offensive, not in the Carpathians, but in the central theatre. A second-line division and 3. Caucasus Corps were wrenched from Alexeyev's jealous clutch, but even then with great delays, as transport-officers of the north-western front put these troop-movements low in their list of priorities. Ivanov's front, for the Carpathian offensive, had to help itself, and the result was a strategic isolation of the western part of III Army—the two corps south-east of Cracow, holding the lines of the rivers Dunajec and Biala near Gorlice. It was here that the Germans concentrated their forces. At the point of break-through, they had ten divisions of their XI Army ready, with eight Austro-Hungarian ones in IV Army to the north, against five and a half Russian ones, at that second-line troops of poor quality. On the Central Powers' side, there were 120,000 soldiers (in XI Army alone) with 370 light, 144 medium or heavy guns and 96 *Minenwerfer* to 60,000, with 141 light guns and four heavy ones, which blew up when men attempted to fire them, and of course no *Minenwerfer*.[13]

It was later said that German material superiority had been so crushing that even the most stoutly-led army could not have withstood it; that the only way for the Russian army to make its weight tell was for it to get some of the shell and artillery that the western Powers had begun to manufacture in such quantities. This was a refrain heard again and again from Russian representatives, and, increasingly, from the 'easterners' in British political circles. It was of course true that, in this period of the war, the Russian army faced a munitions-crisis. On the other hand, there was a great deal that simple strategy and tactics could do to make up for material shortages, and these possibilities were, on the whole, ignored by senior Russian commanders. In the instance of the Germans' May offensive, for one, it was strategy and not material weakness that had gone wrong on the Russian side. The Russian III Army, as a whole, had in fact a respectable quantity of artillery and shell:

Russian III Army: 219,000 men; 18½ infantry divisions; 5½ cavalry divisions; 675 light and medium guns; 4 heavy guns.

German XI Army: 126,000 men; 10 infantry divisions; no cavalry
divisions; 475 light guns; 159 medium and heavy guns.
Austro-Hungarian IV Army: 90,000 men; 8 infantry divisions; 1
cavalry division; 103 light guns; 150 medium and heavy guns.

Including part of the Austro-Hungarian III Army (which faced the left
wing of the Russian III), the Central Powers had 733 light and light-
medium, 175 larger-medium and 24 heavy guns to the Russians' 675
and 4.[14] If the Russian III Army had had its guns in the right place, there
would have been much less difficulty.

Superiority in artillery certainly did exist on the Central Powers' side.
But the superiority—both here and in the later, similar, campaign on the
Narev—was much less than the superiority which the western Powers
enjoyed over the Germans in France, a superiority that, in the offensives
of 1915-17, was turned to remarkably little account. In the Allied
offensive of May 1915, the attackers' superiority was considerably greater
than the Central Powers' superiority in their May offensive against
Russia: 664 guns of up to 149 mm. calibre on the German side, to 1,554 on
the Allied, and respectively 119 and 203 in larger calibres (i.e. larger
medium and heavy). In 1916 and 1917, the attackers' superiority in
artillery was sometimes vast. At Verdun, the Germans had 488 light
field guns to the French 242; 254 light-medium to 57; 939 larger-medium
to sixty-nine; 170 heavy to ten, and the proportions are still more in
the Germans' favour when age and type of gun (trajectory) are considered.
On the Somme, the British IV and French IV Armies had 1,655 light
guns to the German II Army's 454; 510 light-medium to 206; 423 larger-
medium to 166; 393 heavy to eighteen; and when it came to Haig's
Flanders offensive of July 1917, he had 2,112 light to 612, 1,295 heavy to
536 and 128 very heavy guns to fourteen. Despite these enormous super-
iorities, the western Powers' offensives in France and Flanders made much
less progress than did German offensives in the east in 1915, based on
incomparably smaller superiority in artillery, which strongly suggests
that there was a great deal more to the Russian army's poor performance
in that year, and overall, than simple inferiority of matériel.[15]

Shell provided a rather similar story. It was undoubtedly true that the
Russian army lacked munitions in this period of the war; but it was not
the case that lack of shell led to loss of defensive battles, provided they
were properly-waged. As a matter of fact, the shell-reserve of III Army
in the battle of western Galicia in May was far from trivial. According
to Tarachkov, director of the Army's artillery, the various corps had an
average of 400 rounds per gun in their depots, front and rear, and if the
army's own reserve is included, 500. Langlois, a French observer,

asserted that III Army was rather better-off for shell than other armies, since it had been inactive for much of the time, and he cited this an instance of mismanagement's complicating shell-shortage. Rerberg, who was chief of staff in 10. Corps—one of those attacked at Gorlice—asserted that 'not once, in my nine months' service as chief of staff, was there a shortage of shell'.[16] But of course the delivery of this shell was another matter. Everyone in the rear suspected that, if it were delivered to the front, it would be wasted. Corps artillery chiefs held shell back from batteries, army artillery chiefs from corps, and the front artillery managers from the armies. Huge quantities were stock-piled in the fortresses, and then frequently concealed from inspection by commanders worried that they might have to give it up. Thus, although the quantities of shell were probably sufficient for a well-managed defensive operation, deliveries to the front were so irregular as to compromise the best tactician's plans.

In any case, even a sizeable German local superiority in this war, need not have produced the wholesale collapse of the Russian army that followed from the May offensive. A break-through was, of course, always possible provided that the local superiority were great enough. In this early period of the war, trenches were not usually very complex or deep, and defence-tactics were not subtle. Assembly of sufficient weight could usually procure a break-through, in the sense that nothing living would be left on a given stretch of enemy line. One reason why the western generals continued with their attempts at break-through was that success always seemed to dance before their eyes: one more effort, and victory would be there. The British did, technically, break through in May 1915; the French did break through on 25th September, in Champagne, when they took many thousand prisoners and ninety guns; again, the British did break through on 13th–14th July, in the Battle of the Somme, near Thiepval, when their cavalry made a rare appearance on the field. The difficulty came, not with the initial break-through—provided preparations had been good—but with exploitation of it. The defenders' reserves would arrive by rail and road; the attackers would be moving up through mud, pitted with shell-holes, and their every movement could be painful. Hence, the defender would have time to construct a new line, and the process would have to begin again. When the British broke through in Artois, their reserves were far from this new German line; and when the French broke through in Champagne, they lost 100,000 men in 'grignotage' against it. The defenders' reserves were the key to the problem of break-through.

For a variety of reasons, the Russian army in summer 1915 was unable to handle reserves with the same kind of flexibility as the Germans in the west. It was partly a simple problem of numbers: there were not enough troops both for the front and for reserves. Indeed, resistance to break-through and resistance to exploitation of it demanded almost contra-dictory solutions, or so it seemed. The break-through could only be prevented if there were a 'thick front line', i.e. sufficient fire-power in the first position to defeat enemy penetration. But if the front lines were thickly-held, there would be little to spare for reserves. In eastern con-ditions, a break-through was generally more baneful in its consequences than in the west. Since there were fewer railways, and particularly fewer roads, and since weather-conditions often created mud, it was difficult for defenders to retreat with any speed. If their line were broken through, then troops to right and left of the break-through area could be out-flanked and surrounded before they could withdraw—hence the large number of prisoners that distinguished this front. The only way of resisting seemed to be the 'thick front-line' principle, to which the Russian army, and the other two, adhered for most of the war. Conse-quently, the proportion of troops used by the Russian army as reserves was much smaller than in the German or French case. To create reserves, it was necessary to withdraw troops from the front-line of a passive theatre, with all the complications of rivalry between the front-commands that this involved.

Furthermore, the functioning of railways on the Russian side was much less efficient than on the German, so that even when reserves did slip through the jealous clutch of a front-command, they could not be shifted rapidly. The assembly of IX Army in the Bukovina, in May 1915, appears to have taken a month, as had the assembly of XII Army on the borders of East Prussia in February. Even in 1916, transfer of a single corps of two divisions took twenty-three days or, if complete priority were given, a fortnight. This had little to do with the actual speed of trains—even slow trains could cover the whole length of the front from Vilna to Cherson in three or four days, if the journey were not interrupted.[17] It occurred because of bottle-necks in rolling-stock: not enough could be freed at one time for the movement of a division in four days. The contrast with German handling of reserves were plain, for all to see. When the Germans shifted their IX Army early in November from just north of Cracow to their jump-off points around Toruń for their Łódz offensive, they sent four army corps in five days, with 800 troop-trains, and had performed much the same feat when they set up IX Army late in September. In the last ten days of April, using the relatively poor lines south of Cracow, they sent eight infantry divisions to help the Austrians, with sixty trains daily; and similarly took only four days to send three divisions from Ludendorff's front in East Prussia to southern Hungary—174 trains, at forty-four per day. More significantly, when the Germans were actually in occupation of the railway-lines used by the Russian army in 1914-15, their exploitation of them was much more efficient, even though problems of wartime devastation were complicated by those of the different Russian gauge. In the first week of July 1916, to counter the Russian break-through on the Styr, they sent 494 troop-trains, with ten divisions, and ninety-eight artillery trains on lines to Kowel, Cholm and Vladimir-Volynski that in Russian days were supposed to be painfully undeveloped.[18]

The reasons for this immeasurably superior German performance lay in a combination of misfortune and mismanagement. The quality of labour mattered; and in any case there were always fewer railwaymen in Russia before 1914 than in Germany, although the mileage to be covered was greater and the technical problems more demanding. The army had gone to war with 40,000 men in its railway-battalions, and of these, over a third were wholly or partly illiterate, while three-quarters of the officers had had no technical training. Although the railway-troops did expand, to 200,000, lack of training was always a serious obstacle. Furthermore, the various instances of command did not sort out their priorities. Ronzhin, at *Stavka*, had no assistants at all, beyond his two subordinates and a clerk, sitting in half of a railway-carriage in Baranovitchi. The front railway-directors were in fact supreme, but they too had a limited view of their job, and arranged things without reference to each other. The military, who controlled a third of the country's railway-mileage and over a third of its rolling-stock, also quarrelled with civilians in the ministry of transport, itself run none too efficiently, and an amount of rolling stock fell, unused, between these instances.

But the heart of the railway-problem, at least at the front, was the horse. The Russian army maintained a constant million horses, partly because only horses could overcome the local transport-problems of eastern Europe, partly because the army remained faithful to cavalry divisions long after other armies had abandoned them. Grain was by far the bulkiest item for railways to transport. In December 1916, the army's daily needs amounted to sixty trains, of fifty waggons each. Supplies for the soldiers amounted to about 16,000 tons of flour, grits, fat, salt, sugar, preserved meat, and this took 1,095 waggons daily. Supplies for horses took 1,850 waggons daily, for 32,000 tons of barley, oats, hay and straw. Before an offensive, with a great gathering of cavalry, demand for fodder rose even higher. Ivanov, in December 1915, demanded, for his Bessarabian offensive, 13,700 tons of salt, sugar, grits; twelve million portions of preserved meat; 180,000 tons of fodder. The first two, designed for the men, needed 667 waggons; the last, for the horses, 11,385.[19] The contrast with the

German army was plain. Between 15th June and 15th November 1917, the German IV Army, facing the British offensive in Flanders, took in all 6,591 trains, of which 3,942 carried troops, 1,854 artillery and 795 supplies for men and horses of all kinds. This broke down into 242,185 waggons, of which 51,481 counted as supply of all types.[20] In other words, the horse, which required about a fifth of German transport, needed more than half of Russian transport. Not surprisingly, the movement of reserves behind Russian lines was much slower than behind German lines, because the rolling-stock was preoccupied with carriage of supply for horses. This was, to some degree, a consequence of the nature of the front, with its poor roads. But it also reflected a belief in cavalry that cavalry did little to justify, although there were, including Cossacks, some fifty cavalry divisions in the Russian army at a time when all other armies had converted their cavalry divisions to 'mounted infantry', i.e. dismounted cavalry.

When the Germans sent their eight divisions to the east, they brought a new style to warfare there. These, and their chief of staff, Seeckt, had absorbed western lessons—careful registration of guns, observation, camouflage, co-operation between infantry and artillery. German guns did not strew shell around in the Austro-Hungarian manner, in the vague hope of awakening an impression of unconquerable might in enemy breasts. Nor did they, in the Russian manner, disdain their own infantry as a worthless mob, tediously blundering into the skilled tournaments of their betters. German preparations on the field were also superior, since the Germans did not refrain from digging extensively.

The local weakness on the part of the two Russian corps facing attack was compounded by the primitiveness of their digging, which alone could provide an answer to the Germans' artillery-superiority. But this front had been largely inactive since December 1914, and, as the spring thaws came, Russian soldiers disliked digging into ground that might conceal frozen corpses. In any case, no-one foresaw much action, or thought that it needed digging. Prescriptions from France were ignored; the melting of snow and ice made trenches difficult to keep going; and in any case officers sold off some of the equipment for their own trenches.

There was not much more than a thin, ill-connected ditch with a strand or two or barbed wire before it; and communications to the rear often ran over open ground. Bonch-Bruyevitch was sent to inspect the field-positions of the various fronts in spring 1915, and reported that III Army's was 'not serious'. There was almost no reserve-position, either. 10. Corps had wanted to build one, but was told that, if it could spare the labour for this, it must have more troops than it needed to hold the front line: one regiment was therefore removed from each of its divisions for the Carpathian offensive. A corps—21.—and infantry divisions were removed, replaced at best by cavalry divisions, which required support from the remaining infantry. The infantry that did remain was largely second-line, even territorial, in composition, armed, often, with anti-quated rifles they had been barely trained to use. Yet the tactics of the time were that front-lines should be held as strongly as possible: even the Germans held that 'support-troops should be kept as close as possible to the front-line because they are safer, there, from gunnery'.[21] *Minen-werfer* and field-mortars were to profit from this. Yet confidence was strangely high. The Germans did their best to obtain secrecy, but, with large-scale, slow troop-movements, this could never be guaranteed, and by the end of April intelligence-reports on the Russian side revealed the presence of powerful German forces. Even on 11th April, as the Germans were reaching their decision, Yanushkevitch warned Alexeyev of the threat to western Galicia.[22] Alexeyev did not respond. He 'doubted' the news; in any case he probably wrote off the alarm as yet another of *Stavka's* attempts to make him give up troops for someone else's offensive.

On 26th April Dobrorolski, chief of staff of III Army, said the Germans intended 'breaking through at Nowysącz and north'—exactly correct. The local population of Ruthenes was so Russophil that information came in thick and fast—to such a degree that Seeckt wanted the populace moved out altogether. By 29th April, three German corps were noted; on the 30th desertions from the Austrian army revealed that attack was due to begin on 2nd May. None of this seems to have disturbed Russian confidence. Radko-Dmitriev was told, 'There is nothing in III Army's situation to suggest any danger'; the field-fortifications had been 'strengthened in time'.[23] The best counter would be a renewed Carpathian offensive, particularly by IX Army, with its six infantry and two cavalry corps on the Dniester, far to the south-east.

The German break-through was quite a simple affair. It began with a four-hour bombardment on 2nd May that reduced Russian trenches to rubble, swept aside barbed-wire, cut telephones and prevented local reserves from coming up in time. The bombardment ended with *Minen-werfer* action that scared the ill-trained defenders from their places, and the Russians lost a third of their men through gunfire alone—many of the rest reduced to a state of shock. One German corps attacked the point of junction of the two Russian ones, drove a wedge between them and took 4,000 prisoners in an hour. Since there were no rear positions, the defenders simply moved back into open country, still more vulnerable to gunfire. On that day and the next, the Germans advanced eight miles, and in this area ruined the Russian corps' defence-system altogether—

10. Corps fell from 34,000 rifles to barely 5,000, and a second-line division of 9. Corps further north simply disintegrated. A gap of five miles opened between the two corps. The commander of III Army, was not on the telephone, and was in any case absent for celebration of the St. George Order. But in any case there was little he could do. Local reserves had been pushed in, often through bombardment, in piece-meal style. There was not much else. Two regiments, force-marched into the gap, disappeared in it on 3rd May. Two cavalry divisions, hurriedly summoned, with twenty-four guns between them, also melted away in useless counter-attacks. Half of 63. Division, a second-line one, was marched forward without maps to much the same fate. The only substantial group in reserve was 3. Caucasus Corps, in two groups some way to the rear. It could not arrive until 4th May, and in any case, as Radko-Dmitriev reported, 10. Corps and the cavalry were 'so seriously disrupted that even the arrival of 3. Caucasus Corps can only serve to cover retreat'. Most of the troops had been swallowed up in inadequate first-line defences, let down by their artillery, unable, in many cases, to use their rifles with skill. In any case many of these divisions existed purely on paper —facts known to the army command, but not, it seems, to the officers of *Stavka*.

The Germans had captured huge numbers of prisoners on the first two days. But they too had suffered. They could not exploit the victory with much speed, for their own supplies had to be hauled up over broken country, and at Biecz they encountered 3. Caucasus Corps, which gave a good account of itself, on 4th–5th May. It proved impossible to move fast enough to cut the roads leading north from the Carpathians, and trap the Carpathian part of III Army. Only one division—Kornilov's—was caught, partly because its order to retreat came too late, partly because its supply-routes were taken up with other troops' supplies, partly because Kornilov foolishly counter-attacked: he surrendered on 6th May, with all but five guns.[24] The corps in the region had retired towards the Dukla Pass, and formed something of a line on the river Wisloka, by 6th May.

This line was nearly a hundred kilometres in length, more or less running north-south, fifty miles west of the San. It was outflanked to the south as Austrian groups emerged from the Carpathians. The Germans assaulted its western side. Nothing at all had been done to prepare the line. Almost nothing could come in as reserve—Alexeyev had promised the half-strength, second-line 13. Siberian Division, but only half of it could come in—two regiments, not even full-strength. Two battalions of a hastily-composed 'composite division'—scraped together from oddments found lying around the front—were also sent. But the troops expected to defend the line had been destroyed. Radko-Dmitriev asserted that, while nominally he might have twenty divisions, in fact they were worth five. 10. Corps had been reduced to 1,500 rifles—half of a regiment. He talked of 'the Germans' crushing strength, which with numerous artillery has in a short space literally destroyed our trenches and wiped out the defence in places to the last man'. Dragomirov of 9. Corps said 'territorial troops have been utterly feeble, surrendering in droves'. Ivanov reckoned the army should go back to the San and re-fit. Brusilov was offered command of the entire area. 'On my honour' he turned the offer down. Yet *Stavka* insisted on retention of the Wisloka lines: Italy was about to intervene, IX Army would soon be in a position to attack Austria-Hungary in the Bukovina, such that Romania might come in as well.

III Army had already lost over 200 guns; also, its shell-reserve had been expended much faster than foreseen. It now had to suffer shell-shortage, on top of everything. On 3rd May Radko-Dmitriev complained that he needed 50,000 rounds at once. He was told by Kondzerovski, for *Stavka*, 'Your demands are in the impossible class', and he was sent 22,000. On 5th May the demand was for 31,000, supply 18,000. The next day, demand was for 20,000: 'I know that this cannot square with your earlier warnings on the subject, but my situation is exceptional'. Supply was 12,500, with a demand for proper accounting. This latter came back on 8th May: 9. Corps needed 43,000 and had 4,000; overall, 20,000 were needed at once, and 25,000 daily thereafter. 15,000 were then supplied.[25]

Radko-Dmitriev sought to organise a counter-attack. He took 3. Caucasus Corps and 24. with other divisions that had come out of the Carpathians, and attempted counter-attack near the Dukla Pass. This occurred on 7th-8th May, just as a fresh German division came in, a renewed German offensive prepared, and a German stroke on the northern side under way, Radko-Dmitriev said: 'I have great hopes in this man-oeuvre, the only way of restoring the army's position.' There was a set-piece battle that gave the Germans thousands of prisoners, 24. Corps dropping to less than a thousand rifles, in a force, nominally, of forty thousand.

Further north, the Prussian Guard broke through, forcing a retreat that left the rest of 10. Corps and much of 9. Corps in disorder—the Austrian IV Army, following it, taking thirty thousand prisoners. Only a radical retreat, to the San, could have saved the unbroken part of the army. But *Stavka* would not allow this at all,[26] and Ivanov's credit was so low that he could not behave with normal autonomy: on the contrary, he was now begging desperately for reinforcements from Alexeyev's front. Danilov still behaved as if army corps were of full-strength. He talked grandiosely of counter-attacks. There came a medley of declamation and scripture from the Grand Duke. Ivanov, demanding retreat, was told by Danilov: 'Your views cannot conceivably be submitted for the Supreme Commander's approval'; and from the Grand Duke: 'In view of your staff's continual demands to retreat on this or that part of the front, you are hereby categorically ordered not to undertake any retreat whatsoever without my express permission'—fine, fighting stuff, that condemned III Army to bleed to death.

On 10th May the nerves of Ivanov's chief of staff broke: 'The strategic position is quite hopeless. Our line is very extended, we cannot shuttle troops around it with the required speed, and the very weakness of our armies makes them less mobile; we are losing all capacity to fight'. Przemyśl must be given up, together with Galicia; the Germans would invade the Ukraine; Kiev must be fortified; Russia must 'renounce serious military activity until we have recovered'. He was at once dismissed. But it took more than *Stavka's* fortitude to hold III Army, which on 10th May was given permission to retire to the San. It had lost nearly 200 guns, and the Germans had taken 140,000 prisoners, in six days. Of 200,000 men and 50,000 replacements, only 40,000 unwounded men reached the San—10. and 24. Corps barely existed at all; 9. Corps had lost four-fifths; 3rd Caucasus, three-quarters. 21. Corps had 2,000 men, 12. Corps less than 8,000. Even retention of the San would be difficult enough. However, *Stavka* kept its hopes. On 6th May Alexeyev promised to send a corps and a division (he sent the weak 15. Corps); 5. Caucasus Corps was due to come from Odessa. Above all, the new IX Army would soon be ready for its attack in the Bukovina.[27]

As things turned out, IX Army won a considerable, but irrelevant, success. Its 120,000 men took on 80,000 of the Austrian VII Army, dependent for supply on the narrow-gauge mountain railway through Körösmezö, and always hampered by Hungarian politicians' interference—Count Tisza had forbidden the Hungarian State Railways to transport troops from Transylvania to the Bukovina because he wanted a guard kept against Romania, and feared a rising of the Romanians of Transylvania.[28] By mid-May the Austrians had lost much of the Bukovina, and were forced to use one of III Army's corps on this front, instead of on the Italian front. In the same way, the attacks of *Südarmee* on the Dniester were unsuccessful, for the most part, and losses were high. Falkenhayn disregarded these matters: if the Central Powers could succeed on the San, they would be cleared up. If the Central Powers failed there, nothing else would matter any more. Mackensen's force was assembled for attack on the San, beginning in mid-month. On 9th

May the Kaiser took up headquarters at Pless, to be near the scene of new operations in the Balkans and the east.

Mackensen's shell-reserve was once more brought up to the standard thousand rounds per field-gun: in other words, not far short of a million rounds. The entire reserve of Ivanov's front on 13th May amounted to just over 100,000 rounds of all types, on 20th May to 114,000 field-cannon shell, 118,000 mountain-cannon, 25,000 howitzer, 42,000 heavy. III Army could only be given trivial amounts—60,000 rounds sent from Lwów on 17th May, 15,000 to follow—even then with unpleasant observations: 'Unless you have been throwing away your shell-boxes, there must be enough'. But as yet tactics had not been adapted to deal with this emergency. The San positions had not been prepared at all—on the contrary, Austrian wire, trenching-tools, timber-props and the like, captured in the previous autumn or in Przemyśl, had been sold off to the local populace. Przemyśl itself was still something of an obstacle, but there was nothing much from there to the north. Besides, the line had many peculiar features. On 21st Corps's front, near Radymno, the eastern bank was completely dominated from the western bank, and the river was only a few yards broad. Its defence could only be conducted from the western bank, with all the isolation and difficulties involved.

The San battles opened, more or less, with repetition of the Gorlice pattern. Since the troops were now even weaker—III Army having lost five-sixths of its force—reserves were even fewer than before. Radko-Dmitriev's divisions had merely been assigned bits of the river to defend: reserves, for the whole position between Przemyśl and Jaroslau, consisted of two infantry regiments. A new '29. Corps' had been formed from the wreckage of 81 and 13. Siberian Divisions—together, not 2,000 men. A 'composite division' constructed from a new second-line division and one division of 3. Caucasus Corps, consisted barely of a ring of men round the guns. Alexeyev had, by 20th May, sent ten divisions in all: the three corps involved were now gathered on the lower San, opposite the Austrian IV Army, with a view to counter-attack. This was Radko-Dmitriev's only hope, and yet, with shell in such short supply, not much was to be expected.

A German tactical success between 16th and 19th May led off the San battle. The Radymno salient collapsed, thousands of the defenders being drowned or machine-gunned as they tried in panic to cross the San. By 19th May the Germans had established a large salient across the river, and now sought to extend it to the south—towards the rear communications of Przemyśl. It was a mark of the Russian defence's considerable qualities that this attack was far from being successful. As Mackensen's group inched forward, Falkenhayn grumbled. He told his commander in the central theatre, to the north, to prepare for attack: affairs in Galicia 'do not have good prospects'; 'we can win only if we use great quantities of ammunition and man-power, and we have the best reasons for economising with both'.

Moreover, the Auatrians, in the central theatre, suffered unmistakable reverses, and had to be given help from Mackensen's group, itself under pressure. But a mismanaged Russian counter-attack dispelled some of these advantages now coming the Russians' way. In the night of 19th–20th May they attacked the Austro-German lines with three corps taken from Odessa and Alexeyev's front. Another new Corps had been set to *Südarmee's* front to *Stavka's* annoyance. The Austrians suffered a crisis. retired, lost many thousands of prisoners, and had to be helped out by a German corps. Against the German front, this counter-offensive broke down, reducing the new troops to much the same level as the old ones.

By 25th May it had been contained; indeed, the Germans had profited from it themselves since, just before a Russian attack came, with the troops exposed, waiting to attack, the Germans had launched one of their own attacks and destroyed 5. Caucasus Corps which, in a few hours, saw its regiments sink to a few hundred rifles. Further east, the successes of Ivanov's troops had little relevance, even when won, on the Dniester, against German troops. On the contrary, they were a waste of precious shell. Early in June, the defenders had been pushed back until only a narrow corridor of three miles connected Przemyśl with the armies to the east. On 4th June the Austrians and Germans finally entered the fortress.

On 23rd May, the Italians had finally declared war—perhaps given the final impetus to do so by the reflection, paradoxical, in view of Conrad's strategy, that the Russian position must be saved. But their army was not at all ready for what was to come. Although, to start with, there were over 800,000 men to 100,000—armed at that with old rifles and out-of-date artillery—the Italians failed to gain more than a line of outposts on the Austrian side of the border. The tasks of supply were beyond them, and defenders, in these mountains, had an advantage still greater than elsewhere. For the whole summer, the Italians failed to divert significant German forces from either front, and the Austrians also held their new front with relatively insignificant changes—III Army from the Carpathians, some of their troops from the Balkans. The Serbian army, anxious to seize Albania before their nominal allies, the Italians did, could also give little help to Russia.

In the circumstances, Ivanov could only retire. Conrad and Falkenhayn, on their side, were not sure what to do. Conrad wanted to attack Italy. Falkenhayn would have preferred an attack, by some thirty divisions, on Serbia. They compromised on continuation of the campaign against Russia. Here great successes seemed to come, almost by themselves. Seeckt persuaded Falkenhayn, at Jaroslau station, to pursue the attack across the San.[29]

Ivanov had now used up all of his reserves, either in the fruitless counter-offensive on the San, or in the less ineffective offensives against *Südarmee* in the Dniester valley. The shell-reserve sank to 240 rounds per gun, and of course much less than this at the front. Nominally, he held to the idea of 'stubborn retention of every square foot of ground'. But the troops had lost so heavily that they had not the force to do this; increasingly, too, they had not the will. Now, he withdrew even IX Army back to the Dniester.[30] The chief cause of defeat had been tardy movement of reserves. They had come in little-by-little, and now it was much the same. Alexeyev offered, now, 6. and 23. Corps with a Guard division, to be linked, on the western side, with the troops beaten in the San counter-offensive. Later, the whole of the Guard, 2. Siberian Corps and 31. Corps were offered from Alexeyev's front, and Alexeyev took over defence of western Galicia.

But to concentrate these troops took time, and the Germans mean-while brought three divisions from the Balkans and another two from the west. These were to 'strike the enemy east of the San until we have a decision suitable for our purposes'. In mid-June the German offensive began. Soon, Mackensen was able to conclude that he faced 'completely defeated troops'. *Stavka* on 17th June announced that the whole front had gone down to 500,000 men short; the shell-reserve amounted to forty per cent of complement. Moreover, the forces in Galicia had to retreat eccentrically—VIII Army to the east, III Army towards the north-east, and the new group—under the Guard general, Olokhov—to the north —such that energetic action by the Germans could always strike an exposed flank. Even within the armies, links became strained—particularly in VIII, defending the Wereszyca positions and Lwów.

Within six days, Mackensen's offensive brought the Austro-Germans towards this city. *Stavka* now believed retreat must begin. The Grand Duke told the Tsar that two-thirds of Ivanov's men had dropped out; but 'the quality of replacements, as regards their training, is beneath criticism. Their training has been very hurried, and because rifles are short, they do not even know how to fire'. On 20th June 'energetic evacuation of Lwów and the rest of Galicia' was ordered; on 22nd June the Austro-Hungarian II Army entered it. The six weeks' campaign had turned out to be one of the greatest victories of the war. For an initial investment of only eight German divisions, Falkenhayn had earned, with the forces of Mackensen's group alone, 240,000 prisoners and 224 guns, for a loss of 90,000 men.

CHAPTER SEVEN

The Shell-Shortage, 1915

The disaster in Galicia provoked an immediate outcry within Russia. The army was said to have been defeated because of a crippling shell-shortage, complemented by a severe shortage of rifles. It was, as Bernard Pares,* faithfully echoing respectable opinion in Russia, called it: 'a war of men against metal', in which even the stoutest soldiers and the ablest strategists would have been at a loss—an opinion naturally shared by *Stavka*. At first, shell-crisis involved *Stavka*, war ministry and Artillery Department. But the manufacture of war-material, and conversion of the country to a war-economy, came to involve the State's relationship with private businessmen and the working-classes, and hence opened up a whole seam of economic and political questions that touched on the essence of Tsarist Russia. Some writers have suggested that the shell-shortage proved Russia to be 'incapable, at her then stage of industrial development, of matching the needs of modern war'.[1] Hence the whole question becomes a touchstone for Russian economic development before 1917, although before a direct relationship between shell-shortage and structural faults of the economy can be established, many short-term factors have to be given their due weight.

There was little dispute, at least by spring 1915, as to the facts of shell-shortage. Rennenkampf and Ivanov had already complained in September 1914, and there had been an appeal from the Grand Duke to the Tsar. Usually, such alarms were dismissed by the war ministry and the Artillery Department as hysterical, but their frequency grew. In September 1914, *Stavka* said it would need 1,500,000 rounds per month—about three times

---

*Pares, whose accounts of Russia in the last days of Tsarism are famous, espoused Russian liberalism and its legends. He was sent out by the Foreign Office in 1915 to observe the eastern front, which he toured by bicycle. He sent back lengthy reports, written in indelible ink, which he later published; but they deserve caution. The Foreign Office felt that 'much of his efforts' was 'valueless', and he seems to have been retained mainly because he had an energetic impracticality that gave him unique feeling for Russian liberals.

what had been thought necessary before the war—and in later months this figure climbed to 2,500,000 and then 3,500,000, which remained the 'norm', with some fluctuation, for the rest of the war. By spring 1915, tales from the front revealed that German artillery superiority was crushing. When Mackensen broke through in May 1915, his XI Army alone had a million shells, not counting those of his allies; III Army, at the point of break-through, had less than 100,000 and received not much more than that in the next month, since on 13th May the entire south-western front had barely over 100,000 in reserve. Between January and April 1915, the whole army received two million shells only, and, with the German 'pincer-movement' of summer 1915, Russian troops were either captured wholesale or driven back in panic. Shell-shortage could not have been more clearly documented than by the Russian abandonment of Poland that summer.[2]

The first reason for shell-shortage, and the parallel shortage of rifles, was relatively simple. No-one had foreseen that this would be a long war, and no preparations were made for armaments-production 'in depth'. The supposition that war would be short owed little to purely military calculations, for men were aware that states could field huge armies with vast armament, and the defeating of such would be a long business. The calculation that war would be short owed much more to prevailing ideas of economics—the advanced nations of the west could not possibly allow disruption of trade for more than a few months, or their economies would collapse. Financial calculations were much the same. After a few months, the states' credit would be exhausted—indeed, the Hungarian finance minister said, as war broke out, that it could not last longer than three weeks. The preamble to Russia's 'Great Programme' read: 'the present political and economic circumstances of Russia's main neighbours rule out the possibility of a long war'.[3] Some writers had even argued that, since Russia was less dependent on international trade, she could afford a long war; a strategy of attrition was recommended, even by the perceptive Bloch. The discovery that states could go on fighting the war with bits of paper took almost everyone by surprise.

The immediate consequence of this belief in a short war was that states concentrated on building up their stocks of armament, rather than their factories to produce armament. They used their money to buy shell from existing manufacturers, rather than to develop factories that would, in wartime, produce shell but that would, in peacetime, lie idle. This policy saved every state money, at a time when defence swallowed more and more resources in budgets. In Russia, a factory to produce 20,000 fuzes a day would cost forty-one million roubles, but with the same money the state could add two million shells to its existing reserve of seven million.[4] This problem was less in other countries, because the defence-factories, even in peacetime, would be far from idle: they could count on a considerable export-market. In Russia, excess-capacity would just rust. An informed guess was made, on the basis of 1904–5, that a thousand rounds per field-gun would suit European war, and a reserve of seven million shells of various types was laid in. Even this—which in 1916 would not have kept a single gun going for ten days of offensive action—was not to be mobilised at once, but over 480 days. Shell kept the better, the more its parts were separated. One-third of the shell was kept in complete readiness, one-third in part-readiness, and the rest split up into its parts. Assembly of shell, in 'parks' of 30,000 rounds served by ninety men, would take time, especially in the long winter nights, and until 1912 men supposed that the shell could be got ready in leisurely style. Again, the three State factories for shell were told to produce half a million rounds per month if war broke out. With rifles, it was a similar case. Enough rifles were laid in for the 4,500,000 men to be called up in wartime. Ponderous logic dictated that the army should make money by selling off its surplus stock, and 450,000 rifles of an older model were sold off to officers for use in hunting. Similar logic dictated that skilled labour should be released, and the machinery not used. The State factory in Tula produced, in the first months of 1914, between one and five rifles per month and its manager converted some of his machinery to make gun-sights and pistols, in order to have something to do. Not more than 50,000 rifles could be produced in a month. Once the old stocks ran out, replacement-rates were therefore absurdly low in both rifle and shell—the more so as even the agreed production for wartime could not be carried out at once. By July 1915, over four million men had been called up above the initial set,[5] and by then, *Stavka*'s minimum demand for shell was five times greater than the production 'norms' of 1914.

Shell would have to be produced from somewhere, and the responsibility for this lay, initially, with the war ministry's artillery-department. But a considerable delay in production, from Russian resources, was caused by the department's feeling that the shell-shortage was not a real crisis at all, despite appearances. The department were of course wrong; but they were wrong for the right reasons. In their panic, *Stavka* had exaggerated both the inevitable effects of inferiority in shell, and the quantities available to the Germans; and they also mis-handled the shell that came their way. Battles were not lost uniquely because of shell-shortage, or even mainly because of it.

The over-rating of artillery was of course understandable. The First World War produced a unique disparity between weight and mobility:

huge armies, with twentieth-century supply, but moving with less speed than eighteenth-century infantrymen. Manoeuvre was ruled out; and men concluded that the only way to defeat the enemy was to find him where he was concentrated, and rain shell on him—in the French phrase, 'artillery conquers, infantry occupies'. If this too failed, then the answer must surely be: more shell, and of course heavier shell. There were many drawbacks to this method, as the offensives of 1915–17 showed, but commanders did not see much alternative to the great bombardments with which they initiated their actions. There was an alternative, which boiled down to better training of the infantry, and harmonisation of infantry with artillery. But it took generals a long time to recognise that the new soldiers could be intensively trained, and it took artillery an even longer time to regard infantry as an equal, partnership of which was essential to the winning of a battle. At bottom, it was the same attitude that prevented civilian recruits of 1914–18 from ever achieving really considerable promotion in the wartime armies of Europe. The generals behaved as if they had a monopoly of wisdom, and demanded vast quantities of shell as a consequence of tactical bankruptcy.

Certainly, shell was exaggerated as a feature of Russian defeats in the spring and summer of 1915. The Germans' artillery-superiority on the eastern front was no greater, and indeed was usually smaller, than the western Powers' artillery-superiority in France, which got them nowhere. German shell-production in the summer of 1915 did not exceed four million rounds per month, three-quarters of which normally went to the west; Russian production rose from 450,000 in the first months of 1915 to nearly 900,000 in July and over a million in September. Of course the Germans could concentrate shell-stocks for an offensive, and achieve local superiority at the point of break-through; but this was not a long-term factor, and a truly crushing weight of shell appears to have been established only three times: Mackensen's break-through at Gorlice early in May, Gallwitz's break-through on the Narev in mid-July, and Mackensen's break-through at Cholm and Lublin in late July. Even then Russian accounts over-rated the Germans' quantities of shell—the careful Korolkov, for instance, remarks that Gallwitz's army had three million rounds to use on the Narev, whereas the army did not use even a million in the course of the whole eight weeks' campaign between the Narev and the fall of Vilna on 18th September.[6]

In any case, it was quite possible to counter the attackers' artillery-superiority by tactical devices, as the Germans did in France. Guns were seldom very accurate, and for much of 1915 usually had the wrong kind of shell for the work asked of them—shrapnel rather than high-explosive.

Dummy-trenches, dug-outs with earth ceilings ten metres thick, support-lines, flexible handling of reserves counted for a great deal in the west. In the east, they were more difficult to set up—man-power was thinner on the ground, building-materials more difficult to come by, roads and railways either too few or too over-loaded to permit rapid shuttling of reserves. But at bottom it was lack of will not lack of means that dictated the Russian army's poor response to the challenge of German bombardment. *Stavka* fell into the habit of blaming all of its misfortunes on lack of shell, and seems to have neglected ways by which the German superiority could have been countered, while at the same time many interested but ignorant parties in Russia automatically sympathised with *Stavka*'s view.

A further criticism of the artillerists' was also true, that *Stavka* mishandled its shell, though the fault was often the artillerists' as much as *Stavka*'s. *Stavka* itself had no artillery section until the spring of 1916, when *Upart* was set up, and accounting for shell was one of the many responsibilities of Kondzerovski, the adjutant-general, whose prime function was none the less to take care of senior promotions. When the artillerists asked *Stavka* for details of shell-consumption, *Stavka* had none to give; and contradictory tales came from the front and army headquarters. In September Ivanov said he had used up 1,000 rounds per gun, but inspection of his armies by the artillerist Khanzhin showed that all of his armies, except IX, had quite enough shell for the campaign of late September–mid-October on the Vistula. The artillerists could show that they had sent nearly five million rounds to the front by the end of 1914; *Stavka* could account for only a third of them, and the artillerists concluded that there must be three million rounds left.[7] They suspected, in any case, that the infantry were both grossly wasteful with shell, and that artillery was already, as a result of Sukhomlinov's misdoings, too much dominated by infantry. Artillery experts in the infantry units were not given power to command their guns, but were supposed only to make sure they were in good shape. Not until late in 1915 did artillery brigadiers' establishment contain even two telephones.[8] In some units, individual batteries were commanded by battalion commanders, with the inevitable consequence that the batteries were told to do what the artillerists imagined to be infantry work—the breaking-up of an enemy patrol, for instance. If shell-shortage existed, then it was the infantry's fault; infantry would learn sense, and give the work back to artillerists. At bottom, the shell-crisis reflected the bad relations of infantry and artillery, as much as it caused them.

But the artillerists themselves were far from free of blame. Their crazy insistence on the value of fortresses led to a stock-piling of guns and shell in artillery-museums such as Novogeorgievsk and Kovno, where the Germans captured 3,000 guns and almost two million shells. The commanders of these places seem also to have concealed their stocks of shell, for fear *Stavka* would remove them, and the first time *Stavka* learnt the size of the stocks was sometimes from German communiqués. Of course, some fortresses did quite good work, if the defence were well-planned, as was the case of Osowiec in spring and summer 1915, and Ivangorod in 1914–15. But both were really luxuries—using a thousand rounds per gun, in the case of Osowiec, in a complicated artillery-duel that showed the technical qualities of Russian artillerymen[9] at their best, but that did nothing to help the exposed infantrymen to north and south. The artillerists' attitude to reserve-divisions in particular was shameful. They resented having to waste their precious shell to preserve the existence of these allegedly useless troops. Moreover, if it was true that infantrymen sometimes made gunners spend too much shell, the fault often lay with the over-large batteries that artillerists had insisted upon, for their eight-gun batteries, retained until 1915, wasted shell that six-gun German batteries did not have to waste.*

An initial delay in ordering shell came therefore from the Artillery Departments' private calculation that shell-shortage was unreal, and was quite possibly a manoeuvre mounted by personal enemies in *Stavka* against the war ministry of Sukhomlinov. Responsibility for ordering shell lay with the War Council, an institution composed of, even for Russian circumstances, extraordinarily aged generals, set up to administer the war chest, and chaired by the War minister. It was supposed to examine every order made. In time, with millions of roubles' worth of orders, the Council could not contend with the flow, and the system had to be stream-lined. But throughout 1914, the members of this Council, all of them acutely aware of the sneers of civilian ministers at slipshod military accounting, were determined to do their bit to save the country's money; they remained little corks of pedantry, bobbing in the war-economic storm. A request for two million shells was turned down in September; 800,000 were substituted, even then only on the grounds that the noise they made would be good for troops' morale.

---

*Rifle-bullets were also used more generously on this front than in the west. A figure supplied by Alexeyev to the French, in January 1916, showed that Russian rifles used 125 rounds per man-month, French ones 30 and British ones 50. The Artillery Department suspected that troops also concealed both rifles and ammunition. A great deal of Austrian munition was captured, and so many rifles that Russian bullet-factories were ordered to produce 37 million rounds p.a. for them, until 1916, when Brusilov captured so many that the order was countermanded. Two corps of VIII Army were armed with Austrian rifles, and the Department always suspected that there were many more in existence, undeclared.

In this period, not even the five million rounds that Russia, with her existing capacity, could turn out in a year, had been ordered. With rifles, it was much the same. Meanwhile, a complicated game of buck-passing developed between General Headquarters and Ministry until the shell-reserve per gun fell, by June 1915, to less than two hundred rounds per month, and until the rifle-stock declined to the point where, in July 1915, five men were being trained with two rifles.

Certainly, by the end of 1914, the Artillery Department had woken up to the fact that this would be a long war; generally, too, there was now appreciation that shell would be needed in great quantity. But the experts did not consider extending shell-production inside the country, for the simple reason that they could not imagine Russian businessmen to be capable of producing shell. The Department had faith only in a narrow circle of seventeen Russian industrialists, and it had not much faith in those. In any case, Russian industrialists were already complaining of wartime difficulties: the cessation of trade with Germany deprived them of a vital source of machinery and skills, and conscription of skilled labour within Russia, together with the transport-disruption of wartime, had made life difficult for them. It was characteristic of this period that the Council of Ministers should pass an order for thirty large locomotives to America, since the Putilov factory demanded 1,500,000 roubles per locomotive, and would deliver only late in 1916, whereas the Americans would send them in four and a half months, and would charge 500,000 roubles per locomotive less than Putilov.[10] The Artillery Department could not imagine that Russian industry would be capable of manufacturing war-goods, and therefore had recourse to foreign suppliers, who were supposed to be cheaper and more efficient, and who had also been supplying Russia for many years past.

Not much could be got from France, although Schneider-Creusot did produce for Russia throughout the war, because French industry was almost completely taken up with supplying the French army. Not much—though still a surprising amount—could come from Germany, hitherto a large-scale supplier. It was on England, and then on the United States, that the Russian war ministry counted. Orders both for rifle and shell were passed in great quantity—by the beginning of 1915, fourteen million rounds of shell had been ordered from various British and American firms, together with shell-parts for still more rounds. Large orders for rifles had also been placed, in the United States for the most part, and by November 1914 the English firm of Vickers had received forty-one million roubles' advance-payment. Russian reliance on these foreign firms is shown in the following table, applying to December 1914:

Shell (1,000 rounds) expected by the Department for use at the front:[11]

by 1st May 1915	Russian production:	Vickers:	United States:
3″ shrapnel:	820	490	275
3″ high-explosive:	146	100	75
by 1st September 1915			
3″ shrapnel:	950	400	250
3″ high-explosive:	315	225	350
Totals:	2,231	1,215	950

General Hanbury-Williams, British representative at *Stavka*, even said that Vickers should be sending two million rounds in the first half of 1915, while a further British firm, Kings Norton, was due to send a million 22-cm. time-fuzes by April 1915. Vickers were also directly involved with the Russian government in gun-production. An Anglo-Russian company, *RAOAZ*, was set up to make guns in Tsaritsyn, and extensive orders were made.

If these foreign firms had done their work, there would have been neither shell- nor rifle-crisis. But there were endless delays in fulfilment of Russian orders. Both British and American firms were busy working for the British government; in any case, they were performing even this task inadequately, because they had to expand very quickly, and were not used to the work. In the British case, a withdrawal of skilled labour to the army went together with an ill-suited conservatism of management; in the American case, there were also serious misunderstandings in finance. Moreover, Russian practices did not make things easier. Vickers complained that they could not make Russian fuzes because the powder for them had not come from Russia; guns to test the Russian shell produced by Vickers had not arrived, or had arrived late, and without carriages; Russian blue-prints were difficult to make out, because they came in Cyrillic, and with Russian measurements; Russian experts, sent out to negotiate over contracts, behaved with an exasperating suspiciousness even in trivial matters—a criticism given heart-felt echo by American firms who had to deal with General Sapozhnikov and his technical mission. The links between Russian authorities were often tenuous, such that any negotiation took months, however urgent the business. Writing on the Vickers' fuze-contract, Hanbury-Williams could claim that it was hardly Vickers' fault if—as he engagingly wrote*—'*ces*

---

*Hanbury-Williams was not of course a very perceptive witness. He owed his appointment as British military representative to *Stavka* to nothing other than his distant ancestor's having had some success, as *ambrassadeur*, with Catherine the Great, and his supposed despatches from the front display, apart from weakness in spelling, a very shaky knowledge of eastern-European geography.

négotiations ont déjà duré pour entre trois et quatre mois' (*sic*). Even more engagingly, Vickers explained delays to the Russian government, with reference to their need to conceal things from British factory inspectors, who wanted to make sure that every shell went to their own army. But the real problems were much simpler to define. Without lavish government finance, which, at the time, the firms themselves rejected, the firms could not produce enough to meet all of the demands on their books; and at the same time they did not hesitate to accept all orders, if only because the swelling capital costs involved demanded more and more money in the form of advances. French contracts subsidised British ones, and Russian ones subsidised French ones. Vickers' affairs went into confusion, and it was with justice that Grand Duke Sergey, for the Artillery Department, concluded that 'they have unconscionably lied to us . . . it has been one long, wicked piece of deception'. British government people themselves agreed with this judgment: Sir G. R. Clerk, at the Foreign Office, found that 'Messrs. Vickers have done us enough harm, in all conscience'. American industry did not do any better. Deliveries to Russia came a long way down its list of priorities.[12]

The Russian army in 1915 got very little in the way of finished wargoods from its allies and the United States, despite the large sums poured into them. Three hundred thousand Russian rifles had been ordered from Winchester in America, 1,500,000 from Remington and 1,800,000 from Westinghouse, to be delivered at monthly rates of 100,000 in mid-1915, rising to 200,000 in mid-1916. By March 1917, only nine per cent of the Winchester order, and twelve per cent of the other two, had reached Russia. The Kings Norton fuzes, ordered for April 1915, arrived in August 1916. The *RAOAZ* factory in Tsaritsyn failed to produce heavy guns, and the order (for 167) was passed direct to Vickers in England, who supplied nothing until late in 1916. Meanwhile, the Tsaritsyn factory was put on to production of light artillery, for which the State paid a third above the usual price, and gave an advance of 17,500,000 roubles. In shell, the short-fall was disastrous. In 1915 as a whole, Russia herself produced 11,200,000 shells, and imported 1,300,000—about a tenth of what had been expected. By November 1916, 40,500,000 shells had been ordered abroad, but only 7,100,000 had arrived. Yet this mistaken reliance on foreigners had led the government to neglect ways of developing Russian industry. In Sidorov's words, 'hopes placed in the Allies, in the vast industry of America, had allayed the fears of the Russian government, and had removed all creative energy from the war ministry, the will of which had been paralysed'.[13]

The dishonesty and bungling of foreign businessmen destroyed the Russian people's faith in foreign capitalists. In Petrograd, a repulsive atmosphere of profiteering developed, as one parasite after another descended on the Hotel Astoria: from English tailors, offering to extract rifles from bandit-chiefs in Bolivia via Japanese middlemen, to more highly-placed toilers in the bran-tub of Russian war-orders, such as Raguzo-Suszczewski, friend of the Tsar's mistress, Kseshinskaya, or the comte de Saint-Sauveur, brother-in-law of Schneider. Americans and Canadians arrived in the expectation of a new Yukon trail; the Canadians Mackay and Clergue, with an associate, Allison, described by the British Foreign Office as 'the most notorious black-leg in Canada', arrived to set up a 'Canadian Purchasing Syndicate', which would produce shell for Russia, in factories that would be bought with the advance on the deal. Thanks to 'contacts' with the various ministries, some of these profiteers were amply rewarded; but not much in the way of war-goods reached Russia, at least, until the Russians were already well able to make them for themselves.[14]

The Russians were then expected to pay a huge price for the privilege of having had their industrial development retarded by this vast confidence-trick. In matters of foreign trade, Russia was dependent on Great Britain, and some of the delays in foreign ordering, particularly in the United States, had been caused by difficulties to which this dependence had given rise. Her gold-reserve, though large, was not in any proportion to her needs in foreign trade, and she had virtually no investments overseas that could be converted into imports; while her surplus on balance-of-trade was cancelled out by the interest she had to pay on foreign loans. In the first weeks of the war, when there was still an illusion that it would not last long, the Russian government placed orders abroad and paid for them out of current account, although even then there were difficulties, because the French included Russian assets in the 'freeze' they proclaimed early on. But by October, the source of Russian payments for foreign orders had become questionable, and foreigners jibbed at accepting payment in roubles that they could see depreciating in a few months' time. It became necessary for Great Britain, with her £5,000 millions of foreign investment, to act as banker for Russia. Between 1914 and 1917, Russia's foreign debt increased by some 8,000 million gold roubles—a doubling, within three years, of the pre-war debt. About three-quarters of the increase was due to Great Britain.

It took several months of war before the British were ready to finance Russian ordering—an important cause of the confusions of shell-supply in 1915—and the whole matter was not put on a regular footing until the autumn of 1915, when British authorities agreed to place £25,000,000 per month at the Russian authorities' disposal, although these credits had in fact been anticipated since the early summer. Delays occurred partly because the Russians found British terms onerous. The British, who themselves had a lower gold-reserve than Russia, demanded quantities of Russian gold before they would back Russian purchases; the Russians, who knew that their own currency was much more fragile than sterling, fought against this until October 1914, when £8,000,000 of Russian gold was sent via Archangel to Liverpool (where there was, characteristically, no Russian represenative to meet it), and continued to fight against further British demands. There was also grumbling that the rate of interest demanded by the British was high: five per cent. At bottom, the Russians felt that, since their troops were fighting and dying, while the British army consisted of a mere dozen divisions, the British should forget about commercial considerations and simply hand their allies cash to get on with the war. There was a widespread suspicion that the British were using their favoured creditor-position to take unfair advantages; and there was something in this view, for the meaning of 'business as usual' in Great Britain came perilously close to sharp practice. The British navy would cut off, not only Germany's imports, but also Germany's exports. British goods would supplant them—in China, Latin America, the United States, and in Russia as well, which had been one of the largest takers of German manufactures and of course machinery. British merchants dreamt of capturing Russian trade.[16] The profits made from these enterprises could then be used, via war-loan to the British government, to pay for purchases of war-material in the United States and Great Britain; and this would then be presented, with a bill, to Great Britain's allies, who would do the actual fighting. Great Britain's weapons would be—first the blockade, and then an export-drive. British exports did in fact undergo a period of buoyancy in the middle of the First World War, where every other ally's declined sharply:

British exports in the First World War (£ million)
1910–1913 average: 474; 1914–431; 1915–385; 1916–506; 1917–527.
Russian exports and imports in the First World War (million roubles)
Exports: 1914–1,000; 1916–600.
Imports: 1910–1913 average: 1,200; 1916–2,800.

It was in this light that Russians saw, for instance, Great Britain's long refusal to introduce conscription, which would have bitten severely into the export-trade, or to apply it very seriously in 1916.

In time, the British, no doubt recognising that there was a danger Russia would make a separate peace, supplied Russia generously enough with capital. But it took a long time for the mechanism to work properly, because the British insisted on centralising all orders in a committee dominated by themselves. Almost as soon as war broke out, Grey had suggested a 'Commission internationale de ravitaillement', with French, Belgian and Russian sections, which would act as clearing-house for all allied orders placed with British industry. It was sensible enough; for otherwise the allies would be bidding secretly against each other and the British government, and prices would rise. A consumer-co-operative made sense, in the circumstances. Later on, an Anglo-Russian committee was formed by which Russian orders, paid with British credits, were passed to British industry; finally, when the bulk of Russian orders was passed, again with British credit, to the United States, the committee was established in New York, in June 1916. It came to contain, on both sides of the Atlantic, 700 men, and passed orders worth 7,694,000,000 roubles on 5,386 separate orders. Each step in this centralisation was carried out only after much black-mailing of the Russian authorities.[17]

The Russian war ministry, Artillery Department, and various other ministries greatly resented British attempts to interfere with their ordering abroad. Each one was only concerned with its own section of affairs, and was concerned above all to secure goods immediately, so as to avoid discredit. There were frequent cases of Russians' conniving—sometimes with suspicions of corruption—in breaches of British regulations. Captain Kostevitch was said to have exported toluol from England, in tea-chests, via Norway. Vickers' doings with Russia were often underhand. Wyldbore-Smith, chairman of the 'Commission internationale de revitaillement', remarked early in 1915 that 'At present there seems to be no cohesion between the various Russian delegates, they all seem to take a pride in each going his own way and keeping his actions as secret from his colleagues as he possibly can, while the central Authorities at Petrograd are showering orders on this country without informing any of their delegates what they are doing.'[18] The Artillery Department resented British centralisation of orders, because, often enough, it meant paying huge prices. For instance, in February 1915 Lord Kitchener offered his good offices to Stavka to obtain ten million rounds of artillery munition in America. The Artillery Department obstructed the affair, on the reasonable grounds that Kitchener would do better to get the shell already ordered, and not delivered, in Great Britain. Moreover, Kitchener's supposedly generous offering was to cost the Russians 732,000,000 roubles, more than twice what they normally paid for shell.* At its most

---

*Grand Duke Sergey opposed the order. But Stavka sent a telegram to Kitchener, informing him that he should go ahead. The first that the Artillery Department heard of this was two months later, when the British military attaché, Knox, arrived to ask for blue-prints of Russian shell.[19]

extreme, the Russian attitude was simple: that the Russians would be expected to pay back British money, and therefore should spend it as they liked, instead of going through tortuous processes that usually caused Russian wants to come last on the list. On the other hand, the British could claim—and were supported both by Benckendorff, the ambassador in London, and Yermolov, the military attaché—that independent ordering by Russia would merely drive prices up still more. The British, in the event, won, because the rouble declined in value (early in 1916, to half its pre-war value against neutral currencies), such that Russian ordering had willy-nilly to pass by the British agencies. But it was not until early 1916 that the system worked with much efficiency.

The Russian government itself was unable to work a system of planned foreign trade, and this too prevented British finance from being as effective in launching a great Russian war-effort. The various ministries bid against each other, the banks, and industrialists. The possibility of getting some piece of foreign machinery often made the difference between prosperity and bankruptcy for many smaller firms, banded together in *Zemgor* or the War-Industries Committees, and there was a desperate fight for foreign currency on their part, which the government, with the interests of its main suppliers, usually resisted.[20] The banks earned impotent *lapalissades* from finance ministers because of their refusal to let the State even know what they were about in matters of foreign trade; and it was only when the fall of the rouble imposed foreign exchange-control from without that the centralised system of ordering promoted by the British really began to work. Throughout 1916, government agencies and business wrestled with each other, the War-Industries Committes and the rest; there was a prolonged fight to see whether the War-Industries Committees would even have the right to maintain a representative on the New York Committee. It was a measure of the confusion that no Russian Ministry of Supply came into existence, since the whole field became much too complex. The British lifted a corner of the confusion in December 1916, when they sent a high-level delegation to Petrograd to confer with the Russians and other high-level delegations on the needs of the Russian war-machine. Pokrovski, who was supposed to be chairman of the conference, did not learn of his appointment until just before it began, by gossip in *Stavka*. Because the Russians had not been able to centralise their affairs, they had to maintain their full delegation, in plenary sessions, in order to have the right information. They separately sorted out their needs, pronouncing them to amount to over ten million tons' worth of goods; and it took the British to point out that Russian railways, from the points of entry, could manage at most a third of these in a year. By the turn of 1916–17, there were heartfelt British complaints to the effect that 'our work has resembled swimming in glue'.[21]

When in 1916 some kind of order was imposed on supply-questions, the problem of transporting goods to Russia occurred as a final complication of the whole matter. In 1914, the ordinary trade-routes through Odessa or Petrograd were closed; and the remaining routes were weak. The Trans-Siberian railway, from Vladivostok, could take only 280 railway-waggons daily, of which 100 were reserved for railway-material and 140 for government stores, leaving 40 for all other purposes (as a standard of comparison, the Putilov factory alone required 900 waggons of supply every month). This line could not take more than a tenth of the ten million tons wanted by Russia in 1917.

There remained the ports of northern Russia, particularly Archangel, at the mouth of the river Dvina. It had been used as an entry-port for British coal, which could be shipped by canal to the south, but its great drawback for other purposes was that the navigation-season was only seven months, because ice prevented movement of ships between December and May. There was a narrow-gauge railway but it had been built very cheaply: when the concession for exploitation of the Moscow-Vologda line was running out at the end of the nineteenth century, the government had insisted, as a price for renewal, that the company involved should build a railway to Archangel, and this was done in the cheapest possible way. The railway did not even have a bridge across the Dvina to Archangel: the terminus was at Bakaritsa, but, in the spring thaws, the station itself became flooded, and the terminus had to be moved eight miles back, to Isakagorka. Goods would be unloaded at one or other of the wharves—'Ekonomiya', a saw-mill at the mouth of the Dvina, Bakaritsa, opposite Archangel, 'Birzhevaya', a further small wharf on the Archangel side, from where goods would be taken by barge to the railway. In winter, goods could be moved by horse over the ice, as happened with automobiles in the winter of 1914–15: unloaded directly onto the ice and dragged by horses over it, to the railway. As millions of tons of goods arrived in Archangel, the port became a scene of chaos. There were not enough wharves, warehouses, electric facilities, or even rails along which the boxes could be wheeled through the rudimentary streets of the town. The railway itself, with its capacity of twelve small trains daily, could manage only a fifth of the minimum requirement, 500 waggons.

It was typical of financial management of this period that neither the ministry of transport nor the Council of Ministers developed a plan for

Archangel, but simply met its needs with one 'extraordinary' grant after another as the needs appeared. In the course of the first year of war, a series of demands reached the Council of Ministers: in October 1914, 1,500,000 roubles for two Canadian ice-breakers, in November 272,000 for iron barges, in December three million for the wharves, in January 20,000,000 to extend the railway-gauge, in February 800,000 for more ice-breakers, in April one million for a floating dock, in July 12,000,000 for more gauge-broadening. Lack of foresight distinguished the whole matter. It was not until July, for instance, that any effort was made to carry out what was a very obvious step—using the now redundant rails of the old narrow-gauge railway to form lines along which goods at the wharves could be transferred to the railway-terminus. It was not until October—after 7,000 tons of saltpetre had blown up—that a grant was asked for fire-fighting equipment. The whole business went through endless delay, and was treated in the most rudimentary of empirical styles. Just the same, a new Archangel railway functioned by spring 1916, and was capable of taking 2,700,000 tons per annum.

This was still not enough—the more so as the blockage of Archangel was such that 'mountains' of goods already existed to be transferred by rail at the turn of 1915–16. The government thought of developing an ice-free port: the Catherine Harbour at Alexandrovsk, subsequently known as Murmansk, offered reasonable possibilities for navigation all the year round, and the government picked up pre-war plans for construction of a railway between it and Petrozavodsk, on the way to the capital. But to construct this railway was difficult. It had to pass through the Kola peninsula and along the shores of the White Sea, and the frozen rock splintered when drilled. To ship the material, a provisional line had to be built across the ice of the White Sea, but the tides caused even very thick ice to shift its position, and the provisional line buckled. Labour gave immense problems. Austrian prisoners-of-war were used for some time and the British company given the task of building the difficult northern section suggested bringing back Russian emigrants from Canada. But the war ministry said they would be at once conscripted, if they returned to Russia. The British company (Paulings) gave up the job, after much mutual recrimination with the ministry, and the government then went ahead with the line. By March 1917 it was theoretically open, and its theoretical capacity for 1917 would be 1,300,000 tons per annum. But the line did not function properly until 1923. Meanwhile, huge quantities of material built up both at Murmansk and Archangel: at Murmansk alone, 100,000 tons by March 1917, which could be shifted at perhaps 3,000 tons per day. Altogether, about 3,500,000 tons per annum. could now be shifted by various routes, Archangel, Murmansk, Trans-Siberian in par-

ticular.* However, just as the system began to work, German submarines
interfered with it. Allied transport became centralised, and Russian
requirements came low on the list of priorities. In 1917, control of
Russia's supply from outside became rigorous, and in the Russians' view,
petty. By March 1917, Russians were even using the postal services, in
an effort to evade controls—American suppliers of boots for the Russian
army were reduced, for instance, to sending their boots, in packets of
three, via the parcel-post.[22]

Allied help was, in the long run, of vital assistance to the Russian war-
economy, despite all of the dislocations with which it arrived. British
and, particularly, American machinery was essential for development of
Russian production;[24] so, too, were certain vital raw-materials, even
copper, of which Russia herself at the time produced little. The Russian
railway-system almost depended, for a time, on imports of American
locomotives and rolling-stock, and a whole range of modern industries—
automobiles, aircraft, wireless among them—could not have been developed in Russia without the plant and skills that arrived from the west.
This was not a token of Russia's economic backwardness. The share of
Russian economic growth in the First World War that was directly
attributable to western help was not, probably, very much greater than
the share of British economic growth brought about by imports of
American goods and skills. It was the economy's capacity to adapt to
imports, and not the imports themselves, that revealed whether it was
still 'backward' or not; and the story of Russia's development of her own
resources shows that the country had—despite much legendry to the
contrary—become capable of sustaining modern war, at least in very
narrowly economic terms. Of course, the shell- and rifle-shortages of
1915 were an unmistakable fact. But it was a whole range of non-
economic factors that had led to them: lack of foresight, before the war;
mistrust between General Staff and war ministry; mistrust between

---

*Routes through Sweden counted for something, when the Swedes were not in a black-
mailing mood; and a further possibility, of suitable picturesqueness, occurred when the
authorities discovered that reindeer-sledges, driven by Lapps, could transport goods
from the western harbours of the White Sea to the railheads of Rovaniemi or Uleaborg
in Finland. The Lapps at first resisted conscription for this, because they had a statute
guaranteeing them against it, but Admiral Roshchakovski threatened to hang their
chiefs, and they submitted. In December 1915 the British were informed that they
might use this route: 'Enquiries should be made to the Archimandrite Jonaphan, Prior
of the Tripheno-Petchengy monastery', and early in 1916 the sledges carried 100 tons
daily, being particularly useful for aircraft-parts. The French were very taken with this
system. The British were much less impressed with it, and itched with disapproval.
In the context of the 10,000 tons a day to be shifted, it was not worth hanging Lapps
in order to move 100.[23]

infantrymen and artillerymen; mistrust between businessmen and government; exaggerated reliance on allied assistance in the form of finished war-goods; transport-problems; the vast incalculable of allied war-finance. All of these contributed to the Russian army's suffering from material shortages from early 1915, and of course the clumsy handling of the army in the field resulted in these shortages' acquiring a greater importance than need, in defensive warfare, have been the case.

The greatest problem, in the long run, was that the Russian people were saddled with a huge international debt incurred for war-material that did not arrive when it was needed, despite contractual obligations on the suppliers' part, but that did arrive when much of it was redundant. More serious, in the short run, was the government's initial failure to develop Russian resources for war, because of reliance on foreign suppliers. The war ministry behaved as if Russian industry would be quite incapable of producing war-material, although already Russia was producing more coal, steel, iron than France, where, in 1915, four million shells per month were produced, and although Russia had already begun to develop sophisticated electrical and chemical industries. Three State rifle-factories (Tulski, Izhevski and Sestroretski) and three Arsenals, with trivial contributions from private business, were supposed to supply the war-material, and it was only later that the government discovered how ludicrous was the disproportion between needs on the one side, and the 50,000 rifles per month or half-million shells per month that came from these sources. To meet the gap, recourse was had to foreign suppliers who proved to be inefficient and untrustworthy, and it was not until the failure of this recourse had been shown by events over the next seven months that the government were forced to consider how Russian industry might be developed.

In August 1914, the war ministry knew only a small section of Russian industry, and relied on a smaller section still—a handful of factories, mainly in the Petrograd region.* Two main factors dictated the government's behaviour: an overwhelming cost-consciousness, and a desire for the highest quality of war-material. Neither the Council of Ministers nor the War Council were prepared for lavish expenditure. For instance, the Council of Ministers were told in mid-August that the preparatory period for mobilisation had cost 5,600,000 roubles and were also asked to give the war ministry a credit of 1,000 million roubles for the war-fund.[25]

---

*The Putilovski, Baltiyski, Nevski, Obukhovski, Petrogradski-mekhanicheski, Sormovski, Izhevski, Izhorski, Nikolayevski, Aboski factories, the firms 'Vulcan' and Löwenstern, and the *Russkoye obshchestvo dlya izgotovleniya snaryadov*, which between them had contracts, for 6,650,000 shrapnels and 1,060,000 high-explosive shells, by October 1914, at a cost of nearly 100,000,000 roubles.[26]

The Council queried the figure for the preparatory period, and agreed to assign at once only 200 million roubles, to which the rest might be added when 'details' were given by the ministry. Even in 1915, 200 million roubles would not have paid for ten days of the war. But the officers of the Artillery Department in particular—Grand Duke Sergey, Inspector-General of the Artillery, Kuzmin-Karavayev and Smyslovski—had been trained in a very hard school, and could not get used to the idea that money must be spent. Before the war, each gun had been allowed to use only forty rounds of shell per annum, in order for money to be saved, and even in 1916 the Artillery Department had not rid itself of its passion for preposterous economies. A flavour of its attitude came when it announced that a programme for construction of 37 State factories would cost '607,126,083 roubles and 15 kopecks'.[27] Russian business could clearly not be converted to produce for the war unless it got money to pay for equipment; difficulties of transport, finance made the acquisition of such equipment from abroad difficult enough, and the sudden switch of suppliers from Germans, who were known, to Englishmen or Americans who were not, made the problem all the greater. Yet, by law, the State was forbidden from giving more than ten per cent of the value of a contract in advance; and all contracting had to go through a complicated set of legalistic and traditional rituals before anything could be concluded with a particular company.[28] Grand Duke Sergey and Sukhomlinov could only see an endless process stretching ahead of them, by which endless State money would be poured into firms inside Russia, who would merely produce more expensively and less reliably than foreign firms already known to them.

Moreover, they could not imagine that manufacture of war-material could be anything other than extremely difficult. A rifle had nearly 1,000 different parts, a machine-gun over 3,000 and each had to be made accurate to within a few thousandths of an inch. Shell-fuzes were more delicate still, especially as the Russian field gun shell had a fuze, the '3 G.T.' that combined safety and quality to the great pride of the artillerists. It had a built-in safety-device that prevented the shell from exploding,[29] even if there were premature detonation of the fuze, unless it were already on the downward path of its trajectory. This fuze was expensive, since it needed the best quality of steel and the least volatile explosive, trotyl. But the experts were very proud of it. They could not imagine Russian industry to be capable of producing it. Even the best Russian factories had sometimes made a fool of themselves before the war, when it came to war-contracts. The Kolomenski factory, although capable of producing Diesel engines, failed to produce the '3 G.T.' fuze; the Ayvaz factory, already producing automobiles and aircraft before

1914, could not make rifle-sights; even the Tula arsenal had turned out 900,000 defective fuzes before anyone noticed the defect. Manikovski, who came to dominate the Artillery Department later on, wrote that 'In this field, all the negative qualities of Russian industry emerged in plenty—bureaucratism, mental sluggishness on the part of management, ignorance sometimes bordering on illiteracy on the part of labour.'[30]

Wartime disruption, far from convincing the war ministry that a different attitude was needed, instead confirmed its original judgment: if Russian industry was unreliable to start with, then wartime disruption would make its performance hopeless. The quality of labour was not high: even in the State's advanced Izhevski factories, 3,000 workers trekked back to their villages at Easter for celebrations there, and of course the prevalence of workers who also owned land meant that there was constant leakage to the countryside at harvest-time—a process that high wages, far from halting, merely subsidised. Russian workers were not used to putting in regular labour. They might have very long working days (in the mines, for instance, women and children were 'dispensed' in March 1915 from laws forbidding them to work over ten hours a day), but there were also countless holidays—in the month of May, fifteen. The ways of industrialists were not much better. As was perhaps inevitable in an economy dominated by State finance, corruption was frequent. The Sormovski factory regularly reserved five to six per cent of its orders' value as 'compensation' for the 'collaboration' of officials of the State.[31] Confusions of foreign trade, conscription of labour, transport and raw materials combined to make the wartime picture still more difficult than the peacetime one. When in spring the minister of trade and industry, Prince Shakhovskoy, was offered 'full powers' by the Council of Ministers, he refused them in horror.[32] The war ministry took the simple view that, to rely on Russian industry would be to pay high prices for shoddy goods, irregularly delivered.

There were of course protests. In December 1914, the banker Vyshnegradski, the businessman Putilov, and the 'étatiste' bureaucrat Litvinov-Falinski had visited Stavka to find out what plans were being sketched by General-Headquarters, since they could find little encouragement from the war ministry. Many Moscow magnates—Guchkovs, Ryabushinskis, Tretyakovs, Polyakovs—wanted to find their place in the war-economy: they offered skills, machines, raw materials that were, they alleged, only waiting for some understanding on the war ministry's part.[33] There were also grumbles within the ministry: General Vankov, head of the Bryansk Arsenal, had noted what civilian industry could achieve if the war ministry prepared to relax its attitudes both to prices and standards. Early in 1915, a fillip was given to these men by the arrival of a French technical mission, headed by Captain Pyot. He was sent out to show the Russians how to make the simplified French three-inch high-explosive fuze, which could be made in one piece and did not need the complicated screwing-together of Russian fuzes. Of course, introduction of the French fuze would not be easy to begin with, since it needed hydraulic presses that industry often did not have, and no-one could imagine industry producing the presses. But Vankov, and far-sighted industrialists in Moscow, saw a chance to make shell on a great scale, and Vankov went off to prospect things in Moscow and the south. The Artillery Department resisted. Pyot was received with scant courtesy; Vankov's blandishments were ignored. The French fuze was treated as fraudulent; the possibility of using cheaper explosives, such as Schnei-derite or Yperite, regarded as laughable.[34] The French military observer, Langlois, who had frequent dealings with Pyot, wrote that Grand Duke Sergey *appartient à cette catégorie d'esprits imperfectibles, à qui des mois de guerre n'ont absolument rien appris*'; there was '*un prodigieux esprit de routine*' at work;[35] and the Department as a whole was made up of officers '*fatigués ou ignorants*'.

It was not until three months after his arrival in Russia that Pyot achieved anything at all; only in mid-April did Vankov receive any kind of authorisation from the Department to involve civilian industry in an organisation to produce shell within Russia. Meanwhile the Department went on resisting initiatives even by highly-placed Russians. A Prince Obolenski wrote officially to offer the services of his factory in war-work, and received his letter back, on the grounds that it had not been furnished with the required government stamp. The bulk of private industry went on producing on pre-war lines, in so far as wartime disruption allowed it to, because there was no alternative. As a result, important items in a war-economy went on being wasted in civilian industry. The chemical industry was still producing, in 1916, 1,500 tons of cosmetics, from materials that could have gone to explosives.[36] Almost no beginning was made in exploiting the various by-products of coal to make explosives, the Department denying, for instance, that benzol could be got in significant quantities in Russia, whereas the chemist Ipatiev found out, a few weeks later, that Russia could have enough benzol for all purposes and to spare. It was these conditions that kept back Russian shell-production for longer than was true of other countries,* for, between January and April 1915, the Russian army received less than two million shells, which was hardly a fifth of its minimum demand for the period.

---

*Germany profited, in this connection, almost at once. Paradoxically, this occurred not because of the German soldiers' foresight, but because of the allied blockade. Germany could not rely on foreign suppliers; she developed her own. Moreover, the blockade not only stopped imports from outside Europe; it stopped exports. This delighted the British, and depressed the Germans—even in September 1914, there was forty per cent unemployment in Nuremberg because the Franconian pencil-makers and pencil-sharpener-makers, who supplied the world, were deprived of markets. But the pool of skilled labour that this created, and still more, perhaps, the quantities of now unusable raw-materials, were of the utmost service to the war-effort, and areas such as Franconia became important centres of the munitions-industry overnight, and to everyone's surprise. It would be interesting to speculate how much less war-goods Germany would have produced if the British had allowed her to go on exporting.[37]

CHAPTER EIGHT

The Retreat, 1915

Constant talk of shell-shortage, and the blaming of everything upon it, concealed a much more important factor: the increasing crisis of authority in the Russian army. Shell-shortage, lack of officers, and the increasing restiveness of the men were the three factors that most influenced the shape of affairs in 1915, and it is not surprising that *Stavka*, with respectable public opinion in general, concentrated its attention on shell-shortage which at least had an obvious, material remedy, and one moreover that could profit respectable public opinion. But the shell-shortage had itself been greatly complicated by the nature of the army, which in the long run mattered much more than shell-shortage.

Officer and man began to draw apart, almost as soon as the initial patriotic euphoria had vanished. Revolutionary urges began to affect the men: not yet in the form of mutiny, but certainly in the form of *je m'enfoutisme*—malingering, passive resistance, dumb insolence, over-staying of leave. To measure such things is of course difficult. There are several collections, in print, of soldiers' letters home in this period, but both they and the censors' comments on them present the historian with a well-known trap, since much depends on the methods of sampling. Some of the printed collections have the reader wondering why revolution failed to break out in December 1914, and others equally have him wondering why it broke out at all.[1] Just the same, there are clear indications that, in 1915, 'incidents' multiplied. Sick-lists lengthened, with 85,000 men evacuated to the rear in 1914, and 420,000 in 1915. More revealing still, the Germans and Austro-Hungarians captured, in 1915, over a million prisoners, so many that the Russian authorities lost track of them. There was a widespread demoralisation of the army, that had inevitable effects on the commanders' strategy. In some ways, 'shell-shortage' was a mere technical translation of the great social convulsion within Russia.

The difficulties were blamed on 'agitators', and at the generals' conference in Cholm, just before the evacuation of Lwów, arrangements were made for construction of barracks in provincial towns, 'so that reserve-battalions can be kept away from the populace'. Hitherto the troops had been kept mainly in Moscow, Petrograd, Kiev, because these alone had housing and supply-facilities, and the bulk of troops continued to be placed there, for lack of anything else. Naturally, their contact with the populace, particularly in Petrograd, and particularly with the women, who were more uncompromising revolutionaries than the men, caused trouble for officers. Still, at this time the soldiers were still overwhelmingly 'patriotic' in their orientation, and though they resented their officers' behaviour, they shrank from full-scale mutiny. There were riots, drunken outbreaks; there was some desertion. But, just as in this period there were not many strikes, so these outbreaks were confined to a sort of continual revolutionary murmur.

It was not agitators, but the collapse of the old army's structure, that produced trouble. The army's numbers went up, beyond the capacity of the administrative machinery even to count. The standing army, the first class of the reserve, the recruit-years (by anticipated conscription) of 1914–18 were called up. Beyond these, there was the enormous mass of territorial troops, the *opolcheniye*, who had little or no training, but who found themselves bearing arms—of a sort—as the man-power crisis bit deep. Altogether, nine million men seem to have been called up by July 1915. On the other hand, the number of officers, inadequate even for the peacetime army at its full strength of two million men, went down because of officer-casualties, of which there were 60,000 by July 1915. The 40,000 officers of 1914 were more or less completely wiped out. Replacements from the officers' schools could proceed only at a rate of 35,000 per annum. Wide recourse was had to 'warrant-officers', men with little fitness to become officers, promoted straight from their high schools. But by September 1915, it was rare for front-line regiments—of 3,000 men—to have more than a dozen officers. The training-troops of the rear were similarly few in number, because officers were not enough for the purpose. The whole of Russia supported 162 training-battalions, which would take in between one and two thousand men for a training-period supposed to last six weeks. It is therefore understandable that a large number of the hundreds of thousands of troops arriving every month in army depots had nothing to do for most of the day.[2] Moreover, the army leaders would not, until the turn of 1915–16, promote men from the ranks on a sufficiently lavish scale to make up; and even when men were promoted in this way, they never attained substantial posts. It is sometimes astonishing to see how many men, sometimes due for brilliant careers in the Red Army two years later, failed to rise above a non-commissioned post in the Tsarist Army. Zhukovs, Frunzes, Tukhachevskis were available to the Tsarist army, but they never rated more than a subaltern's job, much as Napoleon's marshals had done in the days of the ancien régime.

But the problem with officers was only part of the structural problem. There was also a problem, perhaps more serious, with N.C.O.s. As Dragomirov said, 'this vital link in the chain of command was missing'. N.C.O.s were appointed *ad hoc*, shared the men's facilities—there was no sergeants' mess, certainly none of its ethos—and usually were among the first to go Bolshevik, unless they were in the privileged cavalry or artillery. It was partly the blindness of the old régime that was responsible for this, for officers could not imagine that an N.C.O. could appear in less than ten years of service. It was also a consequence of the social development of Russia, where the N.C.O.-type had not emerged to nearly the same extent as in western countries. France and Germany had a whole range of artisans: men, certainly not of officer-status, who none the less had their own parcel of responsibility, over a counter-help, a Polish maid-servant or seasonal labourer. In the German army, artisans made up two-fifths of the N.C.O. corps and in some regiments even more; independent peasants made up most of the rest. The State offered its support for this process, because it guaranteed a man who served for seven years, and became a Reserve-N.C.O., a job in the Prussian postal or railway-services, which suited many men of artisan-background at a time when excessive competition was eating away their livelihoods. What the Prussian bureaucracy had done for the economically-pressed Junker, it also achieved for the artisan or small farmer in difficulties, and it acquired thereby the most solid N.C.O.-corps in Europe. Russia was a different case. Only three per cent of her peasant population was in the habit of hiring labour, and the village commune indeed existed to dismantle properties that looked as if they would proceed on western lines.[3] More-over, where Russia had the egalitarian commune, western Europe had a plethora of trade-unions, churches, schools, boy-scout organisations where men could learn discipline and also learn how to transmit it. At N.C.O.-level, there was a smudgy copy of the officer-class, which did excellent service in turning a mass-army into a serviceable military unit. In Russia, this caste was much weaker: in 1903 there existed only 12,109 long-serving soldiers in the army, in place of the 23,943 there should have been —two per company, where the Germans had twelve.

Russia lacked officers, and lacked still more N.C.O.s who could link them with the men. The gap between the Russia of the officer-class and the Russia of the private soldiers widened throughout 1915. 'The officers have lost all faith in their men', wrote a well-informed staff captain in autumn, 1915. Officers were often appalled at the ignorance and savagery they encountered. Telegraphs would suddenly stop working; and investigation of the lines to the rear would reveal a party of soldiers cooking their tea with pieces of telegraph-pole. The chief of staff of 2. Corps said, in September 1915, that 'when we sent the *opolcheniye* yesterday to take station near Leipuni, they burst into tears; a senior officer reckoned that, with a single heavy shell, the whole lot would run away'. Prince Kochubey thought 'they hold their rifles like peasants with a rake'; and a host of orders from the various army commands reveals what officers thought of their men, who were told, for instance, to make sure that they cleared vegetation before trying to fire their rifles from a field-position, and to make sure that their rifles were clean. Artillery-officers thought the infantry not worth expensive shell; again and again, when the Germans attacked second-line divisions, there would be thousands of prisoners, but no guns in the Germans' hands, a clear indication that artillery was leaving the 'cattle' in the lurch. The phenomenon was noted at the Wroclawek engagements of 11th-13th November 1914, and again in Yepanchin's corps on the right of X Army in the battle of the Masurian winter, where the two second-line divisions were abandoned, not only by their own guns, but by Leontovitch's cavalry as well. The officers very frequently remarked, not only on the number of prisoners taken by the Germans, but on the fact that these prisoners made no effort to escape, even when they might have done. They worked happily enough in kitchens and labour-camps behind the German lines. When the three divisions of Scheffer and Litzmann were almost surrounded by the Russian army east of Lódz in November 1915, one reason for their escape was that Russian cavalry supposed the Germans twice as strong as they were—mistaking for Germans the 16,000 Russian prisoners carried by the three divisions, who made no attempt to escape. The disintegration of III Army in Galicia was similarly written down by its chief of staff, and corps commanders, to the *opolcheniye*'s surrendering in droves.[4]

The officers over-reacted. This was a situation that called for the utmost finesse, sympathy and sense; men should have been promoted to high posts who understood what the front-line feelings were. The generals reacted, instead, by applying force, more and more viciously, and, in the short run, this did produce results of a sort. 'His Majesty ordains that there should be no hesitation before the harshest punishments in order that discipline should be restored.' Leave was cancelled, although there were too many soldiers as it was for the existing rifle-stock. General Smirnov, octogenarian commander of II Army, issued a general warning that sanctions would be taken against the families of prisoners, who would also be court-martialled on their return to Russia. Guns took to bombarding their own side. At Opatów in June 1915, a battalion, ordered to

attack, fell into uncut wire and enemy machine-gun fire. The survivors
fell into shell-holes, and were bombarded by enemy artillery. A few
white flags then appeared above the shell-holes; and Russian officers, in the
rear, ordered Russian guns to fire on the troops, as well as the German ones.

Harshness of this kind might have succeeded—as it did in the Prussian
army—if there had been some sign that the officers' business was itself
being adequately transacted. But the shell-shortage and the rifle-crisis
were themselves notorious enough, indeed publicly used by *Stavka* as an
excuse. The treatment of wounded remained primitive: men were
bundled into filthy sanitation-trains and dumped on straw when they
arrived at the Warsaw station in Petrograd—though maybe with the
comfort that a Grand Duchess would look after them.* *Zemgor*, the
union of municipalities and county councils, was supposed to look after
the wounded as a voluntary operation. It took lavish government subsidies, despite its voluntary claims, and exempted from military service
a large number of liable young men who worked with *Zemgor*. The
wounded would have clean clothes put on them as they arrived in *Zemgor*
hospitals, but they would be given their rags back, uncleaned, when the
time came to shift them to an army hospital. Leave was always un-
generous, and the wounded would be taken back into service even if
their case had been quite severe. Not surprisingly, hospitals were places
of low morale. Sandetski, chief of staff of the Kazan military district,
reported that spies he had placed among the wounded came back with
endless tales of woe: 'the absence of real capacity on the part of commanders is felt more strongly than lack of shell'. Alexeyev wrote at
length to Brusilov on the state of morale, as reported by his own son:
commanders were thought imbecilic, 'and there is hardly a single general
you can name who has become popular with the men'. There was a
similar want of understanding between the men and the censors who
read their letters. The Moscow Board, covering selected letters, soon saw
that the men were appalled at their losses. The censors wrote off the
figures given by the men as obvious examples of wartime hysteria. Then
they examined the affairs of a single regiment, to see what bearing these

---

*It may not have been much comfort. In the days when people expected the war to be
short, there was a rush of charitable offers: rich ladies would run hospital-trains, and
their daughters would do the nursing. Princess Shcherbatova operated, for her group
of ladies, eighteen hospital-trains, costing 150,000 roubles per month. As the war lasted,
she became disgruntled, and demanded that the army authorities should take some of
the cost. They disliked the idea, because the trains were heavy, and took only one-third
the wounded that army trains could take. Each sister had her own coupé, and the trains
had a way of finding themselves in the rear of the ultra-marriageable Guard Corps.
Ordinary wounded men were sometimes dumped on to army hospital trains; and the
nurses were allowed to accommodate only 'cases of light wounds, above the belt'.[5]

figures had on the reality. They discovered that this regiment—the 226th Gryazovetski—had contained 2,389 men on 19th August 1915; on 27th August, 665.[6]

For army morale, supply-considerations were often the decisive ones. Men might put up, as they did in other armies, with the brutality and inefficiency of their officers, provided they at least had something to eat and something to wear. By 1917, the overall economic crisis of the country had made survival even in the army questionable, since food and clothes did not arrive. By 1915, the problem had emerged, though not in the dimensions of 1917. It arose partly because the army authorities treated their men on a lavish scale: they supposed that each soldier must have 4,000 calories a day, twice the standard diet of today, and therefore arranged for soldiers to have one and a half lbs. of meat every day, and a pound of sugar, as well as exaggerated quantities of other food-stuffs, though only one ounce of soap per week. There was not much sense in these quantities, which were meant for a soldier marching and fighting in the manner of the past century. Yet they required 15,000 head of cattle per day to be sent, where the authorities could not really supply more than 5,000 per day,* and armies lurched around eastern Europe with huge herds of cattle clogging their lines of retreat. Supply-attempts broke down in the face of exorbitant demand, and the men would be fed extremely badly for days on end, after which they would have a feast of food already going bad. The supply-depots, with huge stocks, often sold them off before they went bad: indeed, 'they had a whole mechanism for robbing'. For similar reasons, an army group indented for 2,500,000 pairs of underpants in spring 1916, regardless of its casualties' having made a great number of these superfluous. Supply-officers then made a profit out of this particularly ghoulish version of Dead Souls.[8]

All of this went together with an insistence that, if things went wrong, it was the men's fault. 'The officers look on us as soul-less lumps, without any feelings at all'; there were savage beatings, 'sometimes of old men with long beards'; 'We throw our rifles away and give up, because things are dreadful in our army, and so are the officers'. The diary of one soldier, Shtukaturov, shows what life must have been in the Russian army in 1915. Shtukaturov was the type of man who usually made an excellent soldier—honest, intelligent, patriotic, enterprising. He had risen from his village to become a skilled workman of the Putilov factory, of which he was proud. He happily went off to do his duty in war. But his diary for the second half of 1915 shows what obstacles he met while doing so. After a stay in his village, he went back to the front in June, going through

---

*An Austrian calculation was that each beast gave 500 portions, but this included gristle, which was turned into 'Dauerwurst'.[7]

Moscow, where, thanks to an error in his railway-pass, he was stranded. He took the problem to a railway-official 'who looked at me with majestic contempt' and ignored him. Thanks to the kindness of a guard, he managed to go on without too much delay, after a night in the station. He arrived in Novocherkassk, meaning to pray in the cathedral, but found it closed. The supply-command in Kiev behaved brutally towards soldiers who grumbled; that in Podwoloczysk, near the front, made him pay forty-one kopecks for a meal that ought to have been free. In July he went to Vilna, where he witnessed the beating of a cretinous soldier, noted that even the N.C.O.s rifles were dirty, and heard from his wife in Smolensk a rumour that she, with the rest of the village, was to be evacuated to Siberia. In October he moved from Molodechno to Kherson —third-class, because someone had again blundered over his railway-ticket. He was then given a medal, but the wrong one was sent to him, and was taken back without replacement. He was finally killed in December 1915, in the offensive of the Strypa, one of Ivanov's perfect little jewels of ineptitude. Maybe Shtukaturov's case was merely one case of misfortune, but the authorities' comments at the time suggest otherwise. Men began shooting themselves in the finger, as Brusilov complained, and were then 'helped' off the field by other men, there being (characteristically) no field gendarmerie to stop this until spring 1916.[9] Such phenomena, as desertion and malingering, could only be stopped, ultimately, by the disapproval of the men themselves, as seems to have happened in western armies. But in Russia there was increasing polarisation of officers and men. The problem of men running away already perturbed Yanushkevitch sufficiently for him to put to the Council of Ministers a suggestion that soldiers should be guaranteed twenty-five acres of land if they fought well—a proposal received with ribaldry.

The army, in this situation, had now to take on strategic difficulties going far beyond its leaders' comprehension. It was not only that Galicia had been lost. A substantial German threat had also developed in the Baltic, which threw planning into confusion. In mid-April, Ludendorff[10] had been told to do what he could to take Russian reserves away from Galicia, or to prevent them from going there. He decided on the one area of his front that had not seen serious action so far: the stretch of barren land along the Baltic coast, to the north-east—Courland. Neither side had done much about it, and the two lines consisted of block-posts, at intervals, ten miles apart. The Germans had had nothing to spare for the area, and the Russians in any case thought no threat would ever come there, because the fortress of Kovno was ostensibly an imposing obstacle, and because communications were even scantier in Courland than elsewhere on the front. Ludendorff launched a strong cavalry force into

Courland in mid-April, with some infantry support. The force was known, somewhat grandly, as *Armeegruppe Lauenstein*, and subsequently became the *Niemen-Armee*.

Russian blundering converted this feint into a strategic menace. Alexeyev himself wrote off the whole thing as a waste of troops on the Germans' part. Even if Lauenstein advanced some way, he would not achieve anything other than conquest of some barren miles, at expensive lengthening and exposure of his communications; later, indeed, the Russians could make an effective counter-stroke from Kovno into his flank. Only after prodding from *Stavka* did he agree to send a cavalry division to support the territorial troops holding the province, but it had only six guns. But he was forced to engage more troops, in the end, for a local collapse led, not only to outraged patriotic clamour, but even to fears for Riga, the one substantial prize at stake in this affair, but even then a hundred miles to the north. The naval authorities did not share Alexeyev's view of the dispensability of Courland, and decided to hold on to the fortress of Libau—an antiquated affair on the coast—no doubt because they had been doing nothing else but sink German fishing-smacks since the war had begun. One set of Russians evacuated it, destroying the telegraph-link, while another set moved into it, to defend it, and in the confusion an enterprising German commander, Schulenburg, took it. Alexeyev would have liked to wash his hands of the whole affair, but *Stavka* pushed him into defending the province, and large numbers of Russian troops were poured into it—by early June, nine infantry and nine cavalry divisions to Lauenstein's five and a half and seven and a half. Meanwhile, the Germans had spread out to the north-east, capturing thousands of unresisting territorials, and the town of Szawli (Schaulen), a railway-junction between Riga and Vilna. A Russian counter-offensive was mounted there, to no great effect. Russian cavalry and infantry failed to collaborate. Gorbatovski, the infantry-commander, took foot-soldiers from Oranovski, the cavalry-commander, and thus made the cavalry largely ineffective; but the cavalry none the less demanded their full-share of exiguous supplies, and deprived the infantry of weapons. In this way, Ludendorff achieved a line, from which he could not be dislodged, and which, at no great cost to himself, enabled him to level threats both at Riga and at Kovno, until in the end the Russians were driven to set up two armies in the area, one to cover Riga and the other to cover Kovno. Neither was strong enough for its task.

By mid-June, with disaster in Galicia and threatened defeat in Courland, *Stavka*'s situation was perilous. The Cholm conference of 17th June recognised that the army was half a million men under strength, roughly what Ivanov's front had lost in six weeks. Moreover, chill winds were

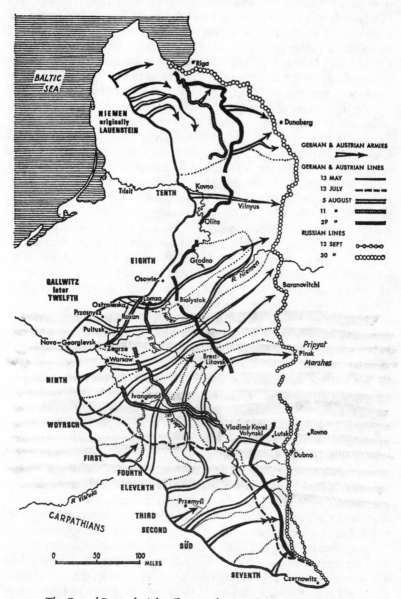

The Central Powers' triple offensive of 1915 and the Russian retreat.

now blowing in Poland. The Russian armies of the central theatre stood in a salient, of which East Prussia and the newly-lost Galicia formed the northern and southern sides. It was now possible for the Central Powers to mount a pincer-movement from East Prussia and Galicia—much as Conrad von Hötzendorf had wanted in August 1914—with a view to surrounding the Russian troops of the central theatre. The danger in the northern sector was all the greater because Alexeyev had been forced to transfer troops on a considerable scale to the south, as Ivanov's front collapsed. In May, Alexeyev had had two-thirds of the troops in this theatre, but by mid-June he had lost twelve divisions, not counting 3. Caucasus Corps and a second-line division sent from *Stavka's* reserve; and by 5th July, with the departure of four corps to make up a new army (Olokhov's) against Mackensen, Alexeyev's troops were reduced to forty-three infantry divisions and thirteen and a half cavalry divisions out of a total 116 and thirty-five and a half operating on the eastern front. The south-western front now contained thirty out of forty-nine and a half army corps, where in May it had had nineteen. To give better central control to the front as a whole, Alexeyev was now given charge of the whole of the Polish salient, instead of half of it, as before. But the troops of his old front, from west of the middle Vistula to north-west of the Narev, appeared to be very exposed to German thrusts.

Voices were raised, first timorously in mid-June, and then with increasing shrillness, in favour of retreat. 'The foremost theatre'—the Polish salient—ought to be given up, because the front could be pierced, and the troops of I, II and IV Armies surrounded. A bold policy of retreat, put into effect in mid-June, might indeed have saved the Russian army from the disasters of summer 1915, and loss of hundreds of thousands of prisoners. But *Stavka* shrank from such a policy. It would mean letting the Germans take Poland. It would mean abandoning forward positions at the very moment the western Powers were likely to take the Dardanelles; Russia would lose her arguments for eventual annexation of Constantinople; moreover, if the Italians, now, broke out into Austrian territory, Russia would maybe lose control of areas the future of which she desired to shape. The French and British talked of launching an offensive in the west, with quantities of artillery that the Russians regarded as fabulous, and a Russian retreat could not therefore be opportune.

Moreover, on the ground there were solid arguments against retreat: the fortresses of Poland.[11] The men surrounding Grand Duke Nicholas had strongly opposed Sukhomlinov's proposal to scrap these; they were now foist with the consequences of their own proposals to retain them. Novogeorgievsk, down-river from Warsaw, was a great fortress, with 1,680 guns, and almost a million shells. Ivangorod, though smaller, had been restored in the course of the war, and had many partisans because of its stout defence in the previous October. These two, with Grodno, Kovno, Osowiec and Dvinsk, contained 5,200 older fortress-cannon and 3,148 modern high-trajectory guns, as well as 880 large-calibre modern cannon. These fortresses had been constructed with just the present emergency in view, and it seemed precipitate to abandon them (and thus confess the enormity of pre-war errors) at the very moment they were required. Moreover, Schwarz in Ivangorod and Sveshnikov in Osowiec could point to singular successes against the Germans, in October 1914 and February-March 1915, while in any event the evacuation of fortresses could take an unconscionable amount of rolling-stock—Prince Yengaly-chev, governor of Warsaw, said that he would need 2,000 trains to evacuate Warsaw, and 1,000 for Novogeorgievsk, quantities which supply of the ineffable horse obviously forbade. It would in any case be highly embarrassing to give up fortresses at the very moment Sukhomlinov was being charged with high treason for proposing the same thing years before the war. Of course, the fate of fortresses in western Europe should have shown *Stavka* the folly of its course: Liège, Namur, Maubeuge, Antwerp had collapsed after at most a few weeks' defence, and the French ability to hold the town of Verdun was based on correct recognition that the forts ostensibly protecting it were just concrete traps, offering obvious targets for the Germans' heavy artillery, and preventing the defence from behaving flexibly. But *Stavka* knew better: there would be an attempt to hold the fortresses.

There were of course occasional hints of realism. Palitsyn, who had been summoned to advise *Stavka*, thought that 'soberly-considered, it is a mistake for us to fight for the foremost theatre'. But even Palitsyn swung the other way when news from the front seemed to improve. *Stavka* sent him to Ivangorod with an instruction to the commandant to prepare for retreat, but he was told to add, personally, that there should be no great hurry in such preparations. The front commands were meanwhile rapped over the knuckles for suggesting that they might retreat. Ivanov had proposed at least withdrawing the armies west of the Vistula to lines where retreat would be easier, a shortening of the front that would allow him to take some of its troops for reserve. *Stavka*'s response was to give responsibility of this part of the front to Alexeyev. But Alexeyev too thought retreat would be sensible. His I and XII Armies holding lines north-west of the Narev were exposed to a German attack, of which there were already signs. He proposed taking them back to the Narev, again to create reserves on a shorter line. *Stavka* thought that this would cause the German attack Alexeyev feared, and told him to leave the troops where they were. On 25th June Yanushkevitch recommended construction of strong lines, one after another, 'on which our troops can successfully hold out, dragging the enemy into battle for every square foot of land'. Characteristically, nothing much was done to prepare such lines: men disagreed as to where they might be dug, lacked man-power to dig them, and in any case thought they would be bad for morale. Some desultory earth-shifting alone followed *Stavka*'s precepts: the lines offered obvious targets for German artillery, yet little protection for men inside them. Although many highly-placed officers knew, in their heart of hearts, that the shell-crisis, the rifle-crisis, the strategically unfavourable layout of Poland, and the moral crisis of the army could only add up to retreat, nothing much was done to prepare for it. 'The masterly Russian retreat of summer 1915' was a legend, invented by the Central Powers to excuse their own blunders. The Russian supreme command simply waited on events, or rather hoped there would be none.[12]

Stavka's decision to retreat came piece-meal and reluctantly, as a consequence of German action. In July 1915 Falkenhayn elected to launch a double attack on Poland, from north and south, as well as to maintain pressure in Courland. The Central Powers, too, had suffered from indecision, but they needed success, and were therefore prepared to go on against Russia, where originally they had meant to stop on the San. Falkenhayn temporarily forgot his plans for an offensive against Serbia, to clear the way to Turkey, while Conrad also shelved his plans for an offensive against Italy. Even so, Falkenhayn's aims were always very limited against Russia. He did not want to commit himself to an open-ended Russian campaign, for he feared another 1812: 'The Russians can retreat into the vastness of their country, and we cannot go chasing after them for ever and ever';[13] there would be huge supply-problems, and the forces were in any case too weak. Falkenhayn did not believe that Germany could win a two- or three-front war. One of the major enemies must be led to a separate peace; and throughout 1915, he made attempts at a separate peace with Russia, through a Danish intermediary, Andersen. He received dusty answers. Just the same, both he and Conrad were interested in 'building golden bridges' to Russia—no doubt, over the Golden Horn—and their strategy was designed at least as much to show German invincibility as to bring about a complete destruction of Russia— or so Falkenhayn claimed. Ludendorff had different ideas. He was impressed at the Russians' crumbling in Courland, and thought that a bold stroke from the north-east would work. Falkenhayn preferred his own limited strategy of attrition, and the most he would undertake was an attack over the Narev towards Warsaw. The Russians would lose Poland, and many thousands of men. They would not lose much territory—which was as well, for the Germans would not have to lengthen their lines of supply, and the Russians would not be stimulated into defence to the uttermost. By 2nd July this plan, after considerable objection from Ludendorff, was agreed to. Mackensen's group would attack from the Austro-Hungarian border, and, from the front north of Warsaw, a strong group under Gallwitz would attack. On the map, this did not look like an ambitious pincer-movement such as Ludendorff, and, with some reservations, Conrad, hoped for. But at bottom it reflected a much more sensible view of the war.

Three German operations therefore proceeded: Galicia, the Narev, and Courland. Already, Russian reserves had been greatly dispersed, and the three-front attack proved to be an excellent way of dispersing them still more. In the Galician theatre, the Central Powers' forces grouped as *Heeresgruppe Mackensen* were to move north, straight towards Brest-Litovsk. Conrad had different ideas—wanting some of this force to go to the north-east, where something of a 'pincer-movement' could be effective, the rear of the Russians in Poland taken. Some cavalry, and an Austrian army, were vaguely ear-marked for this purpose. Falkenhayn thought that a stroke of this type would merely end up in supply-difficulties, since it had to cross the great marshes of the Pripyat; and he had little faith in the ability of Austrian troops to carry out an ambitious scheme of this type—doubts that the event substantially confirmed. Mackensen himself was against fancy manoeuvres. He had thirty-three and a half infantry and two cavalry divisions in his own Army Group, with eight and three in the Austrian I Army on his right. He faced thirty-three infantry and six and a half cavalry divisions, many of them fresh troops, and he had no doubt that ambitious flanking-schemes in the east would simply mean a subtraction of force that he could not afford. If the flanking operation could make much speed, no doubt it would be different; but the roads were few, and mobility bound to be too little. 'As before', he later said, 'I reckon that a strong centre is suitable for attack, as it will give us the best chance for successful advance.' His method was to assemble a great weight of artillery in his centre. Hitherto, this had worked well enough, and it continued to do so. The Russians not only failed to make a strategic retreat at this time; they also had no notion of tactical retreat, and yet the trenches they built were primitive. In these circumstances, the Germans' bombardment was always extremely destructive. A British observer wrote that at Trawniki, in late July, the Guard and 2. Siberian Corps had been bombarded from 2 a.m. until noon, one Siberian division was 'annihilated'. The Guard did stay put under heavy fire, 'whereas in other corps the men run away and are destroyed by shrapnel'.[14] He added, 'It is unfair to ask any troops to stand this nerve-wracking unless they have a regular rabbit-warren of trenches.'

The Russian trenches were 'graves'. In these circumstances, Mackensen's bludgeon seemed a good policy to use, and Falkenhayn went ahead. Mackensen assembled troops on the Galician border, contained the attack of the four corps that Alexeyev had sent south—they won a success near Kraśnik against the Austrian IV Army, incontinently advancing—and in mid-July attacked towards Lublin and Cholm.

Both places had fallen by the end of the month, after a break-through at Krasnostaw that brought 15,000 prisoners in a day. Conrad again grumbled that more force should be sent towards the north-east, and an attempt made to trap huge Russian forces in the Polish pocket. But Falkenhayn had no time for schemes of this kind. In the days when cavalry was effective, they were all very well: now, they would simply mean infantry plodding forward through difficult country against an enemy going away by railway. It was much better to draw the enemy into a battle somewhere where he would not refuse to fight, and then knock him down by virtue of artillery-superiority. In irritation, he told Conrad—in words that have subsequently been held up as an instance of strategic bankruptcy—'It is endlessly less important where Mackensen and the *Bug-Armee* break through, than that they should merely break through somewhere.' Falkenhayn was a modern general, and had a more sensible view of the war than either Ludendorff or Conrad. He knew that great manoeuvres, as in past wars, could not fit in with present circumstances. The war in the East proved Falkenhayn to be right. What shook *Stavka* was not the ostensibly brilliant manoeuvring of Ludendorff—and certainly not that of Conrad—but the huge losses they suffered in set-piece soldiers' battles such as Gorlice, or Mackensen's bludgeoning before Lublin. They were much more costly, even than Tannenberg. Alexeyev told the Grand Duke late in July—when *Stavka* protested that the new army appeared to be achieving little—'You appear not to appreciate the situation regarding III and XIII Armies (on Mackensen's front). In numbers, they are now insignificant, exhausted in an extreme degree, incapable of further resistance.' 10. Corps counted only 4,000 men 'with almost no officers left'; and so few troops could come in 'that it is all just a drop in the ocean'. The two armies together required 180,000 men to bring them up to their complement. In a world in which Napoleonic envelopment was ruled out, Mackensen's tactics offered easily the best method of knocking Russia out of the war. It was Conrad and Ludendorff that were out of date.

Mackensen's advance from Galicia was very slow, dependent on constant assembly of ammunition and reserve-troops. Until mid-July, the railway functioned only as far as Rozwadów on the San,[15] and even thereafter only to Lwów; everything had to be brought up by cart, and even when a field-railway was constructed—rails along which horses might pull small waggons—it only went as far as Lublin, in mid-August. The attrition-battle was in itself something of an achievement, and there was certainly no room for ambitious schemes in the Pripyat.

Mackensen's attack made sense only if there were a complementary attack over the Narev. The Germans had decided on this early in July, for a break-through here would cause the collapse of the Russian position in Poland; and Falkenhayn calculated that the Russians would make some effort to defend Warsaw and their fortresses. The Narev offered conditions for a successful battle of attrition, the more so as Russian reserves would necessarily be confused between the Kovno front, the Narev, and Mackensen's front. These calculations—despite what Ludendorff subsequently said—were correct.

The Germans put, on forty kilometres, ten and a half divisions, one in reserve, over 1,000 guns and, for the east, 'masses' of shell—400,000 rounds.[16] They had tried to break through in the area west of the Narev in February–March, and had failed; now they were determined to risk nothing. The operation was prepared with characteristic thoroughness, the artillery being in charge of Bruchmüller, the break-through expert. The offensive was to begin on 13th July. Success was based on much the same factors, though on a lesser scale, as at Gorlice in May. *Stavka* and Alexeyev had confused their reserves, partly because they were already undecided as to whether further retreat should be undertaken, partly because they were in no agreement as to priorities. Alexeyev had arranged for reserves to come to the Narev from the central theatre, but he had left it too late. When the Germans attacked, these were still many miles from the front. Tactically, the Russian position was also weaker than it should have been. The German attack fell on the inner wings of two armies—XII (Churin) and I (Litvinov). They did not co-operate efficiently. They had lost 2. Siberian Corps and the Guard for the south-western front. Yet they were deluded by their success in February. There was no inspection of the front line until a week before the Germans attacked, when a commission of 1. Siberian Corps reported that gun-positions were too open, dug-outs were constructed with weak, even rotten, timber, the trench-lines had not been planned with defence in mind, and in the second position the vegetation had not been cleared. Seven divisions with 377 guns held this line, and are said to have had only forty rounds per gun to use; although—as at almost every turn in the Russian material crisis—a great deal of the material shortage could have been compensated for by more agile behaviour on the ground. In this case, the Russians had on their flank the 1,600 guns of Novogeorgievsk, of which no use at all was made.

Litvinov and Churin also mismanaged the battle. As ought to have been foreseen, the bombardment was successfully managed. A Siberian division tried to escape from it in the middle, and lost fifty per cent in half an hour. On 13th July, the two Russian armies were forced two miles apart—the break-through, near Przasnysz. Reserves did not co-operate. Counter-attacks would be launched by the one, while pure defence was maintained by the other. Litvinov demanded 'categorically that all troops should hold their lines'—merely a way of making sure they would be ground down by the German guns. The two central divisions were almost wiped out. Alexeyev had arranged for two corps to come to the Narev (21. and 3. Siberian), but they were too far off to help. Such reserves as did come in were mishandled—taken by one corps commander, then another.[17] By 17th July, the Germans had advanced perhaps five miles, but they had inflicted seventy per cent losses on the defenders (including 24,000 prisoners, a quarter of the Russian numbers). This coincided with Mackensen's successes at Kraśnik and Krasnostaw. Alexeyev pulled back his troops to the Narev, with corresponding withdrawals to left and right.

Maybe the Narev line could have been held, if defensive tactics had been correct. But Litvinov himself could not imagine any other system of defence than that which he had applied—every soldier to stay put until wiped out, after which reserves would arrive to be wiped out—and told Alexeyev that 'My army will be unable to hold out for long on this new line, as it is not fortified and its right flank is altogether unsuitable for defence.' The fortresses of Pultusk and Rozan were museums—though costly enough, before the war—and the river was not deep. On 17th July, both Falkenhayn and Gallwitz—commanding the offensive—felt that they could manage to break through grandly towards Warsaw. But Alexeyev had planned things well enough. As the Germans came forward, they stumbled against increasing numbers of Russian troops, such that the 62 battalions and 188 guns that had faced the initial German attack rose to 100 and 600 respectively once the Germans arrived on the Narev. German attacks fared badly—the guns unprepared for Russian resistance, the troops defeated by machine-gunnery; and, other than an unexpected tactical success near Rozan, there were no gains to report, and only 3,000 prisoners.

It was not the defence that snapped, but *Stavka*'s nerve. Alexeyev had so far fought the battle correctly enough, and Gallwitz would have had great trouble in penetrating the Narev. But there were complications on other fronts—the north-east, where a very original set of blunders led the Germans towards Kovno—and even in the central theatre where, just west of the Vistula, the German IX Army was allowed to win a success with almost no superiority of numbers at all. On the southern side, the railway from Lublin to the east was cut by Mackensen, and for a time even the activity of an Austro-German cavalry force east of the Bug (Heydebreck) was taken seriously. On 19th July Yanushkevitch opined that the German break-through to the Narev meant giving up Warsaw; the Grand Duke himself turned up in Alexeyev's headquarters and said that retreat to the Vistula, in the centre, was now required—otherwise significant forces would be cut off in Poland; and Alexeyev was now told 'You can evacuate Warsaw, if you feel you must'. On 22nd July orders went out for a retreat of the Narev groups to the east (Lomza—Siedlce—Kock) and of the southern armies to a line north of Lublin and Cholm (Ivangorod—Opalin—Kowel). Apart from a minor mishap on the Vistula, this retreat was undertaken. The Germans entered Warsaw on 4th August.[18]

The Russian retreat had been conducted in reasonably good order. The river-system of the northern side held the Germans, and the fortress of Osowiec continued to defy German attempts (even with gas, on 6th August) such that no break-through into the rear of the central Russian armies could be made. The only serious misfortune of the retreat from the Vistula was the fate of Novogeorgievsk. In June, when ideas of retreat were beginning to tell, some consideration had been given to it. Alexeyev, in his heart, knew that fortresses were a trap: if they were at all suitably fortified, they merely reproduced, in a defence-version, the disadvantages normally suffered, in this war, by the attacker—obviousness of target, vulnerability of troops—as well as more traditional supply-problems. But Alexeyev was always easily-swayed by men of higher class than himself. Novogeorgievsk was the symbol of Russian rule in Poland; 'spiritual motives speak for its defence'. The railways did so also. Evacuation had been left too late, for the trains needed to evacuate Warsaw—government services, army goods, much of the industrial machinery—were under way and there was not much to spare for Novogeorgievsk, or so officers made out. *Stavka* seemed to think that Novogeorgievsk would be a Przemyśl, not an Antwerp; it should hold for six months. But Przemyśl had really been defended by mud—heavy guns could not be manoeuvred properly—whereas Novogeorgievsk had no such advantage. Its citadel could be fired on by modern artillery, since the forts supposed to protect it had been built only to keep the older type of artillery out of range of the citadel. A new belt of forts had been begun in concrete, continued in brick, and left unfinished. Alexeyev could not spare proper troops for its defence, and sent only 'the piteous remnant' of 11. Siberian division, and a second-line division, 63rd, that appears to have had the worst record of any division in the army. 58th, another second-line force with a long and calamitous history, was moved in at the last moment. 1,600 guns and nearly a million shells were none the less kept in the place. As the Germans advanced, they enclosed it early in August. Beseler, conqueror of Antwerp, arrived with a siege-train. On the first day, he captured the chief engineer of Novogeorgievsk, doing the rounds, with a map of the defences on his person. The German artillery overpowered the defenders; one fort was blown up by a single shell. Bobyr surrendered on 19th August. *Stavka* learnt the news when the last of the fortress's pilots landed—having been fired on by Russian guns—at Baranovitchi. Alexeyev prayed for an hour and a half.[19]

From the beginning of August, a great Russian retreat went on, which lasted until the end of September. The line shortened as armies moved east from the Vistula: by 7th August the salient had been much flattened, by the 22nd the front ran almost perpendicularly from Osowiec—which acted as 'hinge' of the retreat—to Brest-Litovsk; by 30th August a further retiral had been completed, to east of Bialystok and Brest-Litovsk; and the retreat went on until the Germans had reached Lida, Baranovitchi, Pinsk, some way into White Russia. Whether this retreat was militarily essential is questionable. Suitable tactics probably would have held the Germans further west. But the generals had swallowed their own propaganda regarding material shortages, and felt they could not afford to fight. They had no faith in their men. They regarded the Germans as invincible. They were probably anxious, too, to 'bring sense' to the Russian government and the masses. Finally, they were anxious that reserve-troops should be created, by a shortening of the front, for Courland.

In theory, as the Russian armies retreated, German and Austrian groups to north and south should have broken through, into their rear, and trapped them. Mackensen and Gallwitz, with thirty-three and a half and twenty divisions respectively, were seemingly well-enough placed to achieve this. Falkenhayn himself wanted it—pressure on the centre should stop the Russians from retreating, while the two wings came forward. But on the ground this was not possible. Every day the Russians would retire three miles or so, construct a new line, and wait for the Germans to stumble up towards it; then a new phase of the retreat would begin. As the retreat went on, the line shortened with abandonment of the Polish salient, so that there were too many German divisions for the front— Gallwitz, for instance, advancing towards Bialystok, could put only five of his divisions in line at one time. In time, the Germans came up to primaeval forest—the Bialowieś woods—and the great marshes of the Pripyat. The railway-lines stopped on the Vistula; even field-railways came only to Ostrołęka on the Narev, and supplies had to be dragged forward for the next forty or fifty miles. By 20th August, Gallwitz had lost 60,000 men, well-over one third of his troops; and if the temporarily *hors de combat* are included, over half. His corps commanders were pessimistic. Watter said that his guns were worn-out, his horses exhausted, and the hay of low quality—yet by 20th August he was 125 kilometres from the railheads. Surén produced much the same story: 'Progress takes ages . . . it is not so much the enemy's strength as the complete impossibility of all observation in terrain of this type'. Even water—in this marshy region—was often difficult to come by, since everything had to be boiled. Conrad's forces further south encountered similar problems, and Austrian attacks in East Galicia failed to dislodge the Russians from this part of the province. Tarnopol was still in Russian hands. At most, Russian rear-guards would be pierced, and some prisoners made. The Russian retreat went on just the same, the Germans being lucky to find some broken-down cart. Brest-Litovsk, with the example of Novogeorgievsk and, in the outcome, Kovno, before it, was not retained, although its evacuation was done at the last minute. Mackensen took it on 26th August, the Austrians, Kowel on the 21st and Gallwitz, Osowiec[20] on the 26th. But these places were taken as the Russians retired. There was not much strategic advantage to the capture. The Germans were full of admiration for the 'brilliant conduct' of the Russian retreat.

The Russian Council of Ministers[21] was rather less full of admiration for it. As the army retired, its leaders demanded extension to the east of the area of military administration. Polivanov himself, the war minister, remarked: 'It was pretty bad in Germany and Poland; it would be national disaster to have it close to Tver and Tula.' The minister of the interior, Prince Shcherbatov, thought that 'the picture of military rear-areas is one of sickening outrages, anarchy, arbitrariness'—even children being imprisoned in Warsaw for 'activities against the State'. The retreat itself was 'a mad bacchanalia'—Cossacks dragging off refugee-women with their long whips; 'while thousands of people trudge along the railway-lines they are passed by speeding trains loaded with couches from officers' clubs, and carrying quarter-masters' bird-cages'. General Danilov, the supply-chief of Alexeyev's front, was said to have reserved a train for his mistress. A great flood of refugees—variously estimated at one million people—moved to the east, eventually to be dispersed, in miserable conditions, in the great Russian cities. A British observer noted how one officer, told to manage the movement of refugees over a solitary bridge over the Bug, made each one pay a toll. The army leaders had proclaimed a new 1812. This was not historically accurate—in 1812, the Russian armies had been pushed back, had not really made a voluntary retreat at all, which was a Tolstoyan fabrication. But even the fabrication was not really imitated, now. A 'scorched earth' policy was proclaimed—

all movables to be moved, crops to be burned, and so on. In practice, this meant merely a heightened degree of anti-semitism. Land-owners could usually pay to have their crops survive, their movables not moved; some of the great Polish noble families—Potockis, Sapiehas—had links with all three high commands, and could thus ensure complete survival of their estates. The earth was therefore only selectively scorched, and 'Even the most extreme anti-Semites have been moved to complain at treatment of the Jews'.[22]

But the retreat achieved at least some strategic point. The Germans were led into an infertile area, and their supply-problems became overwhelming as they arrived on the Pinsk–Baranovitchi–Slonim positions early in September. They had captured a large number of stragglers and deserters, but the Russian army had remained intact, while, apart from the guns taken in fortresses, and the 250 of Galicia west of the San, only a few tens of guns had been taken in the German advance: Gallwitz, for instance, twenty only in the course of a six-week campaign.

Only on the northern part of the front was there still a significant German threat. By mid-July, politicians and *Stavka* alike began to fear that Riga would soon fall. The Germans had taken Mitau, and their cavalry also began to sweep towards the approaches of Kovno. Defence was characteristically inept. The cavalry groups of Grabbe, Trubetskoy and Kaznakov manoeuvred with pretentiousness, to no purpose. The troops of V Army were unreliable, such that, with the withdrawal of the central armies, a new army command was set up to cover Riga (XII Army). Threats to Riga and to Kovno pulled the Russian commanders in two directions, leaving a gap increasingly exploited by the Germans; and the Russian commanders did not feel they had the strength for an offensive that could have reduced the danger. Alexeyev, meanwhile, refused to part with troops for this area. He had his hands full in central Poland, and could see no case for giving any greater superiority of numbers to the armies in Courland than they already had: ten and a half infantry and nine and a half cavalry divisions to the *Niemen-Armee's* seven infantry and six and a half cavalry.

The Germans, too, increased their interest in Courland. Since mid-June, Ludendorff had wanted a full-scale offensive in the north: according to him, it would grip the Russian flank, would lead to collapse of the Russian position in central Poland, and possibly to an entrapping of huge Russian forces in the Polish salient. When, early in August, Falkenhayn decided merely to follow the Russian retreat, Ludendorff wrote that 'To us it is obvious that Mackensen, Woyrsch (in the centre) and Gallwitz can probably force the Russians to retreat, but not to a decisive end'. Falkenhayn did not see things this way. The northern attack was out of the question for 'season and terrain'. Mobility was so low that no entrapping-operation of the type planned by Ludendorff offered any more than tactical success—as had indeed been the case with every one of the operations planned, and expensively executed, by Ludendorff since Tannenberg. The Germans would only be led into some wilderness or other. The exchanges became heated. Ludendorff said it was an elementary truth of warfare that flanks were to be preferred to centre. Falkenhayn retorted that 'a rapid advance on the wings is only possible if there is strong pressure on the centre'. Falkenhayn was right, in this case. The reason for Ludendorff's successes in Courland was that the great bulk of Russian troops was tied in the centre by Gallwitz and Mackensen. Moreover, Falkenhayn did not mean to go on into Russia. He thought it would stimulate Russian resistance, that it would give supply-problems. He also had other things to do—planning a campaign against Serbia, to open the route to Turkey. A Bulgarian Colonel had already been sent to Pless, and the terms of a military convention discussed. Already in early August Falkenhayn had said that eastern operations must be stopped 'on the approximate line Brest-Litovsk—Grodno'. Ludendorff objected, as news of the plodding advance of Gallwitz came in; the diarist of his command recorded, 'It all makes us scream with rage'. The Kaiser, Bethmann Hollweg and others were involved. Falkenhayn won the arguments, as, probably, he deserved to. He cut down Hindenburg's power in the east, setting up a separate *Generalgouvernement* in Warsaw under Beseler, and the troops of the German centre as an independent Army Group—*Heeresgruppe Prinz Leopold*.

Ludendorff's plan for a northern attack did not have much sense except in terms of a pinning of Russian reserves in the central theatre more or less as Falkenhayn perceived. With such pinning, the German *Niemen-Armee* did well in Courland, and X Army could advance towards Kovno. Alexeyev was transfixed by the problems of extricating his central armies—I, II, IV, XIII, III—at a time when all had been sharply reduced in numbers[23]—in the case of I Army to 100,000, of XIII Army, to 63,000, of III Army, to 55,000, or less than half their complements, in III Army's case one-third. *Stavka* was deeply worried that the Germans might land on the Baltic coast, even threaten Petrograd; inspection of the defences of the capital revealed that the way at Pskov was quite open to attack. The Duma and the government set up an outcry. Yet the western Powers, who had promised an offensive in France for much of the summer, remained passive. Appeals went off to Joffre in the name of the heroic Russian army, to which the French said 'Amen' and went on as before.[24] The British, in particular, had a cornucopia of inter-Allied banalities into which they delved deeply when they were driving a hard bargain. Their offensive did not take place until the end of September, even then to little strategic consequence. Yanushkevitch's fears for the Baltic coast were now boundless. He interfered again and again with Alexeyev's conduct of operations there, even wondering why commanders did not lead their men from the front line—a curious observation from a chief of staff who never once saw the front line. He told Alexeyev to send the Guard Corps —then counting 27,000 men—to stave off a quite imaginary threat to Pernau. Alexeyev, who needed the Guard to cover his retreat against Mackensen, temporised. A categorical order caused him to send it to Vilna and a division to Kovno, 'with an extremely heavy heart, and only in view of the alleged indispensability of the transfer'.[25] *Stavka* now felt that the responsibilities were too great for Alexeyev alone; a new, northern, front must be set up. As befitted the national emergency, an orthodox relic was selected to command it—Ruzski. The division of fronts occurred on 17th August, and in this period Ruzski's front rose to twenty-eight divisions, Alexeyev's sixty-one, Ivanov's twenty-five.

But before the northern front could be built up to such proportions, a German offensive was under way in the north. It occurred at a time of abnormal confusion on the Russian side, since Alexeyev had washed his hands of the northern front before Ruzski took it over. X Army and V Army were not co-operating—V drawn into the Courland battles, X into those on the Bobr, near Grodno. The fortress of Kovno co-operated with neither army. It was an object-lesson in the non-role of fortresses in the First World War. It contained a large number of guns—1,360, 350 of them heavy—and had received desultory fortification before 1914. It was too imposing to be abandoned, in the way Osowiec or Pultusk might be abandoned. But it had serious weaknesses—no barracks, other than those for gunners, no underground communications, and a basic belt of forts built for the conditions of 1880. Grigoriev, the commander, was aged nearly seventy, and had learned little of modern war except that Germans could not be defeated. He prevented initiatives by his subordinates—particularly the artillery commander—but took none himself, visiting one of the forts, at that only once. The defence lacked management—as Germans took one fort, guns of another would fire by mistake at a fort still maintained by Russians. Grigoriev seems to have given up hope because of the garrison he received—a second-line division and a mob of territorials, most of them arriving in Kovno only a week before the siege. On one of the forts, preparation for gunnery was such that only one battery had even a brick emplacement, the others being not camouflaged at all. In another area woods half a mile away had not been cleared. The German bombardment was effective, in circumstances of this kind. The garrison panicked, and on 17th August Grigoriev himself fled, having to be chased, subsequently, by the gendarmerie—for which he was sentenced to fifteen years' hard labour. The German X Army took, here, over 1,300 guns, 53,000 rounds of heavy shell, and over 800,000 of light shell.[26]

The fall of Kovno marked the end of the old *Stavka*. It is impossible to tell the course of events, here, since the Tsar did not reveal what was in his mind. But Polivanov appeared in *Stavka* by train, failed to call on Yanushkevitch, commandeered the *Stavka* Rolls and motored to consult Alexeyev. Shortly after, the Tsar sent word that Grand Duke Nicholas would henceforth be Viceroy of the Caucasus; and, to universal shock, the Tsar declared that he would take the supreme command himself. His motives for doing so can only be guessed at. He knew that Grand Duke Nicholas enjoyed much popularity in 'enlightened' Russia—the students of Petrograd University went on strike when he was dismissed[27]—such that to get rid of the Grand Duke would need a very high card. The Grand Duke had engaged in political activity—had promoted the cause of capitalists in war-contracts, had supported the Duma liberals. In the summer political crisis, he had often been mentioned as a possible replacement for the Tsar. The Tsar would no doubt have removed him before; the fall of Kovno, and threats to Riga, provided an opportunity when *Stavka*'s prestige was running down. On 1st September, the Tsar himself took over the supreme command. His chief of staff was Alexeyev, who passed command of the new western front to Evert.*

In this period of confusion, the strained situation on the Niemen continued. The German, Morgen, showed much virtuosity, persuading Ruzski that there would soon be a German offensive towards Petrograd, with a naval landing on the Baltic coast, such that Ruzski bunched his new forces at Friedrichstadt and Dvinsk, leaving a fifty-mile gap between V and X Armies that could be covered only by cavalry. X Army had been shaken by the fall of Kovno, and had to execute a complicated manoeuvre from Grodno, protecting its northern flank and Vilna. Ludendorff could also profit from the delay in shifting north the Russian troops of the centre, for Alexeyev was still more worried that their front would collapse than that Ruzski's front might be pierced. Many of these central divisions had lost heavily from German battering, from desertion and sickness. One—27. infantry division of 31. Corps, which was not even particularly hard-hit by the then standards, lost 8,848 men and 90 officers (5,385 wounded, 1,951 missing) between mid-June and mid-September, being reduced from 6,500 rifles on 30th July to 3,500 on 25th September,

*See Note on the Tsar's *Stavka* at the end of the chapter.

and its Corps—nominally with four divisions—to 13,300 men with 354 officers,[28] Alexeyev was still reluctant to divert such troops to the north, an area he regarded as already substantially-covered.

This left an area that Ludendorff could still exploit. Early in September he put into effect the great northern offensive with which he had entertained Falkenhayn since July. He did so against Falkenhayn's will. Falkenhayn had already warned the eastern commanders in August that they would have to stop, and he repeated the instruction on 2nd September. Ludendorff 'misunderstood' the instruction, and Conrad, also anxious to invade Russian territory, did so as well. Even the central commanders—Linsingen, Woyrsch, Prince Leopold—on whom Falkenhayn could normally rely, blundered forward into the Pripyat marshes, although, with a Balkan offensive being prepared, they could not count on much support. The preconditions for success were dwindling.[29] In July and August, Ludendorff had done well in the north largely because of continual pressure on the Russian centre. The pressure now slackened—partly because of the terrain, partly because the quality of German troops was running down, partly because the line had been so shortened—from 1,700 kilometres to 1,000—that Russian reserves could now be freed for the northern sector. Moreover, the Russian output of shell was increasing: 100,000 rounds per week in July, 220,000 in September, while reserve-troops began to come in greater numbers. X Army around Vilna had 105,000 men, most of them with rifles, and 600 guns, with up to 200 shells to use.

The most that Ludendorff could achieve would be a tactical success—certainly not the great advance on Petrograd or Moscow of which he sometimes dreamt. The Russian X Army had concentrated for frontal defence at Vilna, and had also been pinned for some time at Grodno. Its eighteen and a half divisions were therefore weak on the northern side, while V Army was similarly weak on its southern flank. There were only three divisions of X Army north of Vilna, with only cavalry on their flank, towards Sventsiany. Ludendorff achieved a feat of concentration that was remarkable enough given the appalling state of the railways—railways that, even in perfect order, were ostensibly too weak to allow any large-scale, rapid shifting of reserves in the days when the Russian commanders had had use of them. Of Ludendorff's forty-one and a half infantry and six cavalry divisions, respectively twenty-eight and five were concentrated on the 110 kilometres of Eichorn's front against X Army, the rest over 300 kilometres.[30]

The German offensive took the form of a frontal attack on Vilna, which failed, and a flank-attack to the north, which succeeded. On 8th September three German infantry divisions and three cavalry divisions came round the northern flank of the Vilna defenders. By a peculiar Russian mix-up, there was not much in their path. A small cavalry group, under Tyulin, the oldest cavalry commander—despite severe competition —in the Russian army, with a force of 600 Latvian territorials with antique rifles, opposed them. Further to the rear was a colonel, Nazimov, with two companies of a supply-battalion. To the north, Kaznakov's cavalry performed services of a sort. By 10th September the Germans had penetrated as far as the railway-junction at Sventsiany, Kaznakov hearing gunfire to the south, but doing nothing, Sventsiany itself was in German hands on 12th September, and the railway from Vilna to Riga thus cut. Subsequently, the German cavalry raided some way into the Russian rear—Molodechno, Smorgon.

It took some time for Alexeyev to react. Tyulin's performance was at first written down to poor-quality troops, cavalry arrogance, Ruzski's nerves. The main German attack was thought to be the continuing assault on Vilna. But with Germans in the Sventsiany gap, there was a risk that the Vilna troops would be out-flanked, surrounded. Alexeyev over-reacted. He authorised further retreats to the south, in order to free troops for this new area of attack. There were withdrawals, before Prince Leopold's group, to Baranovitchi and Novogródok, Slonim, Lida. The troops thus made free would come to the Vilna side—II Army command, to set up a new army between V and X, followed by two corps each from I and II armies, one each from III and IV. They were to form east of Sventsiany, and on the railway-line east of Vilna. An offensive might be launched. By 16th September Eichhorn's front had eighteen and a half infantry, five cavalry divisions to thirty-four and six, and had lost 50,000 men, mainly in frontal attack on Vilna, in two weeks. Ludendorff fed more troops to the left wing, out-flanking Vilna. But he had learned prudence: there was to be no 'second Brzeziny', the fate that had nearly overtaken the three outflanking divisions east of Lódz a year before. His troops merely pressed south towards the rear of Vilna, while Alexeyev decided on the 17th to withdraw from it. On 18th September the Germans took Vilna. It was their last great capture.

There followed a series of embarrassments that showed how correct had been Falkenhayn's analysis. Ludendorff, again with commendable speed, had mustered a new infantry group (Hutier) to the north-east. But the concentration of Russian troops was now too great. Now, a new II Army had been set up along a line of lakes—Narotch, Svir—and, although its transport was confused, it could now attack. The German cavalry was driven back, losing heavily; and Hutier's infantry was drawn into a defensive battle. Attacks on Molodechno failed, and the Russians later were able to re-take Smorgon. Falkenhayn stepped in to demand thirteen divisions for France; in the Pinsk marshes, a German group was defeated, at Logishin.[31] On 26th September Ludendorff admitted defeat, and ordered construction of a *Dauerstellung*, a permanent line of trenches, on his front. Further south, all German attacks petered out; and there was a Russian offensive in October, which Ludendorff was able to contain only with difficulty. Further south, the campaign ended as it had begun, with an Austro-Hungarian embarrassment that, again, showed how right Falkenhayn had been. Conrad had sought to accompany Ludendorff's Vilna offensive with one of his own, and dreamt of a double envelopment of the twenty-five divisions of Ivanov's front, from north and south. This took no account at all of the terrain, or the declining quality of Austrian troops. On the contrary, it was billed as 'Black-Yellow Offensive'—it would carry the Austrians to Rovno, maybe Kiev. As Hoffmann rightly said, the Austrian high command would see sense 'only when the knife is at their throat'. Ivanov appealed for reinforcements—sending even an eleven-page letter to the Tsar (which he did not read until March) explaining that Kiev mattered a great deal, 'on account of the increasing numbers of pilgrims going there before the war'. But he was given only trivial reinforcement, and Conrad supposed a great victory was to be had.[32]

His troops attacked in eastern Galicia, on the Sereth, and in Volhynia. At first they made reasonable progress, taking Lutsk on 31st August. But the sick-lists rose alarmingly; transport through the marshy valleys was sometimes so slow as to be barely perceptible. Six Austro-Hungarian divisions were also removed to take part in the new Serbian offensive. In Galicia, there was a sudden reverse, with an extraordinarily high number of prisoners taken by the Russians. In Volhynia, IV Army (Archduke Joseph Ferdinand) blundered forward from Lutsk, exposing its left flank. Russians concealed themselves in the reeds and marshes, and attacked this flank between Lutsk and Rovno. By 22nd September 70,000 prisoners had been taken by the Russians, and Brusilov re-entered Lutsk. Falkenhayn had to divert to Galicia two of the Austrian divisions meant for Serbia—they had already reached Budapest—and German troops were turned south to restore the position at Lutsk. In the last days of September, Brusilov retired from Lutsk, and a line was established between it and Rovno. Conrad grumbled, after his strategic genius had once more, in his view, been betrayed: 'We can do absolutely nothing with troops like this. Something so simple, so easy as what we planned has not been seen in the entire war, and yet we were let down'. Falkenhayn had a different verdict on these Austrian extra-tours: they were an object-lesson for Central European soldiers who thought they could defeat Russia. Austro-Hungarian losses were astonishingly high: between 1st and 25th September their force in the East fell from 500,000 to 200,000, and the proportions of loss were also remarkable—in IV Army, 30,000 'missing', 10,000 wounded, 7,000 sick, 2,000 killed. It was already notable that, in the Austro-Hungarian army, twice as many officers reported sick as were wounded. In the German army, this proportion was reversed. It was good evidence of the different quality of the allied armies. Falkenhayn, not surprisingly, was glad to be relieved of the need to co-operate with Austria-Hungary on the eastern front.

The armies now looked elsewhere, the Central Powers to Serbia, the Russians to an internal re-organisation of their forces. Actions, sometimes of some scale, were undertaken in Courland and on the river Styr, north of Lutsk. But even these died down when winter settled in. Between 1st May and 1st December, the Russian armies had lost a million prisoners and in all over two million men. Falkenhayn's strategy had proved itself, and would have done even better had Falkenhayn been allowed to end the campaign where he had hoped, and intended, early in August. The Russian armies would be unable to interfere effectively with Falkenhayn's operations for many months to come. Their great superiority on the German front—on the 600 kilometres of Ludendorff's, sixty infantry and fifteen and a half cavalry divisions to thirty-seven and seven and a half— was useless to them, and a whole force of 126 infantry divisions with 4,650 guns (1,136,000 men) could not be active again for months to come.

Note on the Tsar's *Stavka*[33]

The Tsar's command was a largely formal affair: as Langlois said, '*c'est à Alexéieff qu'on obéit, ou plutôt à qui on désobéit*'. The Tsar was usually too busy with home matters, and in any case knew little of army affairs. If I guess right, his decision was a way of trumping the Duma politicians' military ace, as a climax to the summer crisis, at home and at the front. The question of an effective commander—chief of staff to the Tsar—was more difficult. Evert was considered, but ruled out because he had a German name, or perhaps because even the Tsar quailed at the nomination of a general so unmistakably valetudinarian. Alexeyev was perhaps chosen because he would show more sympathy for the needs of the Riga front than he had done as commander of the north-western front, if he were given full responsibility at *Stavka*—a calculation which, if consciously made, proved correct. But if the Tsar wanted an a-political *Stavka*, he unquestionably got one in Alexeyev and his aides (as similarly in the war ministry, where the Duma politicians' friend, Polivanov was replaced by the a-political supply-expert, Shuvayev). Alexeyev was a very simple man of humble origins. He knew little of any foreign language, was sometimes embarrassed when he was saluted in the streets, found *Stavka* dinners an effort (not knowing, for instance, that coffee was usually drunk after dinner) and tended to join the officers only once a week. It was typical of him also that he paid his own mess-charges, instead of living at army expense in the Yanushkevitch manner: even now, mess-charges were thirty-three roubles per week, the cost-price being up to fifty roubles more. He was assisted by Pustovoytenko, Quarter-Master-General—also a man of very simple background—where the Tsar would have preferred the General Staff professor, Shcherbachev, commander of VII Army. Alexeyev's closest confidant was V. Borisov, dismissed by Grand Duke Andrey Vladimirovitch as 'a prole'. He had assisted Alexeyev throughout the war, and did good service at the time of the Sventsiany break-through, admiring Alexeyev's iron nerves. Alexeyev, Pustovoytenko and Borisov were the kernel of *Stavka*. The rest, in Lemke's words, 'are either clerks or furniture'. But Alexeyev's great defect was inability to de-centralise. He worked himself into a continual migraine, and left himself no time to think things out—his response to the great Brusilov victories of 1916 being extremely unimaginative. It is difficult not to regard his *Stavka*, never the less, as a great improvement on its predecessor. The aristocratic furniture was removed—only survivor being a Count Kapnist, skilled at devising pompous missives. The various parasites knew that they would get nowhere with Alexeyev—Prince Yengalychev, redundant Governor of Warsaw, or Count Bobrinsky, redundant Governor of Galicia, both given their salaries and demanding military appointments, were shown the door. Rasputin was not allowed in *Stavka*. The staff functioned rather better than before—partly because it now had a stronger complement, of seven Generals, thirty senior officers, thirty-three *oberofitsers*—in all, eighty-six persons, with Kondzerovski's department taking fourteen. Information was now (despite the previous *Stavka*'s habits, and despite a nightly film-show) taken in after 9 p.m. Alexeyev was an incorruptible man, with only the good of Russia at heart. He was disliked by the cavalrymen and the associates of Grand Duke Nicholas; in a way, this was a shadow-play of the *Sukhomlinovshchina*, though without the baroque personnel-management that had perpetuated the *Sukhomlinovshchina*. Alexeyev was a charmless effigy of the virtues his predecessors ought to have displayed.

The conditions in which *Stavka* lived were not much more comfortable than before. Various towns had been inspected—including Kaluga and Orsha—to see if they had suitable buildings. Only Mogiliev turned out to have these, and it was there that *Stavka* was installed—hardly a happy choice, since the root of the town's name was the Russian word for 'grave'. The mess was in the café-chantant of the Hotel Bristol, and meals were as before extensive—although only wine, not vodka, was now served. Mogiliev was a 'filthy, poverty-stricken place' with no library, only four horse-drawn trams, and a youth that 'hooliganstvuyet'. It was here that Tsarist Russia was to be ended.

CHAPTER NINE

The Political War-Economy, 1914-1917

The great retreat of 1915 coincided with a great political crisis inside Russia. It had been imminent since the turn of 1914-15, and broke, over the question of shell-shortage, in the spring of 1915. To start with, patriotic euphoria had led to something of a 'civil truce' in Russia, as elsewhere. But the strain of months of war began to tell, and provoked many problems for Tsarist Russia. In the Duma, Russia's parliament, there were many politicians who wished to limit drastically the powers of the Tsar, and the Constitutional Democratic Party was self-confessedly Republican. These men had always feared that they might be engulfed in waves of populist nationalism, set in motion by the Tsar; it was therefore their best course to put themselves at the head of a rival patriotic movement. Such a movement, which materialised later on in the shape of a 'Progressive Bloc' in the Duma, which included 235 of its 422 members, would demand reform: cabinet government, with ministers appointed from the Duma and responsible to it; the Tsar's power restricted to narrowly constitutional functions, and possibly even abolished altogether. Shell-shortage gave these men a wonderful chance to show that the existing régime was corrupt and incompetent. There were attacks, particularly on Sukhomlinov and the detested minister of the interior, Maklakov.

But the political movement was supported by powerful figures within the régime, and it was this support that gave it such success as it obtained in the summer. The army generals also groused at Sukhomlinov's régime, and were determined to replace it with one of their own. This was a fundamental quarrel, almost on class-lines, that went back to the clash of patrician and praetorian before 1914. The army generals pursued their vendetta against Sukhomlinov, and exploited the army's material weakness to suggest that Sukhomlinov should be removed, along with his partisans. This led the generals into an informal alliance with the Duma men. It was an alliance that also received powerful support from industrialists. They resented the war ministry's unbending attitude in war-contracts. Businesses were going idle because of wartime circumstances, but were not getting war-contracts to make up, because the war ministry relied only on foreigners and its own tiny set of Petrograd protégés. The magnates of Moscow industry, in particular, resented this exclusion, on which they blamed the crisis of matériel; and their resentment was matched lower down the industrial scale, where thousands of the country's smaller businesses grumbled that they were on the edge of bankruptcy because of the war ministry's attitude. The industrial opposition promoted a scheme for 'War-Industries Committees' in the spring of 1915, which would bring private enterprise into the war-effort. The elected town and county councils of Russia joined this agitation, and set up a union, *Zemgor*, to show that they too could provide sinews of war. The alliance gained support from within the government: Sazonov, the foreign minister, recognised that some reform must come within Russia, if only to show that the Entente's declarations to the effect that it was fighting 'for Democracy' meant something; Bark, the finance minister, also thought that the placing of foreign and internal loans would depend on men's confidence in the régime, and he too supported demands for moderate reform.

The shell-crisis triggered off political as well as economic explosion in Russia. Politicians, generals, ministers of the Tsar, businessmen great and small demanded change, and blamed Sukhomlinov's régime as Russian soldiers abandoned Poland and the frontier districts of the empire. Besides, the economic crisis of revolutionary Russia had already appeared. Inflation was already a severe problem; and some essential commodities, among them sugar, had increased in price, in the capital, by fifty per cent in a few months of war. Wages had gone into a bewildering pattern as well. Fuel supply became irregular, and there were cases in southern Russia of factories not working full-time because they had run out of coal. Transport bottle-necks occurred, particularly with the events of September 1915, when the last and most confused stage of retreat at the front coincided with evacuation and establishment within Russia, not only of millions of roubles' worth of industrial plant, but of hundreds of thousands of refugees. At this stage, labour-agitation had not become uncontrollable—there were a few strikes, but, as Goremykin told the Council of Ministers, 'our labouring population has so far shown the utmost willingness to prosecute the war'[1]—but businessmen were already worried by the pattern of wage-increases, and the government's apparent unwillingness somehow to 'control' the workers. Shell-shortage, for politicians and businessmen, was as much a short-hand version of economic and social crisis as a grievance in itself. It all produced an economic-military-political alliance of 'respectable' Russia that foreshadowed the Provisional Government.

Since the end of 1914, there had been signs that such an alliance would develop. The visit to *Stavka*[2] of politicians such as Rodzyanko and Varun-Sekret, President and Vice-President of the Duma, the industrialist Putilov, the banker Vyshnegradski and the 'technocrat' Litvinov-Falinski had occurred at the end of December; it was followed by a memorandum of the great banks', urging 'collaboration' of business in the war-effort and, by extension, appointment of ministers sympathetic to this programme. In February and March, these themes were taken up lower down the scale: lesser businessmen, under great economic pressure, lobbied Guchkov and the Moscow industrialists, and hoped to see something similar to the German system of local war-industries committees established in Russia. Duma politicians began a campaign of agitation for constitutional change: the Octobrists, party of big industry, came together with the Constitutional Democrats, a left-liberal party that supported small business, to form an opposition coalition, later known as Progressive Bloc; and, gradually, it acquired the sympathies of allied diplomats, *Stavka* generals, 'even the Imperial Yacht Club on Morskaya'.

The government might have resisted Duma 'chatter' if the times had been normal. But they were not. Now, powerful figures whose rôle in 1905 had been counter-revolutionary, were prepared to enforce reform: *Stavka*, on the one side, and big industrialists, on the other. Both had their reasons for resenting Sukhomlinov. The peculiarly obstinate refusal of the war ministry and the artillery department to recognise that there might be angels in the marble of Russian private enterprise was hardly affected until the end of 1914. They continued to believe that Russian businessmen would be inefficient and expensive. They were not prepared to spend money, and therefore would not pay more than ten roubles per shell—a price at which most Russian firms could not make a profit, since they lacked the experience and tools. Moreover, they would not pay substantial advances on the contract: not more than ten per cent, for which there was legal justification. They felt that, if money had to be spent, it would be much better-spent on State factories, and developed something of a programme for building these.[3] If private enterprise were involved as well, it could only mean wasteful competition for scarce stocks of skills and raw-materials, and of course for the machinery that had to be imported. In fairness to Sukhomlinov, Russian businessmen behaved more or less as predicted, once they were involved in war-work. Their advances were considerable, and their prices rose far beyond what the State was used to paying. Three-inch shell rose in price to at least fourteen roubles and twenty-five kopecks, where the State could turn them out for 6·40; field cannon cost, from State suppliers, between 3,000 and 6,000 roubles each, whereas private suppliers charged from 7,000 to 12,000.[4] In England, by contrast, the price of eighteen-pounder shell declined from £1. 12s. 0d. early in 1915 (c. 16 roubles) to £1. 0. 0d. in June 1915, and 12s. 6d. (c. 6·50 roubles)[5] at the end of the year, as private producers learnt how to mass-produce it; and Russian expensiveness was quite often matched by inefficiency and even corruption.* Of course, many of these difficulties were simply the price of economic progress; but that was not how Grand Duke Sergey saw things at the time. He cold-shouldered both Vankov and Pyot, for their standard shell-price would be 18·50; and the most he would do was to form a 'special executive committee,'[7] in January 1915, that did little more than remove some of the more indefensible pieces of ritual in contracting, with slight increases in the advances that the State was prepared to pay on its contracts with already-established firms.

But defeat at the front, and non-delivery of foreign goods, provoked crisis. *Stavka's* power extended, with every reverse at the front, since these reverses were 'explained' with reference to the limitation of *Stavka's* powers. Highly-placed generals slipped to *Stavka's* side—among them, Polivanov, who had been refused the appointment of governor of Warsaw by the Grand Duke, but who subsequently made his peace with *Stavka*, serving first as assistant to the head of the Red Cross, Prince Oldenburg, and then becoming the Grand Duke's candidate for Sukhomlinov's succession. Even Sukhomlinov's regiment of journalistic housecarls slipped off: Prince Andronikov writing winsomely patriotic articles in praise of the Grand Duke. *Stavka*, in any case, wrested control of the army's promotions-machinery from Sukhomlinov, and now played this instrument with much virtuosity. In February, there was a considerable political scandal that destroyed Sukhomlinov: the Myasoyedov affair. *Stavka* (with Polivanov in a prominent rôle) controlled justice in the army area, and it arranged to have Myasoyedov arrested as a spy. The charge was trumpery. A Russian, who had been allowed to leave Germany after agreeing to spy for the Germans, was allegedly conscience-stricken when he returned to Russia, and revealed that there was a highly-placed spy in the north-western front. After prodding, he identified the spy as Myasoyedov. Myasoyedov was certainly unpleasant and corrupt. He had served Sukhomlinov† before 1914 by spying on the officers' corps, and had been

---

*One example was Solodovnikov, owner of the Revdinskoye factory in the Urals. He took large advances from the State, but could not use them properly. He devoted them to speculation in commodities—sugar, grain etc.—which, in time of inflation, offered quick profits. Then the State wanted to know what had happened to its contract. He at once decreed, in his factory, that there would be parity of wages between men and women; and used the resulting strike as excuse for non-delivery of the contracted war-goods.[6]

†It is evidence of the often curious link between *Sukhomlinovtsy* and the Red Army that Myasoyedov's brother taught for years in a Soviet military academy.

provoked to a duel by Guchkov. His corruption led to his dismissal, but —whether out of blackmail or loyalty—Sukhomlinov found him other employment, in the gendarmerie on the German border. In this capacity, he was attached to the north-western front, which of course was commanded by Sukhomlinov's protégés, Ruzski and Bonch-Bruyevitch. The decline of Ruzski coincided with Myasoyedov's arrest by *Stavka*, and both Ruzski and Bonch-Bruyevitch were shifted to lesser posts in the aftermath. In March, with full-scale publicity, Myasoyedov was condemned and executed, after trial before a *Stavka*-staged court in Warsaw. The affair was, as Polivanov subsequently confessed, judicial murder.[8] But for the time being, it discredited Sukhomlinov whose incompetence now received the lining of treachery. Duma politicians rode off against him, and colleagues within the government came to regard him and three other 'reactionary' ministers, as simple liabilities. The Tsar held on to him until early in June. But against demands from *Stavka*, the government, Allied envoys and the big industrialists, he could not prevail for ever. The degree to which the Tsar's own power had waned was shown when, almost immediately, Sukhomlinov was arrested, and made subject of a 'High Commission of Investigation'. The wishes of the big industrialists were now met. In May, there assembled a 'Special Council for Examination and Harmonisation of Measures required for the Defence of the Country'.[9] It included Duma politicians and representatives of industry; it was supposed to take control of all ordering for the war-effort. In June, it was extended to include further business and political representatives, and it seemed as if the body would promote political reform and economic progress at the same time.

But the alliance of politicians, *Stavka* and Special Council was short-lived. The politicians lacked mass-support, and some of them would have repudiated it if they had had it. Their talk remained no more than talk, so long as they had neither military nor industrial allies to influence the government. The military ally, never in any event staunch for constitutional change, was appeased by the old régime when Sukhomlinov fell, and Polivanov took his place. In any case, *Stavka* was discredited by the great retreat, the chaos of refugee-evacuation, the German threats to Riga, Moscow, Kiev. Late in August, the Tsar knocked the *Stavka* card from the Duma politicians' hands, when he sent Grand Duke Nicholas off to the Caucasus, and himself took charge of the army. Grand Duke Nicholas was too remote and powerless in Tiflis, and although his old associates of spring 1915 sometimes travelled there to find out his attitude to a military or palace coup, there was not much that he could do. There would be no 'officers' plot' against the Tsar—at least, not until the revolution had actually been started by someone else.

Of greater importance in home affairs was the failure of the Special Council to act as agent for constitutional reform. This occurred because the Council itself split, and essential elements in it, which had hitherto favoured the cause of reform, now swung back to adopt a waiting attitude. The first Special Council, in May, had been dominated by representatives of business that the war ministry already knew and favoured: mainly the great bosses of Petrograd, Putilov, Vyshnegradski, Meshcherski, Plotnikov, Davydov. They were quickly attacked by their Moscow rivals, who did not wish to see defence becoming a Petrograd monopoly; and the Moscow men—Ryabushinski, Guchkov, Tretyakov, Tereshchenko and other magnates—denounced the new system, and promoted attacks upon it by thousands of lesser businessmen throughout the country, who formed War-Industries Committees to assert their willingness to furnish war-material. The industrialists' newspaper, *Commerce and Industry*, and the 9th Congress of Representatives of Commerce and Industry, in May, were loud with complaint at a system that permitted businessmen from a rival region to award contracts to each other, more or less naming their prices. *Zemgor;* the Octobrists who were in league with the large Moscow firms; and the Constitutional Democrats, who supported the lesser firms of the War-Industries Committees, added their voices to these protests.

The Moscow magnates apart, this was essentially a quarrel between big industry and the rest—a quarrel that did more and more to divide the businessmen, and to drive the more important of them to take the government's side. The industrial 'outs', in this case, had very good arguments. Moscow was not being properly-used for the war-effort; the Petrograd men, on the other hand, used the Council to favour themselves. The first two orders given by it went to Putilov and Vyshnegradski.[10] Putilov and his factory group were ordered 113,250,000 roubles' worth of shell, with an advance of thirty-four millions; each shell was to cost thirty-three roubles and seventy kopecks, which gave a profit of 5·70—itself not far from the standard State price for shell. Vyshnegradski's *RAOAZ* company similarly took an order for guns—to be made in a non-existent works—that would cost forty per cent more than usual; and the banks behind them both took eighteen per cent of the profit, as well as the State's advance-payment, which was deposited at a low rate of interest. It later turned out that Putilov used shell-contracts to subsidise other parts of his factories. Before 1914, he had laid in too much ship-building machinery, much of which he could not now use. The works were converted to shell-work, and even then did not perform very well. The affairs of his firm became more and more complicated; he took on loans to the value of more than five times his capital. Attempts were made to cut costs. Workers' wages in the Putilov works stayed almost exactly the same as in pre-war days—3·16 per day, on average—although the cost of living had risen by fifty per cent by the middle of 1915. There were strikes. The firm also neglected its less profitable contracts of pre-war, pre-inflationary days, and in 1916 was, after a long wrangle, placed under sequestration. When the government managers moved in, they found 1·50 roubles in the till, and 137 in the current account. Meanwhile, Putilov and his co-director Dreyer went off to the south of the country, with the million roubles which they had been given as 'bounties'.

Episodes such as this were particularly discreditable, because they came at a time when business was under very great pressure. The Russian economy had always been dominated by great monopolies and very large firms.[11] They faced unstable profit-rates, lack of skilled labour, bottle-necks of various kinds, and combined to make conditions easier. Prices were maintained by *Prodameta*, the metals-cartel, *Produgol*, which united 711 coal-firms in the south, *Prodvagon*, which produced railway-material, and *Med*, producing copper, because they would restrict production in order to create sometimes artificial scarcities; and the method was so successful that by 1914 there were some thirty monopoly-organisations in Russia, which naturally strove to subjugate competitors. The First World War generally favoured large firms at the expense of lesser ones. Skilled labour was rare enough in Russia, and conscription bit into the stock of it; but firms employing a thousand men, and able to pay higher wages, were naturally less affected by this problem than lesser firms. Fuel and transport offered bottle-necks. The country's performance in both fields was, in fact—and despite legends to the contrary—superior to its performance in 1913, in so far as there was more coal, much more petrol, more rolling-stock and greater railway-mileage during the First World War than before it.* But demand also rose, even further, and it was large firms that could survive the problem better than others. Foreign machinery presented a similar version of the war-time problem. Scarce supplies of foreign exchange could not meet the demands of every firm needing plant from abroad—although such plant was often essential for a firm to take part in production of war-material. Monopolies, fearing competition, also used their position as a weapon to compel independent firms to subject themselves.

These bottle-necks—some traditional, some wartime in origin—brought about concentration of capital, as small firms were forced to amalgamate with larger ones. In 1913, thirty-one factories had opened, and twenty-one had closed. In the First World War, many more factories

---

*These issues are more fully discussed in chapter 13.

closed than opened, but the number of workers in the factories that opened
greatly exceeded that in the factories that closed:[12]

| | Factories: | | Average number of workers in those | |
	opening	closing	opening	closing
1914:	215	356	88·8	45·1
1915:	187	573	96·8	28·7
1916:	276	298	78·5	37·6
1917:	264	541	81·5	69·9
War-years, overall:	942	1,788	86·4	47·8

These figures represent only the tip of an ice-berg, for they make no
reference either to the great extensions of capital occurring in existing
companies, or to the great difficulties that many lesser companies experienced, without quite going bankrupt. In particular, they ignore the hundreds of thousands of cottage-industries that folded up, without ever
disturbing the statisticians of the Special Council. It was this movement
that underlay much of the agitation of the War-Industries Committees,
and their allies in *Zemgor* which were, first and foremost, unions of small
or, at best, middle-sized industry. In May 1915, both sets gained the ear of
the Moscow magnates, who had their own interest in War-Industries
Committees. The resulting agitation against the Petrograd monopoly in
the Special Council was successful. Early in June, as Sukhomlinov fell, the
body was widened to include representatives, not only of great Moscow
industry, but also of the War-Industries Committees and *Zemgor*. In
theory, Russian industry was now organised for war. In practice, its
performance was frequently more impressive than legend allows. But
little of the performance was owing to War-Industries Committees or to
Zemgor, whatever the legendry of the time. The Special Council began as
an engine for utilisation of free enterprise; but it ended by inaugurating
the Soviet economy.

War-Industries Committees and *Zemgor*, despite the claims of their
propagandists, did not provide the sinews of the war-economy, but were
rather its greatest casualty.[13] Where they succeeded, they were unnecessary; where they did not, they were a nuisance. In theory, the system
looked good enough when it began in spring 1915. A Central War-
Industries Committee, in Moscow, undertook to farm out contracts
from the war-ministry departments to its own subordinate Committees—
33 district ones, 220 local ones—which would in turn report on their
capacity and their needs, in terms of raw-materials and labour. The
Central Committee had a staff of 2,000, and its labours would be paid for

by one and a half per cent of the value of any contract passed through it, or by subsidies from the great Moscow men who had promoted the system. To begin with, the Central Committee also included representatives of the metals-cartel, *Prodameta* (Darcy, Theakston, Vvedenski, von Dittmar), in the hope that *Prodameta* would support the new system and break with its own restrictive practices. The system also enjoyed political power, by virtue of the Moscow magnates' links with the Octobrists, and the lesser businessmen's alliance with the Constitutional Democrats. It was the Progressive Bloc on the factory floor, which no doubt accounts for the inflated reputation that it came to enjoy in the west.

In reality, the large firms did not need War-Industries Committees, and soon began to regard them as tiresome. The many lesser firms imagined that War-Industries Committees would permit them to acquire government money, lathes from abroad, raw-materials (at favourable prices) from *Prodameta* or the coal-owners, whereas the larger firms knew that these things could be much better used if devoted to themselves rather than to thousands of lesser producers scattered over the face of European Russia. They had their own contacts with the monopolies and the Special Council, and found the Central War-Industries Committee almost irrelevant, and sometimes bothersome, whilst the local Committees, with a heavy admixture of lawyers and academics, seemed to be meeting-places of barrack-room lawyers. The system worked well only where it dovetailed with already-existing sub-contracting links. This meant in practice the large towns, particularly Moscow. Here, by virtue of advanced transport-possibilities and the magnates' links with cartellised suppliers of fuel and raw-materials, a certain de-centralisation could be carried out within the industrial concentration that Russian circumstances promoted. The forty-five local Committees of the Moscow region existed, informally, before the system was formally introduced, and Vankov made use of these links among the Moscow men in February 1915, when he began to set up his shell-producing organisation with Pyot. Even before May, 1915, 500 of the 1,200 Moscow firms eventually included in the War-Industries Committee were already on war-work, and the rest would have been included, committee or no committee, as the flow of government money increased. The same was true, though on a lesser scale, of Kiev or Odessa; and as for Petrograd, it, though forming the country's source for the most intricate war-goods and machinery, scarcely troubled to have a War-Industries Committee at all.

Elsewhere, the War-Industries Committees were little more than a nuisance. The large firms by-passed them, and the lesser firms, unless they could do sub-contracting work for the larger ones, were left high-and-dry. Of course, the lesser ones could grumble, legitimately enough, that if they had been given greater State assistance, they would be able to produce more. But this was not an argument that had much appeal, either to large firms or to the State. It was characteristic that, in Ivanovo-Voznesensk, the largest textile-centre of Russia, the whole War-Industries Committee network supplied Vankov's organisation with less shell than two independent factories[14]—the *Kuvayevskaya manufaktura* and the *Ivanovo-voznesenskoye tovarishchestvo mekhanicheskikh izdeliy*, which supplied 150,000; in Samara and Saratov, it was the same story. In Yekaterinoslav, the Elworthy railway-works supplied Vankov, virtually without rivals on the War-Industries Committee side. Sometimes, political influences on the Special Council did secure contracts for War-Industries Committees, but their record of delivery was poor. The Reval one, by August 1916, had given only 500,000 roubles' worth of orders totalling four million; the Vyatka one gave nothing; the Rostov-on-the-Don one, less than five million roubles' worth out of twenty-four millions. The Baku Committee offered to undertake production of benzene and toluene by pyrolysis of petroleum, but failed;[15] the work was taken over, successfully, by the local Nobel company. Once inflation bit into the economy, the performance of lesser industry became still less impressive; and the War-Industries Committees appeared to be almost parasitical. The *Prodameta* men abandoned the Central War-Industries Committee; Ryabushinski and von Dittmar even denounced the Constitutional Democrats, and left the Party, for its links with wasteful small enterprise. Altogether, the Central Committee took less than ten per cent of war-ministry orders, and fulfilled less than half of those. The system survived by virtue of the sub-contracting networks of Moscow or Kiev, which were disguised as War-Industries Committees, and even then needed considerable charitable hand-outs from the local millionaire. For better or worse, this kind of business was being slowly throttled in Russia, and by the end of 1916, the War-Industries Committees, their needs neglected by *Prodameta*, their representatives abroad spurned by the government purchasing-committees, their wages derided, relapsed into querulous isolation. Their assemblies were marked by 'coarse attacks on the working-classes',[16] who, by going somewhere else for better wages, made life so difficult for War-Industries-Committee people; equally, there were attacks on the government, the monopolies, and the Special Council, who lacked 'understanding'. Not surprisingly, this agitation took, in the end, political form. But by then, the Duma Octobrists had lost sympathy for the War-Industries Committees, and the Constitutional Democrats, who remained faithful to them, were powerless.

Zemgor, also a subject of inflated claims, was victim to much the same situation. Large army suppliers already supplied the army; lesser ones had at best a sub-contracting rôle to play. *Zemgor* put forward the claims of

lesser, and even tiny, industry in matters of army supply, and at the same
time ran much of the army's hospital service. Both cost the government a
great deal of money—to the beginning of 1916, 500 million roubles,
although operation of hospital services was supposed to be voluntary,
based on rate-payers' money. In industrial matters, *Zemgor* could not make
sense. It was a collection of small-producers, spatch-cocked together by
groups of *désoeuvré* territorial magnates, who knew little about industry.
Zemgor's men worked expensively and inefficiently. Producing great
amounts of clothing for the army was beyond them, at least at prices
that would make sense. Their price for a blanket was almost seven
roubles, where ordinary army suppliers charged 1·50; and *Zemgor* had an
engaging habit of taking State money in advance, ordering the goods in
question from the United States, but without warning to the foreign-
exchange section of the finance ministry. It too found the government's
refusal to give it representation on the purchasing committees abroad
incomprehensible. Indeed, *Zemgor's* own incomprehension of its own
limitations was such that would-be producers of war-material, who did
not get contracts, suggested that the only reason could be that the government 'feared to let weapons into the hands of the people'.[17] *Zemgor*
received only a tiny fraction of orders for war-material.* Just the same, it
and the War-Industries Committees launched a legend, of humble and
patriotic entrepreneurs, frustrated at every turn by a corrupt and frivolous
régime. This claim was frequently accepted in the Entente countries. A
German observer had it more accurately when he wrote that, in the
public organisations, 'the talk is overwhelmingly of plans and intentions,
appointment of committees, sub-committees, sections, special conferences
etc., and relatively little of practical results'.[18]

The division between Moscow and Petrograd, between large concerns
and War-Industries-Committee men, prevented the Special Council from
surviving as a united agent of constitutional change. The industrialists who
dominated it feared political interference on the lesser producers' behalf,
and several of them found it much easier to work with the government
than with the Duma. Duma allies were therefore regarded as expendable,
and the political crisis stopped, in August 1915, when the Tsar took control
of the army, prorogued the Duma, split the Special Council into four, and
left the industrialists to quarrel among themselves. But at least some mechanism had been found for running the war-economy. The Special Council

---

*242,000,000 roubles, of which it fulfilled 80,000,000 by 1st January 1917.

†This percentage is sometimes taken to apply to *all* industrial enterprises. Had it done so,
there would have been no trouble with the War-Industries Committees, for whom
'non-war-industries-committees' would have been a more suitable title; but it applies
only to the larger firms of Russia.

for Defence was dominated by large producers, monopolies. 2,290 enterprises were involved in its labours, with a work-force of over two million men—in other words, the average number of workers in the Special Council's factories was about one thousand. Of such enterprises, eighty-six per cent worked for defence,†[19] and the Council became an instrument in the hands of the large firms and monopolies. The basis of its existence was the State's willingness, now, to spend money lavishly on defence-industries. Men took charge, who understood that, for industry to convert, money must be offered beyond anything imagined by Grand Duke Sergey or Sukhomlinov. The Special Council spent 15,000 million roubles between 1914 and the summer of 1917 (1st September) on armaments, which represented a third of all government spending in this period; the railways —fostered to help industry—took almost 2,500 million roubles between August 1914 and March 1917. Russian industry received, in other words, more direct assistance from the government between 1914 and 1917 than it had had in the whole of the nineteenth century.

This money was channelled through large firms and monopolies, who co-operated with each other, and at the same time could spread out the State's money rationally. *Prodameta* could arrange for those firms to receive metal who would make the best job of it; fuel-suppliers (who formed a monopoly, with the State, at the end of 1916) could act similarly. The Special Council divided the country into eleven regions, each with a plenipotentiary at its head, who had powers to dictate prices and wages, and if need be to take factories under sequestration (which happened in almost 100 cases, usually of foreign-owned factories). If State and monopolies worked together, they could subjugate factories that tried to retain their independence; and power to inspect factories' books, though opposed by some businesses on the grounds of the sanctity of profit, enabled the plenipotentiaries to dictate their prices with reference to real circumstances.

Of course the co-operation of State and monopoly was not always easy.[20] The State, despite a new attitude, was not always prepared to put up prices at the monopolies' dictation; and the monopolies were also not always prepared to have their prices dictated by the State. There was endless wrangling: threats, on the one side, of nationalisation, and on the other, of production-cutting. Wogau and *Med* resisted the State's attempts to put a ceiling on copper-prices. *Krovlya* in the Urals actually refused to produce sheet-iron for defence, until its protesting managing-director, Erdelyi, discovered that the Special Council's notion of a maximum price was to take the highest demands of the least efficient producers, add on a little bit to be safe, and then pronounce the result to be a fixed price —a method also tried with the farmers. Some Soviet writers have seen in this price-policy of the monopolies a simple piece of profiteering. Metals and fuel were barely enough to go round the various government agencies, and the civilian market would hardly have a look in. The government agencies bid against each other—war-ministry and ministry of transport taking equal shares of the metal—and prices were, naturally, forced up, until agents of rival ministries were requisitioning each other's supplies. But the two main factors behind the monopolies' price-policies were, first, the overall cost-push of world trade, raw materials and wages; second, the need to create, out of profit, investment that would carry not only the expensive conversion-process and its post-war counterpart, but a general expansion of industry in all kinds of new ways. The State attempt-ed to decree a fixed price for sheet-iron, and a technical commission of the Special Council, under Professor Baykov,[21] 'costed' roof-iron at 3·90 roubles per pood (16 kg.). This price, though suitable for ordinary factor-ies, would do nothing to attract the more backward ones, the more expensive processes of which would rule out a serious profit; *Prodameta* then pushed up the standard price to a level at which such factories—those under *Krovlya* were a case in point—would be able to make a profit, despite the raw-materials, labour, and transport-problems which they had to face. In spring 1916, *Prodameta* pushed up the price to 4·05 and then to 4·90. At such a price, less-than-ordinary factories would just scrape through with a profit; an efficient factory, such as the *Dniéprovienne* or *Providence Russe*, would make profits of 141·3 per cent of its basic capital on a single contract for shell-casings. The State grumbled that these factories should accept less; *Prodameta* could reply, first that this would be to penalise them for efficiency, and second that the money would in any case be re-invested. Moreover, this second point was generally true, for, through the banks, the profits were indeed channelled back to industry, to create a large number of new companies, with a wide spread of activities.

The political outcry against these profits was, of course, vast; and the figures are still repeated as evidence of the peculiar wickedness of Russian monopolists, savagely exploiting for private profit the country's wartime emergency. Ryabushinski's companies quadrupled their profit-rates in two years alone. The annual of the ministry of finance reckoned that, in 1916, profit-rates as a percentage of basic capital, had attained the 'improbable' average figure of 77 per cent, where before 1914 ten per cent would have been regarded as healthy. Strumilin,[22] the great statistician of the Soviet period, examined six large metallurgical works in Petrograd, and found that their turnover profits rose from 10·4% in 1913 to 18·6% in 1914, 28·5% in 1915 and 79·5% in 1916. He then turned to a group of 21 large enterprises of all kinds, and found the results as shown in the table.[23]

It was not only in war-material that firms made huge profits. The banks in particular also made profits out of speculation in commodities. This was brought on by inflation, in 1915 and particularly in 1916. Holders of grain, sugar, salt tended to hoard, knowing that a price-rise was inevitable.

year: 19:	−13	−14	−15	−16	% of 1913
Capital: (m. gold roubles)	72·4	72·5	72·5	83	115
workers: (thousands)	29·6	30·0	36·0	44·0	149
average wage: (roubles p.a.)	423	483	607	1066	252
total wage-bill: (m. roubles)	12·5	14·4	23·9	47	376
net profits: (m. roubles)	12·5	16·3	29·7	54	431
gross profits: (m. roubles)	27·3	38·5	72·6	137·8	504
real wages: (% of 1913)	100	115	115	132	—
dividends: (% of 1913)	100	113	167	225	—

The banks often bought from the hoarders, reserving the sellers a certain percentage of the eventual profit; and since the banks had great storage-space available, as well as some influence over the railway-mechanism, they were in a good position to profit. The Moscow branch of the Russian Bank for Foreign Commerce bought and sold 3,658 tons of sugar in 1916, and made a profit of 183,000 roubles; and its dealings in 5,174 waggons containing cotton bought a similar profit, without much effort on the banks' agents' part. Indeed, the banks' activities in such speculation was such that, in 1916, Bark had their vaults inspected by the police.

These profits provoked an outcry—from State agents having to supply them, from War-Industries Committees not sharing them, from workers whose labours allowed them, from ordinary consumers exposed to all the rigours of the black-market. From time to time, the Special Council was moved to protest. But any protest would be met with a display of rectitude on the monopolies' part, usually followed by concealment of books. If the State wanted goods, then it must 'see things as they are, for theoretical considerations are of no interest to us' (Erdelyi).[24] Industries' costs had risen, their expectations higher still; and, short of nationalisation, the government could do little against them. By the end of 1916, an uneasy marriage of State and monopoly had arrived. The State, unable to control its own priorities, handed much responsibility to *Prodameta*, the statistical section of which was simply taken over by the Special Council's metals-committee. It is difficult, and perhaps not very profitable, to determine which partner dominated the marriage, for the State ultimately joined the monopolists in enforcing a certain kind of industrial growth on the country.

The profits themselves, though sometimes indefensible, were in fact of considerable help to the economy as a whole. They were passed back into the firms, or sometimes invested through the banks in a variety of industries. However astonishing it may appear in retrospect, the Russian Stock-Exchanges went through something of a boom in the First World War, a process noted elsewhere only in the United States. 2,500 million roubles of new share-capital appeared; and, according to Vyshnegradski, the banks alone invested 9,000 million roubles in industry during the war.[25] There was a considerable expansion of the number of companies formed. In 1913, 241 had been chartered, with a capital of 403,140,000, as well as twenty-one foreign companies, with a capital of 36,500,000. In the war-years (excluding the freak conditions of summer, 1917), 1,138 Russian companies were chartered, with a capital of 2,032,400,000, and forty-five foreign ones (mainly in the extractive industries) with a capital of 77,650,000.[26] It is generally reckoned that about a third of these companies did not start to operate, and were founded for speculative reasons. Just the same, the capital stock of Russia rose, between 1914 and March, 1917, by one-third—1,256,000,000 roubles, of which roughly half (628,000,000)[27] represented new machinery.

The wartime crisis of the Russian economy is of course a stock theme of the documents and historical literature. Men saw the railways not working; they knew that coal was not enough to keep the factories working; the metals-shortage became such that output of civilian goods declined sharply; finally, there came great food-crises in the large towns, which in the end produced revolution. But these confusions did not represent an irreversible decline of the economy; rather, they were crises of growth. There was no absolute decline in any of these sectors, not even the harvest; on the contrary, virtually all sectors of the economy grew, and some very fast. But their growth was not even, and a series of bottle-necks threw the economy into chaos as it encountered them. The Tsarist régime had little idea as to how such crises might be surmounted, and in any case they provoked the final crisis of an already badly-strained society. It remains none the less true that they came, not from industrial backwardness, but rather from a too-rapid industrial advance.

The overall growth-rate of the Russian economy during the war-years has been estimated by Sidorov:[28]

(1913: 100) 1914	1915	1916	1917
101·2	113·7	121·5	77·3

Excluding the special circumstances of 1917, the output of coal rose by almost thirty per cent, although some of the mines were occupied by the Central Powers; the output of petroleum similarly rose, in Sidorov's words, 'to save the country's economic life'. There was a vast expansion of engineering and chemical industries. Vorobiev,[29] who examined 123 factories, reckoned that the output of the engineering industry rose, in gold roubles, from 200,200,000 in 1913 to 709,900,000 in 1915, 954,160,000 in 1916. In 1913 there had been, including Poland, 2,420 companies in Russia involved in metal-working, and they employed 386,000 workers. By 1917, not including Poland and other occupied territories, there were 2,332 such companies, employing 546,000 workers.[30] A substantial part of this was simply response to the government's demands for war-material. But a growing, and impressive, part was creation of new machinery; and Russia's capacity to substitute her own for imported machinery showed how far her backwardness was a thing of the past. Imports of foreign machinery declined almost at once, as trade with Germany was curtailed; and thereafter the expensiveness of British or American machinery made it profitable for Russian industry to pioneer its own machine-tool industry. Imports of machinery of all types showed the following pattern (m. Gold roubles):

1913	1914	1915	1916 (including tariff.)
156·3	114	42·4	108·2

Russian output of machinery of all types rose from 308,200,000 roubles' worth in 1913 to 757,000,000 in 1915 and 978,200,000 in 1916, of which industrial plant, 69,300,000 roubles' worth in 1913, took 163,200,000 in 1915 and 218,500,000 in 1916.[31] In chemicals, there was, overall, a doubling of output. The work-force rose from 36,000 to 58,400, and output per man rose from 5,729 roubles' worth to 7,590. A survey conducted in 1918–19 concluded that industrial output had risen during the war on lines indicated in the following table: (gold roubles, rounded)[32]

	1913	1914	1915	1916	1917
Overall: (m. roubles)	1819	1862	2139	2177	1542
Per man: (roubles)	2349	2355	2590	2496	1690

It is not surprising to find, in 1916 as distinct from 1917, many well-informed voices being raised with much optimism. Ryabushinski produced a plan for future collaboration of State and great industry, with a view to freeing Russia from dependence on foreigners; Litvinov–Falinski sketched a similar plan for great import-substitution, and ended, 'It is with cheerful anticipation that we await the very near future.'[33]

The expansion of engineering and chemical industries permitted the Russian army to receive increasing quantities of war-goods. There was 2,000 per cent growth in out-put of shell, 1,000 per cent in artillery, 1,100 per cent in rifles.[34] Four Russian factories—Shetinin and Lebedev in Petrograd, Dux in Moscow, Anatra in Odessa—produced 80 per cent of the monthly 222 aircraft Russia was said to need in 1915–16; five large automobile factories produced not only lorries, but in the end also tanks for the Red Army; similarly, the army's 10,000 telephones became 50,000 in 1916.[35] Artillery showed the advance best:[36]

Russian Artillery 1914 – 1917

	1914	1917
light (field, horse, mountain) ..	6,278	7,694
(batteries of light guns ..	959	1,868)
light mortar	512	1,054
heavy field	240	1,086
very heavy	nil	344
anti-aircraft	nil	329
Totals	7,030	10,487

The Russian figure for 1917 (1st January) is actually higher than the French one for August 1916 (10,330) and is well over double the British one for that month (4,290). A certain amount of Russia's artillery was foreign in origin. In light calibres, Russia herself produced 20,000 guns, and foreigners sent 5,625. But of the modern howitzers, production was 100 per cent Russian, and was still three-quarters Russian in the heavier varieties. By 1917, the economy could provide 900 guns per month.

Shell-production provides a similar story. Once the State and the large firms co-operated, shell could be produced in respectable quantities. Of 54,000,000 light shells sent to the army, foreigners provided 15,000,000; nine State factories 8,300,000; eleven large private factories 26,500,000— mainly, the Vankov[37] and Putilov organizations—and seventeen others, 5,200,000 (mainly the War-Industries Committees and *Zemgor*). Of 11,700,000 medium-calibre shells, nine million came from Russian factories; and even in the heavy category, over half of the shell came from within Russia, mainly from Vankov's collaborator, Vtorov, whose factory near Moscow could fill 12,000 of them in a day. Manikovski,[38] the Artillery Department's principal expert, gives the following table for Russian shell-output: 1915: 11,230,000 three-inch shells, production rising from 358,000 in January to 440,000 in May, 852,000 in July, 1,197,000 in September and 1,512,000 in November:

1916: 28,300,000, production rising from 1,740,000 in May to 1,980,000 in June, and 2,900,000 in September.

In September 1916, 320,000 light mortar shells were produced; and if all categories of shell—including gas-shells—are counted, the country could produce four million rounds of light shell, and 500,000 heavy shells, by the autumn of 1916. By January 1917, there was a reserve of shell, at the front alone, of 3,000 rounds per gun; in November 1917, the Bolsheviks inherited a Tsarist shell-reserve of eighteen million. Of course, there were continual gumbles from the front. The generals went on overrating what artillery could achieve, and when in 1916 they still failed to break through, they discovered a shortage of heavy artillery, which they had not talked about before. But, by 1916, the Russian army had achieved considerable superiority, not only in men, but also in matériel. The superiority was achieved at the cost of a gigantic industrial effort, which brought its own social consequences in 1917. But over the facts of the industrial effort itself, there could be little dispute.

CHAPTER TEN

The Second War-Winter, 1915-1916

By the winter of 1915-16, the basis for a successful war-effort had been laid—at least, in narrow terms of war-material. In January 1916 Alexeyev informed the French, through Zhilinski, that his front-line strength was now 1,693,000, of whom 1,243,000 had rifles; a few weeks later, the Russian front-line strength became two million, virtually all of them with rifles. The main armies against Germany—I, II, X, IV, and III— had over a million men in February, and of these, only 110,000 lacked rifles; most of the 110,000 were in any case supernumerary. With shell, too, confidence grew, as the correct amount for an offensive operation— 1,000 rounds per field-gun—seemed to be secured. Other essential items, from aeroplanes to wireless-sets, gas-masks, barbed-wire, bandages, were now arriving in quantities that led to universal hope that the Russian army could soon take the offensive again.[1]

But all of this weight needed muscle; and the characteristic feature of the pre-war army, the growing dichotomy between its ostensible strength and its efficiency of organisation, became, now, still more clearly evident. Legend has a picture of countless millions of peasant soldiers being thrust into battle, armed with long-handled axes, against overpowering German artillery and machine-guns. It is a legend that owes almost nothing to reality; indeed, reality was the very reverse of legend. The army, by the beginning of the 1916 campaign, was not suffering from material short-ages of any significance, any more than other armies; it did, however, experience remarkable difficulties in using the countless millions of peasant soldiers alleged to be available for conscription. The front-line strength was less than that of France, with less than a quarter of Russia's population, until mid-1916.

The pre-war system of conscription lasted until the end of 1915, and in effect even longer. It had been introduced in 1874, at a time when European armies reckoned, following the example of Prussia, that a large trained reserve had become essential. Theoretically, all physically-fit young Russians then became liable for conscription. But it is tempting to add that they were then exempted from it. The army authorities would have had to take in, annually, about 600,000 men—and, later on, even three times as many—if conscription had been genuinely universal, for these figures represented the number of fit Russians reaching the military age in any one year between 1874 and 1914. But to take in this many was unthinkable. The army did not have officers and N.C.O.s to train them; it lacked barracks. Above all, it lacked the money to supply them. Supply ('intendantstvo') took up over 100 million roubles out of the army's total revenue, 172 millions, in the 1870s, and 'administration', at nineteen millions, took more than all matters of artillery put together. Later on, the demands of supply grew: in 1913–14, they took 450 million roubles out of 580 millions spent by the army.[2] To take in many hundreds of thousands of conscripts every year would be to consume in food, blankets, fodder money that was desperately needed for guns (and of course also for pensions and promotions). Consequently, the army authorities found ways of cutting down their recruit-contingents. On the one side, they generously exempted minorities—Finns, Menonites, Central Asian peoples and, usually, Jews. On the other side, they proclaimed a generous system of exemptions for family-status. Only sons, men with a close relative already in the ranks, men who had lost a father or an uncle in the Polish revolt, only grandsons were all exempted. Finally, in the grandest exemption of all, 'bread-winners' were not taken in to serve, i.e. married men. Thus, in 1914–15, one million new peasant households came into existence—a circumstance still bewildering to agricultural economists, but one wholly comprehensible to students of the Draft.[3] Together with exemptions for educational reasons these exemption-classes proved to be so numerous that the authorities had difficulty in finding even the small recruit-contingent on which they had decided (150,000 in 1874), and seem to have taken in men whose physical standard was not high. The 150,000 produced among them 76,000 appeals, most of which turned out to be justified.[4] In later years, the recruit-contingent rose—320,000 in 1900, 450,000 in 1906 and 585,000, under the terms of the 'Great Programme' in 1914—but it did not represent much more than a third of the available man-power.

Conscription is often put forward as one of the chief factors causing Russia's economic problems in the First World War. It is alleged to have caused fearsome problems both for agriculture and industry; and no doubt did bring about severe, local disruption. But it has to be put into perspective. Russia called up just over fourteen million men between 1914 and 1917, from a population of almost 180 millions. This was barely more than France, with a population of forty millions, and less than Germany, with one of sixty-five millions. As far back as 1902, the surplus rural population of Russia had been reckoned to be twenty-two millions, so that Russia should have been more able than either western country to sustain real mass-conscription. In reality, the baneful effects of conscription were yet another hard-luck story, exempting government from its responsibilities. It was not so much an economic as an administrative problem, one calling in question the whole relationship of government and people. The government shrank from the creative effort that real conscription would have involved. Like most autocracies, its great strength was, not that it governed harshly, but that it governed less. Its tax-collectors and recruiting-sergeants were little more than a nuisance; and the government rightly feared that, if they became more, it would be swept away in a tide of popular indignation. Real conscription was possible only where a partnership existed between people and administration. A partnership of this kind existed in England, but not in Ireland; in Germany, but not in Austria; in the Red Army of 1918, but not in the Tsarist one of 1916. In 1918, there was a great rush of volunteers for the Red Army, and men who failed to report for it would be 'informed' on by their fellows. After 1914, there was a rush to benefit from the various statutes of exemption, and most of the Russian people seem to have sympathised. The Tsarist army thereby came to suffer from a shortage of man-power that no-one could honestly explain.

A large part of the difficulty was of course the authorities' simple incomprehension of it. They had never supposed, before the War, that they would need to call on more than a fraction of Russia's available man-power, since they foresaw neither the casualties nor the length of the war to come, and in any case could not imagine supplying more than a million or so men at the front. They had, indeed, been criticised by progressive critics not for producing too few soldiers, but for producing too many, who swamped the training-facilities. They called up less than five million men in 1914, and thought this would suffice, since both France and Germany called up much the same. The active army—i.e. the conscripts of the years 1911, 1912 and 1913—went off to war, with the trained reserve of the first class, i.e. men who had served in the ranks between 1904 and 1910, respectively, some 1,500,000 and 2,800,000.* Numbers were made up with Cossacks and classes of territorial troops, called up to guard bridges and depots. Altogether, mobilisation in 1914 thus affected some 4,500,000 men.

---

*Liability to military service extended in Russia between the ages of twenty-one and forty-three. Men would serve three years in the line; then they would be liable for service with the 1st class of the reserve for seven years, and with the 2nd class for eight. This would be followed by three years' liability for service with the 1st class of the territorials (*opolcheniye*). Most exemptees served in its second class, in so far as they had to serve at all.

Casualties in 1914-15 went far beyond what anyone had imagined possible, indeed far beyond what the authorities were capable of counting. The authorities became aware of constant demands for more men, and lurched about in a fog. The army's statistical office was the *Glavny Shtab*, which was run, almost by definition, by incompetents, who had failed to make a career in anything other than this department, which was regarded as a waste-paper-basket. The few dozen dim-witted officers of this department attempted to keep up with losses by installing an enormous set of filing-cabinets, where they faithfully recorded every man's career—his medals, promotions, permits, wounds. When casualties ran into hundreds of thousands per month, the *Glavny Shtab* succumbed, and could produce nothing beyond unenlightened guess-work. There is, as a result, much confusion as regards the army's losses in the First World War—figures between four and eleven million being quoted. Most authorities, Soviet and émigré, inclined to the higher figure—no doubt to display that allied money had not gone in vain, and therefore need not be repaid—but a sober Soviet investigation results in a figure of between 7,000,000 and 7,500,000 for losses of all categories to the armistice of December 1917. Of these, three million were caused in 1916, and the bulk of the rest in 1914-15. With losses running at between 300,000 and 400,000 per month, of whom forty per cent would not be able to return to the front, the authorities were therefore faced with a situation in which each month of the war was eating up the recruit-contingent of a single pre-war year; and the situation was quite possibly more serious still, in so far as the casualty-returns did not include men who were cured at the front-hospitals and returned to their units within a short time.

The authorities were thus driven to make a much more profound effort of conscription than they had thought possible. They had certain obvious openings. The trained reserve of both classes represented fifteen recruit-contingents of the period 1896-1910 inclusive, and these were taken in. They should have amounted to five million men, but because, in the course, of their liability to reserve-service, many had become physically less able than before, or had acquired a right to exemption, or had simply disappeared without trace, no more than 3,100,000 men were taken in from this set during the war, of whom more than two-thirds were affected by the initial call-up of August 1914. A second obvious opening was for the army to anticipate the conscription of future recruit-contingents, i.e. to summon to the colours in 1914 or 1915 young men who would not normally have served until they reached the age of twenty-one in the years to come. The 'recruit-contingents' of 1914-18 were all called up in 1914-15, and were mustered in the usual way, i.e. exemptions and deferments carried on as before, so that each contingent counted 585,000 men, although three times as many Russians would reach the military age in that year. This gave the army a further three million men to use, who were put into the army during 1915 and 1916. Delays in the delivery of these new troops caused difficulties, even in 1915; but in any event they could not cover the demands of modern war. The army would have to conscript some more, from somewhere.

It would have to delve into the ranks, first of the older men (forty-one— forty-three years of age) who had completed their term of service with the reserve and who had gone into the first class of the territorials. This was duly done, though without much return in terms of numbers. A second step was to call up elements of this class of the territorials who had not served in the army at all, who had not been taken in for full-scale military service, although physically able for it, because they were 'supernumerary' to the army's requirements in recruits in that year. Both sources gave, together, a further three million men. The next step would be to exploit the vast sea of the second class of the territorials: men who had been exempted altogether from military service, or who had dropped out, for one reason or another, from one of the other classes while liable for service. The territorial force was vast, since it accounted for more than two-thirds of the male subjects of the Tsar; but the second class, though presumably including, in every year, 400,000 men, gave only three million men for the army in the First World War. The army's failure to exploit territorial troops properly is a considerable puzzle. Of course, some soldiers simply wrote off the untrained *opolchentsy* as quite useless in the field. But the real problem was failure of will. The authorities did not want to bring upon themselves the unpopularity that conscription of this kind could bring; more pertinently, it is doubtful if any kind of serious record existed of these millions of men, scattered all over Russia. The *Glavny Shtab* and the military districts had not imagined, before 1914, that such a record would be needed, and now, in wartime, was hardly the point where one could be set up. Even in countries more advanced, and easier to survey, than Russia, the military authorities made all kinds of blunders in conscription—serving call-up papers on cripples, dead men, lunatics, convicts. In Russia, the dimensions of this would make the State ridiculous as well as detestable. In fact, the territorial troops could be conscripted only if they reported for duty, which they might do for the Red Army, but not for the Tsarist one. It was only in places where records were reasonably good, and where the police could do their work, that territorials were conscripted in any numbers. In practice, this meant the big towns; and of course was followed by complaints from factory-owners working for defence that their skilled workmen were being removed, so that even attempts to conscript the territorial troops of whom the army had some record would produce clouds of demands for exemption—two million, or two-fifths of the contingent that the big towns were expected to produce for the army. Had Russia been able to conscript in the French manner, she would have called up sixty million men; but she called up less than a quarter of this.

These confusions also affected the recruitment of officers. For most of the time, deferments by reason of education were maintained, and the universities of Russia continued at full blast, disturbed at best by ineffective appeals for volunteers. The war ministry grumbled that it needed officer-material. The other ministers asserted that it would be unfair to conscript senior students just as they were about to take their final examinations; and that it would be equally unfair to conscript their juniors while the seniors were being exempted. Neither set was therefore affected—partly because ministers resented the waste of talented men on the army, partly because they feared what the educated classes would do if the State leant on them, and it was not until the end of 1915 that any encroachments were made on the universities. The army of 1916 therefore had 80,000 officers, more than double those of the army of 1915.

The authorities were at a loss, and could only screw up their existing methods as far as possible. They extended liability for service to the age of fifty; they anticipated conscription, and took in seventeen-year-old boys—thus arriving at the situation, peculiar to Russia, of grandfathers and grandsons leaving for the front, being waved off by the middle, exempted, generation. They exerted increasing pressure, not on the men who had escaped their net before 1914, but on the youngest classes. In June 1915 they extended their recruiting for the classes 1915-18 to include all men who were physically fit, i.e. the standard recruit-contingent of 585,000 with a supernumerary element that would usually have gone to the territorials. In October 1915 they produced a law to allow revision of past exemptions (and then, characteristically, failed to operate it, since re-combing gave them less than 250,000 soldiers throughout the war); finally, in December 1915, they made a new military law that allowed a recruit-contingent of 985,000, applicable to the 1919 class. The Russian army was thus overwhelmingly made up of men aged from seventeen to twenty-five, but its commanders were not often less than sixty years of age. More important in the short run was that the army was coming to an end of the possible recruits. The army for 1916 included 4,587,145 men, and there was a reserve of 1,545,000. But behind it, there was only the anticipated recruit-contingent of 1919, and a further batch of territorials, together not 3,000,000 men. If the war did not end in 1916, the State would have to undertake some conscription of the huge classes of territorials of which there was little record.[5] Not surprisingly, *Stavka* was pressed to win the war before the State had to make this effort. 1916 was the last chance.

It was an equal paradox of this war that men's war-aims ran up parallel with the difficulties of attaining them. Theoretically, a State in the vulnerable situation of the Tsarist one should not have exposed itself any longer to war. But there seems to have been very little thought, in circles that mattered, of a separate peace with the Germans, and peace-feelers never went beyond surreptitious and insincere conversations, although the Germans kept trying for more. On the contrary, Russian aims went up, parallel with the sacrifices being demanded of the people; and ministers feared that the whole system would be overthrown if they did not offer satisfaction to the national aspirations. Sazonov and his associates wanted to set up a range of Russian satellite-states in eastern Europe—independent Bohemia, enlarged Serbia, semi-independent and enlarged Poland—and to assert Russian control of the Dardanelles. Much to their surprise, the British took the lead in offering Constantinople, in spring 1915, though themselves making off with the oil-rich areas of the Turkish empire. Somewhat later, as a result of provisions of the inter-allied economic conference, Russia was promised part of the reparations to be exacted from the Central Powers; and by the beginning of 1917 the French were prepared to underwrite a huge Russian empire from Stettin to Trieste and the Straits, in exchange for Russian guarantee of French supremacy in seventeenth-century style, over the Palatinate and the Saar.[6] Even many left-wing members of the Provisional Government secretly approved of these aims, and it was not until the November Revolution that they were seriously disavowed.

In the old days, governments under pressure could always make peace before the crisis bit too deep. Now, they had the physical power to carry on the war for a long time, with hundreds of thousands of recruits, the capacity to supply them, and boundless possibilities for joyous arithmetic in paper-money. Moreover, the First World War both coincided with, and caused, a social dislocation that did much to make war-aims a matter of life and death for important sections of each country, and as the war went on, the increase in social dislocation, far from producing demands for peace, instead produced still greater war-aims, almost independently of vicissitudes at the front. Already before 1914 the comfortable gold-standard world had been under strain, as the process of levelling between sections of the working-class and sections of the middle-class went ahead. This was shown, for instance, in the threefold rise of servants' wages between 1870 and 1910; it was also shown in the decline, marked from the 1880s, of the middle-class birth-rate, as, particularly in France, middle-class families became prepared to forego children in order to maintain a nanny. The First World War vastly increased these tensions. Wartime inflation—which reduced the value of the pound by almost two-thirds in four years, and the value of other currencies still more—knocked away the great prop of the rentier world, the fixed income. Taxation became more severe; and many middle-class occupations became, in wartime, almost redundant. The wages of actors in Austria, for instance, remained exactly the same throughout the war, although prices rose five or six times; the salary of high bank officials doubled, but the wages of a plumber's assistant quadrupled.[7] Middle-class property was sold off, as the rents on it declined in value: there were considerable rises in peasant-held land in France, and in Italy agricultural 'squatting' came to an almost complete end during the war, as even small peasants became able to buy property. At the same time, government spending opened up a whole range of new employment-possibilities for the working-classes; and the decline of middle-class buying-power on the one side, and the opening of these new possibilities, on the other, resulted in a considerable drop, in most countries, of domestic servants. In England, there had been over a million domestic servants in 1914, but by 1920 there were not 400,000. It is not irrelevant to war-aims that half a million middle-class women were having to do the washing-up for the first time in their lives.*

After the initial euphoria of 1914, the Left merely tolerated the war, for reasons of national defence; and the sting of their opposition to it was usually removed or lessened by the social benefits that the war conferred. The parties of property, on the other hand, produced great, imperialist war-aims and were less, not more, prepared to compromise as the war proceeded, and Imperialism acquired a more obvious social dimension than ever before. Men assumed that acquisition of an empire would make up for all the supposedly temporary social dislocation of the war. It was, for instance, an almost universal assumption, from Marx to Cecil Rhodes, that the British were wealthy because they had an empire, not that they had one because they could afford it. The state's rents must be put on their old secure footing; markets must be captured; sources of vital raw-materials acquired; foreign competition eliminated. Each country produced war-aims that summed up its own version of imperialism in the previous century. The British demanded confiscation of the German fleet, and the German merchant-marine; an end to Germany's colonies; and, particularly, control of the vast oil-areas of the Middle East. The

---

*The English encountered a smaller problem in this than other, more traditionalist countries, for middle-class women could work without demeaning themselves as much as in France or Germany. Middle-class women invaded the bureaucracy, and emancipation of women in England tended to mean paying wives with the money they extracted, in the form of taxes, from their husbands.

French demanded lesser versions of the same, and put most of their passion into a demand for German gold, a demand dressed up as 'reparation'. It was again an almost universal illusion that Germany's industrial advance had been 'caused' by French gold, exacted in 1871; now the French would become prosperous at Germany's expense, and 'reparations' continued to be the great indivisible aim of the French rentier class. Similarly, the Germans went on a quest for land in the east, which they sometimes dressed up in their own peculiar version of idealism. It was a German who best expressed the realities of war-aims in the First World War: Bussche-Haddenhausen, of the Foreign Office, who instructed agents in the occupied areas, 'Russia's railways, her industry and her whole economy must come under our control. We have no alternative, but to exploit the East; it is there that we shall find the interest-payments for our war-loan'.[8] To the Mr. Gulbenkians of Europe, all of this might mean a fabulous five per cent; to the middle-classes, it meant an end to the washing-up. The appeal to force was becoming irresistible, just when force was at its least decisive.

Despite the war-time problems it encountered, the Russian government was committed to much the same game as its allies, and bid for more gains, the less favourably the war went. Russia's dependence on the western Powers was now complete, and could not be broken short of a total repudiation of debts or submission to the German empire. One instance of this dependence was the despatch of Russian troops to the western front, more or less nakedly in the style of the Hessian mercenaries sent to fight England's colonial wars in the eighteenth century. The French had long grumbled that Russia's front-line strength was no greater than that of France, despite the difference in population-figures; Joffre also grumbled to Zhilinski that France alone was fighting the war. The Russians replied that they would send more men to the front if the men had arms; and the French, in December 1915, proposed instead that a contingent of Russian troops should go to the western front. Doumer, visiting the country late in 1915, even made it clear that despatch of war-goods would be dependent on despatch of a Russian contingent, of 300,000 men, to fight in the west. In the end, four brigades* were sent off, to France and to the new front at Salonica—an obvious exercise in cannon-fodder that Alexeyev would have liked to prevent, but could not, since 'we are so dependent on the French for war-material that the categorical refusal we should give is out of the question'.[9]

---

*Under Marushevski, Diederichs, Lokhvitski and Bobrikov. Some of these troops later took a rôle in the unrest of the French army in 1917, and there was also trouble in Salonica. Some were repatriated; others were sent to the Sahara for penal service unless they agreed to serve with the Whites.

At this stage, the allies were bankrupt of strategic ideas. All of them waited for one reason or another. The French had had enough of fighting the war on their own; they wanted the British to take a greater rôle; and they expected the Russians to resume their offensive some time. Operations in 'the side-shows', particularly Gallipoli, were a clear failure, but the battle between 'easterners' and 'westerners' went on regardless. While the western Powers were simply waiting, Falkenhayn struck at Serbia. With 180 battalions and 900 guns, Mackensen attacked the Serbian army, with 120 and 330, in the early days of October. As the offensive succeeded, six double-strength Bulgarian divisions attacked Serbia in flank, in mid-October. The army was pushed towards the south-west, eventually into Albania, where, with the loss of all but 150,000 men, it reached the sea and safety. The Entente were at a loss. They wished to do something to help Serbia, but lacked the will to send serious forces. They pushed Greece into declaring war on the Central Powers, but fumbled the process, and almost caused a Greek declaration of war upon themselves. They then violated Greek neutrality, occupying the port of Salonica with a view to directly assisting the Serbians. But transport-problems, wrangling among the allies, and the failure to contribute substantial troops made this ineffective: in the whole Serbian campaign, there were thirty British casualties. In the end, the Serbian army was moved to Salonica, from its refuge on Corfu, and this front remained a monument to the bungling of autumn 1915.

There was much grumbling that Russia had done little to help Serbia, a country that came within her sphere. At this stage, Alexeyev was principally concerned that he should not be left in the lurch, as Russians alleged had happned in the summer of 1915, when the Germans attacked Russia without disturbance from the western Powers. It became necessary to document both Russia's power and willingness to act, so as to exact from the allies a promise that, in 1916, all the Powers—England, France, Italy and Russia—would synchronise their offensive against Germany, which was planned for April. This led Alexeyev to exaggerate his strength* and also to attempt something for the Serbians' benefit. As the Germans attacked Serbia, he staged some minor offensives in the north-east and in Volhynia, without effect; then, in response to foreign ministry prompting, he decided to assemble a new army on the Black Sea coast, as a

---

*He informed Zhilinski, for the allies' benefit, that the Russian army would have a front-line strength in April of 2,750,000. The French had, correctly, estimated it at 1,500,000; and Zhilinski was much embarrassed when they showed him their source—a telegram from Paléologue, their ambassador, quoting a Russian war ministry source. Zhilinski, to prevent further publication, 'without ceremony took the telegram, hid it in my wallet and refused to discuss it.'

general menace to Bulgaria. There were plans for a descent on the Bulgarian coast. On the ground, this operation made less sense than it did in foreign ministry heads, for there were two Turco-German battleships, *Goeben* and *Breslau*, in the Black Sea, and their submarines were a threat to the long supply-lines of any amphibious operation on Russia's part. The Russian navy had, characteristically, too many great battleships and too few smaller vessels capable of dealing with submarine-threats; since the beginning of the war with Turkey, it had done not much more than raid Turkish light-houses and coastal traffic; now, the admirals would not countenance an amphibious operation, and Alexeyev threatened to turn the Black Sea fleet into an infantry brigade. VII Army remained disposed along the Black Sea coast, doing nothing in particular as the Serbians were pushed, throughout November, towards Albania.[10]

To achieve at least something—perhaps the intervention of Romania—the new force was sent instead to the Austro-Hungarian front. It was to launch an attack in eastern Galicia and along the Dniester, IX Army co-operating. This operation showed that, although the Russian army might to a large degree have already overcome its material crisis, its commanders had no serious idea as to how this recovery might be put to good use. It began almost as a political manoeuvre, rather than as a military one; there seems to have been little thought as to difficulties of season and terrain, merely a vague confidence that the Austrians would collapse. This vague confidence was not shared by Ivanov, commanding the south-western front. The order for attack came from *Stavka* on 23rd November; the three corps of VII Army were diverted to eastern Galicia, on the river Strypa; Ivanov did not order the offensive until 12th December. He did so, moreover, only after presenting a bill for supplies no doubt designed to make the most ardent proponent of the offensive stop in his tracks—12,000,000 portions of preserved meat, over 11,000 waggons of fodder.[11] He quarrelled with Savvitch, his chief of staff, whom he replaced (by Klembovski) just before the attack was to begin. The new army commander, Shcherbachev, was full of ill-defined fight; but he arrived barely a week before action started, and his troops also knew not at all the ground they were expected to fight on. Commanders seem merely to have felt that Austrians would be easy to defeat.

Both this battle,[12] and that of Lake Narotch that followed in March, illustrated one of the most unfortunate consequences of shell-shortage—the generals' tendency to blame all their woes on it, and corresponding expectation that, once shell-shortage were no longer in evidence, all would necessarily be well. Men assumed that, once a thousand rounds per field gun were laid in, then a ten-day operation would be possible, and victory only a matter of wrecking enemy defences so that they could be occupied by the infantry. But no-one had any idea how a break-through operation should be planned. It was only in July 1916 that *Stavka* issued a manual (*nastavleniye*) on infantry action, one that replaced the pre-war ones hitherto used for instruction of infantry-officers. The troops are said to have left its pages largely uncut. Similarly, the *Stavka* manual on break-through operations was not much more than a muddled translation of a German manual of 1915. There were of course visits to and from the French front, but to date these had not resulted in the absorption, at the Russian front, of significant information. The problem of combining infantry and artillery still evaded solution, since artillerists and infantrymen would not agree. It was only early in 1916 that *Stavka* set up an artillery section, *Upart*, and even then there was not much agreement. The differences between infantry and artillery were to some degree composed only in a demand for huge amounts of shell—4,500,000 rounds per month—which, if realised, would have worn out the army's guns in a few months. *Stavka* itself was not only too puzzled, but also too busy, to think things out. Alexeyev worked all but six hours of the day at boxes of telegrams and letters; and, merely to keep pace with the millions of details coming in, the officers of *Stavka* were kept going fast enough—on 15th February 1916, for instance, *Stavka* had to send 442 telegrams, with 45,473 words; on 10th March 140, with 14,240 words, and on 13th March 504 with 52,814 words. During March, 1916, II Army Headquarters had to receive 3,000 persons a day.[13] It was not surprising that staffs failed, on the whole, to think things out, while planners in the rear were too remote from events to write manuals that could be taken seriously. The result was that each front had a different system, sometimes privately-printing different manuals of instruction. Trench-systems, for instance, were, even in June 1916, 'childish'—sited on the sky-line in places, and often over-looked by the Germans.[14] There was almost no concept of digging great dug-outs to hold the reserves—in the Bessarabian offensive, these were merely marched over open ground for three miles before they came up to the first Austrian trench.

In the present case, generals assumed that with crushing numerical superiority and one heavy shell for every square yard of the front—both of them now attained—all would be well. The artillery would pulverise Austrian defences, and the infantry would easily pick up the wreckage. Nine infantry and two cavalry corps were mustered for attack, beginning on 27th December in eastern Galicia. The attempts went on for a fortnight, in which 50,000 men were lost. The initial attacks failed, or at best took a stretch of enemy front trench. Infantry and artillery failed to co-operate; reserves were too far off, and, when they reached the front, not concealed. The Austrians' guns were well-handled, did not reveal themselves until the last moment, and then did powerful work against the attacking Russians. Shcherbachev and Lechitski reacted by bunching their troops closer together—2. Corps, for instance, took all of VII Army's heavy guns for the front of one division, hardly more than a kilometre, and used 11,000 heavy shells.[15] The Austrian front trench was naturally enough levelled and occupied. But thereafter, the attackers were enfiladed from either side of their kilometre, could not bring their reserves up either in a concealed or in a rapid fashion, such that they had to fall back, in the open, from their gains. An attack of this kind was described:

> After artillery preparation, we went about a mile forward under heavy enemy gunfire. Once we were within five hundred yards, we were hit, suddenly, by devastating machine-gun and rifle-fire that had hitherto been silent. There was the enemy, in solid trenches with great parapets and dug-outs; sitting behind ten or fifteen rows of uncut wire, waiting for us. We lay on the frozen ground, for hours, as the snow drifted down; if we were wounded, there was no help because we were so close to the wire. But behind us, there were artillery colonels and captains of the General Staff, drinking rum tea, and writing their reports—'After brilliant artillery preparation our glorious forces rushed forward to occupy the enemy trenches, but were held up by counter-attack of strong reserves.'[16]

The generals had been led to error by the myths of shell-shortage. They had not noted the need for intense preparation, for disruption of enemy reserves in particular. They now responded by supposing, on the whole, that yet more shell would be needed for break-through. They do not appear to have altered their tactics in a significant degree. After the failure of the offensive in Bessarabia, a document was produced by VII Army command and by Ivanov's headquarters, discussing failure. Lack of shell was mentioned, particularly by Shcherbachev, as taking first place—although in practice he was to break through in the same area a few months later, with brilliant results, with barely more shell than he had had in the Bessarabian offensive. Obvious truths were stated—the need for reserves to be closer to the front line, for better observation of the enemy artillery. But it needed the genius of Brusilov for anything to emerge from this but stale imitations of French practices of 1915.

A new Russia was indeed beginning to emerge in 1916. But its shape was not at all clear. There were now large numbers of junior officers and General Staff men who were thoroughly discontented with 'the system'—men of high military competence, whose services the Bolsheviks knew how to exploit to the full. But for a variety of reasons, they did not get much authority in the army. Much of the officers' corps was made up of sprigs of the middle-classes, not used to exerting authority; and there were not many officers, in any event—in the specially-favoured 'descent-force' on the Black Sea coast, ninety-nine officers for 2,890 men in the 3. Turkestan Rifle Brigade, 157 for 5,026 in 41. infantry division; officers, at that, barely-trained for the job. In the Russian army, with its immense problems of untrained man-power, the authorities always tended to prefer old regular soldiers to civilians. The civilian intake might be more adaptable; but it had not the habit of authority that alone—it seemed—could make the Russian soldier into a good fighting machine. Promotions tended therefore to be a battleground between the rival cliques of the army—the Grand Ducal men on the one side, the remnants of the *Sukhomlinovshchina* on the other. The crisis of 1915-16 did make for some change, but the authorities reacted with extraordinary conservatism just the same. They went on promoting strange figures to commands.[17] For instance, in this period the Guard was taken out of line for re-training, due to last nine months. It was now made into two corps, with a cavalry corps, and contained men of the highest physical standard. It was then extensively trained, by veterans of Plevna, in the methods of 1877. One corps command went to Grand Duke Paul, an aged cavalryman. His chief of staff was a man to whom staff-work was quite new—Count Ignatiev, appointed mainly because the commandant of the Tsar's Palace, Voyeykov, wanted him removed from the post he had at Tsarskoye Selo, where his influence on the Tsar had not been in Voyeykov's interest.

The pride of this collection was General Bezobrazov, appointed to command the whole of the Guard Army, as the two infantry corps and the cavalry corps were collectively known. He was in his late sixties when appointed to this position. His previous history did not justify such honour—he had been among the men who had led the Tsar into the gross bungling of war with Japan. In war, he commanded a Guard division, with Olokhov as corps commander. He refused to obey Olokhov's orders, and the two men fought publicly at a station. Bezobrazov was then removed from his command. He used his influence with the Tsar, and was appointed to command the entire Guard Corps. In the retreat of summer 1915, he quarrelled with the commander of III Army: Lesh, its commander, wanted the Guard to retreat, covering another corps. Bezobrazov announced that the Guard never retreated, and the other corps was badly let-down, while the Guard underwent a futile sacrifice. The two men then had a competition in insulting telegrams, as result of which Bezobrazov was removed from his corps command. But he was apparently a man of astonishingly high influence—the Tsar regarded him as 'charming', although in junior officers' eyes he was 'a ruin, with the dull gaze of a gourmand, hardly able to drag his log-like legs around'. He represented to the Tsar that the Guard 'should only be commanded by people of class'; and for the sentiment was rewarded with command of the Guard Army itself. He used the position, moreover, to appoint as divisional commanders favourites of his who had been removed, for incompetence, from regimental commands. Bezobrazov's case was only the most notorious. There were a great many similar ones—commanders removed from one position, only to be given another, and sometimes higher, one after using their influence at Court or Ministry. Radko-Dmitriev, removed from III Army in spring 1915, went to XII Army a few months later. Ruzski was a boneless wonder, three times appointed to command the northern front—the third time because the Tsar wished to remove Kuropatkin from it, but without making him feel that it was because he was too old. Ruzski, being older than Kuropatkin, could reassure him that he had been dismissed for inefficiency, not for age. Artamonov, of East Prussian fame, surfaced as governor of Przemyśl; both Pflug and Sievers got corps after losing armies. Langlois, the most acute of foreign observers, wrote this '*particularité curieusement fâcheuse*' down to *Stavka*'s not having power—able to dismiss, not to appoint. But this was not the whole story, as *Stavka* could arrange appointments. The difficulty came with the division between the front and the rear military authorities—the rear authorities, inheritors of Sukhomlinov, suspected, quite rightly, that their friends were being unfairly removed, just as *Stavka* suspected that, when its friends were removed by war ministry fiat, incompetence was not at all the whole story. When incompetent commanders slipped through, they did so by playing off one side against the other. When the system was challenged, the commanders could always retort that it was shortage of shell, or shortage of officers, and the low quality of the men that were responsible for defeat and retreat. In this way, the shell-shortage came to be an excuse for everything; and, even when the shortage was demonstrably less acute, the commanders still reacted—as they did after the Bessarabian affair—by blaming shortage of shell. A thousand rounds per gun could not be enough; there must be a great deal more before an offensive could be launched. In the meantime, elderly generals had a wonderful time inventing ways of winning the war. Kuropatkin, whose conduct of affairs in Manchuria had not been of the best, surfaced, after eighteen months' pulling of long faces to war ministry and *Stavka* alike, and was given command of the Grenadier corps. He distinguished himself by a suggestion that attack should be made at night, with the aid of search-lights—these would be shone, presumably to dazzling effect, in the Germans' eyes. The Russian attackers were silhouetted against their own lights; the corps lost 8,000 men in a night.

The last real effort by the old Russian army—as distinct from the new, which emerged in summer 1916 on Brusilov's front—was the offensive staged at Lake Narotch in March 1916. It was an affair that summed up all that was most wrong with the army. There had been talk of a spring offensive for some time—*Stavka* had felt that the results of Sventsiany in September 1915 justified a renewal of the offensive in this region; and the French were even told that it could well win the war outright. Now, the bulk of German troops had gone against France, had lost heavily at Verdun. Evert, commander of the western Front, was full of rather ill-defined pugnacity—though also, by one account, 'gaga' to the point of writing 'Mariya' for 'Armiya'. Moreover, the French had been told, in December, that if one ally was attacked, the others must launch immediate offensives to save it—an argument designed to save the Russian army from the isolation of summer 1915, and now turned against Russia. French appeals for help went out as soon as the German offensive began at Verdun. Alexeyev could not refuse his help. *Stavka* was now prisoner of its own arguments. Alexeyev had told Zhilinski to suggest that Russia was now strong enough to attack. Privately, he did not feel this at all—there had been delays in the re-organisation, and the army, now counting 1,700,000 men at the front—with 1,250,000 rifles—was not yet strong enough for offensive action. Evert, too, began to quail at the thought of attack once he was asked to bring his pugnacity to some concrete expression—no doubt he had, in the interim, read the south-western commanders' reports on the failure of their winter offensive, where a thousand guns with a thousand rounds each, and two-fold superiority of numbers, had failed to make much of a dent in the Austro-Hungarian lines. But not much could be done: an offensive would have to be staged for the benefit of the French. On 24th February—three days after the Germans launched their attack on Verdun—there was a conference in *Stavka*. The Russian superiority of numbers was now considerable—on the northern front, 300,000 to 180,000; on the western, 700,000 to 360,000 (917 battalions to 382) with 526 cavalry squadrons to 144; and on the south-western front, about half a million men on either side (684 Russian battalions to 592, and 492 squadrons to 239).

It was felt that the western front—Evert's—should attack. The shell-reserve had now been built up to 1,250 rounds for the 5,000 field guns, 540 for the 585 field-howitzers, and 685 rounds each for nearly a thousand guns—a force that, if concentrated, must surely bring great results. It would be Evert's duty to ensure concentration of this force. There were also, now, increasingly, rises in the number of battalions and divisions, of which there were 152 in March, 163½ in summer, with forty-seven cavalry divisions, later fifty. The area of attack[18] was much the same as in

September 1915—east of Vilna. The two army groups, Kuropatkin's and Evert's, must co-operate in attacking, one to the south-west against Vilna, the other due west from the line of lakes east of Vilna. The Russians' superiority was a considerable one—II Army, on the line of lakes, assembled 253 battalions and 233 squadrons of cavalry, over 350,000 men, with 605 light and 282 heavy guns—982 in all if two corps in reserve are included. There were ten army corps involved, over twenty divisions. The German X Army, here, had four and a half infantry divisions, subsequently built up to seven: 75,000 men, with 300 guns, subsequently built up to 440. It is, in the first place, notable enough that the Russian superiority at Lake Narotch—in men, guns, and shell (since each gun had a thousand rounds and more) was considerably greater than had been the Germans' superiority in May 1915 at Gorlice, or even in July 1915 on the Narev.

The difficulties came, as usual, with command and operations. In the first place, the promised co-operation of Kuropatkin's front did not come into much effect, beyond a feeble demonstration at Dvinsk that cost 15,000 men. II Army was commanded by General Smirnov, born in 1849, 'a soft old man with no distinction of any kind'. Usually, he played patience while Evert's chief of staff did the work; Evert, himself elderly, resisted attempts to have him dismissed by reason of age; and he was removed from command only just before the attack, to be replaced by the younger Ragoza—a man altogether unfamiliar with II Army, and subsequently replaced in turn by Smirnov. The corps were drawn up in groups, each commanded by the commander of one of the corps involved —as usual, on principles of seniority. In this case, the groups were taken by Pleshkov, Sirelius, Baluyev. Of Sirelius, Alexeyev wrote, 'It seems unlikely that he will be able to manage the bold and connected offensive action or the systematic execution of a plan that are needed.' But attempts to remove Sirelius broke down because, it is alleged, 'some old granny still has flutterings about the heart when his name comes up'.[19]

The offensive was carried out at a time of the year that could not have been less suitable if it had been chosen by the Germans. It opened on 18th March. The winter conditions had given way to those of early spring— alternating freezes and thaws that made the roads either an ice-rink or a morass. Shell would explode to little effect against ground that was either hard as iron or churned to a morass; gas was also ineffective in the cold. Supplies presented problems that the best-trained army would have found impossible to solve: the man-handling of boxes of heavy shell through slush that was a foot deep. The Russian rear was a scene of epic confusion—complicated by the astonishingly large masses of cavalry deployed there, to no effect whatsoever at the front. It was altogether an episode that suggests commanders had lost such wits as they still possessed.

Preparations had gone on for some time, or so Evert alleged. In practice, the Russians' positions were sketchy—some parts of their line were protected only by staves in the ground, and Kondratovitch, who inspected II Army's positions, said that, when snow fell, rifle-fire became impossible. 20. Corps was sited in a marshy region, with its rear in full view of German artillery. There had been almost no preparation of dug-outs[20]— nor, in view of the season, could there be. But the elderly commanders, their mental digestions still coping uneasily with the lessons of 1915, were in no condition to think things out. The Germans received a fortnight's warning of the offensive—it was even discussed by the cooks in Evert's headquarters three weeks before it began.

The attack began with bombardment on 18th March, the northernmost of the corps groups—Pleshkov's—leading off. Of all bombardments in the First World War, this was—with strong competition—the most futile. It was subsequently known as 'General Pleshkov's *son et lumière*'. A subsequent investigation of the artillery-affairs in this battle revealed that only in Baluyev's group had there been discussion between senior artillery and infantry officers on the ground—as distinct from maps—as to how things should go. Almost no reconnaissance had been conducted, so that the guns fired blind—on Pleshkov's front, they were even told to fire blind into a wood, behind which the Germans were thought to be. On Sirelius's front, the guns registered on their own infantry's trenches, in case the Germans came to occupy them. The guns were useless against German enfilading-positions and communications-trenches, since no-one knew with any accuracy where they were; even observation-posts for the guns were, as things turned out, vulnerable to machine-gun fire. It was only on 7th March that Pleshkov's artillery was told what to do, and the instructions were changed on 13th March, the guns having to be hauled over marsh and slush to new positions. A further peculiarity was that artillery was divided into light and heavy groups: the heavy artillery of Pleshkov's group was mainly concentrated in the hands of Zakutovski, the light artillery mainly in the hands of Prince Masalski, corps artillery commander. The two men quarrelled—Zakutovski believing that, as commander of the whole group's artillery, he should be giving the orders, while Masalski reckoned that, being commander of artillery in the corps mainly involved (1.), he should have the task. There was almost no co-operation between the two men; and shell-delivery became difficult enough, since heavy rounds would be delivered to Masalski, light ones to Zakutovski, and not released by them—even if the morass had allowed it. One Corps (1st Siberian) got half the shell it needed; another (1st) twice as much as it could use. This was more than a battle of competence. It reflected the poor state of relations between infantrymen and gunners,

Masalski protecting the one, and Zakutovski the other. In this way, many gunners' tasks were not carried out at all, and many duplicated. Light artillery tried to do the work of heavy, heavy of light.[21]

Pleshkov had supposed that a narrow concentration of guns—on two kilometres of his twenty-kilometre sector—would create a break-through. His guns fired off their 200 rounds per day, commanders feeling that a weight like this—after all, equivalent to three months' use of shell, as foreseen in 1914—could not go wrong. With four army corps on a front of twenty kilometres, against a German infantry division with one cavalry division, there ought not, in commanders' view, to be any difficulty. By sending in waves of infantry on two kilometres, Pleshkov merely gave the German artillery a magnificent target; and when, as happened, these occupied German trenches, they would be fired on from three sides by German guns on the sides of the salient—guns that had been registered previously on the trenches, which were found evacuated. One division attacked before the other, because of an error in telephone-messages; it even attacked, on 18th March, under its own bombardment, no doubt because liaison between Zakutovski and Masalski was so poor. A further corps assaulted the woods of Postawy, also in vain—German guns being concealed by the woods. In all, Pleshkov's group lost 15,000 men in the first eight hours of this offensive—three-quarters of the infantry mustered for attack, although fifteen per cent of Pleshkov's total force. On 19th March the attacks were continued, although trenches now filled with water as rain came, with a thaw. There were minor tactical successes—600 prisoners being taken—and losses of 5,000 in a few hours, equivalent to a whole brigade. On 21st March Pleshkov tried again, and even Kuropatkin stumbled forward. Each lost 10,000. In the rear, confusion—brought about mainly by the presence of 233 cavalry squadrons, who monopolised supplies and transport—was of crisis proportions, the hospital-trains breaking down, troops going hungry while meat rotted in depots. Over half of all orders were counter-manded.

The only success of any dimensions came on Baluyev's front, on Lake Narotch, where artillery and infantry had co-operated. At dawn on 21st March Baluyev attacked along the shores of Lake Narotch, using the ice, and helped by thick fog. His gunners sustained an artillery duel with the Germans, and a few square miles were taken, with some thousand prisoners. Sirelius, to the north, would not help at all, relapsing into cabbalistic utterance, and losing only one per cent of his force—through frost-bite. In the next few days, there were repeated attempts by Baluyev and Pleshkov; then the affair settled down to an artillery-duel. Later on, in April, the Germans took what they had lost. In all, they had had to move three divisions to face this attack, ostensibly, of 350,000 Russians. Not one of these came from the western front. The Russian army lost 100,000 men in this engagement—as well as 12,000 men who died of frostbite. The Germans claimed to have lifted 5,000 corpses from their wire. They themselves lost 20,000 men.

Lake Narotch was, despite appearances, one of the decisive battles of the First World War. It condemned most of the Russian army to passivity. Generals supposed that, if 350,000 men and a thousand guns, with 'mountains' of shell to use, had failed, then the task was impossible—unless there were extraordinary quantities of shell. Alexeyev himself made this point to Zhilinski, saying that the French Army itself demanded 4,200 rounds per light gun, and 600 per heavy gun,[22] before they would consider an offensive, and Russia had not these quantities. In practice, even Russia could have assembled such quantities on a given area of front had the generals managed their reserves properly. But they had no way of arranging sacrifices by one part of the front to the benefit of another; they did not understand the tactical problems; and, certainly, recognition of the extreme incompetence with which affairs had been combined in March, 1916 remained platonic. As before, artillery and infantry blamed each other, the only positive consequence being a demand for yet more shell. The way was open to *Upart's* demand for 4,500,000 rounds per month, and also to the eighteen million shells that were stock-piled, to no effect save, in the end, to enable the Bolsheviks to fight the Civil War. Now the western and northern army groups would have no stomach for attack. It was only the emergence of a general whose common-sense amounted to brilliance, and who selected a group of staff-officers who were almost a kernel of the Red Army, that gave the Russian army a great rôle in 1916.

CHAPTER ELEVEN

Summer, 1916

Lake Narotch paralysed much of the Russian army for the rest of the war. Both Evert and Kuropatkin now disbelieved in the possibility of breaking through at all—indeed, Kuropatkin resigned in despair, to go and practise against Central Asian rebels the military talents that had been of so little service against Germans. Evert stayed at his post, though disbelieving in his troops, his guns, his positions. Both of the fronts against Germany were now beset by crippling feelings of inferiority. If nearly 300,000 Russians had failed to defeat 50,000 Germans—figures that Alexeyev gave to Zhilinski—then the cause was lost in advance. Yet by now there was a superiority, on these two fronts, of almost 800,000 men. No-one had any idea as to how this might be used. Inevitably, the generals fell back on their standard excuse for failure—shell-shortage. Alexeyev told Zhilinski early in April that 'the latest details I have concerning shell-output, particularly for the heavier calibres, compose a quite hopeless picture, since our own production would not suffice even for a three-week operation'. The army would just have to sit back until enough heavy shell were produced to make an utter wreckage of even the best German positions. This was a dangerous illusion. Shell, even in the mountains assembled on the western front in 1916—the French used 10,500,000 rounds in some eighty-four days in the Verdun fighting— did not have decisive effect at all. But as news came into *Stavka* of the vast quantities assembled by the British and French for their summer offensive, Russian commanders grew ever more depressed. They could not compete with these mountains of shell; better therefore to do nothing. Then the British might send some more supplies.

But younger officers of the Russian army did have some notion that this pessimism was unnecessary. On the two fronts north of the Pripyat, they did not make much showing. But on the south-western front, their voices were heard. The south-western command did not altogether share the view that shell-shortage had caused defeat on the Strypa and on the Bessarabian border in December 1915. A report issued by Klembovski, chief of staff to this command, announced that 'It must be said that our constant complaints, to the effect that failure was brought about only by shortage of mortar and heavy shell, are far from being invariably correct'.[1] In one case, twelve shells had been used per square yard of front, and 700 rounds per gun in a day. Shelling had even been counter-productive— ploughing into a morass the ground that infantry had to cross; and in any case they had had too much ground to cross, since the attackers had often started from a mile away, with predictable effects. Preparation of the attack was much more important than the simple strewing of shell. In the early months of 1916, these officers began to get control of the south-western front. In the first place, Ivanov was removed from command in April, his place taken by Brusilov. It is notable that officers of this front, in particular, formed a strong kernel of the Red Army in 1918–19. Brusilov, who had begun life as a scion of south-Russian gentry, married a cousin of Stolypin's and Izvolski's, and studied in the Tsar's corps of pages, ended up as inspector-general of Trotski's cavalry. Klembovski, corps commander in 1914, Velichko, engineering-chief of the front Karbyshev, chief engineer of VIII Army, Kirey, senior artillerist of IX, and a large number of the divisional commanders and chiefs of staff all took prominent places in the Red Army, a mark of the Bolsheviks' considerable ability to attract all that was best in the Tsarist army, elements, that in *Stavka*'s day, were sacrificed to the attitudinisers and the senile.

A new Russian army was coming into existence, one where modest and sensible technicians were coming to power, men who could use the immensely promising natural qualities of the Russian soldier. Yet its emergence in 1916 broke a Tsarist pattern of much durability, and the dismissal of Ivanov, and his replacement by Brusilov, is a remarkable enough occurrence in the circumstances. Ivanov was a powerful figure in the army—associated with Sukhomlinov, yet careful to keep his links with the Grand Ducal side; in Lemke's phrase, 'a diplomat pretending to be a peasant'.[2] But he, too, was something of a 'great poster'—supposed to be very popular with his men, no doubt kept on for that reason. Alexeyev had no faith in him; and after the Strypa failure, his position weakened very greatly. He fought to retain his command—decorating the little Tsarevich for inspecting the wounded, dismissing a succession of chiefs of staff. The Tsar was persuaded to release him in spring 1916, and Brusilov arrived in Berdichev to take over the front—Ivanov sobbing throughout dinner. He went to *Stavka*—'Ivanov has become a complete old granny and needs doping'—and sat ostentatiously in his motor-car as conferences went on, until in the end the Tsar appointed him 'adviser', and included him in the *Stavka* deliberations. In March 1917, because of his alleged popularity with the masses, he was entrusted with pacification of Petrograd—not a successful venture.

The removal of Ivanov was a sign that, as far as questions of command went, a new type of officer was emerging. In the south-western command, sense and modesty prevailed. Brusilov himself is something of a surprise in this context. He had been a very successful commander since 1914, taking VIII Army and at times being responsible for the whole of the Carpathian front. Before 1914, he had clearly been intelligent and agile in exploiting the promotions-system to arrive at high command without falling foul either of the cavalry-General Staff clique or of the war ministry clique: of course his social origins helped. He shared with Count Ignatiev—military attaché in Paris, Guards officer, and then Red major-general—an ability to cut free of class-considerations, and to identify in good time which side would be the stronger; he had a gift of choosing able subordinates, and to enforce their will on recalcitrant conservatives. Himself unmistakably, and in the end fatally, part of the world of 1914, he none the less had enough of the new Russia to him for its elements to break through in the front under Brusilov's command. A new style came at once to the headquarters in Berdichev. Headquarters was a small building with a mere two sentries at the door. Right away, a new style came to front orders—crisp, organised prose in place of Evert's meandering literature.[3]

On 14th April Alexeyev summoned a meeting of the front staffs in Mogiliev. The French and British had demanded some Russian help in the summer, and this meeting was to discuss what form such help should take. Ostensibly, it should be considerable—there were now 1,700,000 men with rifles, and soon, with the arrival of the new conscript classes, the overall superiority would rise to 745,000, on the front north of the Pripyat, and 132,000 south of the Pripyat. Alexeyev himself said, 'We are capable of decisive attack only on the front north of the Pripyat',[4] and put forward a plan not unlike that of March—double offensive from the Dvina and the front of II and X Armies. Neither Evert nor Kuropatkin agreed. Kuropatkin said, 'It is quite improbable that we could break through the German front, the lines of which have been strongly fortified and so developed that success is hardly imaginable'. Evert remarked, 'Without superiority in heavy artillery, there is no chance of success'. In the end, Evert was pushed into agreement. He would take a very small area, send in two waves, each of three corps, assemble almost all of the thousand heavy guns behind his front, and take two months over preparations. The front of attack would be no greater than twenty kilometres. Even so, he was not happy.

The gathering was heartened by Brusilov. He said he would attack in the summer, that he would need only trivial reinforcements in men and guns. Kuropatkin 'looked at me and shrugged his shoulders, in pity'. Brusilov was told to go ahead, although, since he had not much superiority of any kind—except leadership—over the Austrians, no-one expected from his offensive much more than a tactical success, and quite possibly only a repetition of the Strypa failures. Yet Brusilov's team had come up with new ideas that made for the most brilliant victory of the war. They had studied the failures of December and January, which—as Zayonchkovski says—served something of the same purpose as the Russo-Japanese war had done. In reality, the Russo-Japanese war had led men often enough merely to a more vigorous repetition of the same views as before, whereas Brusilov's command seems to have thought things out radically. Whatever the reason, these men came onto methods that were used—without acknowledgment—by Ludendorff in 1918, and then by Foch. To some degree, these new methods were forced on Brusilov by his very weakness. He could not hope for a crushing superiority of shell, and so had to think things out in other terms; in a sense, he had an advantage of backwardness, of being forced to move from 1915 to 1918 without passing through the stage of sacrificial *Materialschlachten* between them.

The military problems of the First World War consisted of a number of circles to be squared. A successful offensive needed both surprise and preparation. These were incompatible: preparation of millions of men and horses took so long that surprise was impossible. In the same way, mobility and weight could not be reconciled. A huge weight of guns could be assembled. The enemy might be defeated. Then the guns could not be moved forward. In other words, armies would be mobile only if they had not the weight to make their mobility worthwhile. Brusilov's staff noted that, in a break-through operation, there were too main problems—the break-through itself, and the exploitation of it. These demanded almost contradictory solutions. A break-through could only, it seemed, be achieved by assembly of great weight—enough shell to knock down thick belts of barbed-wire, destroy concrete enfilading-posts, dominate the enemy guns, destroy the defenders. But assembling this weight of guns and shell—and of course hundreds of thousands of men—would mean that the enemy knew what to expect, and when: just before Lake Narotch, for instance, German pilots had had no difficulty in spotting the long columns of Russian infantry marching through the snow towards the west. The defence would know where to put reserve-troops. Consequently, even if the break-through were achieved, the attackers would stumble onto a new line, not reconnoitred, with their own lines of supply complicated, crossing shell-torn ground known to the enemy, while the attackers' artillery would be too far behind. Counter-attacks would follow; enemy artillery to right and left would enfilade the attackers in the area of break-through and the attack would collapse, despite its initial tactical success. This had happened on the Strypa in December.

The essential difficulty was that attackers were not sufficiently mobile. The internal combustion engine could not be used for front-line purposes. Certainly, by 1917, tanks were in use on the western front. But, unless the enemy were surprised, and to some degree also demoralised, they were not effective enough. They moved too slowly—five miles per hour—and were vulnerable, at that slow pace, to well-handled field artillery. They tended to break down, or to stick in mud (it is notable that, in eastern European conditions, cavalry could be more effective than tanks, as was shown in the Russian civil war, and to some extent also in the Russo-Polish war of 1920); in the Nivelle offensive of spring 1917, half of the tank crews were grilled alive, such that Ludendorff wrote off tanks as a fancy civilians' scheme of no value. In other words, there seemed no alternative to the horse—hence the clutter of cavalry squadrons that waited in attacking armies' rear, complicating supply to an intolerable extent, merely as insurance against the event of break-through. But the horse was too vulnerable except against armies that had been so badly demoralised that they surrendered as soon as a Cossack *sotnya* appeared to whom surrender might be made.

In the circumstances, there seemed no solution at all except 'attrition'— to attack the enemy where he could be hit hardest, where he would be obliged to fight, i.e. his strongest point—and then make him lose many thousands of men by heavy bombardment. This was the method chosen by Falkenhayn in summer, 1915, and executed particularly by Mackensen. A great phalanx would be assembled in the central part of the front, with thousands of shells for up to a thousand guns—Gorlice; Radymno; Krasnostaw; Przasnysz. The validity of this method had been impressed on Russian commanders in the most direct possible way, and most of them now could only think of producing some imitation of the German phalanx-system. Shcherbachev had tried it on the Strypa, and Pleshkov had tried it at Postawy. Now Evert had much the same in mind for the summer offensive. It was certainly true that these methods more or less announced in advance that attack was coming, and gave the enemy time to move up reserves, if he had any (as the Russians believed, in 1915, that they had not, at least none with sufficient mobility). Consequently, the break-through operation would have to be attempted again, as Mackensen had seen.

In December and March, the Russians had failed with these methods. Of these failures, various interpretations were possible. On the south-western front, the view was taken, by Brusilov though not by some of his subordinates, that the break-through operation had failed precisely because strength had been too narrowly concentrated. Pflug, commanding 2. Corps on Shcherbachev's front, had attacked on a single kilometre of front; Pleshkov in March had really attacked only on a front of two kilometres, out of twenty. The theory, here, had been that a great weight of concentrated shelling would at least remove anything living from the small space involved—which was usually true enough—and that the Russian army did not have shell for more than two or three kilometres of front to be the object of such concentrated fire. It needed 400 heavy shells to tear a gap of fifty yards on three-strand barbed-wire, or 25,000 light shells; and when Austro-German wire was stepped up to nineteen or twenty strands, as came to be the case late in 1915, with not one but three different belts, the quantity of shell became literally incalculable, the more so as heavy artillery was not particularly accurate. Officers thought that only an extreme concentration of fire could bring results. In December, this had proved to be true: two, three Austro-Hungarian trench-lines would be occupied. But, in a small area like this, the attackers became highly vulnerable to enemy artillery to right and left, since it could rake them from both sides and front, while they were un-protected, and their supply-lines, reserve-lines and the rest were open to bombardment. Yet to deal with this problem—enfilading fire—seemed to demand a contradictory solution—attack on a front sufficiently broad that troops breaking through would not be within range of guns to right and left—in other words, a front of at least thirty kilometres. But a front of this length could not be broken through, since there would not be enough shell—or so the theory ran. Most commanders preferred to believe that the break-through operations had failed for a variety of other causes—not enough shell in particular; reserves not moved into support fast enough; troops lacking in 'elan', and so on. Each of these had sufficient validity to be convincing to many experienced observers. But they were far from being the whole truth.

Brusilov and his staff came up with good answers to all of this. It was, first, vital to disrupt the enemy's reserves—his local reserves and his frontal ones. When the break-through came, the attackers would not therefore have to face the resistance and counter-attack of fresh troops. This could be achieved, first, by surprise—the enemy must be caught off his guard. Preparation must be concealed as far as possible—if it had to be done, it must proceed along the whole length of the front. Then, there must not be one single attack, but several, at more or less the same time, so that the enemy would not know where to expect the main blow. As regards the problem of breaking-through, the blows must be delivered along a front of not less than thirty kilometres, so as to avoid the problem of enfilading-fire. Reserves must be brought close to the front line, hidden in great, deep dug-outs ('*platsdarmy*') with excellent communications to the front line. When troops got through a breach in the wire, they must be immediately followed by reserves. The artillery must co-operate closely with infantry—gunners living in the front trenches, carefully studying the problems, getting to know the infantry officers involved. There was one drawback to this method—that it entailed not assembling huge forces of infantry and cavalry at any point, so as not to draw the enemy's attention to the point of attack. If a break-through came, it could not be exploited very greatly. Moreover, Brusilov not only failed to make use of cavalry, but seems even to have forbidden more than a division or two to take part in his offensive, at least on the main front, near Lutsk. He lost mobility, though no doubt gained endlessly better supply-arrangements.

The preparation ordered by Brusilov's staff was thorough beyond anything hitherto seen on the eastern front. The front-trenches were sapped forward, in places to within fifty paces of the enemy lines—at that, on more or less the entire front. Huge dug-outs for reserve-troops were constructed, often with earth ramparts high enough to prevent enemy gunners from seeing what was going on in the Russian rear. Accurate models of the Austrian trenches were made, and troops trained with them; aerial photography came into its own, and the position of each Austrian battery noted—an innovation, since on the other fronts pilots were not given any training in aerial photography at all. The fact, too, that reserve-troops were under the same command for a number of months also helped organisation—another comparative rarity.

Preparation of this intensity was comparatively rare on the Russian front. According to Klembovski, on most of the other front-sectors, communications-trenches were primitive; there were not even notice-boards showing where troops should go. In some areas, foreign observers were astonished to find gaps of three miles between the enemy lines, on occasion even with inhabited villages in no-man's-land. It took much pressure from Brusilov himself to make sure that subordinates undertook novel work of the type he had in mind; and Brusilov himself appears to have been the best type of commander—striking the fear of God into his subordinates, but never to the point where they became terrified of responsibility. He was himself a tireless worker, but not one like Alexeyev —for whom work became an end in itself. He and his staff paid continual visits to the very front lines, again a considerable rarity, although Brusilov, as the example of 1917 was to show, lacked the common touch. He had to deal with innumerable objections from his subordinates. Kaledin, commanding VIII Army, showed little stomach for action; Lechitski, of IX Army, complained continually of poor heavy artillery; Shcherbachev, one of the cavalry-General Staff would-be imitators of French methods, also had his own schemes and grumbled at Brusilov's challenge to French supremacy. Only, perhaps, Sakharov of XI Army had much sympathy with what Brusilov was attempting. For Brusilov to force, not only the three dissenting army commanders, but also the dissenting Alexeyev, to accept his methods shows tactical skills of an unusually high order. By mid-May preparation was complete.[5]

The Russian plan was for four separate attacks to be made, by each of the armies on the entire front; and the front of attack was not to be less than thirty kilometres. The plan seemed impossible—what had eluded a single, immensely strong group on one short front was now to be attempted by four much weaker groups on longer fronts. Overall, the Russian superiority was not at all marked. Brusilov reckoned it at 132,000 men. In terms of divisions, it was a superiority of insignificant proportions—forty infantry and fifteen cavalry divisions to thirty eight and a half and eleven, 1,770 light and 168 heavy guns to 1,301 light and 545 medium and heavy. There were over 600,000 Russian soldiers to about 500,000 Austro-Germans. The separate armies certainly lacked decisive superiority of any kind. VIII Army, which had the main task of breaking through towards Lutsk, had fifteen divisions to thirteen, 640 light guns to 375 and 76 heavy guns to 174. On other fronts, the Russian superiority barely existed at all. IX Army had ten infantry and four cavalry divisions to nine and four, 448 light and forty-seven heavy guns to 350 and 150, VII Army with seven infantry and three cavalry divisions was roughly equal to the defenders, while XI Army was actually weaker than them in all ways. Brusilov, seemingly, would merely bombard for a short while and then his troops would walk forward. It is true that, for light shell, there were now no alarms. VIII Army had 2,000 rounds per gun—160,000 light and 40,000 heavy shells surplus to a requirement of 100 rounds per day, and there were also 52,000 Japanese shells. IX Army had a similar surplus of light shell—87,000. Austro-Hungarian guns are reckoned to have had 400 rounds apiece, though in the confusion many of these were not fired. Certainly, such quantities of shell were much less than had been present in March, 1916. The enemy line was also very strong. Alexeyev raised continual alarms, up to the last moment begging Brusilov to attack only on one front,[7] at that shortening his front of attack to twenty kilometres. Kaledin seemed near the verge of break-down at times, and Brusilov had again and again to go to Rovno to put heart into him. Lechitski, for IX Army, rose from his sick-bed aghast at what had been done in his name and protested that he would have to face 100,000 Austro-Hungarians with 'an extremely insignificant quantity of heavy artillery'. It is curious, and significant, to note that the Austro-Hungarian commander subsequently put down his immense defeat in this area to 'enemy heavy artillery of undreamed-of effect'[8] of which there was 'a huge superiority'. None the less, attacks were set by Brusilov to begin on 4th June.

The great victory that followed was simply put down by all observers to the low quality of the Austro-Hungarian army. Victories against these troops could not have any lessons for the serious belligerent states, any more than victories over Neapolitan troops in the nineteenth century could. The opinion was widely-held in Germany—beginning, of course, with Falkenhayn. But it was also, most curiously, put about by the Austro-Hungarian official historians; and similarly Berndt, chief of staff in IV Army, reckoned that 'the main cause' of defeat was the surprisingly low fighting quality of the troops.[9] The Slav soldiers are held to have surrendered at once: an opinion, naturally enough, supported by Slav propagandists. Conrad himself was usually too loyal to blame his own men for letting him down; but he slipped all too easily into such talk when the situation required.

But what was said later does not at all accord with what was said at the time, by the units involved. Neither IV nor VII Army—which faced the greatest defeats—show the slightest record of shell-shortage in June 1916. More surprisingly, there is not the slightest indication in either force of fear for the morale or the fighting qualities of the men—at divisional level, or at corps or army level. There had of course been worries before, in September 1915 particularly. In May 1916, there appears to be not the slightest alarm.[10] The incidence of desertion was less than normal, and in any case trivial—from 15th to 30th April, for instance, losses came to 439 killed and wounded men, 2,476 sick, thirty-nine missing, for an army of over 100,000 combatants. Yet on one day there had been 129 Russian deserters, which appears to have been the rule. The sick-lists could be an important indication of morale. It is true that the command of IV Army noted, on 22nd April, 'the surprisingly high sick-lists' of 10. Corps (Martiny) and 2. Corps (Kaiser)—1,048 in 10. Corps in the first half of April. But these ran down again as the spring drizzles gave way to summer —losses of all types, in this force of 30,000 men, came to 689 in the first half of May, 674 in the second half. Far from being alarmed about its troops, IV Army command recorded in mid-May that 'reports on the troops' fighting qualities read relatively favourably'; and an order of the high command itself singled out a largely Czech unit, 25. infantry division, as an example of how commanders could, with the help of priests, 'ethically influence' their troops. IV Army was offered more of such 'appropriate clergymen', but turned down the offer. If morale was as bad as subsequently made out, then clearly the commanders were not doing their jobs. As things were, sick-lists, soldiers' letters, discipline in general seem to have offered few signs for alarm—at least, none were reported. It could of course be that alarms were not reported by divisional and regimental officers so as to avoid trouble, discredit. But on the whole it seems unlikely. The truth of the matter seems to be that if such troops were ably commanded, they fought well. If they were not ably commanded, then they collapsed much more than other troops might have done—partly because of the language gap, partly because of the class-gap between officer and man. In the outcome, it was probably easier for Ruthenes to surrender since they knew they might expect favourable treatment at Russian hands. But the heart of the matter was leadership.

What is much more evident in the records of the defeated Austrian forces than concern for morale is the almost Spanish-Habsburg combination of serenity and incompetence they reveal. There were of course innumerable reports of impending Russian action—the arrival of troops was noted perfectly accurately on the Austrian side, despite Brusilov's precautions. Deserters announced, for instance, two days before the attack that clean underclothing had been issued—the event that had made them desert. Austrian pilots noted the construction of Russian dug-outs, the famous *platsdarmy* for reserves. In particular, the units reported continual Russian sapping-forward, as, following Brusilov's instructions, Russian trenches were being brought to within seventy-five paces of the Austrian front line. What is curious is the Austrian units' failure to stop this sapping, which, evidently, would give the attacker an advantage. Commanders seem to have reported when they stopped it, not when it continued—no doubt for fear they would be driven into troublesome minor actions. Indeed, IV Army command and the command of *Heeresgruppe Linsingen* seem to have learned of one or two quite large-scale events from the Russian press—which called down a severe reprimand from Linsingen, and subsequently also IV Army command, that 'reports should be accurate and detailed'. It is no doubt this failure to stop Russian sapping that brought losses to such trivial figures in May—not 500 men killed and wounded in a force of over 100,000 men that should have been stopping Russian night-work and patrolling. Perhaps, too, this holiday-camp atmosphere had something to do with the drop in desertions.

Certainly, the affairs of the Austro-Hungarian IV Army command were conducted in a spirit of wonderful frivolity. The chief of staff, Berndt, left a diary that is very revealing.[11] He had been put in this command, under Archduke Joseph Ferdinand—godson of Emperor Franz Joseph—

much against his will. After the catastrophe before Rovno in September 1915, Conrad had wanted to dismiss Archduke Joseph Ferdinand.[12] But he had—for obvious reasons—been given such prominence in army communiqués that Conrad would have lost some credibility had he dismissed the Archduke. Instead, he dismissed Paić, the chief of staff, and moved in Berndt, in whom he had faith. The Archduke subjected poor Berndt, to continual slights—would not use the same automobile as Berndt, preferring to drive with the automobile-officer, 'the Jew, Strauss', gossiped and joked with subalterns at the expense of senior officers, treated horses with savagery, making low conversation at table before a prudish Berndt and still more disapproving German officers. He surrounded himself with aristocratic playboys—his brother Heinrich, Prince René of Bourbon-Parma and *Kommandant* Graf Berchtold, son of the foreign minister—of whom Berndt pertinently observed, 'That the foreign minister who began this war has got his son taken out of its dangers, is painful'. The Archduke's relations with his German superior officer, Linsingen, were extremely tense. He resented Linsingen's position. On 26th February he was gazetted 'Colonel-General'—hence superior to Linsingen, no longer subject to the army group commander's orders, and likely to take over the group himself. 'Like lightning' there came back a German response—Linsingen also promoted Colonel-General (*Generaloberst*), the appointment pre-dated to 20th February. Linsingen's chief of staff, Stolzmann, turned up to inspect IV Army. Archduke Joseph Ferdinand objected to his 'snuffling around' and took him, through heavy rain, in an open motor-car. Then he went on a three-day hunting trip, in a boat along the river Styr, with his brother. All this reflected vast confidence in the strength of the defences built up since autumn 1915. There were three positions, each with three trenches. The dug-outs were buttressed with concrete, the officers' quarters even had windows. There were concrete enfilading-points for machine-guns. Stolzmann turned up in Teschen to report to Conrad just before the Russian attack opened. The Russians had no numerical superiority; 'they attack quite stupidly in thick masses, and they can't possibly succeed this time'. Linsingen similarly explained to the German Kaiser that 'our formidable positions' would 'automatically hold' against an enemy 'of the present strength'. Even an 'Anfangserfolg' was 'impossible'.[13]

The truth was that the Austrians had passed into a mood of almost grandiose confidence. By the middle of 1916, old tunes were being played in Vienna; in Teschen, Conrad's headquarters, the voices of Prince Eugene and Radetzky were once more heard—the Prussians snubbed, the Balkans ruled, the Poles about to join the Habsburg Empire. An expedition against northern Italy was almost automatically the outcome of this mood, and it was towards this that Austrian efforts were now bent. It produced a fatal diversion of the Central Powers' war-effort, from which Brusilov could greatly profit.

The Central Powers' alliance had begun to weaken towards the end of the Serbian campaign, late in 1915. Conrad had been irritated that Germany took such preponderance in the area; he resented depending on Bulgaria, feared Bulgarian ambitions in Albania and elsewhere, and even considered making a separate peace with the Serbians in order to contain these ambitions. Falkenhayn was not concerned, and also rejected a plan of Conrad's for invading Greece, capturing Salonica. All he wanted to achieve, from the military viewpoint, was some kind of passable situation in the Balkans; while indirect German control over Bulgaria, perhaps even of Albania through Bulgaria, suited him politically much better than direct Austrian control of anything. The two powers also quarrelled over matters of peace. The Germans hoped to win the war outright. This meant an offensive in the west. The Austrians were not nearly so pledged to this end—on the contrary, an outright German victory would worry them almost as much as an outright allied victory. They were in much the same position as Italy in 1942, 'if England wins, we lose; if Germany wins, we are lost'. They took a quite different view of the military situation. Conrad and Tisza agreed, at the turn of the year, that 'There can be no question of destroying the Russian war-machine; England cannot be defeated; peace must be made in not too long a space, or we shall be fatally weakened, if not destroyed'.[14]

But when the Austrians charged off in the direction of peace, as they frequently did throughout the war, they were always brought up short on the Italian rope. Italy was the major enemy as far as almost all the peoples of the Habsburg Empire were concerned. Czechs, Germans, Slovenes, Croats were alike enthusiastic to fight Italian pretensions—indeed, the popular enthusiasm among Slav peoples such as the Slovenes for war with Italy was such that even the army authorities were on occasion embarrassed, fearing that the formation, for instance of Slovene volunteer groups using Slovene national colours, was a hidden prelude to some challenge to the German character of much of the army. The heroic defence of the frontier against Italy had given the peoples of the Monarchy a cause that united them as no other did; as in 1848, an Italian campaign could do much to settle internal discontents, to make the Austrian army genuinely popular. It was not surprising that Conrad should have profited from the long months of inactivity in winter 1915–16 to plan an attack on Italy, intending it no doubt as prelude to some acceptable peace. He could not hope for superiority of numbers, but he could assemble sufficient force in the north-western sector of the front for some break-through to be thinkable: Austrian troops would emerge from the mountains of the north-west, and cut off much of the Italian army on the northern and north-eastern sectors of the Italian front, particularly the attackers of the Isonzo. Contrary to legend, he did not detach for the Italian offensive significant numbers of men and guns from the eastern front. But he did remove a few of his better-class brigades and some heavy artillery; in particular, he diverted much shell to the Italian front, where each gun now had to have over a thousand rounds in its immediate reserve. He neglected to strengthen the eastern front as the Russians were strengthening it.

But what mattered more than this was the almost complete diversion of Germany from the Austro-Hungarian part of the Russian front. Late in 1915, Falkenhayn had decided to resume German attacks in the west. He knew that Germany could not win the three-front war; there was only one way of making an acceptable peace, to weaken England's will to win, which he regarded as the motor of the enemy coalition. This could be achieved if he could knock out 'the sword of England on the continent' —the French army. But a straight-forward break-through operation in the west would not work. Falkenhayn adopted the plan he had used with such effect in the east, in summer 1915. He would attack a point where the French army could not afford retreat—in this case, Verdun—and assemble a huge force of heavy artillery that would bleed the French army white. German attacks would be designed merely to force the French to bring up more and more reserves, to be pulverised by the heavy artillery, perhaps also forced into costly counter-attacks. It was a method that owed much to German experience of summer 1915 on the Russian front. Falkenhayn's analysis was also perceptive. The French would not carry out the retreat the situation demanded of them: they behaved as Falkenhayn had predicted, and lost much more heavily, in the first six weeks of the Verdun campaign, than the Germans did—almost the only case in the First World War where the ostensible defenders lost more heavily than the attackers. But the analysis went wrong in so far as Falkenhayn under-rated French capacity to resist, for the French army brilliantly survived the bleeding-white that Falkenhayn had prepared; moreover, the British, far from having their will to win weakened, merely brought in armies of their own for the summer offensive of 1916. The offensive had begun on 21st February; by early April, it was clear that, while Falkenhayn might cause the French high losses, Germany would lose very greatly in terms of prestige, since Verdun had held out so well. Falkenhayn allowed himself to be dragged by the local army commanders into attempting a break-through operation at Verdun, again and again, such that German losses began to exceed French ones—and still Verdun held. Falkenhayn was drawn into a costly blunder, not unlike the pattern of late summer 1915, when he had also been drawn into the Sventsiany-Vilna affair against his better judgment. This was not a war in which generals with limited aims could, in the end, make the pace.

The diversion of Germany's effort to the western front was much more important, in the eastern context, than Conrad's Italian venture. There was an almost complete withdrawal of German support for the Austrian front against Russia,[15] and the front against Russia, overall, was weakened greatly. In August 1915 there had been as many as twenty German divisions (to around forty Austrian) on the front south of the Pripyat. After August, Falkenhayn demanded most of them back, and left only a token force—82. reserve and 48. reserve. But at the same time German commanders still controlled much more of the front than these numbers warranted—Linsingen's Army Group accounted for the Austrian IV Army and troops to the north (including 82. reserve division) and *Südarmee* still controlled, with the German Bothmer as commander, a section of eastern Galicia. Falkenhayn would probably have removed such German forces as he left on the Austro-Hungarian front, had it not been for his interest in maintaining these German commands. Even so, he successfully demanded that Conrad should leave equivalent forces on the German side of the front—the two divisions of the Austro-Hungarian 12. Corps, operating under Woyrsch's command to the north of Linsingen's army group. There was even a suggestion that Austrian troops should go to the Vosges—a suggestion not taken up until the summer of 1918, when Austro-Hungarian forces did arrive in the west, having to be given boots by the German command in Metz. These removals mattered more than the removal of six Austro-Hungarian divisions from the Russian front. The Austrians would be deprived of the vital German support, and there was only a vague agreement, late in May, that troops from the other parts of the eastern front might be sent to Linsingen's front if required. Relations between Conrad and Falkenhayn were very tense. Conrad complained, as ever, that the Germans were 'brutal, shameless, ruthless'.[16] He resented being told so little of Verdun, and resented even more the little he was told. Falkenhayn's disapproval of the Austrian offensive against Italy annoyed him, and for some time there had been such coolness in relations that Conrad was driven to send a letter of apology—the text of which has never been seen again. At bottom, the Austrians did not want to face the total war Germany now prepared to fight; at the same time, they could see no alternative to it—they too could now see that a 'neutral' peace would mean the end of the Monarchy. For better or worse this meant alliance to the bitter end with imperial Germany.

Neither Conrad nor Falkenhayn worried very much over the Austrian front in the east. It was known that two-thirds of the Russian army had concentrated against the German front, and that forces in the southern sector were roughly in balance. Overall, Conrad reckoned there were eighty-eight German and Austrian divisions to between 127 and 130 (with six others in the interior of Russia), with forty-nine German and Austrian divisions on the German front, to eighty-five Russian, and thirty-nine Austrian ones on the front south of the Pripyat—that controlled by Conrad—to thirty-nine or so Russian divisions. Correctly enough, no great change was noted in Russian dispositions before June 1916. Conrad went on with confidence. He set great hopes in his Italian offensive. His troops were groomed for a great victory. But the snow caused some postponement, and the offensive did not get under way until mid-May. Once it did get under way, results were impressive. The Italians laid out their defences mistakenly—they held the mountains, while the Austrians resolutely went forward in the valleys, causing one mountain position after another to collapse from inanition. By the end of May, 380 guns and 40,000 prisoners had been taken, and the Austrians had reached the plateau of Arsiero-Asiago, almost on the edge of the mountains—about, it seemed, to emerge and cut off the retreat of huge Italian forces on the Isonzo to the north-east.

This Austrian offensive caused Alexeyev in the end to shelve his doubts as to Brusilov's methods. From 20th May, a series of appeals from Italy[17] reached *Stavka*, 'each more peremptory in tone than the last'. Joffre, through Laguiche at *Stavka*; the Italian representative there; the Italian embassy in Petrograd; finally the King of Italy in a personal telegram to the Tsar prevailed on Alexeyev. It seemed that only an immediate Russian offensive could help Italy; and if Italy dropped out of the war, then large numbers of Austrian divisions would be free to take up the battle against Russia. Alexeyev grumbled; he told Joffre that the situation was surely better than Italians said; in any case, the western Powers were supposed to attack on the Somme, and this would bring relief. 'With our ineradicable weakness in heavy artillery the execution of an immediate, unprepared attack cannot promise success and would only lead to the disruption of our plan in general.'[18] Evert, of course, would do nothing. In the end, Alexeyev had to ask Brusilov; and Brusilov agreed to attack at once, asking only for one corps more, to arrive after the offensive had opened. Alexeyev called him on Hughes' apparatus and asked him to lessen the area of attack. Brusilov refused: he had confidence enough in his methods, felt at least they ought to be tried. Kaledin, Lechitski, Shcherbachev were also over-borne—the first two suffering from extreme nervousness, the other from a desire to imitate French methods too closely, on a relatively narrow front. Brusilov, showing a detailed knowledge of their fronts that took them by surprise, refuted their arguments. The offensive was to begin on 4th June with bombardments on the front of all four armies: VIII Army with the main blow, on the front in Volhynia between Rovno and Lutsk; XI to the south, at Sopanów where a bridgehead over the river Turya offered a convenient jump-off point; VII in eastern Galicia, on the roads west of Tarnopol; IX on the Dniester, and near the Romanian border.

Alexeyev had ordered, on 31st May, 'a powerful auxiliary attack on the Austrians . . . the main blow being delivered, later, by the troops of the western front'. But the supposed 'auxiliary' attack succeeded far beyond expectations, and certainly—as happened quite often in the First World War—far beyond the supposed 'main blow'. This was, for a start, because enemy reserves had been disrupted. The Germans had drawn their troops against the northern and western fronts. The Austrians had of course sent six divisions to their Italian front, and beyond this had only two divisions that could be shuttled from one part of their eastern front to the other—both being sent, at first, to the wrong place. Moreover, Brusilov's attack—being launched in four different places—caused great confusion with reserves, and first two, then four divisions spent their time going from one rear-area to the other, never even being engaged. There was, in particular, to be great confusion of reserves between Volhynia and the Dniester, contributing largely to the ineffectiveness of their intervention. Even tactically, within the area of each separate army— except in the case of VII Army—there was confusion of local reserves, since the fronts of attack were long, and reserves were either engaged in the wrong place or not engaged at all—being swallowed up in calamity before they could even retire, and staging at best an ineffective, piece-meal counter-attack. From this point of view, Brusilov's methods were a brilliant success.

But the first task was to break through. The Austro-Hungarian lines were strong, and VIII Army, with 704 guns, was not significantly superior to the Austro-Hungarian IV Army, with 600; nor was the superiority in man-power—200,000 to 150,000—of much moment in a war of fire-power. The corps of VIII Army were drawn up on a long front—almost thirty miles for the three central ones, 39., 8. and 40., which had over half of the guns and some 100 battalions between them. Also, in much offence to orthodoxies of the First World War, these corps did not have anything like an overwhelming weight of heavy artillery—206 field guns, forty-four field-howitzers, four Austrian medium howitzers, forty-four heavy howitzers and twenty-two heavy cannon (42-cm.). The defence, with 600 guns and thirteen divisions, was absolutely, and of course relatively, much stronger than at Lake Narotch in March, where II Army, with a third more guns, had faced half those of the Austrian IV Army, and less than half the numbers of that army.

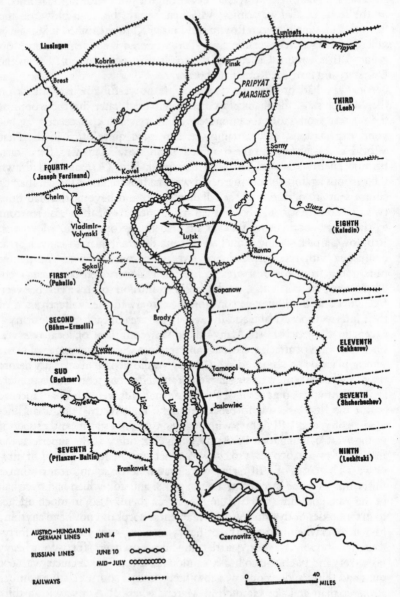

The Brusilov campaign.

The break-through succeeded by virtue of careful preparation.[19] The guns knew what to achieve; they knew their targets; they co-operated with the infantry; reserves were hidden very close to the line in great dug-outs, and further reserves had a whole network of communications-trenches, duly sign-posted, along which they could move; the front lines were only seventy-five yards away from the Austrian ones; Russian guns operated no further off than two kilometres—all an innovation as far as Russian operations were concerned. On 4th June, the Austrians were astonished to discover that the Russians had even tunnelled below their own wire-obstacles—'the first time they have been so thorough, for previously, when they meant to attack, they took the obstacles away themselves'. Now Brusilov was determined on surprise, and he unquestionably succeeded in some degree. On 4th June the Russian bombardment had much success. The Austrian artillery was either silenced in the opening phase, or its gun-teams ran out of shell in an effort to persuade the Russians that they had a great deal. The forward trenches were levelled, and even some of the dug-outs knocked in by heavy shells. Fifty-one ways were opened in the wire opposite the three main corps of VIII Army. An Austrian investigator subsequently discovered that 'there was drum-fire of hitherto unequalled intensity and length which in a few hours shattered and levelled our carefully-constructed trenches'. Chaos had broken out: 'Apart from the bombardment's destruction of wire obstacles, the entire zone of battle was covered by a huge, thick cloud of dust and smoke, often mixed with heavy explosive-gases, which prevented men from seeing, made breathing difficult, and allowed the Russians to come over the ruined wire-obstacles in thick waves into our trenches'.[20] Sand fell into rifles and machine-guns, and made them difficult to work.

The Russian bombardment continued for most of 4th June. The next day, infantry attack followed—preceded by 'testing' patrols. In practice, the Austro-Hungarian defence had already been ruined. Two-thirds of the available troops were put in the front position—the three foremost trenches, in a belt perhaps a kilometre in depth. There were huge dug-outs in this belt which could sustain the heaviest artillery. But two great errors had been made: the Russian lines had been allowed to within seventy-five paces of the Austrian trenches, and the reserves did not emerge from their dug-outs until the last moment. Not surprisingly, the defenders of the very first trench were over-run, the dust and confusion affected defenders of the second trench and the reserves in their dug-outs, and the Russians—pumping reserves in fast from their own dug-outs only a few hundred yards away—came up to the dug-out mouths only shortly after the bombardment had ended. The Austrian dug-outs were therefore traps, not strong-points: each a miniature Przemyśl.[24] This happened with one division of 10. Corps, near Olyka, and the collapse of this division allowed Russian troops into the third belt of trenches even on 5th June—an advantage they exploited to attack the flanks of other divisions. By the end of 5th June, 10. Corps had lost eighty per cent of its men in consequence, and of course in the chaos, language-difficulties came to the fore, with non-German troops surrendering perhaps more easily than they might otherwise have done. In circumstances like this, there were no defences for the local reserves to pick up—they were merely involved in a retreating mass of men. Szúrmay's corps was equally badly-treated, such that, by the evening of 5th June, virtually all three Austrian positions had fallen. In the first two positions, it was later found, eighty-five per cent of the casualties had been caused by gunnery and rifle-fire. In the third, a hundred per cent of the loss was prisoners. There were even tales of officers running back ahead of their men, artillery galloping away to the rear, and other signs of calamitous demoralisation. On 6th June the Russian central corps followed up their success, as far as the river Styr and Lutsk. Here the Austro-Hungarian disaster was completed. There were reserve-positions around Lutsk, the pride of Archduke Joseph Ferdinand. Belts of wire had been set up, with concrete fortifications, around the place. But it was defensible only if heights to the south, at Krupy, were free of enemy artillery; and yet Krupy was indefensible—it could be approached easily, and the attackers would even be invisible as they moved through long grass. No answer had been thought necessary for this. Szúrmay's corps retired to the Krupy positions, and lost them in panic on 6th June. Russian guns occupied them. They fired on the defences of Lutsk. The Austrians panicked—hundreds fleeing over packed pontoon bridges across the river Styr. The defenders were also seized by panic, but could not get away so easily, since they were blocked by their own wire. Austrians soldiers were even impaled on it as they ran back; and their officers, naturally, chose to save themselves. In Lutsk, another huge packet of prisoners was taken by the Russians, who in two days had been able to claim 50,000 men and seventy-seven guns. Kundmann did not altogether exaggerate when he said that 'the whole of IV Army has really been taken prisoner'.[22] Szúrmay's corps announced, 'It's a complete débâcle, we can do nothing with the troops'. The defence had simply disappeared. IV Army even after reinforcement came to 27,000 men; and so much Austro-Hungarian ammunition was captured that Russian factories hitherto making it—for the weapons already captured—were now told to convert back to Russian ammunition.[23]

What gave this disaster a new dimension was that it came together with disasters elsewhere that ruined the effectiveness of reserves. XI Army, to the south of VIII, attacked after short bombardment on 4th June. It had not even the slight superiority that VIII Army had had; even so, it broke through at Sopanów, where a favourable tactical position—a bridgehead, where movements were protected by woods—could be exploited. The Austrians' local reserves were drawn into action further south, and the forces at Sopanów broke through, two corps co-operating well and together taking 15,000 prisoners. This, combined with the defeat of the Austrian IV Army, led to the fall of Dubno. The initial defeat at Sopanów had even led Conrad to direct the front's reserve to this area, and not to IV Army's, so that it was of no use to the defenders of Lutsk. Similarly, there was a tactical success on the Strypa at Jazlowiec. In its way, this was a revealing affair. Shcherbachev and his chief of staff Golovin had been full of French talk; they would imitate French methods (the 'chablons' of 1915). The bombardment was much longer than elsewhere—forty-eight hours—and the enemy—Südarmee—knew what to expect. On the main front of attack, Shcherbachev failed. It was a subsidiary attack, forced on him by Brusilov, that succeeded, an entire Austro-Hungarian corps on the southern flank of Südarmee being surprised and destroyed—this success being achieved, revealingly, by rather less force than had been mustered in much the same area in December 1915. But since Shcherbachev had lost 20,000 men with his 'chablons' further north, he could not do much to exploit the gain.

Further south, on the front of IX Army, there was a success almost as great as that on VIII Army's in Volhynia.[24] This was a revealing affair, for the army that lost—Pflanzer-Baltin's VII Army—was the most solid of the Austro-Hungarian armies, one well-known for its comparative freedom from problems of morale, and composed mainly of Hungarian and Croat troops whose loyalty was never questioned even by commanders looking for excuses. Pflanzer-Baltin, in his diary, referred to 'the enemy's great superiority in long-range heavy artillery . . . of unprecedented effectiveness'. In reality, IX Army had only forty-seven heavy guns to Pflanzer-Baltin's 150 medium and heavy. Many of the Russian guns were very old, and they did not have generous amounts of shell—such that Lechitski wished not to attack at all when, rising from his sick-bed, he found what his chief of staff, Sannikov, had carried out. There was some numerical superiority (150,000 to 107,000) and some slight superiority in light artillery overall; and of course at the points of break-through, the Russians could assemble greater weight than the defenders who had to maintain a strong front everywhere. Even then, it was not of decisive proportions. After Lechitski had won an astonishing victory, men did not know what to conclude. A British report ran,[25] that if the Russians 'have obtained such results with so small a number of antique guns, what would they not have done if properly armed'. In a sense, this was the very point. Russia's inability to amass these huge quantities of heavy artillery or the crushing amounts of heavy shell (Lechitski had at most 300 rounds for his heavy guns, whereas the standard French quantity—without which there would be no attack—was 1,700 per gun) had forced commanders to think of something else, often despite themselves. In the case of IX Army, preparation had been as thorough as on VIII Army's front, the director of operations (Kelchevski) having gone to France to study western trench-systems. The gunners were well-trained, and this army's manuals of instruction for artillery co-operation were models of good sense. It is thought that artillery behaved with 'unprecedentedly good timing and thoughtful preparation'.

The Austro-Hungarian VII Army had already done quite well at the turn of the year—it had held the December offensive, at that without German help. Pflanzer-Baltin therefore supposed that his defensive tactics were correct. His guns had caused the Russians much harm, firing off a great deal of shell at once; and his 'thick frontline' system had worked well enough, for the Russians had been unable to break through significantly on any part of the front, while minor penetration was always held by enfilading fire. Two-thirds of the reserves were always kept close to the front line—the three trenches of the first position, or *Kampfstellung*. The troops seemed to be in good enough heart—an official investigator subsequently wrote that they had fought with 'heroism deserving of recognition'.[26] However, training had not been effective. As new troops appeared, they would be set to shift snow in the base-towns, and training took the form of repetitive drilling. Also, as rumours of an attack spread, a tense atmosphere developed, fostered by telephonists who listened-in to officers' conversations and spread alarming rumours. 'Tatar' troops were supposed to be coming; and there was a persistent tale to the effect that the Russians would scalp any soldier they took who had on him a favourite Hungarian weapon, the *fokó* or bill-hook. On the whole, however, it was a tactical rather than a moral problem that ruined VII Army. The defence had been too far concentrated in the *Kampfstellung*, and the army's front was bisected by the river Dniester, co-operation between the two halves being poor. The commander, Pflanzer-Baltin, was generally good, but he had not got over the lessons of 1915, and in any case had fallen ill just before battle began.[27]

Lechitski's attack began with a tactical victory near the town of Okna. In a bend of the river Dniester—the 'Samuszyn-Schlinge'—the Austrians had taken up a highly unfavourable line, over-looked by the Russians. It was held because retreat here would have meant retreat elsewhere; but the sector did not even have a separate divisional command. Lechitski's troops sapped forward to within thirty paces of the Austrian lines, and

nothing could be done to prevent this. On 4th June bombardment began
—200 guns south of the Dniester firing 100,000 shells, in an ably-pro-
grammed style. The bombardment was much more effective than before,
since light and heavy guns stuck to their tasks. the heavy ones maintaining
fire on the Austrian rear to prevent reserves from coming in, while the
light ones were well-timed—stopping for fifteen minutes as supposed
prelude to attack, firing again once the Austrians had come out of their
dug-outs. After several such episodes, the defenders did not come out of
their dug-outs, and many were captured in them. On 5th June a considerable tactical success was achieved near Okna, where the Austrian salient
was taken, with 11,000 prisoners and fourteen guns.

But the dimensions of Lechitski's victory turned out to be much
greater. Pflanzer-Baltin now committed all of his troops to the area south
of the Dniester, where two heights buttressed his line. He was led to
commit all of his forces by continuing Russian attacks on these heights.
The attacks, generally, failed over the next few days. None the less, there
was nothing to spare for his front north of the Dniester, and a well-staged
attack by Russian forces there on 7th June brought collapse—the Austrian
corps retiring in disorder over the Dniester itself. As they retired, they
bared the left flank of the defenders to the south, and collapse set in—a
collapse that found most of the troops already committed to their front
line and almost unable to escape. The tactical victory on Lechitski's front
was therefore as great as on VIII Army's. But, because Brusilov had seen
the importance of disrupting enemy reserves, of confusing the Austrians
as to the direction of attack, the victory turned out to be a still greater one.
Pflanzer-Baltin ordered retreat on 9th June. But he ordered retreat to the
south-west, into the Bukovina, which he imagined Lechitski wished to
take. The Austro-Hungarian high command, however, was told by
Falkenhayn that retreat must be towards the west, where Pflanzer-Baltin
could keep his links with the German *Südarmee*. Retreat therefore had to
go first south-west and then west—a confusion of transports that brought
the entire movement to a stop. By mid-June VII Army had almost
disintegrated, parts of it holding the river Prut to the south, parts of it
fleeing west, on the side of *Südarmee*. Lechitski's troops arrived on the
Prut. On 17th June an Austrian bridgehead fell, with 1,500 prisoners, for
Russian loss of one man, wounded. Demoralisation was such that the
artillery now ran off: a Russian observer noted that 'although the
artillerists knew their business well, they did not now have the courage to
do their duty by the infantry. Batteries made off to the rear much earlier
and more rapidly than they should have done, and left the infantry to its
fate'. There were even cases where Cossack troops seized whole batteries.
Now, part of VII Army had gone off to the west, and another part retired

to the southern reaches of the Bukovina. Pflanzer-Baltin himself reckoned that he had lost 100,000 men, talked of his 'ruinierte Armee'. That morale alone had not been responsible for this was shown in that only forty per cent of the loss could be ascribed to capture—at that, mainly in the confused conditions of retreat. It was tactical and strategic mishandling that brought about this defeat.

By 12th June two Austro-Hungarian armies had been broken up almost completely. Brusilov's command reported its captures (and perhaps under-stated them) as:[28]

Army	officers	men	guns	machine-guns	Minenwerfer
VII	716	34,000	47	106	9
VIII	437	76,000	87	276	90
IX	1,245	55,000	66	172	32
XI	594	25,000	16	91	64
	2,992	190,000	216	645	196

In other words, the Austro-Hungarian army had lost over a third of its men as prisoners in less than a week of action; with other casualties, the losses came to over half of the forces in the east. The blow to Austrian morale was irreparable: from now on, Austrian troops fought with an ineradicable sense of inferiority, and the loss of positions which had been universally thought impregnable led to a deep disbelief in commanders and in fortifications of all kinds. From now on, the Austrian army was useful only in so far as it could be joined with German troops—which happened, increasingly, even to the degree that companies of Austrian and German troops were joined to make mixed battalions. It is probably not an exaggeration to state that the Austrian army survived, now, by grace of the Prussian sergeant-major. Except on the Italian front, the heirs of Radetzky were not much more than stage-props pushed around, often contemptuously, by German managers. Pflanzer-Baltin had Seeckt foist on him as chief of staff;[29] Südarmee, under its German commander, Bothmer, took over most of the east-Galician sector; the command-area of Linsingen's Army Group—though theoretically under Conrad's orders—came to include the Austrian I as well as IV Army; and IV Army itself had most of its units mixed with German ones, under German command—although the Austrian army command, again theoretically, remained in existence. In time, pressures for establishment of a German command of the entire eastern front came up—Falkenhayn proposing first Mackensen, then late in July having to preside over the extension of Hindenburg's powers to include the bulk of the Austrian front as well as the whole of the

German one. Austrian independence, late in July, was shown only in the existence of 'Army Group Archduke Karl'—south-eastern Galicia and the Bukovina—and even this had Seeckt as its chief of staff. Conrad sometimes grumbled that peace would have to be made, that the Germans should abandon their 'limitless' plans for conquest in Europe.[30] But it would have been difficult, on the ground, to withdraw the Habsburg army from action, since it was already so much intermingled with German troops; and in any case the junior officers of the Austro-Hungarian army were probably more loyal to the German alliance than they were to the wreckage of the supra-national Habsburg Monarchy. Hitler's satellites existed before Hitler.

But, even though Austria-Hungary had almost collapsed, Brusilov could not follow up his victory at once. The losses of VIII Army had not been insignificant—35,000 by 8th June, of which two-thirds were wounded —and much of the shell-reserve had been fired off. The rapid advance to Lutsk, and later Dubno, brought the infantry beyond their supply-lines, and when the advance went over the Styr at Lutsk, the problem was still more complicated. It was true that the defence had been shattered; Russian cavalry even reached Vladimir Volynski, headquarters of IV Army. But there was not much cavalry, and as usual it could be held up even by platoons of infantry in passable condition. The infantry could not move fast enough, and so the Austrians were able to retire until no Russians were following them. In later years, Brusilov was much criticised for his failure to have reserves of infantry and cavalry to exploit his break-through—he had only one cavalry division in reserve, that of Mannerheim, later President of Finland. But he did not have reserves, partly because his was meant to be an 'auxiliary' attack for which no great reserves were made available, and partly because his very method ruled out assembly of reserves—most of the men took part in the immediate, long-front attacks, instead of waiting behind the lines for someone to break through on a tiny sector, as had happened at Lake Narotch. As far as cavalry was concerned, Brusilov had simply dismounted his divisions and used them as infantry: again from a reasonable judgment that cavalry divisions—for instance Smirnov's preposterous 233 squadrons of cavalry in March 1916 —merely complicated supply to an intolerable degree. In this case, failure to exploit the break-through was almost a direct consequence of breaking through in the first place, and it was unfair to ask more of Brusilov.

Faced with the physical impossibility of going on against the remnant of IV Army, Brusilov turned his attention to the north. Here was the vast weight of Evert's front, with its three-fold superiority in guns and men. Some way must be found of bringing that superiority into play. Brusilov allowed his forces to halt their advance to the south-west, against the Austrians, in order to turn to the north-west, in the direction of Kowel—his main aim being to dislodge the defenders of this area, and thus roll up the German line opposite Evert's front. In later years, he was accused of missing a great opportunity, for going on south-west to destroy the Austrians. But supply-problems cut across this; in any case, Kaledin, commanding VIII Army, was nervous that the Germans would come to attack him as he moved on, baring his flank to the north. In September 1915, VIII Army had re-taken Lutsk, and had then been humiliatingly expelled from it when German forces moved south into VIII Army's flank. Kaledin seems to have thought much the same would happen now— as a trickle of German troops was reported—and even ordered that positions should be dug just west of the Styr. Brusilov himself was in two minds. He knew that Evert, not he, had the main task in the summer offensive; he acquiesced in Kaledin's halt, and even confirmed it—telling Kaledin, somewhat later, that he might move towards Kovel but 'you are on no account to advance towards Vladimir Volynski'—i.e. against the Austrians. Typically enough, Brusilov himself had won a brilliant victory by methods that had been intended almost as a *ballon d'essai*; and now he too relapsed into orthodoxy, fear for his flank ruling out the energetic pursuit that might have been organised once VIII Army had got over its supply-problems.

Brusilov turned to the forces of the western front, and decided that his main task must be to unlock the German defences on his own northern flank. But the difficulties of this were considerable. In the first place, Evert himself showed no stomach for action; and in any case Brusilov's own northern group—a mixed force of cavalry and infantry divisions on the bend of the Styr north-east of Lutsk—was unable to get over the Austrian defences. This was mainly a matter of terrain—the marshes of the Styr, with only a few ways through them. Two cavalry corps and an infantry corps attempted without success to force the Styr salient, but succeeded, at best, in seizing villages on its perimeter.[31] The one break-through that did occur brought eighty per cent loss against barbed-wire hidden in the marshes, and the attackers lost so heavily that their success could not be followed up. Brusilov blamed this on the cavalry commander, Gyllenschmidt, for his 'feeble activity and bad management'. But in country of this type, there was not much that Gyllenschmidt could achieve. The Styr salient would require investment of greater force, and it was an error—a cruel one—of Brusilov's to suppose otherwise.

With this salient on his flank, Brusilov seems to have thought that German troops would use it to debouch far in his rear. He recognised that Gyllenschmidt could do little, and therefore summoned Evert to attack— Evert, with two-thirds of the army's heavy artillery, and a huge force of nearly a million men groomed for offensive action, prepared—according to conference instructions—since mid-April 1916. Evert had no stomach at all for his attack. He demanded 'quantities of heavy shell that go beyond our wildest dreams'. He switched the main area of attack between one place and another—on 1st June announcing that the Narotch area was unsuitable, that Baranovitchi, in the centre of his front, was to be preferred; and preparations were switched to this area. The transfer of reserves from Lake Narotch to Baranovitchi naturally was allowed to take weeks. He was asked to attack in June, but said that this attack must be postponed—'it would be unseemly to attack on Trinity Sunday and All Souls' Day'. On 4th June, attack was put off until the 17th and then the end of the month. It was switched away from Pinsk—because the marshes were not dry—and then switched back again a week later. As early as 5th June, men on Brusilov's front regarded Evert—with his German name—as a traitor; Brusilov complained to Alexeyev that 'he will turn a won battle into a lost one'. On 16th June Evert was telling Alexeyev that his attack would be 'only frontal blows, promising only very slow progress with the greatest of difficulty'.[32] Kuropatkin, still in charge of the northern front, was even more prudent—even announcing that the Germans had reinforced their front here by four divisions. No-one noted how Brusilov had won his victories—in some ways, not even Brusilov himself. Evert in particular could only imagine some great set-piece offensive. His gestures towards attack were feeble—a few sporadic corps-actions in the latter part of June, leading nowhere in particular. Insistence on great preparation meant that the Germans were not at all surprised, and the preparation was in any event perfunctory as Evert switched the stage of his pusillanimity from one place to another—his deliberations being followed by transport, hither and thither, of great quantities of matériel. It was the legacy of Lake Narotch in March, 1916.

In the event, he agreed to attack near Baranovitchi, early in July. In the meantime, he and Kuropatkin—no doubt partly as excuse to relieve themselves of any need to attack—parted grudgingly enough with reserves for Brusilov's front: 5. Siberian Corps, which arrived on 12th June, followed by two others on 18th June and 1. Turkestan Corps on 24th June. 5. Siberian Corps took only a week to arrive in full—much the same time as reserve-troops took on the German side, a sign that, when the transport-officers were made to do their work properly, reserves could be shifted at speed.[33] These four corps were only the beginning of a considerable shift of reserves to the successful front. Even so, there were still 400,000 men on Kuropatkin's front to 200,000 Germans, and Kuropatkin would not shift more than a division or two, in this decisive phase.

By mid-June, the disorientation of Kaledin and the confusions of

Evert's front had stopped Brusilov's advance in the northern sector. None the less, the great confusions brought to the Central Powers by Brusilov's methods continued to work much harm to the decisions of Falkenhayn and Conrad. Their reserves had been altogether disrupted—some went to Volhynia, for counter-attack; others were sent to eastern Galicia, to stop the threatened collapse; others again went to the area south of the Dniester, in an attempt to shore up the collapsing Austro-Hungarian VII Army.[34] It was this confusion of enemy reserves that allowed Brusilov more successes, in July, despite the confusion of his advance.

Falkenhayn was still committed to his western campaign, and in any case an Anglo-French offensive on the Somme was about to come—the preliminary bombardment beginning on 24th June (lasting until 1st July). Conrad was likewise committed to his offensive against Italy. Neither man wished to break off in order to save the eastern front. There was an initial delay as Conrad tried to get Falkenhayn to send reserves—Verdun had failed, Asiago was working. Falkenhayn responded icily: he had nothing to spare from the west; moreover, there had been no Russian troop-movements to Brusilov's front from Evert's, such that the Germans north of the Pripyat still faced a great superiority of numbers. A series of small-scale grants was made—Linsingen's front received five battalions from marshes to the north, a *Landwehr* brigade, an Austrian brigade, and the Austrian reserve division that had first, erroneously, been put in against XI Army. For four days, nothing more was decided. Conrad met Falkenhayn in Berlin on 8th June and was forced, almost like 'an errant schoolboy',[35] to give up troops from his Italian front, where in any case the offensive was slackening. Four German divisions would be sent, four and a half Austro-Hungarian ones, including two and a half from the Italian front at once. A trickle of German troops began on 6th June, and by 20th June ten and a half new divisions, Austro-Hungarian and German, had been moved to the threatened eastern front. Even so, there was a new dimension to the disaster with the collapse of Pflanzer-Baltin on the Dniester. Reserves were not even sent as a block to Volhynia: three divisons, one of them German (from Macedonia) had to be diverted to hold up the remnant of VII Army. The reserves were not much, in the context of two shattered Austrian armies, of the four corps sent to Brusilov as reinforcement. But Falkenhayn would not give anything away from the west; increasingly, too, Ludendorff, jealously controlling his independent front, would not part with significant reserves. In this way, he could embarrass Falkenhayn and take over command of the whole eastern front himself, perhaps even of the whole German army. If, to cut them down to size, the Austrians and Falkenhayn were defeated, so much the better for Ludendorff.

The Central Powers did what they could, Conrad attempted to restore the morale of his men by moving into commands antiquated fire-eaters such as Tersztyánszki, who rapidly discovered that they did not speak the same language as the dejected and bewildered soldiers. By 10th June 10. Corps had 3,000 men left, Szúrmay, 2,000. The largest division of the army was the Viennese 13. Rifle Division—with 1,400 men of an establishment of 12,000. Tersztyánszki sent back ever more alarming messages to Conrad—the Germans were looking, now, 'queerly' on the Austrian efforts. Tersztyánszki told his men:[36] 'My patience is exhausted and I refuse to have my and the senior officers' reputations dragged in the mud.' The men, who in any case might legitimately have supposed that they were not fighting for their commanders' reputations, remained unaffected by such literature. By the end of June, IV Army ceased to exist, except in so far as there was a German framework for it. To plug the gaps both here and in VII Army, Conrad had to stop the offensive against Italy, and obtain troops. He told Archduke Eugen, commanding the offensive, that the three divisions already sent (by 16th June) must be followed by another five, in two corps. 'We are now forced to stop your offensive, having waited to the uttermost limits for you to fulfil your promises' was Conrad's instruction to the Archduke. On 24th June the Austrians in northern Italy had to retire to a suitable defensive line, and to fend off another Italian offensive. Eight divisions went back to the east.

Falkenhayn had instructed men to hold 'every square foot of line'—not a sensible policy, since the Austrian soldiery was simply taken prisoner while doing so. He had in mind a great counter-stroke, against the northern flank of Kaledin's salient—a flank that now reached the river Stokhod. By 20th June, twelve and a half Austro-German divisions were gathered, under a German, Marwitz. Most of the German divisions were either second-class troops, or tired units from the western front. In any case, the Central Powers' effort was split—of sixteen and a half fresh divisions sent by 20th June, nine went to Volhynia, two to *Südarmee*, the rest to the Dniester front. The counter-offensive on the Stokhod went wrong—at best a few miles forward, for very high losses. 2,000 prisoners were made, and four guns taken; but losses reached 40,000, and the Austrian IV Army, bewildered at the experience of advancing, was counter-attacked and driven far beyond its starting-point. The offensive was switched from the northern to the southern side of Kaledin's salient on 22nd June. It made no difference, even though Austrian groups now came under German commanders. On the Dniester, the Russian advance continued throughout the latter part of June: reserves were too few to stop it. The only thing that saved this area was the supply-difficulty encountered by Lechitski.

In reality, the first wave of reserves, sent in various directions and in packets by Conrad and Falkenhayn, had failed to serve any useful purpose. Marwitz's counter-attack merely broke up the reserve-forces still more. The way was therefore open for a renewal of Brusilov's offensive, again along the whole front. The four new corps were put into line, attacking the Styr salient early in July. Between 3rd and 6th July the salient collapsed, the troops of III and VIII Armies being drawn against it—III Army with five army corps, against two. The guns had been well-prepared, the troops trained; the marshes had also dried, and threw up clouds of dust that obscured the defenders' view. 30,000 prisoners and thirty guns were taken, even German troops' morale now collapsing. Now the Russians came up against the Stokhod, base of this salient. Two German divisions came to hold the line, and succeeded, with the loss of a bridgehead or two, in achieving this. In the south, there was also a minor repetition of early June. Lechitski's army drove against VII Army late in June, encountered divisons that counted less than a regiment at half-strength, and captured a series of towns leading to Halicz. A German counter-attack failed, the three reserve divisions (Kraewel) being largely wasted and the Russians being treated even to the unusual spectacle of German troops fleeing, having to be sabred back, by Austrian generals, to their front lines.[37] Most of the Bukovina was taken by the Russians, and the southern flank of *Südarmee* turned on the Dniester. Now Falkenhayn could not refuse to send troops—four German divisions were sent to the Dniester front, two Turkish divisons were promised as well. In this period, even the weak Russian XI Army did well, advancing over the Galician border to take Brody in mid-month. The northern flank of *Südarmee* was turned, and that army had to undertake a retreat—such that it stood only thirty miles east of Lwów.

On the other hand, attempts by the Russians to break out on the German part of the front failed. On 2nd July the promised offensive of Evert began, at Baranovitchi. It was a piece of fatalism, not unlike Lake Narotch. Ragoza, the army commander, had prepared an attack on Vilna, for over two months. He was now given two weeks to prepare one instead in the marshy region north of Pinsk. At Baranovitchi, there was some tactical advantage—a German salient, occupied, as it happened, by two Austrian divisions. Otherwise, there was only marsh. There was no time to sap forward, no time for guns to register properly. A huge force of cavalry clogged the supply-lines. Twenty-one and a half infantry, five cavalry divisions were gathered. A thousand guns opened the bombardment, with a thousand rounds each. This was not effective. Two German divisions were brought in as reserves just before the attack began; the bombardment, though lasting for several days, achieved nothing in particular. A few initial tactical successes came—3,000 prisoners, a few guns, On 4th July one of the two Austrian divisions collapsed, and the line was held by reserve Germans. Then the attack stopped—resumed again with bombardment on 7th July, and again stopped. By 8th July the Russians had lost 80,000 men, the Germans 16,000. Yet this attack had used up more shell than the whole of Brusilov's front in the first week of his offensive.

With this, efforts to involve the other two fronts came virtually to a stop: troops were now diverted to Brusilov's front, as the other two commanders parted with troops in order to avoid having to attack again. In the south, Lechitski carried on along the Dniester, to take Halicz in the latter part of July. In East Galicia, there was an advance from one tributary of the Dniester to another. But Brusilov decided that the time had come for a great attack towards Kowel[38]—north-east from the Stokhod positions. If he could take Kowel, the German line to the north would be turned, and Evert's front would be allowed forward. After the fall of the Styr salient, his troops occupied the Stokhod and hoped for great things. Brusilov himself seems to have given up his own methods—preferring to believe that, now that his front had been guaranteed unlimited reinforcement, a direct attack of the battering-ram type should be attempted. He was given control of III Army, the southern-most of Evert's front. He set VIII Army, as before, to move west against the Austro-Germans; in between, he would have a new force, the Guard Army.

With this, he achieved almost two-fold superiority of numbers, the more so as the Austrian troops were still in woeful condition. The front as a whole had taken 40,000 men and sixty-three guns in the offensive of 4th to 7th July, and since early June, nearly 260,000 men with 330 guns. But Brusilov's own losses had been high—5,000 officers lost, 60,000 men killed, 370,000 wounded, 60,000 missing. The trained men were running out, and untrained recruits were not able to continue the attack on previous lines. Brusilov's great hope was the new, Guard Army—60,000 men of the highest physical standard, supposedly given competent training in the rear for the past few months. But the training had been entrusted to officers who knew little of modern war; and the command of the Guard lay in the hands, similarly, of men who were not even very competent in the out-of-date methods they prescribed. The commander was Bezo-brazov, with his ineradicable pantomime-*machismo*; the chief of staff, Ignatiev, who, in Brusilov's words,[39] 'knew nothing whatever of staff work'; the chief artillerist, the Duke of Mecklenburg-Schwerin, 'a worthy man who had not, however, grasped the importance of artillery'; the commander of 1. Guard Corps, Grand Duke Paul, 'an exceptionally fine man with no real knowledge'; the commander of 2. Guard Corps, Rauch, 'capable but losing his nerve under rifle-fire'.

The Guard Army arrived on the banks of the Stokhod, and was set the task of breaking through towards Kowel,[40] with the help of III and VIII Armies—together, 250,000 men to 115,000. The attacks of mid-July had failed, and the Guard was expected to attack towards the end of the month after some preparation. The Russians' weight was now far beyond anything seen in the eastern front, and the German commander (Marwitz) subsequently said it was 'like conditions in the west'. The Guard used a hundred guns of the heaviest calibre, whereas no German operation in the east had never used more than forty of these great-guns. Aircraft began to come into their own, although those on the Russian side seem to have been dominated by numerically-inferior German fliers, who on one occasion even caused 200 casualties in the headquarters of the Guard Army, and who caused much damage to Russian morale by flying low over the field, machine-gunning the infantry. Overall, there were six Russian shells to one German. This great battering-ram was levelled at Kowel from late July until early October, offensives being made again and again, usually at fortnightly intervals. But the terrain was manifestly unsuitable. The river Stokhod itself was not much of an obstacle, being shallow and slow-moving. But to either side there were marshes, and although this sometimes meant that the defenders could not drag their guns away to safety, it also meant that attackers lost so heavily that most writers dismiss the offensives as criminal. One Guard officer remarked that 'you could cross the region in a plane, never on foot', and paths through the marshes allowed men to go only in single file. The Guard attacked here on 28th July, continuing the process until early August. On 28th July, with losses of over half the men, a minor height at Trysten was taken—500 prisoners and eight guns. The other Guard Corps profited from this to drive a wedge in the German line to take forty-six guns and 5,000 prisoners as well. But both of the Guard Corps lost 30,000 men in this affair, and the attack could never be repeated with the same weight.

It was only on the front of the Austrian IV Army that successes of real effectiveness could be gained—early in August, VIII Army resumed its drive to the west, and took 12,000 prisoners of one division (and only two guns). Hell, chief of staff to Linsingen's army group, described the front as 'a powder-barrel'; the Austrians were 'indescribable'. From now on, German and Austrian troops were mixed, even at company level. The Austrian IV Army, while still theoretically in existence, was in practice run by Marwitz, then Litzmann, both Germans; and it appears that, with Prussian N.C.O.s and officers, even Czechs and Ruthenes would fight against the Russians. In August, despite uneasy moments, even this front began to show some solidity; while the German troops of Linsingen's command contained all of Bezobrazov's attempts to get beyond the Stokhod bridges towards Kowel. In eastern Galicia, there were also uneasy moments throughout August, *Südarmee* having to retreat. But reserve troops, even including a Turkish corps, arrived to stabilise the line on the Zlóta Lipa. In August, it was mainly in the south, Lechitski's front, that the great advances of the Brusilov offensive were continued. Halicz was taken, and neither the Austrian nor the German groups offered much resistance—even cavalry was effective. By late July, Lechitski had penetrated even the Carpathian passes leading into Hungary; and although four German divisions were sent—the *deutsches Karpatenkorps*—and a new Austro-Hungarian army (III), the only way Lechitski could be held was the increasing difficulty of terrain as he entered the Carpathians. It seemed that all this, occurring on the borders of Romania, would at last bring Romania out of her neutrality.

CHAPTER TWELVE

The Romanian Campaign, 1916–1917

At the end of August 1916, Romania declared war on Austria-Hungary, and shortly afterwards found herself at war with all four Central Powers. Since 1914, men had been waiting for this. Romania awaited national unification, and coveted the tracts of Austria-Hungary inhabited by Romanians. So long as the Central Powers appeared invincible, Romania could not risk intervening against them. Her strategic situation was peculiarly vulnerable. But with the great run of Russian victories, her confidence rose. Moreover, by August 1916, the western Powers were prepared to guarantee much more territory than hitherto: the French, in particular, with an eye to the post-war situation, wanted to establish a greater Romania as a bulwark against Russia. On 17th August, a military convention was signed, providing for extensive Entente assistance, financial and military. The twenty or so Romanian divisions would, it was thought, decisively affect the eastern front as a whole.[1] With 366 battalions of infantry, 106 squadrons of cavalry and 1,300 guns (half of them modern) the Romanian army could invade Hungary and turn the Central Powers' lines to the north.

It is not altogether easy to see why men expected the intervention of small powers to be so decisive. No doubt it was an illusion that—like much else in this war—owed something to misreadings of Napoleonic history. The nationalistic vibrations of Madrid and Lisbon were thought to have shaken the French Empire at its foundations; the Peninsular War to have exposed the 'soft underbelly' of Napoleonic Europe. In reality, nationalism had been much less important than the heavy pounding to which the French armies had been subjected in Austria and Russia; and men also forgot that the Peninsular War involved an army that was, by the standards of the time, large and efficient. The Romanian army could not stand comparison. Of its 620,000 soldiers, a third would be taken up in supply-lines, and almost all were illiterate. The officers lacked experience, and were also inclined to panic. All foreigners noted the incidence of what was delicately known as 'immoralité': indeed among the first prescriptions, on mobilisation, was a decree that only officers above the rank of major had the right to use make-up. Langlois, not an unfriendly observer, thought the '*soldat excellent, officier dépourvu de toute moralité militaire, Etat-major et commandement presque nuls*'.[2] British observers felt that the operations of the Romanian army would make a public-school field-day look like the execution of the Schlieffen Plan; while the comments of Russians who had to fight side-by-side with the Romanians were often unprintable. As things turned out, it was the Russians, and not the Central Powers, who suffered from a Romanian ulcer. Almost a third of the Russian army had to be diverted to the south. This did not save Romania. On the contrary, the Central Powers conquered the country easily enough, and, in the next year and a half, removed far more from it than they could have done had it remained neutral: over a million tons of oil, over two million tons of grain, 200,000 tons of timber, 100,000 head of cattle, 200,000 goats and pigs, over and above the quantities requisitioned for maintenance of the armies of occupation.[3] Romanian intervention, in other words, made possible the Germans' continuation of the war into 1918.

The essential reason for this, as for the halting, overall, of Russian victories, was the Central Powers' capacity to shift their reserves quickly. In Napoleonic days, sea-power had allowed the British to shift their troops faster than the French, who were dependent on horses. Now, railways gave much the same advantage over sea-power that sea-power had had before over horses. Provided the railways were properly-managed, they could shuttle troops within a few days from Italy to Volhynia, France to the Balkans. It had taken the Germans, in spring 1915, hardly more than a week to assemble their XI Army against the Russian lines at Gorlice, whereas it took the western Powers six weeks to assemble an equivalent force for their assault on the Dardanelles at the same time; and even the Turkish railways were such that the western Powers had to face a superiority to two-to-one within a few days of their landing at Gallipoli. In September 1916, the Central Powers sent 1,500 trains through Hungary—not far short of the number used by Austria-Hungary to mobilise against Russia two years before—and assembled a force equivalent to the entire Romanian army within three weeks of Romania's intervention. In the First World War, it was the great profusion of reserves that counted for most. Contrary to legend, it was not so much the difficulty, or physical impossibility, of breaking through trench-lines that led to the war's being such a protracted and bloody affair, but rather the fact that even a badly-defeated army could rely on reserves, moving in by railway. The conscription of whole generations, and particularly the enlarged capacity to supply millions of soldiers, meant that man-power was, to all intents and purposes, inexhaustible: even the total casualties of this war were a small proportion of the available man-power.

The basis of Brusilov's great successes in June and July 1916 had been the Central Powers' inadequate use of their reserves. To some degree, this was a consequence of Brusilov's own methods: a broad-front, well-prepared, many-front offensive between Volhynia and Romania. Local reserves had been frittered away between the various points of attack. In the southern sector, on both sides of the river Dniester, the Central Powers had been particularly embarrassed by Brusilov's methods. They left troops to cover the Romanian border, as well as troops to cover the Dniester flank of *Südarmee*, on which their Galician lines depended. Seven Austro-Hungarian divisions, and even a German force, the *Karpatenkorps*, had been pushed in to defend the Hungarian border and the southern Bukovina: a force contained, as things turned out, by little more than a Russian cavalry corps. The Russians had been able to win further great victories along the Dniester, which had forced a further diversion of German and Austro-Hungarian reserves and thus allowed the Russians in Volhynia to win successes in July. It was of course true that the Russian army, by following Brusilov's methods, itself dispensed with reserves that might have followed up the victories it won. But the prizes were great enough: by the end of August, the Austro-Hungarian army had lost 614,000 men in the east, and the Germans, by their own account, 150,000.[4]

More important, however, had been the confusion among the Central Powers' leaders. Ludendorff would not help Falkenhayn, and Falkenhayn would not help Conrad, since each one had his priorities, of which even military disaster produced merely a re-statement. Falkenhayn's priorities had been in the west: Verdun, then the Somme, preliminary bombardment for which had begun on 24th June. He resented any diversion of troops from France, and demanded that Conrad should give up his Italian offensive first. Conrad was reluctant to do this, because that offensive seemed to promise real success. In this way, only five divisions were sent from the west for most of June, and initially only two and a half from Italy. The divisions were also tired from fighting—in the case of the German divisions, tired from Verdun to the point of virtual uselessness in the field, as the fate of Marwitz's offensive on the Stokhod showed. At the same time, both Conrad and Falkenhayn appealed to Ludendorff, commanding the greater part of the Germans' eastern front. But Ludendorff also made out that he could not afford to part with troops, and in June sent only two under-strength divisions to help in Volhynia. He had good excuses. His troops faced twice their numbers, and although Kuropatkin and Evert seldom bothered to attack with any seriousness, the threat was always there. In any case, none of the men in Ludendorff's headquarters felt any sympathy with Falkenhayn. Hoffmann thought that 'the Austrians' defeat is no doubt deplorable, but that is no reason for us to tear our hair out'.[5] On the contrary, since Falkenhayn had reduced Ludendorff's sphere of responsibility, the business must be settled by him and Conrad. Maybe, too, Ludendorff secretly calculated that withholding reserves would so embarrass Falkenhayn and Conrad that they would have to let Ludendorff once more control most of the eastern front. Whatever the case, throughout June 1916 the Austro-Hungarian front acquired only a dozen reserve divisions, at that frittered away between the Dniester and the Stokhod. This had allowed Brusilov to win a further set of victories in July.

However, these conditions were not to be repeated. In the first place, the realisation—as distinct from the threat—of allied offensives allowed troops to be made free from the other fronts on a scale that few people had imagined possible. In the west, the Anglo-French offensive on the Somme was effectively contained by half the numbers of men and a third the number of guns that the attacking armies used. Similarly, the Russian offensive at Baranovitchi turned out to be a bungled, ineffective affair that cost the attacker 100,000 men for nothing in particular. On the Italian front, a renewed Isonzo offensive, though leading to the fall of Gorizia in August, did not prevent departure of another four Austro-Hungarian divisions for Russia in July, and more than that later on.

In any case, the divisions among the Central Powers' leaders were overcome by establishment of an increasingly united command, dominated by Ludendorff. This was the outcome of a crisis inside Germany and Austria-Hungary that owed its existence to much more than military factors. Discontent inside Germany had been building up throughout 1916. Emergence of a large-scale left-wing opposition to the war—the creation of a dissident socialist group, the strikes of spring 1916—prompted demands for a military dictatorship that would at once win the war and control the working-class. The run-down, relative and absolute, of the comfortable middle-class world had now progressed so far, as inflation bit into 'fixed incomes', as to drive a large section of propertied Germany to desperate courses, in which the existing, relatively moderate leadership of men like Bethmann Hollweg and Falkenhayn had little place. There were demands for unlimited war-aims, for use of any and every weapon, however barbaric, that could win the war: hence the widespread campaign for resumption of unrestricted U-Boat warfare, the sinking of any ship, neutral or not, within the 'war-zone' of British and French waters.

Characteristically, this situation drove Bethmann Hollweg and Falkenhayn further apart than ever, as each sought to sacrifice the other for his political life.[6] Falkenhayn tried to pin the blame on Bethmann Hollweg, and picked up the cause of submarine-warfare. Bethmann Hollweg knew in his heart that this weapon would fail. It would provoke the United States into declaring war, and that would be the end of Germany. At the same time, the desperate temper of propertied Germany was now such that a demagogic campaign for U-Boat warfare could sweep Bethmann Hollweg away. He had to try for something equally popular, and hit on the scheme for putting Hindenburg and Ludendorff back in charge of the eastern front. These two men enjoyed a vast, and not wholly deserved, reputation: they were the men who produced newspaper-headlines, and public opinion resented the whittling-down of their power in 1915. By championing them, Bethmann Hollweg could pose as nationalist demagogue. At the same time, he appears to have had secret schemes. He knew, now, that Germany had little chance of winning the war. But to obtain peace, with the atmosphere as it was, would be impossible. It was not just that the Entente's demands would be impossibly high; it was also that a large and powerful section of German public opinion demanded crushing victory, and resented any whisper to the effect that Germany's gains could be renounced for the sake of a compromise-settlement. Bethmann Hollweg seems to have supposed that, by putting Ludendorff in Falkenhayn's place, he could satisfy the nationalists; then he could smuggle peace in through the back door. In this roundabout way, Bethmann Hollweg came to support the ostensibly *'jusqu'au-boutiste'* generals, but for the sake of his private limited goals. The tone was altogether that ascribed to Low to Baldwin: 'If I hadn't told you I wouldn't bring you here, you wouldn't have come.'

Falkenhayn's position really depended on his having the Kaiser's confidence, and the confidence of military leaders whom the Kaiser respected. His victories in 1915 had strengthened his position; but defeat at Verdun, and the embarrassments of the summer of 1916, much weakened his hold on power. Above all, the eastern front showed that Falkenhayn' methods had failed. His relations with the Austro-Hungarian high command were so bad that, in the decisive days of the Dniester collapse, not a single communication between Falkenhayn and Conrad von Hötzendorf was made for several days. Relations with Ludendorff were such that Ludendorff, with forty-four infantry divisions, would do nothing to help: he sent a few battalions in June, and two divisions early in July. The Verdun campaign had to be abandoned. It also became clear that matters in the east would not be settled until Ludendorff somehow got sufficient responsibility to make him part with reserves for the front south of the Pripyat: and from Falkenhayn's viewpoint, the difficulty was to combine extension of Ludendorff's responsibility with containment of Ludendorff's power.

One obvious way was for Falkenhayn to promote schemes by which the whole of the eastern front—including the Austro-Hungarian army—would come under Hindenburg's command, and then to stir up opposition from the Austro-Hungarians. This method was tried early in July. Ostensibly, it succeeded. Conrad von Hötzendorf produced a litany of grievances against the scheme: German command in the east would make the war one of 'Germandom against Slavdom', and would therefore offend the Slavs who made up half of the Austro-Hungarian army; German command would mean that the Habsburg dream of reigning in Poland would be rudely destroyed; it would prevent free movement of troops against the hated Italians; it would prevent a separate peace. Instead, schemes were promoted by which Archduke Friedrich, nominal commander of the Austro-Hungarian army, should nominally take over the whole of the eastern front, with Hindenburg as his chief of staff for the German part. This did not meet an enthusiastic response from Hindenburg. Falkenhayn seemed to have parried the threat: he had ostensibly promoted Hindenburg's cause, and the Austro-Hungarians had turned out to be the obstacle. But his calculation went wrong. With the disasters of mid-July, indignation in Berlin, Vienna and Budapest rose beyond Falkenhayn's barriers. Highly-placed Austro-Hungarians—including Andrássy—demanded establishment of a Hindenburg-front; Bethmann Hollweg also demanded it, as did the Kaiser. In the end, Austro-Hungarian resistance gave way. By the end of the month, after a meeting in Pless, a new system of command was adopted, by which Hindenburg ran the eastern front virtually as far as the Dniester.[7] In theory, he accepted orders, as far as the Austro-Hungarian sector was concerned, from Conrad. In practice, this was as meaningless as it had been in the days of Mackensen. The only area still commanded by Conrad was the front of Archduke Karl's Army Group, on the southern sector of the front; even it had a German chief of staff, Seekt; and an increasing proportion of its troops was German. Later on, the system was extended to take into account other allies. When Romania intervened, the German Kaiser became commander-in-chief of all of the Central Powers' forces, a device to prevent the Bulgarians from making separate arrangements. At the same time, Falkenhayn was finally dismissed, and replaced by Hindenburg, whose place as *Oberbefehlshaber Ost* passed to Prince Leopold of Bavaria.

In this way, central control of reserves became increasingly possible, and in August there was little of the confusion that had marked June and July. In June, a dozen divisions, mostly tired, had been sent; but by mid-August the eastern front had received a transfusion equivalent to the entire Austro-Hungarian Galician army of 1914: thirty infantry and three and a half cavalry divisions, of which ten infantry and almost all of the cavalry divisions came from Ludendorff's front once Ludendorff was made responsible. This transfusion matched what Brusilov was sent: three divisions to mid-June, fifteen more to mid-July, eight more to mid-August. When the Romanians intervened, the Central Powers' system for pooling reserves worked equally well: the Romanian offensive was stopped in its tracks a mere fortnight after the declaration of war, as all four Central Powers mustered substantial forces against Romania almost at once.

At the same time, the Russians now abandoned the Brusilov method that had brought such remarkable results: they returned to the old system of attacking a narrow front in a predictable way with a huge phalanx. In the first half of July, repetition of Brusilov's methods had brought, again, great successes. The Central Powers' salient on the Styr had collapsed; there had been great advances along the Dniester; and even the German *Südarmee* had been forced back in Galicia. But the Brusilov method could succeed, in the first place, only if new troops were constantly fed to the front. But this would depend on the generosity of the other two army group commanders, who effectively controlled the reserves. As usual, the only way of achieving this turned out to be appointing them to command the offensive. Consequently, Evert was now put in charge of the northern part of Brusilov's front, and was given responsibility for the offensive of III Army, the Guard Army and VIII Army against the Central Powers' positions before Kowel. With this, the Brusilov offensive came to an end, since Evert had no faith in Brusilov's methods. On the contrary, he, with Alexeyev's blessing, returned to the 'phalanx' system: a vast attack on a very narrow front, with so much artillery mustered that nothing living would remain on the enemy side. III Army deployed eighty-six battalions against sixteen, and was to attack on only eight kilometres; the Guard Army deployed ninety-six battalions against twenty-eight and attacked on a front of fourteen kilometres.[3]

Stavka could either renew the Kowel offensive or, particularly after Romania's intervention, attempt some repetition of the Brusilov successes by attacking virtually everywhere along the line, if need be diverting substantial Russian forces towards the new Romanian front. In practice, Alexeyev opted for the renewal of the Kowel offensive, and continued to place most of the reserve troops with the three armies engaged in this. Later, when that offensive produced huge casualties for no significant return, and when Romania collapsed, this decision was made out to be criminal. It did, certainly, betray much want of imagination. On the other hand, from *Stavka*'s point of view, it seemed to make sense. The British and French were attacking on the Somme, and Russia must also mount some powerful offensive at a point where the Germans could not afford retreat. A proper offensive would also prevent the Germans from shifting troops against Romania. It was true that the Brusilov methods—a many-front offensive, with long fronts of attack at each of the points—had succeeded in June and July. But they needed extensive preparation, for which there was no time; and in any case the fact that they had succeeded against Austro-Hungarian soldiers damned them in professional soldiers' eyes, for the Austro-Hungarian army was now thought to have reached such a state that it could be beaten by an army commanded by a rocking-horse: victories won against Austro-Hungarians proved nothing. Now that the Germans had arrived, something serious must be tried. The 'phalanx' levelled at Kowel was the only answer to this problem, or so *Stavka* supposed.

There was a further justification for renewal of the Kowel offensives, which gave them a prima facie case of unfortunate strength. In the offensive of late July, there had been respectable tactical successes. The two Guard Corps had lost heavily towards the end of July, but in doing so they had captured over fifty guns and some enemy bridgeheads on the Stokhod. If the troops could get over the Stokhod marshes into easier country beyond, then they might turn such tactical successes into a strategic victory—the more so as the Central Powers' defence still depended to some degree on the soldiery of the Austro-Hungarian IV Army which, as Hoffmann said, resembled 'a mouthful of hyper-sensitive teeth: every time the wind blows, there's tooth-ache.[9] In the fighting of late July, almost a whole Austro-Hungarian division had been captured—12,000 men—with only two guns: a sign that the forces were simply not fighting. Hell, Linsingen's chief of staff, regarded the whole thing as 'a powder-barrel'; and Marwitz himself thought that the Russians' weight was now such that battles before Kowel 'resemble conditions in the west'. Alexeyev opted for renewed attacks on Kowel, and neglected the chance of winning victory further south. To some degree, he even managed this with Brusilov's consent.

Offensives against Kowel were mounted on 8th August and at more or less fortnightly intervals for the next three months.[10] The Russian super-iroity, overall, was two-to-one at least: north of the Pripyat, 852,000 to 371,000 and south of it, 863,000 to 480,000. On the Kowel front, a great local superiority was built up: III Army, the Guard Army and VIII Army had, together, twenty-nine infantry and twelve cavalry divisions to twelve Austro-German infantry divisions. This, rather than the Romanian front, constituted *Stavka's* main effort. It was a complete failure. Heavy artillery would be concentrated on a narrow front. But the shell was not particularly effective, since marshy country masked the explosion. The attacking troops had to stumble across marshy country, pitted with shell-holes, and found in the Stokhod marshes an impassable obstacle. Moreover, the tactics used were much like the strategy itself: theoretically the obvious answer, in practice calamitous. Troops advanced in 'waves', one after another, and were therefore very vulnerable to heavy rifle-fire, traversing machine-guns, high-explosive shell. The Guard—and especially the Semenovski and Preobrazhenski regiments—attacked seventeen times, with wild courage, and made none but trivial gains, So many Russian corpses lay stinking in no-man's land that Marwitz, the German commander, was approached with a view to establishing a truce, so that they might be buried. He refused: there could be no better deterrent to future offensives than this forest of rotting corpses. But for *Stavka*, these tactics seemed to be the obvious answer. It was easy enough for men simply to walk forward from a trench, in a long line; and troops that followed them into the trench would walk forward similarly. Again, a long, thin target was seemingly less vulnerable to artillery-fire than the thick masses which had been the rule for attackers in 1914-15. But at bottom, these tactics reflected the commanders' opinion of their men. Generals—who had found that it took ten years to make a 'real' soldier of the kind of volunteer they had found before the war—could not imagine that the raw recruits of 1916 could perform any manoeuvre but the simplest. If anything complicated were tried, the troops would break down into a useless mob, given to panic. It was easy to have the troops walk forward in a long line, dressing to the left, their officers in front and their sergeant-majors behind, ready to shoot any man who left his place. Commanders therefore neglected tactical innovations—in particular, the principle of fire-and-movement, by which small 'packets' of infantrymen, moving forward in bounds, diagonally, from shell-hole to shell-hole, could alternately offer each other cover. These principles were used, first, in the German army, mainly because it suffered from a severe crisis in man-power and had to think of some way by which lives could be saved. Other armies, with a longer 'purse', were saved the effort of thinking things out, or of applying doctrines the truth of which they half-suspected. Yet in 1918, the allied victory owed at least as much to tactical innovations as to improvements in weaponry, including tanks.

In these circumstances, the Kowel offensives turned into an expensive folly. The Germans were able to re-form their weak Austro-Hungarian partners, to the extent that the Austro-Hungarian IV Army became infiltrated, even at battalion level, with German troops. Its Austro-Hungarian command became a stage-prop, contemptuously shifted around by one German general after another. The method worked. Czech and Ruthene soldiery did not respond to Austro-Hungarian methods. But the arrival of competent German brigade-staffs, a battery or two of German artillery, and some Prussian sergeant-majors was generally enough to lend the Austro-Hungarian troops a fighting quality they had not shown hitherto—'corset-staves', in the current phrase. In August, there was an extension of this method to all parts of the eastern front, and on the Kowel sector there were no more easy Russian victories. Just the same, Alexeyev went ahead, into mid-October. When huge losses were recorded, the commanders reacted as they had always done: there must be more heavy guns, and then everything would be all right. Evert, indeed, learnt so little from Kowel that for 1917 he demanded sixty-seven infantry divisions for a further offensive, with '814,364' rounds of heavy shell, to be used on a front of eighteen kilometres.[11] As ever, when the old formulae failed, generals did not suppose that this was because the formulae were wrong, but because they had not been adequately applied. In the end, Russian soldiers were driven into attack by their own artillery: bombarding the front trenches in which they cowered.

The successes won by the Russian army in August were on parts of the front still subjected to the Brusilov method. XI, VII and IX Armies in eastern Galicia and the Bukovina 'walked forward', as before. XI and IX Armies in particular did this to great effect. Brody fell, and Halicz, in the south, as the multiple offensive on a broad front disrupted Austro-German reserves. It was the victories of IX Army that finally prompted Romania to intervene, since Lechitski's drive almost brought the Russians into Hungary, and hence into occupation of lands coveted by the Romanians. Yet because so many Russian troops were now involved in the Kowel battles, there was almost nothing to back Lechitsky, whose victories were achieved with a mere eleven divisions of infantry (and five of cavalry). By the end of August, his drive had slackened, while the incurable tendency of Shcherbachev and Golovin, of VII Army, to apply French methods meant that Brusilov's prescriptions were ignored, and the attacks against *Südarmee* turned into a minor version of Kowel.

These were the circumstances in which Romania intervened: Russian troops were pinned to the Kowel and Galician offensives; half of them were placed north of the Pripyat with almost nothing to do. Alexeyev himself had been told again and again that Romanian intervention would be decisive. Joffre had said that 'no price is too high to pay for it'; Russian diplomats had been induced to promise Romania the areas of Austria-Hungary she coveted, and later on the Entente connived at Romania's acquisition of Russian territory, Bessarabia. Alexeyev himself generally felt that Romanian intervention was not worth this much—on the contrary, it would be a liability.[12] At the turn of 1915–16, he had opposed schemes for bringing her in—the front would be lengthened; southern Russia would thus be exposed to a German attack through Romania; the

Russian army was not large enough to cover all of the area; the Romanian army was useless. In June, his attitude had changed to some extent, but he was never willing to make sacrifices for Romania, and now preferred to concentrate his troops on Kowel and Lwów. In any case, the railway-links between Russian and Romania were too weak to allow any rapid diversion of Russian troops. There were only two single-track lines connecting the two countries, even then with the usual problem of differing gauges. Late in November, Joffre managed to extract from Alexeyev a promise that Russian troops would assist in the defence of Bucharest; but since the Romanians could not offer even the sixteen trains per day needed for these troops, the proposal fell through. Alexeyev would give Romania only a small force—50,000 men (two infantry divisions and a single cavalry division) under Zayonchkovski. Otherwise, the Romanians must help themselves. The nearest Russian force was Lechitski's IX Army, but it had only eleven divisions, was already engaged on the Dniester front, and in any case could not receive troops with any speed since communications were very poor and winter-conditions had already set in. Grudgingly, *Stavka* sent an extra corps to Lechitski, and concentrated its main efforts as before against Kowel.

Romania was virtually indefensible. The richest part of the country, Wallachia, jutted out in a long tongue between Hungary and Bulgaria: neither the Carpathians—traversed by many passes—nor the Danube offered real obstacles to an invasion, yet the Romanians could not simply abandon Wallachia, since this would mean loss of their capital. Their army could be easily split up between different functions, each of them difficult to discharge, and the Romanian high command complicated this problem still more by failing to give constant priorities to the various strategic tasks. Half of the army was switched, bewilderingly, between one front and the other. Romania's intervention could only matter if the initial offensive against Hungary won an immediate success.

This did not turn out to be the case. To start with, nearly 400,000 Romanians crossed the Hungarian borders, and met opposition in the shape of the Austro-Hungarian I Army: 34,000 man, with a corps of miners volunteering to defend their pits to the west. Frontier villages were occupied, and the old Saxon town of Kronstadt, which lay in the south-eastern tip of Transylvania. But supply-problems turned out to be crippling. There was not much railway-communication between Hungary and Romania, and that little was badly-managed. The paths through the mountains could often accommodate only troops moving in single file, not carts or guns. Commanders behaved ineptly, and seemed to think that the prospect of meeting German troops dispensed them from further activity. Some of them even thought that, once they reached Central

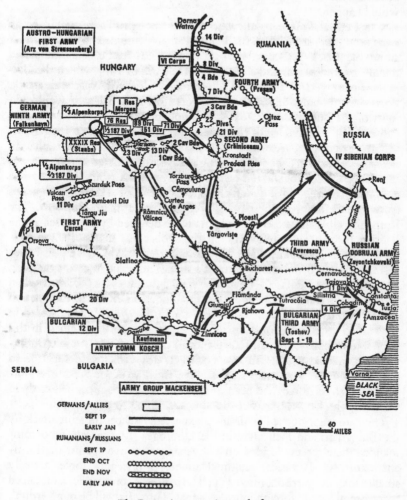

The Romanian campaign, end of 1916.

Transylvania, they would be so far from their supply-routes that catastrophe would intervene. In consequence, the Romanians did not even choose to occupy Hermannstadt, defended only by gendarmerie. They occupied the south-eastern tip of Transylvania, and waited to see what would happen.

The Central Powers' plan was obvious enough. There would be an attack on the Romanians in Transylvania, combined with an attack along the Black Sea coast, into the Dobrogea—fertile lands, inhabited mainly by Bulgarians and stolen from Bulgaria in 1913, which the Bulgarians were keen to recover. The Romanians did not expect this attack. First, they thought that western Powers' forces in Salonica would pin most of the Bulgarian army. This was not the case. The western Powers had enough on their hands to contain mosquitoes, let alone Bulgarians; in any case, their Greek allies were of such doubtful allegiance that an entire Greek army corps refused to fight at all, surrendered in toto and was interned in Silesia for the rest of the war. The attack from Salonica was a complete failure, and did not prevent Germans, Turks and Bulgarians from concentrating a substantial force against southern Romania. The Romanians had also expected Bulgaria to be deterred by the presence of a Russian force, Zayonchkovski's, in the Dobrogea. In theory, the Bulgarians were Russophil; men even thought they might make peace once Romania entered the war on Russia's side. This again was not the case. The Bulgarians hesitated about intervening; they even protested when German and Austro-Hungarian units stationed in Bulgaria took action against Romania (bombing Bucharest, for instance). But they decided in the end to declare war on Romania, a day or so after their allies. In this way, a joint offensive of all four Central Powers became possible. Moreover, the railways that fed reserves to Transylvania were superior to anything on the Romanian side. By the third week of September, the Central Powers' forces had been stepped up to 200,000 men, half of them German. The Kowel offensive did almost nothing to prevent this.

The campaign opened with an unexpectedly successful feint attack by the Bulgarians and their allies in the Dobrogea. Mackensen, who commanded these forces, decided on a diversionary move against the Romanian fortress, Tutracăia, on the Danube. A besieging force, actually smaller than the garrison, moved up. The fortress's commander announced to an assemblage of foreign journalists that 'Tutracăia will be our Verdun'. It fell the next day, eighty per cent of the garrison surrendering, and the rest fleeing, their commander in the lead. By 8th September, Silistria also had fallen, this time without even spoken resistance. The Bulgarians and their allies crossed the border and invaded the Dobrogea. Here they were due to encounter Russian forces. But the collaboration of Russians and

Romanians almost constituted an object-lesson in how not to run a multi-national force. Zayonchkovski, though doing his best to maintain polite forms, complained again and again to Alexeyev that his task was impossible: to make the Romanian army fight a modern war was asking a donkey to perform a minuet.[14] Ordinary Russian soldiers regarded their allies with the utmost contempt, not least when these allies surrendered to Russian units, mistaking them for Bulgarian ones. Russians sacked the countryside in a dress-rehearsal for the agrarian atrocities of 1917: estates laid to waste, wine-cellars ruthlessly plundered, beasts' throats cut, drunken soldiery drowned or boiled to death in vats of burning spirit. Russian officers quoted an old tag on Romania—'*des hommes sans honneur, des femmes sans pudeur, des fleurs sans odeur, des titres sans valeur*'. The Romanians, at their allies' mercy, could only exaggerate the Central Powers' strength in the hope that more Russian troops would somehow be sent to save them. But Alexeyev was adamant: he felt that Wallachia and the Dobrogea should be given up, and the Romanian army withdrawn into the Moldavian mountains until it had absorbed the facts of modern war. A division was sent from Kuropatkin's front in mid-September, and Lechitski was told to make better progress south of the Dniester. Otherwise, Russian help consisted mainly of renewed, futile attempts against the Kowel marches.

Threats to the Dobrogea compelled the Romanian high command to think again. On 15th September a crown council in Bucharest determined that wanderings in Transylvania should be suspended, to permit transfer of half of the army against Bulgaria. A 'Southern Army Group' of fifteen infantry divisions would be assembled under Averescu to cross the Danube into Bulgaria. Meanwhile, Zayonchkovski's Russo-Romanian force (six and a half Romanian and three Russian divisions) would contribute an offensive against the Bulgarians who had arrived in the Dobrogea. A real enough superiority was gradually built up: 195 battalions, 55 squadrons and 169 batteries to 110, 28 and 72 on the Central Powers' side. An attack was to be made between Zimnicea and Flămândă. It was a burlesque. Bridges were inadequate and broke down under the weight of guns and horses. Austro-Hungarian gunboats did much damage to the infantry as it tried to cross. Boats leaked. Such initial success as the crossings had was owing almost entirely to the deduction made by Kosch, German commander, from the Romanians' behaviour that they were only there to defend Bucharest. By 3rd October, after a few hours' action, the Flămândă enterprise had to be abandoned. In the Dobrogea, things took a similar course, with the complication that Romanians misunderstood Russian orders, and in any case were not keen on obeying them.

This strategic manoeuvre had been achieved at the cost of Romanian positions in Transylvania. Here, only ten divisions had been left—less than the Central Powers, with twelve. Moreover, the Romanians' advance had been of the worst possible kind. It had brought them beyond their own lines of supply, but it had not brought them forward to any point where they could disrupt the arrival by rail of the Central Powers' troops. By mid-September, a German IX Army had been established (as a grim joke under Falkenhayn's command) to co-operate with the Austro-Hungarian I Army. The various Romanian groups stood in isolated blocks just north of the Carpathians: usually in utter ignorance as to each other's whereabouts, and with no possibility of establishing rapid contact in battle. Falkenhayn drove against one of these isolated corps, at Hermannstadt, and pushed it back through the Turnu Roşu pass. The Romanian corps to its right, near Kronstadt, did not learn anything of this, and was itself driven back with much loss over the mountains. By 6th October, Transylvania was once more virtually completely in the hands of the Central Powers. Now Falkenhayn could cross the mountains into Wallachia, and join up with Mackensen's forces on the Danube. To avoid this, the Romanians decided to take back from the Danube the troops they had sent in the second half of September—such that nearly half of the Romanian army spent the first six weeks of war travelling between one front and the other. In the short term, this succeeded. The passes into Wallachia were blocked, and throughout October Falkenhayn's groups had a difficult time, pushing through the snow from one defence-position to another on their way through the mountains. From time to time, Conrad von Hötzendorf suggested more ambitious plans: a great offensive towards Bucharest, from the passes just to north-west of it. This plan, though subsequently praised by Liddell Hart, made too little sense on the ground for it to be adopted. Throughout October, the Central Powers' action here was more important for the troops that it pinned than for the ground it gained.

On the other hand, on the southern front the Central Powers' offensive achieved considerable results. An offensive into the Dobrogea was prepared, and launched, mainly with Bulgarian and Arab divisions, on 21st October. Zayonchkovski's army had not been strengthened: on the contrary, his demands for help had met only sarcastic remarks. He complained that his force was 'only the bone thrown to the Romanians to get them into this war'; he went on at length about the 'repulsive impression as regards military matters' that he had gained of his allies, and about their 'utter misunderstanding of modern war, their appalling inclination to panic'. But *Stavka* merely answered that, since the Romanians were not in any position of numerical inferiority, there should be no complaints. Defence of the Dobrogea was another piece of burlesque. Bombardment struck Romanians on the right, who retired without informing Russians in the centre. The Russian centre fell back in confusion, and the race to retreat was then won by the Romanian left, which fled back along the Black Sea coast, pursued by Bulgarian cavalry over the sands. In no time, the railway-line between Cernavoda and Constanţa, the Romanians' main port, was broken. Constanţa itself was not defended. Russians had ordered it to be destroyed, but the Romanians regarded it with too great pride to let this happen, and no doubt felt that their allies would make a thorough job of the destruction, if allowed to do so. They therefore surrendered the port, intact and with huge stocks of grain and oil, before the Russians could knock it about. The Russians' naval detachment supposedly guarding it then sailed away, leaving the Romanian defenders to their fate.[15] By the end of October, the Central Powers had captured more or less the whole of the Dobrogea, and threatened to cut off Bucharest from the sea.

Alexeyev now began to recognise that he would have to do something. The Kowel offensives had failed, and attacks in eastern Galicia were also dying down in failure; now the Central Powers had almost reached the Danube delta, and seemed to threaten southern Russia. *Stavka* first sent VIII Army to the Dniester, and then agreed to send another army, under Sakharov, to constitute, 'Army of the Danube' with a view to the defence of the delta and Gălăti. Finally, IV Army was ear-marked for Romania. Throughout November, a great movement of Russian troops was under way—thirty-six infantry and eleven cavalry divisions.[16] But the railway-lines, through Reni and Benderi, could take only 200 waggons a day, at a time when supply alone needed 433.[17] The management of these lines was such that a French railway-expert suffered a nervous break-down when he was detailed to sort them out. It was not until mid-December that the Russian troops had arrived in full strength, and even then they were badly under-supplied. Early in November, what arrived could suffice only to prevent further Bulgarian progress along the Black Sea coast.

But this stability could not change things in Wallachia. The Russian troops could not reach Bucharest in time, nor indeed did Alexeyev particularly want them to, for he was concerned only to defend Moldavia and the approaches to southern Russia. A cavalry corps was sent, but it was exhausted in covering 400 miles, and even re-shoeing of the horses could take up to a week in Romanian conditions. Early in November, German troops penetrated the passes into the western part of Wallachia— Oltenia—and by mid-November had reached the plains. A cavalry corps moved east towards Bucharest, dislodging the defenders from the southern parts of other passes. On 23rd November the Germano-Bulgarian force crossed the Danube, and found the task easy enough, since the Romanians had now diverted most of their forces back to the Carpathian front: there were only eighteen battalions to forty, and forty-eight guns to 188 when the Germans crossed at Ruščuk. By 29th November the two armies of the Central Powers were threatening Bucharest.

There was a final episode of drama. The Romanians had now been sent a French military mission, under Berthelot, Joffre's chief of staff during the battle of the Marne.[18] Berthelot was full of fight; he wished to build up the Romanian army—so much so that *Stavka* found his talk dangerous, and requested his removal. He had visions of a Balkan Marne: a flank-attack on the Germans as they approached Bucharest, crossing the Argeş river. In the first days of December, Berthelot built up a *masse de man-oeuvre:* divisions scraped from the Danube and the Carpathians. Amid grandiose announcements of national heroism, illiterate peasantry were driven forward by stage-heroic staffs into an affair that only consumed what was left of the reserve-divisions. Apart from a minor embarrassment, the Germans barely noticed 'the Romanian Marne'. Socec, who led one of the Romanian divisions, led his men in flight, was subjected to preliminary investigation for court-martial, and was then absolved when the dossier of his case was 'stolen' from the war ministry archives. As a background to all this, British military representatives prudently toured the oil-areas of Ploieşti, setting light to the wells. In clouds of smoke, the remnants of the Romanian divisions withdrew to the north, leaving Bucharest to Mack-ensen who entered it on 7th December. Of the twenty-three Romanian divisions, six had 'disintegrated', two had been 'captured', and the rest contained, together, 70,000 men. Mackensen plodded after them. But with the arrival of Russian troops, the Germans' progress was slow. They were held up at Urziceni, and then, in a battle over Christmas, at Rîmnicu-Sărat. By early January, they were lodged on the Siret, border of Moldavia, and could not progress beyond bridgeheads.

Thereafter, the Romanian campaign died down. Both sides suffered from difficulties of supply that prevented them from undertaking further action. On the Central Powers' side, the cold caused casualties of twenty-five per cent. Mud, lice, appalling roads, lack of railways, hovels made up the picture. The Central Powers also quarrelled bitterly over spoils: Bulgarians and Turks wrangled over the future of the Dobrogea, many Germans and Austro-Hungarians wished to restore Romania as an ally of the Central Powers. At the same time, Mackensen was told to send troops to other fronts. On the Russo-Romanian side, there was also little appetite for action. The Romanian army had been put to flight; it could count on a man-power reserve of less than 250,000 men, most of them quite untrained. The Russians, who now dominated the area completely, had no stomach for further offensive action. Their only action of any scale between early January and the Kerenski offensive of mid-summer was a stroke on the

Baltic coast. Early in January they profited from withdrawal of German troops to stage a coup in Courland, against Mitau and Tukkum. They attacked by surprise, in an area of sand-dunes that masked the attackers' activity; did not bombard in advance; did not attack in 'waves'. In return for a few thousand casualties, they won a respectable success: thirty-six German guns and 8,000 prisoners. It was a symbol of the patterns prevailing on the eastern front. Minor attacks, launched by surprise, generally achieved far more impressive results than major ones preceded by heavy bombardment. The campaign of 1916 thus ended, fittingly enough, with a demonstration of Brusilov's correctness.[19]

CHAPTER THIRTEEN

War and Revolution, 1917

Early in 1917, Russian generals were full of fight. Conferences with allied soldiers at Chantilly, and with allied politicians in Petrograd, confirmed suspicions that the Entente had now become vastly more powerful than the Germans: the western, eastern, Balkan and Italian fronts each showed an allied superiority of at least sixty per cent in men and guns. Even Evert's mouth watered, as he contemplated the great amounts of shell with which he would plaster a few square kilometres of German line in the coming spring offensives. Moreover, the prospect of American intervention against Germany gave Russians and western Powers alike a hope of final success in 1917. None the less, there was to be little fighting in the east in 1917. Revolution broke out in March; there was a Bolshevik coup in November; Russia dropped out of the war in December, when an armistice was concluded at Brest-Litovsk; and a peace-treaty was signed in March 1918. In the meantime, the front itself was almost wholly inactive. There was some grumbling in March 1917, in Volhynia; an offensive, lasting a few days, in July; a German counter-offensive, which took Eastern Galicia in August, and Riga in September. The Russian economy might, now, be capable of sustaining a world war; but Russian society had not stood the strain. The home front collapsed into class-war; the army at the front could not apparently be got to fight; while the army in the rear joined the forces of revolution. Virtually the whole of the country's working population went on strike, although, with the German enemy at the gates, there was ostensibly every good cause for keeping a united home front until the war had been won.

It was later asserted that the disaster was caused, above all, because of the division of government. After the March Revolution, 'Establishment' Russia—the *Stavka* generals, the Duma, the industrialists—came together as in the spring of 1915, and formed a Provisional Government. The revolutionary masses of Petrograd formed their own council, the Soviet, which faithfully recorded, at regular intervals, the temper of the masses, and which, from the beginning, was dominated by the left-wing parties.

A system of Soviets came into existence, more or less spontaneously, throughout the country: the men in army units, in factories, and, in the end, the villages as well set up such councils to safeguard the revolution and ensure its promotion. The Soviet's order on army matters decreed an end to the humiliating rituals which ordinary soldiers had had to put up with, and henceforth officers' authority could, in most units, be enforced only through agreement with the unit's council, if then. The division of power between government and Soviet was, in fact, unreal. The government had control of the bureaucracy, but increasingly it lost control of the armed forces, and it owed most of its power to the Soviet. But the Soviet did not know how to use its power, and most of its early leaders earnestly wished that the Provisional Government would do the job. The Soviet had pledged itself, quite early on, to 'peace without annexations or contributions'. But, as became increasingly clear, the German government was not interested in this, except from tactical motives, so that, unless the Soviet wanted to see Ludendorff invade Russia, it must go on fighting the war. In this event, power must be left to the generals. In the same way, the maintenance of the economy must be left to bankers and industrialists who understood these things. In due course, many Mensheviks thus found themselves striving to suggest to their followers that they should obey the prescriptions of a régime which they had themselves been elected to repudiate; and in time, prominent Soviet people were to join the Provisional Government—Kerenski being the best-known.

The system did not break down because of Bolshevik agitation alone. To begin with, the Bolsheviks were just as confused as the other parties. They too accepted that the revolution must be defended against German imperialism, and after the March Revolution were eager, to their subsequent embarrassment, to get back to normal—Kamenev and Stalin appealing for 'order' in the army and the factories, Gorki telling people to get back to work. It was only after Lenin's return to Russia in April that the Bolsheviks adopted an out-and-out revolutionary programme: unremitting class-war in town and country, immediate peace, all power to the Soviets. Even then, many Bolsheviks regarded Lenin as a maniac, and in July his name was missed off a list of Anarchists and Bolsheviks drawn up to form a government. It was not until September that the Soviets became, in majority, Bolshevik; and even in November, it was more fear of counter-revolution than desire for power that drove the Bolsheviks into their November coup against the Provisional Government. Russia did not go Bolshevik because the masses were Bolshevik from the start of the Revolution, or because of the machinations of Soviet and Bolshevik leaders. She went Bolshevik because the old order collapsed, more or less as Lenin—uniquely—had foretold it would. By the autumn of 1917, the towns were starving and disease-ridden; stratospheric inflation deprived wage-increases, indeed the whole economic life of the country, of meaning; production of war-goods fell back so far that the army could not fight, even if it had wanted to. Mines, railways, factories seized up. Kerenski and his sympathisers in the Soviets wished to restore things through co-operation with the old order. This programme did not work, for the economy collapsed in chaos, and the way was open to Lenin, who promised a new system altogether. Economic chaos drove Russia towards Bolshevism, sometimes despite the Bolsheviks.

This economic chaos was frequently ascribed quite simply to backwardness: Russia was not advanced enough to stand the strain of a war, and the effort to do so plunged her economy into chaos. But economic backwardness did not alone make for revolution, as the examples of Romania or Bulgaria showed; and in any case, Russia was not backward in the same way as these countries, as was shown in her capacity to make war-material in 1915-16. The economic chaos came more from a contest between old and new in the Russian economy. There was a crisis, not of decline and relapse into subsistence, but rather of growth. There was a sudden burst of progress during the war—much greater commercial activity, much greater labour-mobility, much more investment—and hence much greater exploitation of the country's labour-force than before. Virtually for the first time, the Russian government prepared to spend money, instead of being bound, as in the past, by the narrowest of gold-standard orthodoxies. The result was a considerable economic explosion. It was shown in the wartime statistics of growth overall, particularly the delivery of war-material. It was shown in the great profits of 1915-16, in the boom of the Stock Exchange. It was also shown in the rise of banking, as the general level of economic activity forced banks to extend their business. The number of State Savings Banks doubled, to over 15,000, in the war-years; and more bank-branches were opened, between 1914 and 1917, than in the whole of Russia's past.

There was a parallel movement on the side of labour. The size of Russia's proletariat grew very fast between 1914 and 1916. The registered part of it—which was only a small section, contained in factories with over sixteen employees—rose by one million to reach 3,643,000 in January 1917, and the number of workers in this category may even be larger, since the wartime statistics were not infallible. There were also great increases in the parts of the proletariat not registered with the Factory Inspectorate. State factories, for instance, which had taken 120,000 workers in 1914, employed 400,000 in January 1917—a third of them in Petrograd. The railways employed 1,200,000 persons in 1917, an increase of half a million over 1914, although the mileage operated in 1917 was smaller. The work-force in mines doubled, to 800,000; employees of the oil-firms in the south rose to over half a million, as did men engaged on the country's water-ways. Even the building-industry, normally one to be hit in war-time, employed 1,500,000 people in 1917, a rise of one-third.[1]

The main source for these increases was, inevitably, the countryside; and it is probably not even too much of an exaggeration to suggest that the countryside lost more men of working age to industry than to the army. There was much greater mobility between town and country than ever before: men might go to the towns in search of higher wages in the expanding industries, but they would often return to their village communes so as to keep going their right to land there. Indeed, the whole movement was prompted partly by blandishment, partly by force. Higher wages made the blandishment, though their value was often reduced by inflation. Conscription certainly made for force on the other side, as men strove to get into a 'white-ticket' occupation to save them from the army, or simply strove to escape the recruiting-sergeants in the anonymity of the towns. But the chief element was the collapse of many village occupations as competition from the towns, the dry-up of raw materials, confusions of transport, and inflation hit them. Eleven million Russian peasant households had lived, not from agriculture, but mainly from cottage-industries of one kind or another—rope-making, sack-making, weaving. By 1917, only four and a half million of these were left: in Tula, for instance, three-quarters of the peasant households had declared some kind of cottage-industry before the war, but by 1917, less than a third did so.[2] Conscription, inevitably, was blamed, but in reality much more than that was involved. The large firms produced rope, sacks, textiles more than before, and by modern methods; they acquired raw-materials and machinery, and, with their storage-space, could resist inflationary problems better than cottage-industries that had to sell their goods at once. It is not surprising that many peasants, who had counted among the well-off members of their village community, trekked into the towns in search of work. The vast increase in labour-mobility is best judged by railway-statistics: in 1916–17, there were 113 million more civilian passenger-journeys than in 1913–14, and this was only part of the story, since journeys by road or river and canal are not taken into account.[3] There was, in other words, a burst of economic activity between 1914 and 1917 that brought as much change to Russia as the whole of the previous generation. It was, indeed, the economic 'take-off' that men had been predicting for Russia; that had, in a sense, caused the First World War, since German apprehensions of it had led Germany's leaders into provoking a preventive war. The

First World War provoked a crisis of economic modernisation, and Bolshevik revolution was the outcome.

Some writers have argued that, had it not been for the accident of war in 1914, the Russian economy would have continued to make progress on European lines, instead of having to go through the Stalinist phase. Maybe these writers are right. On the other hand, the war was not such a distortion of Russia's economic patterns as was often thought: on the contrary, economic problems, thought at the time to be peculiar to a wartime situation, were not more than hectic versions of economic problems that have become quite standard in this century. Abandonment of the gold standard—at least in practice—and reliance on printed money were an obvious instance; but there were many others. The cessation of imports from Germany, the difficulty—whether financial, or from transport-problems—of replacing them from other countries, and the increasing inability of Russia to export grain as before, were all versions of a foreign-trade dilemma that any country relying on exports of primary products for its place in the world market was likely to encounter: it had to develop its own industry, because the price-instability of its main exports was such that it could not rely on other people's industry for ever. This, far from being a uniquely wartime problem, was one encountered by all such countries in the 1920s and 1930s, and indeed in the 1950s. Similarly, the ostensibly wartime problem of Russian agriculture was merely a version—and not even in a very altered pattern—of the greatest long-term Russian economic problem of all: how to fit an agriculture that was not structured for production of surpluses to the needs of a modern industrial economy, with millions of urban workers to be fed. In this context, even the supplying with food of an army six million strong would be an incident, not a crippling distortion. Behind the confusion and dislocation of wartime, Russia was encountering, in other words, problems that she had to face, war or no war; the nature of the economy is to be seen, not in speculations as to how the economy would have gone on had there been no war, but in its reaction to the demands of war.

Overall, the war-economy illustrated the force of the maxim, 'il faut souffrir pour être belle'. It required, and got, an expansion of heavy industry, and a concentration of resources on that sector, that could not bring much immediate return—certainly not in the form of consumer-goods and higher living-standards for the masses, for it was on the contrary essential for most workers to put up with lower standards while they were laying the basis for higher ones. The Tsarist government, aware of its isolation, shrank from demanding such a sacrifice, and it refrained from imposing taxes of any seriousness on the populace. But the tax came, none the less, in the most ruthless and dishonest form of all: inflation, which was more effective in transferring resources from consumer to investor than any other mechanism.

Before 1914, Russia had operated a gold standard. Maintenance of this meant strict control of the money-supply, such that circulating money would always be covered by the gold-reserve. In this way, foreigners' and Russians' confidence in the currency and the economy as a whole would be maintained, although the restriction frequently made credit difficult. The gold standard had been under strain before 1914: the volume of economic activity rose, and there was a demand for money that existing gold reserves could not cover. In 1914, ordinary housekeeping had to be thrown to the winds, because the government had to spend far beyond the capacity of Russia's gold-reserve. The circulating currency of 1914— with 106 per cent gold-coverage—would barely suffice to meet one half of the bounties paid to soldiers' families in the First World War; bounties paid at the insulting rate of $1·00 per month for most of the war, but amounting, by 1st September 1917, to 3,264, million roubles. The 15,000 million roubles disbursed on armaments by the Special Council—not to mention the thousands of millions of roubles spent on supply—could only be covered by government borrowing. Pre-war expenditure had amounted to less than 3,500 million roubles per annum. Wartime expenditure rose far beyond this level: 9,500 million roubles in 1915, 15,300 million in 1916, of which the War ministry accounted for 11,400 million. Russia spent $27,800,000 per day in wartime, more even than France or Great Britain.[4] To meet these demands, the government borrowed—partly from the Russian public, through war-loan, partly from its allies, and partly by 'short-term obligations of the State Treasury', usually discounted by the State Bank. The result was a very great rise in the amount of circulating money:

Russian Public Finance 1914–1917

(thousand million roubles, rounded to the nearest hundred million)

Year	Money (all types) in circulation	% rise	price-index
1914: 1st half:	2·4	(100)	(100)
1915: 1st half:	3·5	146	115
1916: 1st half:	6·2	199	141
1916: 2nd half:	8·0	336	398
1917: 1st half:	11·2	473	702
1917: 2nd half:	19·2	819	1,172

In these circumstances, formal maintenance of the gold standard became almost laughable. Russian gold covered less than 2,000 million roubles, and although there was a theoretical loan from Great Britain of a further

2,000 million roubles' worth of gold, the gold itself stayed in the Bank of England—or rather, would have done if the British had had it. Rapidly-expanding money supply, however much men might bewail it, at least secured a much higher level of economic activity than before, was indeed an inevitable concomitant of progress. It generated something of a boom, in which public demand for money came to exceed even the State's willingness to provide it.*

But whatever the immediate, short-term benefits attached to this new policy, it brought about an inflation that went far beyond the experience of any other country in wartime. Prices, overall, rose almost four times by January 1917, and over ten times before the Bolshevik Revolution. The increase in money-supply was not alone responsible; its effects were greater because the structure of the economy was such as to make inflation considerable once the government abandoned its strict monetary policy. The decline of the rouble on foreign exchanges, the rise in basic costs such as transport, shortages that could be exploited by profiteers, the need for firms to obtain relatively scarce skilled labour by offering higher and higher wages, monopolies' tendency to go for quick profits in an era of uncertainty, all made for inflation's being more marked in Russia than in other countries. Finally, the inflation became self-generating, since prices came to include their own counter-inflationary mark-up. The government did attempt to control prices: but the attempt was based on incomprehension of the problem, epitomised by the Governor-General of Turkestan's Saturday visits to the bazaars, and public horsewhipping of traders found to be exceeding his—unpredictable—price-norms. In industrial matters, government—monopoly combinations came into existence in an effort to stop the great traders from hoarding against inflation; but with food, and millions of peasant households, this system did not work at all, and merely dried up supplies unless the government were prepared to equalise its maximum price with the farmers' minimum one. Price-control could work, even modestly, only if accompanied by subsidies; and yet the government's own policy excluded these. Public prices and private prices grew apart, and the background to revolution in 1917 was one of vast queues in the shops, shortages everywhere, and a flourishing black-market.

The government barely understood what was happening, and certainly

---

*By 1917, the pressure was such that the Bank did not have time to cut and number its notes before handing them out. Money was handed over bank-counters in printed sheets containing several notes, which the customer then cut; the Treasury pushed its own 'short-term obligations' onto suppliers, as payment; and the United States government was officially asked, in 1917, to undertake printing of Russian money, on the grounds that the Russian printers were disgruntled and strike-prone.[6]

lacked the statistical apparatus that might have produced a more suitable policy. It fell back on standard remedies: attempts to restore confidence by raising the exchange-value of the rouble; blaming of 'speculators'— i.e. Jews or Germans; in summer 1917, blundering attempts to get the trade-unions to restrict their members' wage-demands—which merely resulted in a loss of confidence in Menshevik trade-union leaders. There was constant talk of somehow absorbing the excess paper-money that was held to be responsible for the inflation, but these measures did not work, since neither the Tsarist régime nor the Provisional Government had the popular base that alone would have enabled them to demand sacrifices.

Taxation,[7] for instance, was barely increased. Before 1914, it had been mainly indirect, and, despite legends to the contrary, relatively trivial. One-fifth of the budget revenue had come from indirect taxes before the war, less than one tenth from direct taxes (mainly on land and property); most of the rest had come from State monopoly enterprises—spirits on the one side, railways on the other. The war brought havoc to the system, since expenses were in ludicrous disproportion to receipts. Yet the government had itself abolished the trade in spirits, which gave it one-third of its revenue before the war; and shrank from imposing taxes on matches, sugar, kerosine to make up. It was only towards the end of 1915 that a variety of such indirect taxes came to make up the loss caused by abandonment of the trade in spirits; and it is thought that the agricultural community gained roughly 1,000 million roubles from prohibition.

It was clearly desirable to substitute a direct tax on income for these indirect taxes. But the government shrank from operating such taxes. An income-tax would hit the section of the community that would invest its savings in industry, or government loan; and would thus merely ensure that the money would reach the government by a roundabout bureaucratic route instead of the simple route through the banking system. In any case, in a country where most people, being peasants, kept their own books and so could not be properly reviewed for purposes of direct taxation, the operation of direct taxes would demand a vast bureaucratic machine that could only be very expensive, and possibly counter-productive.* These arguments were deployed, with effect, by the liberal economists and the propertied classes generally. Much the same arguments were used against the introduction of a tax on excess profits, such as was being gradually introduced in other countries. It was no doubt true that some businesses were making large profits. But it was also true that the government re-

---

*Even in England, which was well-organised, government met the same problem with farmers. Direct taxes (including an income-tax that took 6/- in the £ of incomes above £135) were levied on farmers with a rule-of-thumb that their profits would be twice their rent. Not many farmers objected to this rule-of-thumb.[8]

quired considerable enterprise on its suppliers' behalf, and should therefore be prepared to reward them. Moreover, excess-profits had to cover conversion of industry to war-work, whether directly or through investment in the Stock Exchange; and they would also have to cover the post-war reconversion of industry, and the period of excess-loss that would automatically follow the collapse of the boom. In other words, whatever the demagogic advantages of excess-profits-taxes, they could be damaging to business. It is true that the British operated an ostensibly effective wartime excess-profits-duty. But they had to do so with an allowance for post-war excess-losses; and when these duly came, after 1920, many of the excess-profits-taxes had to be reimbursed. Sir Josiah Stamp, who had been responsible for their operation, regarded the whole enterprise as little more than a forced loan from business to government, and felt that it had quite possibly made a loss.[9] These considerations counted for much in Russia, and direct taxation was never more than a gesture. An income tax was introduced in 1916. It took ten per cent of incomes greater than 400,000 roubles per annum. An excess-profits-duty was also brought in at the same time, again with generous allowances. The income tax gave 130 million roubles, the excess-profits-due, 56 million: together, less than enough to pay for a week-end of war.*

In the circumstances, the only way of connecting wartime expenditure with the nation's wealth appeared to be loan.[10] The Tsarist régime launched six war-loans, with a nominal value of 8,000 million roubles, and the Provisional Government launched a seventh, the Liberty Loan, for 4,000 million: in theory, as effective a way of sucking back excess paper-money as taxation, and one moreover that suited the economics of 1915, i.e. patriotism plus six per cent. But for a variety of reasons, the war-loans not only failed, but may even have added to the stock of circulating paper-money. In an inflationary situation, few propertied Russians would be fool enough to subscribe to fixed-interest, long-dated government bonds. The loans became shorter in term—from forty-nine years to ten—and the true rate of interest rose from five to over six per cent, or even more if they were allowed against tax. Commission alone reduced the value of the loans by almost a thousand million roubles. Even so, the loans hardly worked, and Peter Bark confessed that they did so only through 'a book-keeping operation'. The State Bank was already advancing money to the private banks against securities, in the usual way. War-loan was allowed to count as such security, so that if a bank acquired war-loan, it could get its money back at once, by using the loan as

---

*In England, direct taxation accounted for a quarter of government revenue in 1917 and 1918.

collateral. Moreover, there was little difference between the interest that the private bank would be paying for its loan to the State Bank, and the interest that it was itself acquiring from its war-loan; indeed, for the first three months, the rate of interest on war-loan was actually greater, through devices of various sorts, than the rate on bank-loan, so that the banks were often better-off at no expense to themselves. The banks took a nominal 4,000 million roubles' worth of war-loan, from which their commissions were deducted; they also took 3,700 million roubles of credit from the State Bank. The war-loan operations thus barely dented circulating paper-money, and may even have left the wealthier classes slightly better-off. The governments could rely only on the printing-press: 'short-term obligations of the State Treasury', discounted almost exclusively by the State Bank, which held eighty per cent of them, and forced the rest onto clients not in a position to resist. In theory, these obligations accounted for two-fifths of wartime expenditure; but in effect they also covered the third also alleged to have come from war-loan, and the credit-structure, vital to the maintenance of a capitalist economy, began to sag and collapse. The Tsarist government had put up the money-supply to over ten thousand million roubles by January 1917. The Provisional Government doubled it, to almost twenty thousand million by September 1917, until a classic situation of uncontrollable inflation resulted—wage-demands, bank-credits, government money-supply chasing each other until

it is impossible to say which is the cause and which is the effect . . . The Central Bank is *compelled* to supply the public sector with a growing volume of funds, while commercial banks are *forced* to expand loans to the private sector at an accelerated pace, and wages and salaries *have* to be raised again and again. The three factors originally responsible for the inflationary spiral appear to be simply . . . passive elements in an uncontrollable process.[11]

Russians might have resisted Bolshevism if there had been a real alternative; but the collapse of capitalism was there for all to see. Wages became meaningless: strikes came, one after another, and caused a fall of fifty per cent in industrial production in the summer of 1917.

The principal problem in all of this was that wages could not be translated into food. Industry had done well enough from the inflation, at least in its earlier stages, before the autumn of 1916. Agriculture was not in a position to profit nearly as much, and the result of inflation was to drive the bulk of food-producers back into the subsistence-economy from which they had only recently emerged, if at all. Food-deliveries to the towns ran down after November, 1916; Petrograd had, when the March Revolution occurred, only a few days' grain-reserves, and the bread-riots that sparked off the revolution continued to detonate revolutionary explosions throughout the summer and autumn.

In theory, agriculture, which supplied the most necessary produce of all, should have profited from inflation, and been able to charge what it liked. No doubt, too, had the various legends about Russian agriculture been true, this would have occurred: that is, if the country's agriculture had been controlled by capitalist farmers and great estates fully integrated in the buying-and-selling network. But it is a legend that Russia was dominated by great estates. Only about a tenth of the land sown in Russia belonged to such estates, and even then some of that was peasant land in disguise, farmed on ancient manorial principles.[12] Some of the nobles had made something of a living from exploiting their estates—the Yusupovs in Poltava gained a return of eight per cent per annum on their capital—but many of them, in the face of transport-problems and peasant recalcitrance either sold off the land to banks and peasants, or rented out their huge tracts at tiny sums: the Counts Orlov-Davydov, for instance, renting out 250,000 acres on long leases at three roubles per acre per annum.[13] The quantity of grain coming onto the market from such sources was not great: even taking into account the rôle of land-owners as middlemen for their peasants' produce, it amounted to only thirteen per cent of army purchases in 1914-15, and declined thereafter. Independent smallholders formed a comparable case. They were of course better-placed to exploit their land than the great estates. But there were not many such small-holders, and they hardly supplied more than the great estates: fifteen per cent of army grain in 1914-15.

Both sets of private land-owners suffered from wartime disabilities that made it impossible for them to increase their production. There was, first of all, the question of labour. It was said that conscription had bitten into the stock of labour, but conscription alone was not the answer, for even the absence of eleven million young peasants in wartime could scarcely dent a rural population known to have a surplus of at least twice this. No doubt conscription, by removing a proportion of the able-bodied young workers, caused more damage than the numbers in question warranted; but the heart of this problem was not conscription alone, but the general drift of the rural population towards the towns, where they could sometimes assemble enough money to return to their communes without having to work again for the land-lord or small-holder. Moreover, neither set could expand production by other means, machinery or fertiliser. Resources had been placed, inevitably, in heavy industry; and imports, whether of machinery or fertiliser, had had to be curtailed for similar reasons. In 1916, only thirteen million roubles' worth of agricultural machinery was sold, as against 110 million roubles' worth in 1913, and agricultural machinery as a whole formed about a tenth of all machinery produced in Russia. The stock of machinery on the land aged, and was not replaced. Fertiliser came mainly from abroad, and was reduced, partly because the transport-system had other priorities, partly because foreign exchange could not be made available for it. In 1916, 5,600 tons were used (mainly phosphate) as against ten times as much before the war; the Trans-Siberian railway could accommodate only six waggons of it per day in 1915, and less thereafter.[14] There was even a lack of such items as sacks, allegedly because of speculators, in reality because cottage-industry production had declined. Faced with lack of labour (which half of Russia's provinces complained was 'acute' in 1916), with a three-fold rise in agricultural wages, and a general inability to expand their production by other means, land-owners and small-holders alike found it impossible to produce as much as before. Many nobles faced real hardship, as inflation bit into the rents they collected; a Congress of the United Gentry in November 1916 was only narrowly prevented from passing a revolutionary resolution and the nobles of the south seceded in protest.* Production, both on noble and small-holder land, declined. In 1916, less than two-thirds of noble land sown in 1914 was sown with rye and wheat; and some of the most prosperous regions of small-holding farming cut back their output even more. Stavropol, for instance, one of the most fertile regions of Russia, produced only a fifth of the grain in 1916–17 that it had produced in 1913–14.[16] More and more, the nobles rented out their often useless land. In Tula, for example, 105 of 138 estates were renting out two-fifths of their land, and would no doubt have sold it if a universal conviction that land would soon go the peasants had not deprived them of buyers.[17]

Food-supply therefore came to depend on the peasant plot. In 1914–15, it had supplied sixty per cent of the army's grain, and the proportion rose thereafter: sometimes bought directly by military authorities, but usually purchased through middle-men, and latterly banks. The Russian agrarian question is more encrusted with legend than any other subject in the country's history; and much of the legendry attaches to the question of food-supply in 1916–17. It was suggested that deliveries to the towns and the army were running down because less grain was being produced. This was not at all true. Peasant Russia was not affected by the same factors that affected private land-lords. The peasants were less dependent on sophistic-

---

*Some nobles responded meanly against their remaining labour-force. The Olsufievs took back six cows they had given to their labourers; Prince V. F. Gagarin cut by half the flour ration he gave them; Prince Lvov—of Provisional Government fame—cut back his present of potatoes by six-sevenths.[15]

ated machinery, and they had seldom used fertiliser before 1914—if only because, in Russian circumstances, it blew away. In general, the productive peasant plots did not suffer from a shortage of labour anywhere nearly comparable to that suffered by the private estates. This occurred for reasons that were, by 1914, almost peculiar to Russia.[18] Most of the country's twenty million peasant households lived in communes, either formal or informal. It was the commune that owned the land; peasant families took it over, usually for a dozen years or so, according to their needs. A large family had mouths to feed, and hands to work the land. It would be assigned a much larger number of strips of land than a smaller household. Natural catastrophe—for instance, famine, destruction of the family house by fire, or pestilence—could literally wipe out a peasant family; and in any case, the father of the family would, one day, have to contemplate the day when his children would grow up, have families of their own, and demand their due share of the communal lands. After a dozen years as substantial farmer, he might find the communal assembly re-partitioning his lands; and in a great many communes throughout Russia, men who had farmed sufficient land for them to be known as 'prosperous' peasants* would find themselves reduced to the status of 'middle' or even 'poor' peasant within a few years. A dimension was thus added, in Russia, to the standard peasant problem of sub-division by inheritance; and although reputable economists rubbed their eyes in disbelief, the system suited Russian conditions surprisingly well. The Tsarist régime supported the system for most of the time, because it made administration easier once emancipation of the serfs had been proclaimed. The peasants, or most of them, welcomed it as ensuring some kind of equalisation of chances, and most of them stoutly resisted attempts to abolish it: indeed, according to Professor Shanin, even quite wealthy independent small-holders were sometimes anxious to join communes, because they could get even more land that way than they already had.

This was not a system likely to suffer from labour-shortage. Members of the family might go to the towns, or the army, for some of the year, but they could come back at harvest-time to help the women and old men, and hundreds of thousands seem to have done so—to the factory owners' eternal lamentation. Moreover, the withdrawal from the land of so many people meant that there was more space for animals on it: and the first great surprise of Russian agriculture was the growth recorded, in the census of 1916,[19] in the animal population. The cattle-population appears

---

*The word 'kulak' (fist) is traditionally applied to these people, as a token of their unpopularity with most peasants. It is a misnomer. 'Kulak' meant village usurer, like 'gombeen-man' in Ireland. He might also of course own land, but only incidentally. Prosperous peasants were simply known to the peasants as 'prosperous peasants'.

to have increased by twenty-five per cent, the sheep and goat population still more. This gave many advantages, though it also lessened the amount of surplus grain available for the towns. In the same way, removal of people from the land made it possible for more land to be farmed: and, despite the supposedly savage effects of conscription, peasant land-sowing did not only not decline, but increased by eighteen per cent in the war-years.

It was not at all true to make out the Russian food-problem to be a consequence of low harvests, provoked by labour-shortage. The harvests were, on the contrary, rather higher than before the war, if due allowance is made for the occupation by Germany of the empire's western fringe. Taking the area available in 1916—the forty-seven provinces of European Russia—the harvest of 1914 was 4,304 million poods (1 pood = 16 kg.), that of 1915 was 4,659 million, that of 1916, 3,916 million. Even in 1917, when the food shortage of the towns became crippling, the harvest itself was not too far below pre-war levels—3,800 million poods, not including potatoes.[20] It was certainly true that army demand had risen; but it was also true that exports had fallen by an equivalent amount. If it had been a simple question of dividing the grain available by the mouths that wanted to consume it, there would have been enough and to spare. Lositski quotes the following figures:[21]

Production of, and Demand for, Grain 1917 (million poods, rounded).

Production		Demand	
harvest of 1917:	3,809	army:	501
net, i.e. less grain			
kept back for sowing:	3,124	towns:	263
remainder from 1916:	669	country:	1,472
		livestock:	1,001
Totals:	3,793		3,273

In other words, the harvest of 1917 ought to have been enough to supply all needs, even leaving out of account the reserves that 21 out of the 44 provinces involved claimed to have.

Part of the difficulty in actually carrying out the operation of supplying that section of the country that did not live in the grain-producing areas was brought about by transport; the railways, overburdened in wartime, could not make sufficient grain available both to towns and army: a problem, however, also distorted by legend, to a degree that deserves separate discussions. Certainly, the towns did not benefit from the constant harvests of peasant Russia, but found themselves, on the contrary increasingly deprived of food. In 1913–14 they had taken 390 million poods of grain. In 1915–16 they got 330 million; and in 1916–17, 295 million, although in these years their population, swollen by natural increase, refugees, and migrant labour, increased by one-third. In January and February 1917, Moscow and the Central Provinces as a whole received less than a third of what they needed; by mid-summer, they were receiving 6,256 waggons of grain per month of the 30,000 they were supposed to get. In December, 1916, Petrograd had got 524,000 poods of grain in place of the 3,740,000 it needed, and in January forty-nine grain-waggons per day of the eighty-nine it needed. This was the vital factor in revolution, from March until the end of the year; and it became all the greater in its effects, since the quantities that were delivered were not divided up fairly, or even, sometimes, divided up at all. Suppliers sometimes held it back, at all levels, so as to profit from the inevitable price-increase: rye rose in price in Moscow from a base of seventy-six kopecks per pood in 1914 to 333 per cent in March 1917 and 666 per cent in the autumn. Government attempts to control prices usually caused havoc. The bakers in Petrograd complained that they could not afford to bake bread at the declared price, because that price was out of joint with the price of fuel; and yet if the government tried to control fuel-prices, it would merely provoke a dry-up of fuel-supplies. Moscow and Petrograd developed all the revolutionary symptoms of a town under siege, but without the physical presence of the enemy that usually enforced unity for the duration.[22]

Many explanations—other than the false one of too little grain—were advanced for the dry-up of food-supplies. It was said that the army had taken up too much of the grain. But the armed forces, in reality, took less than had been exported before the war. In 1913–14, 640 million poods of grain had been exported from the area in question; thereafter, exports declined to a trivial figure (in 1916–17, not three million poods). Army demand rose from eighty-five million poods in 1913–14 to 600 million in 1915–16, and fell again in 1916–17 to 485 million. The chief factor was that the peasantry were not marketing grain as before. About twenty-five per cent of the total harvest had been marketed before the war; but by 1916–17, only fifteen per cent was marketed, although urban demand had risen by a third. Where 1,200 million poods had come on the market in 1914, 978 million did so in 1915 and 794 million in 1916. Less than 300 million went to the towns, the rest more or less completely to the army; and the country's animals got a third as much again as towns and army put together.

The peasants preferred to use their grain for livestock or for their own consumption, because inflation had gradually forced this course upon them. Theoretically, they should have benefited from the high food-prices of wartime; in some areas near the large towns, they no doubt did so. But most of the grain was produced in scattered villages, remote from a railway-line and without easy access to markets. The grain would be collected by a local dealer, with a hut to store it and a cart to carry it: this, not the peasant who produced the grain, was the 'kulak'. He would sell it in turn to a larger dealer, who would perhaps pass it on to a bank—and banks, in 1916, held forty per cent of the country's grain-reserve, doling it out according to government willingness to increase the prices. Any profit that the grain acquired would thus stick to innumerable scales, and the peasant would be left with little, unless he were near enough to the market himself, and able to by-pass dealers and banks. To start with, peasants certainly went on selling, to make up for the loss of cottage-industries, or the rise in prices of manufactured items they might wish to buy. But inflation in the summer of 1916 drove prices of this type of item far above what the peasant could pay. In Simbirsk, for instance, a pair of boots that cost seven roubles before the war cost thirty in 1916; in Ivanovo-Voznesensk, calico products rose to 319 per cent of their pre-war price in September 1916; horse-shoe nails, which cost three roubles and forty kopecks the pood in 1914 rose, early in 1916, to forty roubles. There was a 'scissors-crisis', not unlike that of the 1920s, when the price of manufactured items went so far above the prices that the peasant (as distinct from the dealer) would obtain for his produce that many peasants simply relapsed into subsistence: hiding their grain, where they could, or giving it out to animals, where they could not. Government institutions for collecting grain failed;[23] a beginning was made, ineffectively, with requisitioning-squads; in the end, the only part of the economic mechanism that functioned with efficiency was the Black Market, and after a time even it was adversely affected by inflation. A crude system of barter, sometimes through co-operatives, sometimes by 'bag-men', replaced the money-exchange; and it was with this system that the Bolsheviks got through their worst crisis.

It was characteristic of the times that men should have misunderstood the difficulties of grain-supply. These difficulties were variously written down, by civilians to the army, by anti-semites to speculators,* by revolutionaries to landlords and 'kulaks', by liberal economists such as Struve to blundering price-controls, and—most bizarrely of all—by Antsiferov to peasant prosperity. The greatest and longest-lasting such explanation also happened, not altogether coincidentally, to be the one that seemed to remove most of the political heat from the issue: it was claimed that the railways were insufficient to transport the country's grain, because war-time needs, particularly those of the army, cut across grain-supply. The grain-crisis was thus said to have been caused by a railway-crisis. But the evidence suggests that, if anything, it was the other way about.

---

*The anti-semitic 'Black Hundreds' opened their own bread-shops.

Army transport authorities ran the railways of the front area which, generously interpreted by them, came to encompass about a third of the rolling-stock, and that part of the country 'west of the meridian Saint Petersburg–Sevastopol'. The wastage with which these lines were run was notorious: generals wrestled for supply-waggons, and were slow in forwarding empty ones; battles of competence developed; crazy prudence reigned as regards speed and length of trains; unloading was never efficiently carried out. Even so, army transport, as a whole, did not add an extra strain to the railways. The railways of that part of Russia had served importing from, and exporting to Germany, or the needs of western provinces that were quite soon occupied by the Central Powers, and that in any case suffered from an immediate drop in economic activity as soon as war came. The army's railway-traffic did little more than take up slack created by this drop, in Poland and elsewhere, as exporting to Germany (and of course importing) came to a stop. In 1913, these lines had taken ninety-three million passengers and 3,381 million poods of freight. In 1915 they took army traffic similar in scale: ninety-five million passengers, 3,304 million poods of freight; in 1916, 112 million and 3,763 million respectively. There were of course temporary crises of some severity, notably with the evacuation and retreat of September 1915, which caused a general railway-crisis in the country. But army movement alone was no greater than the civilian movement of that section of the country before the war, and, for much of the time, army movement was less.

The rest of the country ought, then, to have had as much rolling-stock available for its purposes as before the war. Indeed, it should have had more, because grain-exporting, which had taken a substantial number of waggons and locomotives in 1913, came to an almost complete stop: in the second half of 1913, 712,000 waggon-loads of grain had to be shifted, but in the equivalent period of 1914, only 353,000. But this advantage was obscured by further legendry, to the effect that the country's railways fell into disrepair, and that the amount of rolling-stock available declined. Neither assertion had a germ of truth in it. On the contrary, the ministry of transport became the greatest spender in Russia, after the war ministry, and its expenditure rose from 400 million roubles in 1915 to 1,100 million in 1916. In all, it spent 2,500 million roubles during the war, and acquired a great deal of mileage and rolling stock. By 1917, 4,000 kilometres of new line, 1,195 of doubletracking, and 1,500 of gauge-broadening had been undertaken; a further 5,000 had been prepared for future construction, and 3,500 were already being built. Rolling-stock followed this pattern. Although the Germans, occupying the western part of the country, made off with a considerable amount of rolling-stock, the quantity of rolling-stock available in Russia actually rose throughout the war, with American imports and Russian construction. In 1918, there were 18,757 locomotives and 444,000 waggons as against 17,036 and 402,000 respectively in 1914, in the territory subsequently to become the U.S.S.R. In 1915–16, 2,188 locomotives and 70,000 waggons were acquired from Russia and America, which added a tenth to the existing stock, and of course, a tenth of higher quality than the rest. It was thus misleading to explain Russia's railway-difficulties in terms of a declining infrastructure, however much it suited both opposition and government to do so.

The railways' principal difficulty was that the patterns of economic life altered very rapidly in wartime, as the country modernised. Grain was an obvious source of trouble. It was, apart from coal, the bulkiest item to be carried, whether by waterway or railway. During the war, traditional suppliers failed to supply as before: the great estates, the northern Caucasus and the Kuban region were all affected by problems of shortages; and yet the railway-system had been geared to transport quantities of grain from such surplus-producing areas to the deficit-areas. In reality, the deficit-areas were often deficient, not in grain, but in farmers willing and able to market it; and if their supplies could be got at—as the Bolsheviks got at them—more grain would have been available, both locally and nationally. The railway network thus had to follow a switch in supply, at a time when all manner of other calls were being made on it. It was not trains, but timetables, that offered problems. Trains chased grain, not the other way about, and although the railways had to carry less grain than before 1914, that quantity needed longer railway-journeys and more trains. The government helplessly watched grain, train and fuel competing, and each falling into chaos. This occurred at a time when economic activity at home was making demands on the railways that they had never experienced before. Labour-mobility brought an increase from 235 million to 348 million passengers in the period 1914–16; increased movement of goods similarly caused the railways to shift 17,228 million poods of freight in 1916, as against 13,826 million before the war. It was not that the railway-network declined—rather the contrary: it was rather that railway-development and railway-usage ran higgledy-piggledy after the economic boom, without plan, and to the confusion of all concerned.[24]

The network as a whole might have stood the strain, if the quality of labour had been higher. But, with the expansion of the labour-force in wartime, from 40,000 to 250,000 in the railway-battalions, and from 750,000 to 1,100,000 on the civilian-run lines, men were taken in who were not in the least skilled. This affected the storage of goods; and it came, also, to affect the maintenance of rolling-stock. One train in four was out of order by 1917, as against one in eight before the war; and although the number of locomotives increased quite substantially, the number of working locomotives declined, at one stage in 1917 to 15,500. Technical labour fell off in quality; the American Stevens Commission, sent in spring, 1917, to assist the ministry of transport in working the railways to better effect, felt that this was the real problem, and not a lack of rolling-stock. It was asserted, for instance, that to turn a Russian train about took twice as long as to turn an American one. The problem of inflation also affected the quality of labour. Railwaymen's wages were directly controlled by the government, and fell behind, as public servants' wages do, in the inflation. At one stage in the summer of 1917, there were complaints that railwaymen were not turning up to work because they had no shoes; and in any event there was a closing of the gap between skilled and unskilled railwaymen that demoralised the skilled, and drove them towards revolutionary courses. The Russian railwaymen had always considered themselves to be the aristocracy of labour: with uniforms, skills, higher pay to mark them off from the rest. Their refusal, at decisive points in 1905–6, to take part in the great strike-movement allowed the government to shift troops from one area to another, and 'pacify' them in turn. But by June 1917, the demoralisation of railwaymen was such that their old self-esteem and apartness dwindled: they too went on strike.

The interaction of railway-problems, failure of grain-marketing, confusions in delivery and use of fuel condemned the old system. It was all very well for soldiers and workers to listen to a speech from Kerenski, demonstrating that the war *must* be fought, the bosses obeyed, and wage-increases controlled. No doubt, most of the soldiers accepted Kerenski's thesis at the time. They would then return to their units, to hear in letters that their wives and families were hungry and cold, perhaps even diseased; if they were workers, they would go home to find that their wages still bought nothing; and yet both soldiers and workers were aware that food was there, if only it could be got at. There was always a curious duality to their behaviour. The soldiers, for instance, did not want to fight the war. On the other hand, they were overwhelmingly patriotic; and it is a complete fabrication to suggest that the army had dissolved in 1917.[25] In November of that year, there were, by *Stavka* census, 6,500,000 men in the front area, excluding civilians. Officers said that the army had dissolved: but mainly because the men had repudiated the more extreme forms of their authority. They mistook questioning for disobedience, committees of the soldiers for mutiny, whereas '*tout au plus, les soldats exigeaient la mort d'une certaine conception de la discipline*'. Of course, the army was demoralised: and this was shown in the high sick-lists of 1917, or the great number of 'delegates' (by one account, 800,000) who found their way to the rear for long periods. But the officers first invented 'the disintegration of the Russian army' and then, by their behaviour, provoked it. Supply-problems completed this picture. The soldiers of 1917 began to receive poor rations, irregularly delivered, in accordance with the country's economic crisis. Living from rotten herring, sometimes even given paper-money in place of rations—paper-money, moreover, that was almost useless in the stores of the rear-area, where only black-marketeering would succeed—the soldiers drank from illicit stills, mutinied, attacked and some-times killed their officers. By November 1917, there was almost no resist-ance to the Bolshevik revolution on the soldiers' part, and, after the December armistice, many of them went back to spread the Bolshevik doctrines at home. In the towns, it was much the same. The huge mass of workers, some long-established, some newly brought into industry, were pushed together by inflation, which reduced differentials between old and new, skilled and unskilled, men and women. The growth of starva-tion and disease in the towns brought them together as a revolutionary force, in a way that no amount of Bolshevik agitation could have done. All were agreed that capitalism had failed, and they became increasingly prepared to listen to a Lenin who offered them hope. The First World War had not been the short outburst of patriotic sacrifice that men had expected. It became, instead, a first experiment in Stalinist tactics for modernisation; and 1917 was a protest against it. In the summer of 1917, virtually the whole of Russia went on strike. The Bolshevik Revolution was a fact before it happened.

Notes

Notes

CHAPTER ONE

[1] K. F. Shatsillo: *Russki imperializm i flot* (Leningrad 1966) p. 44.

[2] A. Kersnovski: *Istoriya russkoy armii* 3 (Belgrade 1935) p. 578.

[3] Generally on the Russian army: Kersnovski op. cit. (and vol. 4, Belgrade 1938); J. S. Curtiss: *The Russian Army under Nicholas II* (Durham N. C. 1965); P. A. Zayonchkovski: *Voyenniye reformi 1860–1870gg.* (Moscow 1952), a penetrating work; H. P. Stein: 'Der Offizier des russischen Heeres im Zeitabschnitt zwischen Reform und Revolution 1861–1905' in *Forschungen zur osteuropäischen Geschichte* (Berlin 1967, vol. 13 pp. 346–507), a very thorough piece of work with excellent bibliography; B. Shaposhnikov: *Mozg armii* (1 Moscow 1926, 2 and 3 1929); L. G. Beskrovny: *Stranitsy boevogo proshlogo* (Moscow 1968); N. P. Yeroshkin: *Istoriya gosudarstvennykh uchrezhdeniy dorevolyutsionnoy Rossii* (2 ed. Moscow 1968) pp. 200ff. for 1861–1904 and 258ff. for 1904–17. G. Frantz: *Russlands Weg zum Abgrund* (Berlin 1926) contains an excellent introduction (pp. 3–132) which should be used to correct the versions of the better-known works of N. Golovin: *The Russian Army in the World War* (New Haven, 1932), in which what is true is not new, and what is new is not true. The most recent work is P. A. Zayonchkovski: *Samoderzhaviye i russkaya armiya na rubezhe 19–20 stoletiy 1881–1903* (Moscow 1973). There is a serviceable, short piece by K. F. Shatsillo: *Rossiya pered pervoy mirovoy voynoy* (Moscow 1974).

[4] Stein p. 380ff.; cf. *Voyenno-statistichesky yezhegodnik* 1912.

[5] V. Zvegintsev: *Kavalergardy* (3 vols. Paris 1936, 1938, 1968) vol. I p. 33 gives the following list of officers in the Maria-Fedorovna Regiment—Dolgorukov, Grabbe, Cantacuzene-Speranski, Golitsyn, Gagarin, Shebeko, Bezobrazov, von der Osten-Driesen, Panteleyev, Bagration, Kochubey, Sheremetiev, Tolstoy, Repnin. cf. P. A. Zayonchkovski: *Samoderzhaviye i armiya* pp. 168 ff., 333.

[6] A breath of these would-be technocrats' world comes from Knyaz Kochubey: *Vooruzhennaya Rossiya* (Paris, probably 1910), a privately-printed regurgitation of half-eaten French doctrines.

[7] Ye. Barsukov: *Podgotovka russkoy armii k voyne v artilleriyskom otnoshenii* (Moscow 1926) p. 17ff; cf. his *Russkaya artilleriya v mirovoy voyne* (Moscow 1938–9, 2 vols.) and *Istoriya russkoy artillerii* (4 v. Moscow 1948). Barsukov is throughout my chief source on matters of artillery, together with A. A. Manikovski: *Boyevoe snabzheniyeb russkoy armii v mirovuyu voynu* (1st. ed. 3 vols. 1920–23, 2 ed. 2 v. 1929 and 3rd ed. 2 vols. 1938. The second edition, edited by Barsukov, is to be preferred).

[8] Barsukov: *Podgotovka* p. 56.

[9] M. N. Pokrovski: *Drei Konferenzen* (Berlin 1920) p. 28 for Izvolski's view of the need for a navy. Shatsillo remains the outstanding source on naval matters (and cf. his articles in *Istoricheskiye Zapiski* 75 (1965) and 83 (1969) on naval matters). There is still much use in M. Petrov: *Podgotovka Rossi k voyne na more* (Moscow 1926); cf. the official

Soviet history: *Flot v pervoy mirovoy voyne* (2 vols. Moscow 1964) which takes a surprisingly pious attitude.

[10] W. A. Suchomlinow: *Erinnerungen* (Berlin 1925); Rödiger: 'Iz zapisok' in *Krasny Arkhiv* 60 (1933) pp. 92–133 esp. p. 93–4; V. Kokovtsev: *Out of my Past* (Stanford, Calif. 1935); V. A. Apushkin: *General ot porazheniya V. A. Sukhomlinov* (Leningrad 1925, French translation Paris 1952) which collects all the legends; Sukhomlinov's 'Dnevnik' in *Dela i Dni* (Petrograd 1920–21) vols. 1 and 2; and various of the hearings in *Padeniye tsarskogo rezhima* (7 vols. Leningrad 1924–27), especially the 'dopros Polivanova' in vol. 7 p. 54ff. Golovin's attacks on Sukhomlinov; *Plan voyny* (Paris 1936) pp. 160f., 178, 212.

[11] A. A. Ignatiev: *50 let v stroyu* (2 vols. Moscow 1955) I. p. 526 quotes this view of Belyayev's.

[12] B. Pares: *The Fall of the Russian Monarchy* (London 1939) pp. 283–4 for a characteristically cracked version of the fall of Grand Duke Nicholas; A. A. Polivanov: *Memuary* (Moscow 1924) vol. 1 p. 62; Rödiger 'Iz zapisok' p. 106, 'dopros Polivanova', pp. 62, 85, 176. Polivanov was one of the most successful tacticians of the Russian army—he identified the winning side well in advance, and always, somehow, managed to keep afloat in that most difficult period of a régime's decline, when the old is clearly going but the new has not yet arisen to replace it. He abandoned the old establishment in time to keep his credit and profit from the changes of 1905–6; then stuck to Sukhomlinov rather than to Palitsyn; then cultivated links with the Duma (Guchkov) in preparation for Sukhomlinov's fall; in 1912, fell foul of Sukhomlinov, had to sit out of affairs for two years or so, and surfaced again as Grand Duke Nicholas's candidate for Sukhomlinov's succession in June 1915; managed to be dismissed by the Tsar in 1916; took only a very modest rôle in the Provisional Government; and surfaced again in the Red Army, to sign the Treaty of Riga for the Bolsheviks.

[13] Voyeykov's 'dopros' in *Padeniye* vol. 3 p. 58ff., cf. p. 313ff. (Beletski) and vol. p. 361ff., 2 p. 9ff. (Andronikov); Sukhomlinov's 'Dnevnik' in *Dela i Dni* I (1920) pp. 219–238 refers to some of these intrigues; the 'Tagebuch des Grossf. Andrej Wladimirowitsch' in Frantz: *Russland auf dem Weg* p. 146 repeats some 'inside' stories; and an irreplaceable source for these currents in the army is always M. K. Lemke: *250 dney v tsarskoy stavke* (Petrograd 1920) pp. 89–90, 476, 485 and passim. Lemke—who edited the works of Herzen and Bakunin—served in *Stavka's* press department, and wrote an immense diary that also contains a large number of documents that came his way. It is a work of great perception, distinguished by the width of its want of sympathy.

[14] Zuyev: *Padeniye* vol. 3 p. 19. He came from the Police Department (usually allied with Sukhomlinov's war ministry) and attained the command of 25. Corps. After confusions near Krasnostaw, Grand Duke Nicholas removed him; but Sukhomlinov and Ivanov then arranged for him to take command of 12. Corps. Bonch-Bruyevitch's career: his memoirs, *Vsya vlast Sovietam* (Moscow 1958 and 2 ed. 1964) and Ya. Lisovoy: 'Revolyuts. Generaly' in *Bely Arkhiv* (Paris) vol. 1 (1926) p. 50. He cultivated Sukhomlinov through Dragomirov's widow, publishing an edition of Dragomirov's work on tactics, and being introduced to Sukhomlinov in recompense. He served with Sukhomlinov in Kiev, and received a high post in III Army—commanded by Ruzski, a friend and client of Sukhomlinov—when war came. In mid-September, Ruzski and Bonch-Bruyevitch went to command the army group against Germany. But *Stavka* seems to have been out for his blood. After the Myasoyedov affair, which, despite Bonch-Bruyevitch's efforts to tack round to the *Stavka* side, discredited all the *Sukhomlinotsy*, he was sent off to be third-in-command of the passive VI Army, and was later demoted

still further, to be garrison commander in Pskov. Here, he declared sympathies with the revolution and, with the help of his brother, a prominent Bolshevik, achieved prominence in the Red Army, Some hints as to the behaviour of the cliques in 'Zapiski N. N. Romanova' *Krasny Arkhiv* 1931 No. 47 p. 159, Lemke p. 220ff. for Rennenkampf's career and cultivation of links with Grand Duke Nicholas and court-figures hostile to Sukhomlinov (Beloselski-Belozerski).

[15]A. L. Sidorov: *Finansovoye polozheniye Rossii v gody pervoy mirovoy voyni* (Moscow 1960) is the outstanding source on army finance.

[16]Shatsillo p. 48.

[17]*Vys. utv. osobiye zhurnaly sovieta ministrov i osobhky soveshchaniy* (minutes of the Council of Ministers, microfilm-copy in the Hoover Institution, Stanford, Calif.) 1915/166 of 6(19) March.

[18]Barsukov: *Podgotovka* p. 66, 75f.; A. M. Zayonchkovski: *Podgotovka Rossii k mir. voyne. Plan voyni* (Moscow 1926) p. 84f. The regular component in a German company was usually five officers and twelve men for eighty soldiers; in a Russian, at best two officers and eight men.

[19]Zayonchkovski: *Podgotovka* pp. 30, 40f. 152; Barsukov: *Podgotovka* p. 70f.; Polivanov: 'dopros' pp. 62–4; Kokovtsev 253f.; F. F. Palitsyn: 'Dnevnik' in *Voyenni sbornik* (Belgrade) vol. 4 p. 267; A. von Schwarz: *Ivangorod v 1914–15gg.* (Paris 1969) pp. 13, 19; S. Khmelkov: *Borba za Osowiec* (Moscow 1939) p. 9; Velichko: *Russkiye kreposti* (Moscow 1926).

[20]Sidorov op. cit. p. 65f. In 1910, the proposals were to spend 81 million roubles on heavy field artillery, 372. 6 million on fortresses; v. also table in Barsukov: *Podgotovka* pp. 56–7, and cf. pp. 88, 94–5.

[21]The authoritative work on planning is Zayonchkovski: *Podgotovka*. Barsukov and Manikovski cover artillery-aspects thoroughly; N. Kozlov: *Snabzheniye russkoy armii voyenno-tekhnicheskim imushchestvom* vol. (Moscow 1926) covers engineering preparations, automobiles etc; K. Ushakov: *Podgotovka voyennikh soobscheniy k voyne* (Moscow 1926) is an invaluable survey of strategic railway-planning; *Materialy po istorii franko-russkikh otnosheniy za 1910–1914gg.* contains pp. 697–718 minutes of the General Staff meetings with France; N. Valentinov: 'Voyenniye soglasheniya s soyuznikami' in *Voyenno-istoricheski sbornik* (Moscow 1920f.) 2, 1920, pp. 94–128 discusses these in a wider context.

[22]G.U.G.Sh: *Voyenniye sily Avstro-Vengrii* (2 vols. Saint Petersburg 1912) vol. 1 p. 126–7.

[23]The 'Great Programme' is discussed by Sidorov op. cit. p. 44ff. and in his 'Iz istorii podgotovki tsarizma k voyne' in *Istoricheski Arkhiv* 1962 No. 2 pp. 120–155; Barsukov: *Podgotovka* p. 81f and 95–6; Barsukov: *Russkaya artilleriya* vol. 1 table, p. 56 and 63ff. In 1914, there were 685 batteries of field cannon (5,480), 85½ of light (48–line) field howitzers (512) and 60 of heavy field artillery (240). After the 'Great Programme' there would be twice the number of batteries, and, generally, a fifth more artillery, with significant increases in high-trajectory types; 1,176 light field howitzers, 468 heavy field guns, 6,048 light field cannon, 666 mountain cannon, such that a Russian army corps of two divisions would acquire a weight roughly equivalent to that of a German first-line army corps of 1914.

CHAPTER TWO

[1]W. Foerster: *Graf Schlieffen und der Weltkrieg* (Berlin 1925).

[2]K. Ropponen: *Die Kraft Russlands* (Helsinki 1968) p. 268.

[3]Reichsarchiv: *Kriegsrüstung und Kriegswirtschaft* vol. 1 (Berlin 1930). pp. 211–236 and *Anlageband*, passim. cf. vol. 2 (Berlin 1925) p. 15f.

[4]M. Schwarte: *Der Weltkrieg Technik im Weltkreig* (Berlin 1920) p. 60ff. for German artillery.

[5]L. Burchardt: *Friedenswirtschaft und Rüstungspolitik* (Freiburg 1970).

[6]A. L. Sidorov: *Finansovoye polozheniye* p. 32.

[7]H. Herzfeld: *Die deutsche Rüstungspolitik von dem Welthrieg* (Berlin 1923) Rüdt von Collenberg: *Die deutsche Armee 1871–1914* (Berlin 1922) Général Buat: *L'armée allenande* (Paris 1920).

[8]K. Ushakov: *Podgotovka* passim, but especially p. 99ff. and appendix Cf. H. von Staabs: *Aufmarsch nach zwei Fronten* (Berlin 1925) p. 26ff. and Reichsarchiv: *Feldeisenbahnwesen* vol. 1 (Berlin 1928) pp. 1–47. The best western-language source for the whole issue of Russian preparedness is G. Frantz *Russlands Eintritt in den Weltkrieg* (Berlin 1924) and the introduction to his *Russland auf dem Weg*.

[9]Kurt Riezler: *Tagebücher* (ed. K. D. Erdmann, Göttingen 1972) p. 184. Lichnowski 'England von dem Krieg'. report of 19 August 1914 in *Auswärtiges Amt, Akten betreffend den Krieg 1914* Band 2 p. cf. *A. A. England No 78 Band 31 Bethmawn Hollweg* to Lichnowsky 10 and 16 June 1914.

[10]A. J. P. Taylor: *War by Timetable* (London 1970) is the best statement of this view of the war's outbreak, but of course there are many other views, the dominant one of which, at the moment, is still F. Fischer: *Griff nach der Weltmacht* (Düsseldorf 1964) and *Krieg der Illusionen* (Düsseldorf 1971).

CHAPTER THREE

[1]F. Franek: 'Die Entwicklung der osterreichisch-ungarischen Wehrmacht in den ersten zwei Kriegsjahren' (*Ergänzungsheft* No. 4 of the Austro-Hungarian official history, *Oesterreich-Ungarns letzter Krieg*, Vienna 1932) p. 10. Sickness rose from 23·5% of losses to 47% in the same period.

[2]*Materialy po istorii franko-russkikh otnosheniy za 1910–1914gg.* (Moscow 1922) p. 698f. give the texts (in Russian and French) of General Staff discussions. At the 9th meeting, in August 1913, Zhilinski undertook to send 800,000 men against Germany 'in the main by the 15th day of mobilisation'.

[3]Ushakov: *Podgotovka* (op. cit. Chapter 1) p. 106f. and *prilozheniye* 6; he shows that the north-western front, by the 13th day, was only sixteen trains short of its complement. S. Dobrorolski: 'O mobilizatsii russkoy armii' in *Voyenni Sbornik* (Belgrade) I pp. 91–116. A. L. Sidorov: 'Zhelezno-dorozhny transport' in *Istoricheskiye Zapiski* No. 26 (1948) pp. 3–64, especially p. 24.

[4]Jean Savant: *L'épée russe* (Paris 1945) p. 18. There are many similar examples; the best-known account of 'unreadiness' is N. N. Golovin: *Iz istorii kampanii 1914 goda na russkom fronte. Nachalo voyni i operatsii v Vostochnoy Prussii* (Prague 1926, English translation 1928) p. 345 and passim.

[5]*Generalny Shtab RKKA: Sbornik dokumentov mirovoy voyni na russkom fronte. Manevrenni period 1914 goda: Vostochno-Prusskaya operasiya* (Moscow 1939) pp. 525–7, and cf. E. Barsukov: *Podgotovka* (op. cit. Chapter 1) table pp. 134–5.

[6]*Sbornik* (as in note 5) p. 540, no. 803.

[7]Ibid. p. 528f. no. 798 (nos. 795–801 on supply). The most thorough contemporary investigation was the report drawn up by General Panteleyev after the disaster. There is certainly no suggestion in it that things went as they did because of the crushing

artillery weakness of which Golovin speaks again and again. The report ('doklad pravitelstvennoy komissii, naznachennoy v 1914 godu dlya rassledovaniya usloviy i prichin gibela 2. armii') appears as document no. 804 in *Sbornik*. Panteleyev's findings that 'materially, everything was complete' are borne out by the dozen special articles devoted to this campaign by various (formerly highly-placed) authors in the Belgrade *Voyenni Sbornik*: v. e.g. K. Adaridi's article in IX (1928) on 27th infantry division p. 162–85, or Rosenchild-Paulin's on 29th infantry division in VIII (1926) pp. 291–45.

[8]Savant op. cit. p. 80. The cavalrymen none the less thought highly of their own activity—e.g. B. Gourko: *Memories and Impressions* (London 1918), and V. Zvegintsev: *Kavalergardy* (3 vols. Paris 1936, 1938 and 1964).

[9]N. Kozlov: *Ocherk snabzheniya russkoy armii voyenno-tekhnicheskim imushchestvom* I (Moscow 1926) p. 7f.

[10]N. V. Abakanovitch: 'Istoricheski obzor organizatsii i ustroystvo provolochnoy svyazi armii' in *Voyenno-inzhenerni Sbornik* vol. 2. (Moscow 1918–19) pp. 197–336 pp. 198 and 201.

[11]*Sbornik* pp. 87f. and nos. 87–133 (p. 129ff.) on deployment.

[12]Sukhomlinov: *Dnevnik* (op. cit. Chapter 1) p. 232.

[13]Life in *Stavka* is best seen from the following: V. Kondzerovski: *Vospominaniya* (Paris 1967); M. K. Lemke: *250 dney* (op. cit. Chapter 1); A. Samoylo: *Dve zhizni* (Moscow 1958); G. Shavelski: *Vospominaniya poslednego protopresvitera russkoy armii i flota* (2 vols. New York 1954); A. Bubnov: *V Tsarskoy Stavke* (New York 1955); N. M. Romanov, 'Zapiski' in *Krasny Arkhiv* 47 (1931) pp. 140–83. The despatches of General Hanbury-Williams (v. Chapter 7) also reveal much of *Stavka*'s ways—including the consumption of spirits, despite official prohibition.

[14]v. note 13 (particularly Lemke pp. 190, 624 and 801, Kondzerovski p. 10, Samoylo p. 142f.); W. Hubatsch: *Hindenburg und der Staat* (Göttingen 1966) p. 24; K. Peball: 'Briefe an eine Freundin' in *Mitteilungen des österreichischen Staatsarchivs* 25. (1972) pp. 492–503.

[15]Planning is best seen from the documents in *Sbornik* p. 27ff. (Nos. 1, 2 and 9 particularly); relations with allies in *Materialy* (op. cit.) and N. Valentinov (Volski): *Snosheniya s soyuznikami po voyennym voprosam vo vremya voyni* (Moscow 1920) pp. 22–3.

[16]My account of operations is taken mainly from the following:

a) *Osnovniye direktivy i direktivniye ukazaniya Verkhovnogo Glavnokomanduyushchego i zhurnaly soveshchaniy*, a set of all strategic orders issued by the first *Stavka* (i.e. until late August 1915), of which a copy is preserved in the 'Archive of Grand Duke Nicholas', with the Golovin-Archive in the Hoover Institution, Stanford, California. This is of course a very important source, although it is less important in those engagements—such as East Prussia in August 1914—that are extensively covered in secondary works and collections of documents. Whenever I refer to a *Stavka* order, it may none the less be assumed that I have used the original version in the *Osnovniye direktivy* (the orders are readily identifiable by their dates and addressees). The instructions regarding IX Army are given, for instance, in Yanushkevitch to Zhilinski of 25th and 28th July (old-style), Danilov to Alexeyev 30th July, by which an attack of six corps was prescribed, four against Thorn—Breslau, two against Breslau—Posen. The source is hereafter identified as 'O.D.'

b) *Sbornik* as quoted in note 5. It belongs to an unfinished series of documentary collections, for Red Army use, on various campaigns of the war in the east, and represents the single most important source on Tannenberg and the Masurian Lakes.

c) I. I. Vatsetis: *Operatsii na vostochno-prusskoy granitse* v. l (Moscow 1929) which is the most solid documentary investigation.

d) G. Isserson: *Kanny mirovoy voyni* (Moscow 1926) which is less solid.

e) Reichsarchiv: *Der Weltkrieg* vol. 2 (Berlin 1925) which is an exhaustive, but still not very reliable, German account.

f) M. Hoffmann: *Tannenberg, wie es wirklich war* (Berlin 1925).

g) Memoirs, such as those of Ludendorff, François, Hindenburg, Morgen. They proved to be of limited usefulness.

[17]Figures for respective strengths are taken, unless otherwise specified, from Vatsetis p. 28f and the Reichsarchiv volume p. 370f: Golovin's figures/*Nachalo* p. 345 are fanciful, based on an assumption that all German divisions were of first-line strength, and that Russian second-line divisions did not count. In reality, nearly half of Germany's infantry divisions, and more than half of those fighting in the east, were second- or third-line, with half or less than half of the artillery of a first-line division; while Russian second-line divisions had as many guns as first-line ones, whatever the differences in quality between them.

[18]Vatsetis p. 29.

[19]G. Frantz: *Russland* (op. cit. Chapter 1) p.128, Kondzerovski p. 52. The famous story that Rennenkampf and Samsonov had come to blows during the war with Japan appears to lack foundation (v. Savant p. 261). The general with whom Rennenkampf quarrelled was Mishchenko. Just the same, it is clear that Samsonov and Rennenkampf came from different cliques of the army—Rennenkampf a well-known protégé of Grand Duke Nicholas, well-established at Court, and able to mobilise many high aristocrats on his behalf when there was a danger of his being blamed for Tannenberg; Samsonov, commanding general in Turkestan—an appointment controlled by the *Glavny Shtab*, and hence a Sukhomlinovite satrapy.

[20]*Sbornik* No. 147 (Rennenkampf to Yanushkevitch, 19th August. Rennenkampf put the blame for it all on Zhilinski).

[21]German plans: E. Ludendorff: *Kriegserinnerungen* (Berlin 1919) p. 37f., but cf. Hoffmann p. 14, 29f.

[22]Vatsetis p. 40.

[23]*Sbornik* p. 210ff. nos. 214–60. Intelligence (p. 211) showed on 23rd August that the Germans had retreated.

[24]*Sbornik* p. 228ff (nos. 261–86) covers I Army until 1. September, p. 245–322 (nos. 287–438) II Army in the same period. There are also useful remarks as to Rennenkampf's behaviour in Savant, passim.

[25]Golovin: *Nachalo* p. 234f., Vatsetis p. 165f. and *Sbornik* no. 356.

[26]*Sbornik* p. 269–70, no. 347 (intelligence showed that there was only one corps before II Army), and cf. Vatsetis p. 134 for Mileant's report that the Germans were retreating, and Bayov's that both 1. and 17. Corps had retired into Königsberg. The group opposing II Army was of course quite small—20. Corps (Scholtz) and two Landwehr groups. It is characteristic of Golovin's methods (p. 206f) that he should reckon that Scholtz's group was actually superior to the centre of II Army—four infantry divisions, with 42 batteries, against five and 36 on the Russian side. First, only two of the German divisions were 'active', with 12 batteries each. The other two were third-line, with three batteries each. Again, each Russian battery contained eight guns; each German, six.

[27]Vatsetis p. 169f and Reichsarchiv p. 184f.

[28]*Sbornik* p. 564f. covers the Russian 4th infantry division, which lost 5,283 men and 73 officers.

[29]Golovin p. 230, and Reichsarchiv p. 170f.

[30]*Sbornik* p. 556f. and 559f.; no. 429 pp. 316–8 is Postovski's report, and no. 428 pp. 313–6 Zhilinski's; cf. Hoffmann p. 80ff. for the surrenders.

[31]O. D. Yanushkevitch to Zhilinski 24 August cf. *Sbornik* p. 791f. and Vatsetis p. 291f.

[32]O. D. Yanushkevitch to Zhilinski 18th August cf. Savant p. 186 and, overall, Reichsarchiv p. 268f.

[33]VIII Army now contained 232 battalions, 124 squadrons and 1,212 guns, of which 184, 94 and 1,074 were concentrated for this battle. The Russians had 398, 288 and 1,492, but failed to concentrate. I Army had, scattered, 228, 173 and 924. *Sbornik* no. 795 gives X Army's strength, somewhat later, as 150,000. These were not really used. In I Army, corps had on average 25,000 men and 100 guns (50 per infantry division), with only 811 officers for 40,000 men (Mileant's figure, *Sbornik* no. 764 p. 791). V. Pflug, '10. armiya v sentyabre 1914 goda' in *Voyenni Sbornik* (Belgrade) V (1925) pp. 231–60 is revealing; cf. Savant p. 286f. and 349f.

CHAPTER FOUR

[1]N. Stone: 'Army and Society in the Habsburg Monarchy' in *Past & Present* 33 (1966) pp. 95–111.

[2]F. Franek: 'Probleme der Organisation in ersten Kriegsjahr' (*Ergänzungsheft* of the Austro-Hungarian official history, Vienna 1932) p. 18; H. Kerchnawe: 'Die unzureichende Rüstung der Mittelmächte . . .' (Vienna 1932) p. 8.

[3]The following account of Austro-Hungarian planning and mobilisation is based on study of the relevant documents in the *Kriegsarchiv*, Vienna: study has been made of private papers (Conrad, Kundmann, Potiorek) as well as of the records of planning in the General Staff, of railway-timetables for individual units, and of the activity of particular armies and army corps in July and August 1914. Full reference to these is made in the author's article: 'Die Mobilmachung der österreichisch-ungarischen Armee 1914' in *Militärgeschichtliche Mitteilungen* (Freiburg i.B.) 1974/II pp. 67–95, which also contains a detailed account of the author's disagreement with versions, hitherto given prominence, of these events. An important but unpublished source is the manuscript, prepared for the Carnegie series on the history of the war, by Emil Ratzenhofer: *Oesterreich-Ungarns Mobilisierung, Transport, Versammlung Sommer 1914*, known as 'Ratzenhofer Deposit' in the archives of the Hoover Institution, Stanford, California. The draft of this exists in Ratzenhofer's *Nachlass* in the *Kriegsarchiv*, Vienna (B/691 Kartons 30–40). Ratzenhofer, as head of the *Russland-Gruppe* of the General Staff's railway-section, was in an excellent position to survey events, and had an important part in them. The original record of the railway experts' transactions is the Straub-diary: *AOK. Quartiermeister-Abteilung, Faszikel 4119*, from which my quotations are taken.

[4]There had also been delay in partial mobilisation, against Serbia. It was proclaimed in the evening of 25th July, but the first day of mobilisation was not until 28th July. Conrad said that the delay occurred because the railways needed it. The railwaymen denied this, at least in private. Probably the delay occurred, like many others on the Austro-Hungarian side in the July crisis, because of 'nerves'.

[5]Conrad had told everyone that 'the fifth day of mobilisation' would be the decisive point. If he knew by then that Russia would intervene, then 'B-Staffel' could go north-

east directly; but if Russia intervened only after then, 'B-Staffel' would have started its road south, and would have to complete the Serbian campaign before going north-east against Russia. He said this more or less word-for-word to Burián, Tisza's representative, on 28th July (*Gróf Tisza István összes munkai* vol. 2, Budapest 1924, p. 35). In fact, 1st August was the fifth day of this mobilisation-programme; and yet the experts found on 31st July—the fourth day—that 'B-Staffel' was irrevocably committed to the Balkans. Maybe it was just blundering; or maybe the whole question of fifth day had not very much meaning, but was merely a technical-sounding justification for Conrad's proceeding to knock out Serbia, despite the threat of Russian intervention, and despite the protests which he knew to expect.

[6]Ratzenhofer, manuscript p. 214.

[7]B. Enderes (and others) *Verkehrswesen im Krieg* (Vienna 1930) p. 60–5 record civilians' disenchantment with the railway-experts' ways. Other details are taken from the war-diaries of army commands: v. Stone, *Mobilmachung* note 41.

[8]e.g. 4th *Armeekommando*, Faszikel 3, op. nr. 33, 37, 114.

[9]M. v. Pitreich: *Lemberg 1914* (Vienna 1924) p. 21. On Jaroslawice, Max Hoen: *Jaroslawice* (Vienna 1921) which should be compared with the (surprisingly numerous) Russian accounts: E. Tikhotski: *Ataka avstro-vengerskoy konnitsy* (Belgrade 1938); A. Slivinski: *Konny boy* (Belgrade 1912); V. Grebenshchikov: 'Noviye danniye o konnom boye 10. K. D.' in *Voyenni sbornik* (Belgrade 1925) 7 pp. 111–9.

[10]The battle of Galicia in August 1914 is best judged in the following, of which I have made extensive use:
a) F. Conrad von Hötzendorf: *Aus Meiner Dienstzeit 1906–1918* (5 vols. Vienna 1921–25), vols. 4 and 5.
b) *Oesterreich-Ungarns letzter Krieg* (v. 2 ed. Vienna 1930)
c) M. v. Pitreich: *Lemberg* (1924) and *1914. Die militärischen Probleme unseres Kriegsbeginnes* (Vienna 1934) which I have found to be most reliable;
d) A. Beloy: *Galitsiyskaya bitva* (Moscow 1929), most reliable work on the Russian side;
e) N. Golovin: *Galitsiyskaya bitva* v. 1 (Prague 1930) and 2 (*Dni pereloma*) (Paris 1940) which have the usual faults of over-estimation of enemy strength and vendetta against Sukhomlinov and his friends in the General Staff;
f) Memoirs, the most useful of which are M. v. Auffenberg: *Aus Oesterreichs Teilnahme am Weltkrieg* (Vienna 1920) and R. Pfeffer: *Zum 10. Jahrestag der Schlachten von Zloczów und Przemyślany* (Vienna 1924).

[11]4th *Armeekommando* Faszikel 34 (Evidenzen 1–330) passim, and the orders issued in Fasz. 4 (501–999) on the basis of this information. The information was sent on to the German VIII Army, with a request that it should attack across the Narev precisely because the Russians were so strong against Austria-Hungary (v. *AOK. Verbindungsoffiziere Oberost.* Fasz. 6180 No. 48 of 14th August).

[12]*Conrad-Archiv* B/6 No. 100 (from Berchtold 18th August) cf. 4th *Armeekommando* Fasz. 3 No, 115 of 13th August and No. 36/1 of 13th August.

[13]Beloy p. 353.

[14]O. D. Yanushkevitch to Alexeyev and Ivanov, 9th and 10th August 1914.

[15]Beloy p. 350, O. D. Yanushkevitch to Zhilinski 31st August.

[16]Beloy's *Vykhod iz okruzheniya* (Moscow 1925) is a special study of this battle. It should be compared with Auffenberg's account (*Teilnahme*).

[17]On Ruzski's behaviour, a controversy developed both in Soviet and émigré publications after the war: for instance, in *Voyennoye Delo* (Moscow 1918–20) especially nos. 23, 25,

and 27 of year 1, and 1–2 of year 2, where Klembovski and Bonch-Bruyevitch kept the controversy going, and in *Voyenni sbornik* (Belgrade) nos. 7f. where Dragomirov added his voice.

CHAPTER FIVE

[1]W. S. Churchill: *The Great War* (1930 ed.) vol. 3 p. 500.

[2]These figures have been taken from the German official history: Reichsarchiv: *Der Weltkrieg* vol. 8 (Anlage 2 p. 629); Oberkommando des Heeres: *Der Weltkrieg* vol. 12 (1939) p. 477 (cf. Beilage 28); Bundesarchiv: *Der Weltkrieg* vol. 13 (1956) p. 47f and from the French equivalent: *Les Armées françaises dans la Grande Guerre* vol. 5 ii pp. 34, 45 and 47.

[3]My account of strategy in the latter part of 1914 is based on the following:

a) *Sbornik dokumentov mirovoy voyni na russkom fronte. Manevrenny period. Varshavsko-Ivangorodskaya operatsiya* (Moscow 1938) and *Lodzinskaya operatsiya* (1939), each with a volume of maps. Like the collection on East Prussia, these are collections, for Red Army use, of the important documents on strategy, individual engagements, and supply:

b) G. Korolkov: *Varshavsko-Ivangorodskaya operatsiya* (1928 edition, Moscow);

c) G. Korolkov: *Lodzinskaya operatsiya* (1928 edition, Moscow);

d) *Strategicheski ocherk voyni 1914–1918 gg. na russkom fronte* vols. 2 and 3 (edited, respectively, by Korolkov and A. Neznamov, Moscow 1922–3);

e) Reichsarchiv: *Der Weltkrieg* vols. 5 and 6;

f) Bundesministerium f. Landesverteidigung: *Oesterreich-Ungarns letzter Krieg* vols. 1 and 2 (1931–2).

[4]P. Cherkasov: *Shturm Peremyshla* (Moscow 1927) discusses Shcherbachev's siege. The Grand Duke forbade attempts against the fortress (O. D. 8th September to Ivanov). He was 'misunderstood'.

[5]*Varshavsko-Ivangorodskaya operatsiya* p. 129f; cf. A. von Schwarz: *Ivangorod v 1914–1915 gg.* (Paris 1969) p. 44f.

[6]*Varshavsko-Ivangorodskaya operatsiya* nos. 81–101 cover V Army, nos. 44–63 IV Army and nos. 64–80 IX Army in this period of transfer.

[7]*Stavka's* attitudes in *Lodzinskaya operatsiya* p. 199ff. (nos. 225f.)

[8]Captain Neilson. His despatches (in diary form) are quite useful: v. WO. 106 nos. 1119–21 (23rd November 1914).

[9]N. Novikov: *6. sibirskaya strelk. diviziya v boyakh pod Lodzyu* (*Moscow 1926*) H. Kraft: 'Brzeziny' in *Wehrwiss. Rundschau* 1966/11 usefully corrects German legends on the subject.

[10]*Lodzinskaya operatsiya* p. 79f. and on II Army p. 149f. covers supply. O.D. 30th November 1914 gives minutes of the Brest meeting of that day.

[11]All of this was cast as a great Austro-Hungarian victory, Limanowa. v. J. Roth: *Limanowa* (Innsbruck 1929). The Russian side is cursorily dealt with in *Strategicheski ocherk voyni*, the account of which is however difficult to expand. Some points can be gleaned from A. Rostunov: *General Brusilov* (Moscow 1964), F. P. Rerberg: *Istoricheskiye tayni: 10. korpus* (Alexandria 1925, manuscript in the Golovin Archive, at the Hoover Institution) and the *Soldier's Notebook* of A. Brusilov (London 1929).

[12]FO. 371/2448 Russia (War): minute on Buchanan's despatch of 28th May 1915.

[13]*Oesterreich-Ungarns letzter Krieg* vol. 2 pp. 30–260 adequately covers the strategic problems of early 1915—the original correspondence between Conrad and Falkenhayn is in *Kriegsarchiv*: AOK. Op. B. Fasz. 512, esp. nos. 5999, 6005, 6052 and 6058–9.

In exchange for the offensive, the Austrians gave up some of their rights in conquered Polish territory, particularly minerals. Ludendorff, as the correspondence of Conrad's liaison officer shows (Fasz. 6182) had doubts as to the Carpathian offensive, but suppressed them, no doubt in order to convince Falkenhayn that his own East Prussian scheme was a necessary complement to Conrad's. *Südarmee* suffered in other ways than from the snows. It had the highest syphilis-rate in the German army, excepting the garrison in Romania (v. Reichskriegsministerium: *Sanitätsberichte* vol. 3 (Berlin 1934) Tafel 47 p. 65.).

[14]*Lodzinskaya operatsiya* no. 516 pp. 447–9 gives the text of this report. Russian operations thereafter are ably discussed in: M. D. Bonch-Bruyevitch: *Poterya nami Galitsii* (2 vols. Moscow 1920 and 1923), vol. 1 p. 20f. and 34f. for Danilov's report, and Kholmsen: *Mirovaya voyna. Nashi operatsii na vostochnoprusskom fronte zimoyu 1915 goda* (Paris 1935). For the Austro-Hungarian sector, Russian sources are not rich, although the work of A. M. Zayonchkovski: *Mirovaya voyna: manevrenny period* (Moscow 1929) fills some of the gaps.

[15]Kholmsen p. 51f.

[16]e.g. a Croat regiment that had to spend the night in the snow lost 28 officers and 1,800 men from frostbite (*Kriegsarchiv* B/50, Nachlass Pflanzer-Baltin, *Tagebuch*, *Mappe* 1, entry of 2nd February 1915).

[17]*Kriegsarchiv*: Conrad-Archiv B/13 Tagebuch d.Obstlt. Kundmann for the period 5–17th March shows the depressed mood of Conrad, who blamed Falkenhayn and Linsingen. II Army lost 40,000 men from frostbite alone in the first few days of March.

[18]Neilson's despatch of 23rd March: W. O. 106/1122. Przemyśl would probably have fallen before if the Russians had been able to manoeuvre their artillery. But it took ten days to move heavy artillery from the naval base of Kronstadt to the nearest railway-station alone, and once it reached the mud of Galicia, it was virtually immobile: Barsukov; *Russkaya artilleriya* p. 204.

[19]v. his article in *Voyenni sbornik* (Belgrade) V (1924) pp. 231–60.

[20]Kholmsen p. 36. The most authoritative account of the battle on the Russian side is N. Kamenski: *Gibel 20. korpusa* (Moscow 1921). The account in Reichsarchiv: *Der Weltkrieg* vol. 7 should be used with care. Budberg, Sievers's chief of staff, wrote an interesting justification in *Voyenni sbornik* VI pp. 148ff.

[21]Kemenski p. 155f; cf. Kholmsen, chapter 7.

[22]A. Khmelkov: *Borba za Osowiec* (Moscow 1939) p. 55f; cf. Bunyakovski: 'Kratky ocherk oborony kreposti Osowiec' in *Voyenni sbornik* V pp. 289–307.

[23]The best source for this period is Bonch-Bruyevitch; *Poterya* vol. 1, but its bias should be corrected with reference to the O.D. series of orders, and the exchanges over Balkan matters with Russia's allies: v. 'Stavka i ministersvo inostrannykh del' in *Krasny Arkhiv* 27 (1928) pp. 3–57, and N. Valentinov: *Snosheniya* I pp. 32, 52–3.

[24]*Vysochayshe utverzhdenniye osobiye zhurnaly sovieta ministrov* 1915 no. 508 (26th June).

[25]*Kriegsarchiv*: Conrad-Archiv B/13 Kundmann diary for 30th March cf. AOK. Op. B. Faszikel 512 nos. 8483 and 8445/I.

CHAPTER SIX

[1]F. Franek: 'Probleme der Organisation im ersten Kriegsjahr', *Ergänzungsheft* 1 of the Austro-Hungarian official history (Vienna 1930) and 'Entwicklung der öst.–ung. Wehrmacht in den ersten zwei Kriegsjahren', *Ergänzungsheft* 5 (1935). Two manuscripts,

prepared for the Carnegie series, but not used, are of some help in this context: Oberst Klose: 'Deckung des personellen Bedarfs' and A. Krauss: 'Kriegsphasen'. Both exist in the manuscript collection of the Vienna *Kriegsarchiv*. A very brave attempt to sort out the confusions of call-up has been made by R. Hecht: *Fragen zur Heeresergänzung* (dissertation, Vienna 1969, of which the *Kriegsarchiv* has a copy).

²Oberst Pflug: *Bewaffnung und Munition* (manuscript, originally designed for the Carnegie series, in the *Kriegsarchiv*) is the most authoritative work on artillery and munitions. Parts of it were used in G. Gratz and R. Schüller; *Der wirtschaftliche Zusammenbruch Oesterreich-Ungarns* (Vienna 1930) and R. Riedl: *Die Industrie Oesterreichs während des Weltkrieges*. (Vienna 1932). Pflug's table p. 109 is revealing.

³R. Lorenz: 'Aus dem Tagebuch Marterers' in *Oesterreich und Europe* (Festschrift for H. Hantsch) ed. R. Plaschka (Vienna 1967) p. 471.

⁴Tisza to Burián, copy to Conrad in *AOK. Op. B.* Fasz. 561 Op. Nr. 19380 30th December 1915. In similar vein, Tisza demanded that, since most of the medals were won by Hungarians, the factories to produce them should be put up in Hungary.

⁵Klose ms. *Beilage* 1.

⁶*Kriegsarchiv: Neue Feldakten: 4 Op. AKdo.* Fasz. 70 Tagebuch 1 p. 14 (9th August).

⁷*Kriegsarchiv: Abt. 3 Kriegsüberwachungsamt* Fasz. 120 No. 8 of 9th October 1915 ('um ein Liebesverhältnis anzuknüpfen').

⁸'Sämtliche kompromittierte Schüler wurden dem Militärgericht geliefert': Coudenhove's report to Stürgkh 21st May 1915, copy to AOK. in *Op.B.* Fasz. 31, Op. Nr. 11352 cf. Fasz. 37 Nr. 13729 of 31st July for further details of the same type. A thorough investigation of the whole matter is C. Führ: *Armeeoberkommando und Nationalitätenfrage* (Vienna 1968).

⁹The whole question of desertion is of course very complex, and not much clarified by rival claims at the time. Czech propagandists made out that all Czechs were waiting for a chance to get away; Austrian soldiers sometimes made the same claim. The documents of the time are not so clear. Pflanzer-Baltin (*Tagebuch*, Mappe 3–4 of 24th May 1915) quotes 10th infantry division as 'striking proof' that Czechs and Romanians could do very well in attack; IV Army command, in answer to enquiry from AOK, thought on 20th October 1914 'the morale and condition of the troops is generally very good'. —*Tagebuch* 3 (Fasz. 70), while Archduke Eugen, on the Italian front, was lavish in praise of the performance of his Slav troops, and was adamant that good leadership could overcome nationality-problems while bad leadership exacerbated them (*AOK. Op.B.* Fasz. 37, 1915 No. 13781 of 5th August). This, probably, touched the heart of the matter, for sloppy commanders quite often seem to have blamed disaffection for the consequences of their own blundering. A famous instance of desertion was that of the 28th Infantry Regiment, recruited in Prague. Thorough investigation has revealed that a combination of Austrian sloppiness and Hungarian arrogance had as much to do with this regiment's well-documented disaffection as initial Czech disloyalty. When they went up to the front, they had had little training, and, as simple Czech townsmen, were singularly ill-suited to mountain-warfare. They were treated, from the beginning, as if they had the plague, being for instance sent to Szeged in Hungary for their training, instead of being left in the Bohemian capital, with its 'malign influences'. When they went up to the front, after a series of incidents with the Hungarian population in Szeged, and particularly with a Hungarian officer—whose reports are more revealing than he supposed—a great muddle was made of their transport. The train pulled out of Miskolc station, with the officers' waggon (and the officers) attached, while the men were still eating in the station itself. There was inevitably much hooting as the crestfallen officers

came back. At the front, the soldiers seem simply not to have defended themselves at all, and the regiment was officially disbanded (though re-constituted, after its nucleus had behaved well on the Italian front). The affair was thoroughly investigated by R. Plaschka: 'Zur Vorgeschichte des Uebergangs von Einheiten des Inf. Regt. 28' in *Oesterreich und Europa* (op. cit. note 3) pp. 455–67. A separate collection of documents concerning this regiment and the 36th infantry regiment exists in the *Kriegsarchiv*, with a substantial selection from Op. Nr. 4329 to Op. Nr. 13016 (1914–15) as the army authorities traced the history of the units.

[10]Conrad's *Denkschrift* of 31st March 1915 in *AOK. Op. B.* Fasz. 551 No. 8577 expounds the view that Italian intervention would mean the end of the Monarchy in six weeks.

[11]*AOK. Verbindungsoffiziere: Oberost.* Fasz. 6182 (unnumbered) of 4.3.15; *Kundmann-Tagebuch* 10.3.15; cf. letter to Bolfras, *Kundmann* 5.3.15.

[12]W. Groener: *Lebenserinnerungen* ed. F. Hiller von Gaertringen (Göttingen 1957) p. 226–7; *Straub-Tagebuch* 5th–11th April passim. In general, Reichsarchiv: *Der Weltkrieg* vols. 7 and 8 supply an adequate account of the origins of the campaign as well as its course, which can be checked from Austro-Hungarian sources in *AOK. Op. B.* Fasz. 551 and 560.

[13]The best source on the Russian side is: *Sbornik dokumentov mirovoy voyni na russkom fronte. Manevrenni period*. Gorlitskaya operatsiya, published by RKKA, for General Staff use, in 1941 (Moscow). Together with Bonch-Bruyevitch's *Poterya nami Galitsii* (2 vols. Moscow 1920–26) it fills in most gaps. The general works of A. Neznamov: *Strategicheski ocherk voyni* (vols. 3 and 4, 1922) and A. M. Zayonchkovski: *Mirovaya voyna* (p. 271ff.) are no more than useful short accounts.

[14]*Gorlitskaya operatsiya* p. 15. There is some confusion as the Central Powers counted their field howitzers as 'light', where the Russians counted them as 'medium' cf. Rerberg ms. p. 291.

[15]These figures are taken from Reichsarchiv: *Der Weltkrieg* vol. 8, *Anlage* 1, vol. 10 *Anlage* 1 ('deutsche und feindliche Artillerie bei Verdun und an der Somme'), vol. 12 *Beilagen* 28 and 29(a).

[16]v. appendices on 'snabzheniye' in *Gorlitskaya operatsiya* p. 504ff.; Langlois's *Rapport* of April 1915 (no. 2) Ch. 3 p. 40 (v. note on sources); Rerberg ms. p. 200.

[17]A. M. Zayonchkovski: *Strategicheski ocherk voyni* vol. 6 (Moscow 1922) p. 12 cf. Bonch-Bruyevitch vol. 1 p. 34; ed. Svechin: 'Dnevnik Shtukaturova' in *Voyenno-ist. sbornik* (Moscow) 1919 vol. 1 p. 132f., esp. p. 180 which records a military journey.

[18]M. Schwarte: *Der grosse Krieg 1914 bis 1918* (10 vols.)—vol. 1, *Organisation und Kriegführung* (Berlin 1921) p. 243, 257. cf. Ratzenhofer: 'Die Auswertung der inneren Linie im Dreifrontenkrieg' (*Ergänzungsheft* No. 2 of the Austro-Hungarian official history, 1931) p. 15.

[19]Lemke p. 310, 494; O. N. Chaadaeva: *Armiya nakanune revolyutsii* (Moscow 1935) p. 19; Sidorov: 'zhelezno-dorozhny transport' p. 24.

[20]Schwarte: *Organisation* p. 259.

[21]K. v. Morgen: *Meiner Truppen Heldenkämpfe* (2 vols. Berlin 1920) 1 p. 50f.

[22]O.D. Yanushkevitch to Alexeyev 31.3.1915 and letter of 14.4. British intelligence apparently reported German intentions before the end of March.

[23]Rerberg ms. p. 240 and *Gorlitskaya operatsiya* pp. 45–7 for the apprehensions of Noskov and Diederichs in Ivanov's command; cf. Bonch-Bruyevitch vol. 2 p. 38.

[24]Ye. I. Martinov: 'Gibel divizii Kornilova' in *Voyenno-ist. sbornik* (Moscow) 1919, I pp. 30–50.

[25]Taken from *Gorlitskaya operatsiya*, passim.

[26]O.D. Yanushkevitch to Ivanov 24th April; cf. Palitsyn, 'Dnevnik' (cit. chapter 1) III, 158–185 esp. p. 158; Bonch-Bruyevitch II pp. 92, 98. 122f.

[27]Bonch-Bruyevitch II pp. 110 and 139. Dragomirov's version: 'Po povodu odnoy zametki' in *Voyenni sbornik* (Belgrade) VI (1927) pp. 152–7.

[28]Pflanzer-Baltin, *Tagebuch* Mappe 1 (of 14.10.1914).

[29]Meanwhile, three divisions left this front for Italy, with Boroević's army command. On overall strategy: K. H. Janssen: *Der Kanzler und der General* (Göttingen 1967) and H. Meier-Welcker: *Seeckt* (Frankfurt 1967).

[30]This retreat—entirely voluntary—appears in the Austro-Hungarian official history (vol. 2) as a great Austro-Hungarian success. There were, on the contrary, frequent Austro-Hungarian reverses both in this theatre and in the central theatre, west of the Vistula. v. D. Parski. 'Operatsiya 30 korpusa na Prute' in *voyenno-ist, sbornik* 1920, 3, pp. 44–63 and 1921, 4 pp. 23–45; Grishinski: '25 korpus' in ib. 1919, 2 pp. 37–9 and G. Korolkov: *Forsirovaniye reki* (Moscow 1935). Of course, these Russian victories were ultimately unimportant, indeed withdrew strength from the main theatre, as *Stavka* continually grumbled.

CHAPTER SEVEN

[1]I. Mayevski: *Ekonomika russkoy promyshlennosti v usloviyakh pervoy mirovoy voyni* (Moscow 1957) p. 63; cf. N. Golovin: *Voyenniye usilii Rossii* (2 vols. Paris 1939), a long demonstration of this.

[2]A. L. Sidorov: *Ekonomicheskoye polozheniye Rossii v gody pervoy mirovoy voyni* (Moscow 1973) p. 16f. very fully documents, particularly with material drawn from the commission investigating the management of things by Sukhomlinov, Smyslovski etc. the account of A. A. Manikovski: *Boyevoye snabzheniye* esp. vol. 3 pp. 26, 76 etc; v. below, chapter 9.

[3]Sidorov: *Ek. pol.* pp. 5–6 and Barsukov: *Russkaya artilleriya* vol. 1 p. 17.

[4]Sidorov: 'Stroitelstvo kazennykh zavodov' in *Istoricheskiye Zapiski* No. 54 (1955) p. 159.

[5]Manikovski vol. 1 pp. 25, 70. To calculate needs of rifles is more difficult than with shell. It is probably safe to conclude, for spring 1915, that 200,000 rifles per month were needed, against the 50,000 (at best) being supplied.

[6]Korolkov: *Przasnysz-skoye srazheniye* (Moscow 1928) p. 12; cf. Reichsarchiv: *Der Weltkrieg* vol. 8, passim, for Gallwitz's army.

[7]Manikovski vol. 3 p. 88; p. 66f. for deliveries; Kondzerovski p. 6f. Barsukov: *Podgotovka* p. 100f. on organisation.

[8]N. Kozlov: *Ocherk snabzheniya* p. 107.

[9]Khmelkov: *Borba za Osowiec* p. 61f.

[10]*Osobiye zhurnaly sovieta ministrov* (Henceforth: SM.) 1914/259 of 17th October.

[11]Langlois, *rapport* No. 2 of 10th April 1915, *Fascisule* 2 p. 9; cf. Hanbury-Williams's statement of 29th December 1914 to Buchanan in FO. 371. 2446 (Russia: War: 1914). Blair (despatch No. 73 of 4th August 1915, WO. 106. 977 appendix A) reckoned that Clergue, for the Canadian Purchasing Syndicate, had had orders for five million shells as well. For *RAOAZ:* SM. 1915/145 (27th February) and 645 (24th August); cf. D. McCormick: *Pedlar of Death* (London 1966), on Zaharoff.

[12]Hanbury-Williams to Buchanan 1st March (and memorandum) in FO. 371. 2447; cf. 2447, Buchanan's despatch of 5th March 1915 with Knox's views; Blair also defended

Vickers, though he disliked them (Nos. 70, 15th March 1915, WO. 106.994 and 68, of 23rd February 1915, WO. 106.992). Clerk's minute appears on Buchanan's despatch of 5th March, and Langlois (*rapport* No. 2) was also highly critical of Vickers. A good Russian view is Sidorov's 'Otnosheniya Rossii s soyuznikami i inostran. postavshchik-ami' in *Istoricheskiye Zapiski* No. 15 (1945) pp. 128–79.

[13]Manikovski vol. 1 p. 44–5 and vol. 3 *prilozheniya* 7 and 11; Sidorov: *Ek. Pol.* p. 20.

[14]Manikovski vol. 1 p. 55 and 3 p. 179; Percy's minute on Buchanan's despatch of 6th May 1915 in FO. 371.2447; cf. Ignatiev: *50 let* vol. 2 p. 119f.

[15]The most thorough investigation of the whole financial question is Sidorov's *Finan-sovoye polozheniye* (op. cit. chapter 1), and my own account owes virtually all to it.

[16]B. Bonwetsch: *Kriegsallianz und Wirtschaftsinteressen. Russland in den Wirtschaftsplänen Englands und Frankreichs 1914–1917* (Düsseldorf 1973) pp. 45–58; generally, G. Hardach: *Geschichte der Weltwirtschaft im 20. Jahrhundert 1: der Erste Weltkrieg* (dtv. 1973).

[17]D. S. Babychev: 'Deyatelnost russkogo pravitelstvennogo komiteta v Londone' in *Istoricheskiye Zapiski* No. 57 (1956) pp. 276–92, which complements Sidorov's work on 'otnosheniya'. There are some pertinent memoirs by Russians: I. Gaidun: *Utyug* (New York 1918)—the title, which means 'iron', refers to Flatiron House, the Committee's headquarters; A. Zalyubovski: *Boyevoye snabzheniye* (Belgrade, stencil, 1932 in the Hoover Library, Stanford) which in general repeats Manikovski, but with some interesting points about the activity of War-Industries-Committee representatives; V. Fedorov: *V poiskakh orudiy* (Moscow 1964) which has interesting statements about missions to Japan, and the Entente powers, but also contains much that is inaccurate (e.g. that 'Second Army had almost no artillery').

[18]Langlois: *rapport* No. 2 fasc. 4 p. 4; Ignatiev vol. 2 p. 202 and Blair No. 65 of 23rd January 1915, WO. 106.989 cf. FO. 371.2447, Wyldbore-Smith's comment on Han-bury-Williams' memorandum of 27th February.

[19]A. Knox: *With the Russian Army* (2 vols. London 1921); Sidorov: *Ek. pol.* p. 246ff. is a thorough investigation; Babychev p. 280f.; Manikovski vol. 3 p. 183; Sukhomlinov: *Dnevnik* pp. 232 (7th May 1915); *Mezhdunarodniye otnosheniya v epokhu imperializma* series 3 vol. 7/1 p. 30ff. (January to March 1915, on supply); Sidorov: 'krizis vooru-zheniya' in *Istoricheski zhurnal* 1944/10–11 pp. 33–57. Overall, Russian officials found that foreigners charged much more for shell than they were used to paying. Clergue offered it at $17 each, the Bethlehem Steel Company at $22. For similar instances of foreign profiteering, Mayevski pp. 50, 67, 128.

[20]v. below, chapter 9.

[21]The most substantial work on this conference is Sidorov's—*Fin. pol.* p. 240ff. and *Ek. pol.* p. 310ff. but cf. V. Yemets: 'Petrogradskaya konferentsiya' in *Istoricheskiye Zspiski* No. 83. FO. 371.2095 contains Buchanan's view (Russia: War: 1917) esp. Locker-Lampson's remarks to him of 19th March. There are a number of English comments. The delegates were appalled at Russian inability to manage committees, and at the same time felt that the great round of banquets etc. was designed to close their eyes both to the confusions of the conference and the signs of revolution outside it:– S. Hoare: *The Fourth Seal* (London 1930); A. M. Gollin: *Proconsul in Politics* (London 1964); C. E. Callwell: *Henry Wilson* (2 vols. London 1927); R. Bruce Lockhart: *Diary of a Secret Agent* (London 1930); D. Lloyd George: *War Memoirs* (1938 ed. vol. 1 p. 928ff.); *History of the Ministry of Munition* vol. 10 part 3 (1922) and vol. II part 4 (1921) discusses, very thinly, the question of British supply.

[22]Zalyubovski p. 25.

NOTES 319

23My account of this problem owes most to reports of British and French observers. In print, there is not much—a few remarks in the British official *History of the Great War* vol. 5 (1931) by H. Newbolt, Sidorov: 'Zhelezno-dorozhny krizis' pp. 32f, Ushakov *op. cit.* p. 40f. The most thorough investigation is Langlois's in *rapport* No. 6, of 16th June 1916, appendix 2, 'Voie ferrée et traînage vers l'extrème Nord', and there are other good French reports in Carton 77 (v. note on sources)—nos. 8560, by Du Castel, 7961 by Lavergne and a further unnumbered study ('Possibilités de transport...') between nos. 10794 and 11106 which appears to be signed 'Guibert'. On the British side, Blair's despatches are the fullest: Nos. 71–74 (17th July to 7th August) WO. 106.995–998 incl. and 78 (7th September) WO. 106.1001 cover the attempts in 1915 to set up a railway to Murmansk, by an English company, Paulings, which was alleged to have got the contract because its chairman was a brother of the English commander-in-chief (the chairman's name was Lord Ffrench, not an easy transliteration). Nos. 90 (10th January 1916) and 91 (16th January)—WO. 106.1012–3 cover Archangel and the sledge-routes, with the report of Major Hallward; cf. No. 95 of 30th March 1916 (WO. 106. 1012). My source for the reaction of the Council of Ministers is SM.—1914/161 10th September opened the discussion, absurdly, with a suggestion that Archangel might be used as a port for export of grain. The subject came up again in 1914 Nos. 259 and 269 (October), 326 (November), 424 (December) and 1915 Nos. 9 (January), 88 (February)— when the picking-around momentarily gave way to visions of a new Ob–White Sea railway system—290 (April), 558 (July), 658 (August), 672 (September), 785/828 and 839 (October), 1076 (December).

24Sidorov: 'otnosheniya' states that whereas 22·5 million roubles' worth of machinery were imported in 1914–15, it rose to 95 million in 1915–16, measured in gold roubles.

25SM. 1914/No. 56 of 19th July.

26Sidorov: *Ek. pol.* p. 36ff.

27Sidorov: 'Stroitelstvo kaz. voyen. zavodov' p. 161 and Mayevski p. 69.

28ed. Frantz: *Russland auf dem Weg* (Polivanov section) p. 263

29Manikovski: vol. 3 p. 195 cf. Barsukov: *Russkaya artilleriya* vol. 1.

30Manikovski: vol. 1 p. 18, 88 and vol. 3 p. 192.

31Pogrebinski: *Monopol. kapitalizm v Rossii* (Moscow 1958) p. 63.

32SM. 1915/No. 294 of 21st April.

33K. N. Tarnovski: *Formirovaniye gos. monopol. kapit. v Rossii* (Moscow 1958) p. 40ff. and cf. below, chapter 9.

34*Istoriya organizatsii upolnomochennogo GAU ... S. N. Vankova* (Moscow 1918) p. 3ff; cf. Langlois's *rapport* No. 8 (19th March 1917) Note 4 on 'La mission Pyot'.

35Langlois: *rapport* No. 3 (June 1915) passim.

36Mayevski: p. 135 cf. V. Ipatiev: *Life of a Chemist* (Stanford 1946)

37Generally, Hardach *op. cit.* and cf. K. D. Schwarz: *Weltkrieg und Revolution in Nürnberg* (Stuttgart 1971) p. 119.

CHAPTER EIGHT

1For an excellent bibliography of these collections, v. G.Wettig: 'Die Rolle der russischen Armee im revolutionären Machtkampf 1917', *Forschungen zur osteuropäischen Geschichte* (Berlin 1967) No. 12. The best collection is probably A. L. Sidorov (ed.): *Revolyutsionnoe dvizheniye v armii* (Moscow 1967) but many of its items stem from September 1915, an exceptionally bad month. O. N. Chaadayeva: *Armiya* (Moscow 1935); *Tsarskaya armiya* (Kazan 1932); soldiers' letters in *Krasny Arkhiv* 17 (1926) pp. 36–54, 4 (1923) pp. 17–24 and 64 (1934) pp. 73–84 and D. Menshchinski: *Revolyutsionnoye dvizheniye* (2 vols. Moscow 1924) all deserve mention.

[2]Questions of conscription etc. are examined in chapter 10. Russian military figures are a jungle, because the *Glavny Shtab* virtually broke down under the strain. Some figures were given in the collection *Rossiya v mirovoy voyne* (Ts. Stat. Up. Moscow 1925) but they are widely regarded as unreliable. Losses are discussed in Kersnovski vol. 4 p. 870f., N. Ya. Kakurin (ed.) *Razlozheniye armii v 1917 g.* (Moscow 1926), and variously in Sidorov (ed.) *Pervaya mirovaya voyna* (Moscow 1968); I take my sickness-figures from *Voyenno-istoricheski sbornik* (Moscow) I p. 175f. while prisoners are best read from the Central Powers' side—v. *Oesterreich-Ungarns letzter Krieg* vol. 2 p. 729, note. By May 1916, there were about fifty men to every officer (in VIII Army, for instance, 225,000 men to 4,750 officers) and this was a great improvement on figures for 1915. Important details can be taken from the record of the Cholm conference: O. D. 'Postanovleniye soveshchaniya v Kholme 4. iyunya 1915 g.' and *prilozheniye* 6 of A. M. Zayonchkovski: *Manevrenni period* pp. 404ff. while P. N. Simanski: *Razvitiye russkoy voyennoy sily* (Moscow 1938) gives a good overall picture.

[3]Teodor Shanin: *The Awkward Class* (Oxford 1972); cf. H. Gauer: *Vom Bauerntum, Bürgertum und Arbeitertum in der Armee* (Heidelberg 1936) p. 48f. The German army recruited 86% of its permanent personnel from towns of less than 20,000 inhabitants, and from the countryside; cf. P. A. Zayonchkovski: *Samoderzhaviye i armiya* p. 122f.

[4]Lemke pp. 178, 518–9; Kochubey: *Vooruzhennaya Rossiya* p. 13; N. Yevseyev: *Sventsyanski proryv* (Moscow 1938) p. 29; I. Patronov: 'Staraya i novaya distsiplina' in *Voyenni sbornik* (Belgrade) II (1922) pp. 221–43; Blair's despatch No. 75 of 15th August 1915, WO. 106–999.

[5]Lemke p. 222.

[6]Yevseyev pp. 30–2; Lemke p. 180ff.; Chaadayeva p. 22–3; *Sbornik dokumentov mirovoy voyni na russkom fronte. Nastupleniye yugozapadnogo fronta v. 1916 g.* by RKKA. for General Staff use: No. 16 p. 25 (of May 1916). henceforth: *Sbornik* (Nastupleniye).

[7]F. Glingenbrunner: 'Intendanzdienst' *Ergänzungsheft* 8 (1933) of the Austro-Hungarian official history, p. 6.

[8]Chaadayeva p. 18, 44f.; Lemke p. 324f., 448, 515f.

[9]Chaadayeva pp. 28–46; Svechin (ed.) 'Dnevnik Shtukaturova' in *voyenno-istoricheski sbornik* 1 and 2; Lemke pp. 721, 800.

[10]The campaign of 1915 is the least-covered part of the war from the Russian side. Neznamov (ed.) *Strategicheski ocherk voyni* parts 3 and 4 (1922–3) and A. M. Zayonchkovski: *Manevrenni period* (Moscow 1929) become essential, although they are thin. The O.D. documents become an original source of much value, together with monographs in the journals. G. Korolkov: *Srazheniye pod Szawli* (Moscow 1926), *Nesbyvshiyesya kanny* (1927) and *Przasnysz-skoye srazheniye* (1928) are essential; cf. *Flot v mirovoy voyne* (1964) I passim. for the navy's rôle and *Reichsarchiv: Der Weltkrieg* vols. 7 and 8, *Oesterreich-Ungarns letzter Krieg* vol. 2 for the Central Powers's side. Important additions to the record come from the 'Dnevnik' of F. F. Palitsyn, attached to *Stavka* and Alexeyev at this time, in *Voyenni sbornik* (Belgrade) vols. 3, 4 and 5 (1923–5), and from 'Stavka i ministerstvo inostrannykh del' in *Krasny Arkhiv* 27 (1928) pp. 3–57.

[11]Barsukov: *Russkaya artilleriya* table 6 p. 216; Schwarz: *Ivangorod* p. 126 and Gerasimov: *Probuzhdeniye* p. 30 (note); cf. Laguiche—GQG. in EMA Carton 77 (unnumbered despatch, of 4th August 1915—the first that Joffre knew of Russian plans to retreat).

[12]Palitsyn 3, pp. 180–1 and 4, 272–3; O.D. to Alexeyev 23rd May and letter to him 12th June; Schwarz p. 118.

[13]K. H. Janssen: *Der Kanzler und der General* (1967) supplies the best German account of these difficulties.

[14]Blair, despatch No. 73, WO. 106–997.

[15]Ratzenhofer: 'Die Auswertung' in *Ergänzungsheft* No. 6 (1933) p. 16.

[16]Korolkov: *Przasnysz-skoye srazheniye* and Reichsarchiv: *Der Weltkrieg* vol. 8 p. 123ff.

[17]Tactics: Palitsyn 5, 308–10 and Lemke p. 299ff.

[18]O.D. to Alexeyev 6th July; Palitsyn 5, 311f. cf. Schwarz p. 140 and 'oborona reki' in *Voyennoye delo* (Moscow 1918) Nos. 16 and 17.

[19]Lemke p. 214; Palitsyn 4, 277; ib. 5, 314; 'B' (probably Borisov) 'Padeniye kr. Novo-georgievsk' in *Voyennoye delo* 1918 No. 12;

[20]Sveshnikov: *Osowiec* (Petrograd 1917).

[21]M. Cherniavski (ed.) *Prologue to Revolution* (minutes of the Russian council of Ministers 1914–15) (N.J. 1967) p. 120ff.

[22]Blair despatch No. 73 (4th August 1915) WO. 106–997; Lemke p. 264, Kondzerovski p. 63f, Palitsyn 5, 308ff.

[23]Yevseyev p. 260 shows that these armies fell to 370,000 men in all—a lack of 600,000.

[24]Valentinov p. 47–8.

[25]O.D. 'Soveshchaniye v Siedlce 15–90 iyulya' (minutes) and cf. to Alexeyev, 18th and 23rd July.

[26]Lemke pp. 223–52 uses the text of Grigoriev's trial; cf. Cherniavski (ed.) p. 75, Khmel-kov *Osowiec* p. 88 for technical details, Palitsyn 4, 276 and ed. Frantz: *Russland auf dem Weg* 'Tagebuch des Grossfürsten Andrej Wladimirowitsch' pp. 184–5.

[27]Cherniavski (ed.) pp. 134–145. The Moscow City Council passed a resolution in the Grand Duke's favour.

[28]Menchukov: *Boy pod Logishinym* (Moscow 1938) p. 62.

[29]Gutor: *Frontalny udar pekhotnoy diviziyey* (Moscow 1936) covers the Lopuszno action which showed how much greater were German difficulties.

[30]Lemke p. 56ff. is a brilliant description of the beginnings of the Sventsiany battle. Yevseyev's is the most thorough account.

[31]Menchukov *op. cit.* covers this action. The Russian 31. Corps had 12,000 men with 91 guns, each with 150 rounds. It took 734 men at Logiszyn.

[32]*Oesterreich-Ungarns letzter Krieg* vol. 3 p. 1–170 and Zayonchkovski: *Manevrenny period* p. 345ff. cover the Galician—Volhynian side.

[33]Lemke p. 30ff. on conditions, cf. Kondzerovski p. 70f, Lemke pp. 170, 188, 140 (on Alexeyev) etc. and Palitsyn *Dnevnik* 3, 160, 180f. and (ed.) Franz, *Tagebuch des Gross-fürsten Andrej Wladimirowitsch* pp. 117, 166–7.

CHAPTER NINE

[1]SM. 1915/144 of 27th February.

[2]V. S. Dyakin: *Burzhuaziya i tsarizm v gody pervoy mirovoy voyni* (Moscow 1967) is an essential modern source; cf. K. N. Tarnovski: *Formirovaniye gos. monopol. kapitala v Rossii* (Moscow 1957) p. 40; A. L. Sidorov: *Istoricheskiye predposylki Vel. Okt. Sots. Revolyutsii* (Moscow 1970); in English, particularly G. Katkov: *February 1917* (London 1967) and Bernard Pares: *The Fall of the Russian Monarchy* (London 1939), which is perhaps more important as a document of the liberals' view than as a history-book.

[3]S.M. 1915/485 of 16th and 19th June shows issue of subsidies to State factories in the Urals, and cf. Sidorov's article: 'Stroitelstvo kazennykh voyennykh zavodov' in *Istoricheskiye Zapiski* 54 (1955) p. 156–69.

[4]S.M. 1915/864 of 3rd November shows Polivanov's figures; cf. *Istoriya Organizatsii* ... *Vankova* pp. 6–7; Sidorov: *Ek. Pol.* p. 36f.

[5]G. Hardach: *Der Erste Weltkrieg* pp. 120ff. for useful comparisons.

[6]S. A. Zalesski: 'Mobilizatsiya gornozavodskoy promyshlennosti na Urale' in *Istoricheskiye Zapiski* 65 (1959) pp. 80—118 esp. p. 105.

[7]'Osobaya rasporyaditelnaya komissiya': Sidorov: *Ek. Pol.* p. 36f.

[8]K. F. Shatsillo: 'Delo Polkovnika Myasoyedova' in *Voprosi Istorii* 1967/4; A. Tarsaidze: *Chetyre mifa* (New York 1969); B. Buchinski in *Voyennaya Byl* (Paris) 1964 No. 67; Lemke p. 190; Katkov, passim.

[9]For the connection of industrialists' and politicians' agitation: Sidorov: *Ek. Pol.* is a basic account, and Tarnovski pp. 43f. is acute. T. D. Krupina: 'Politicheski krizis 1915 goda i Osoboye Soveshchaniye po Oborone' in *Istoricheskiye Zapiski* 83 (1969) pp. 58–75 is a very thorough survey, and Dyakin pp. 218f. adds some points. Of contemporary records, Sukhomlinov's 'Dnevnik' I p. 232 and *Padeniye tsarskogo rezhima* vol. 5 pp. 248ff. contain (vast) speeches by Guchkov and Rodzyanko. Goremykin's reaction—to make Sukhomlinov's trial a 'mise-en-scène' under an occtogenarian general—appears in ed. Cherniavski: *Prologue* pp. 29–31.

[10]*RAOAZ*: SM. 1915/145 of 22nd February and 645 of 24th August; Krupina pp. 60ff; Manikovski vol. 3 p. 160f; Sidorov(ed.): *Ob osobennostyakh imperializma v Rossii* (Moscow 1963) contains a useful work by Shatsillo pp. 215–33 'Iz istorii politiki tsarskogo pravitelstva' cf. his contribution on ship-building in a further collection edited by Sidorov: *Pervaya mirovaya voyna* (Moscow 1968) pp. 192–210; Sidorov: *Ek. Pol.* pp. 55ff. 126. There is not much on this in M. Mitelman and others: *Istoriya Putilovskogo Zavoda* (3 vols. Moscow 1939).

[11]On these problems generally, the latest work is René Girault: *Emprunts russes et investissements français en Russie* (Paris 1973), with a useful bibiliography. On the inter-connections, v. a brilliant essay by Sidorov: 'V. I. Lenin o russkom voyenno-feodalnom imperializme' in his *Ob osobennostyakh* pp. 11–52.

[12]Sidorov: *Ek. Pol.* p. 345; I. Mayevski: *Ekonomika* pp. 101f.; Dyakin p. 91f.

[13]Two articles by A. P. Pogrebinski: 'K istorii soyuzov zemstv i gor' and 'Voyenno-promyshlenniye komitety' in *Istoricheskiye Zapiski* Nos. 12 and 11 (1941) pp. 39–60 and 161–200. Tarnovski contests some of the views expressed here—v. his work on 'Komitet metallov' in *Istoricheskiye Zapiski* 56 (1957) pp. 80–143. Sidorov, by implication (*Ek. Pol.* pp. 191ff.) shares Pogrebinski's view.

[14]*Istoriya Organizatsii* ... *Vankova* pp. 160ff; but p. 156f. explains that in Kiev the local committee worked well for Vankov. It built its own factory in Konotop for 6″ bombs, controlled 56 factories overall and was master-minded by Tereshchenko, who arranged for the committee's factories to make their own plant.

[15]V. N. Ipatieff: *The Life of a Chemist* (Stanford 1946) p. 209. This is about the only work in English or French that discusses the technical side of the war-economy in detail.

[16]Dyakin pp. 92, 126, 174–5, 183 and 190 is particularly revealing. In the end, the government could manoeuvre to split the industrial opposition, in which context the fall of Polivanov, the rise of Stürmer and, in the end, of Protopopov should apparently be read. In 1916, the Congress of Representatives of Industry (Soviet Syezdov) formally cut its links with the central war-industries committee.

NOTES 323

[17]Mayevski p. 291; Zalyubovski p. 16 and Blair's despatch No. 94 of 4th March 1916 (WO. 106/1016) discuss committee-representatives in New York (Astrov) and London (Baehr), who made a nuisance of themselves; SM. 1915/199 (October) shows dealings in foreign exchange; Bruce Lockhart's despatches to Buchanan of 5th January and 14th February 1917 (FO. 371/2995) for a favourable view of the committees: Sidorov: *Ek. Pol.* pp. 201–2 and 288–9 for their rôle in foreign trade.

[18]R. Claus: *Die Kriegswirtschaft Russlands* (Bonn 1922) p. 72. Claus, who served with the German *Wirtschaftsstab* in exploited Russia in 1918, knew the Russian economy better than any other foreign observer. His work is based on close study of valuable contemporary accounts, such as those of Prokopovitch, Katzenellenbaum, Grinevetski, Dementiev; and he was shown a number of government studies, including the memoranda of Litvinov-Falinski.

[19]G. I. Shigalin: *Voyennaya ekonomiya v pervuyu mirovuyu voynu* (Moscow 1956) p. 143f. On the Special Councils: Yeroshkin p. 300ff. for their institutional position; S. V. Voronkova: 'Obzor materialov Osobogo Soveshchaniya po Oborone' in *Istorya SSSR*. 1971/3; Sidorov: *Ek. Pol.* p. 105ff; Tarnovski: *Formirovaniye* p. 90ff,; Manikovski: vol. 3 passim.; interesting—and highly critical—reports from British Vice-Consuls who observed the plenipotentiaries on the spot: eg. Blakey (Kharkov) to Picton Bagge (Odessa) 23rd December 1916 in FO. 371/2995 to the effect that the plenipotentiary assembled 'an enormous mass of statistical data' but was 'incapable of being any actual assistance'. Both Sidorov and Tarnovski, the best-qualified commentators, none the less take a positive view of the system.

[20]Tarnovski pp. 57, 88, 109f.—the essential work; on other questions: V. Ya. Laverychev: 'O gosudarstvennoy regulirovanii ekonomiki' in Sidorov (ed.) *Pervaya mirovaya voyna* pp. 50–62 on textiles; M. Ya. Gefter: 'Toplivo-neftyanoy golod' in *Istoricheskiye Zapiski* 83 (1969) pp. 76–122; P. B. Volobuyev: 'Produgol' in Ibid. 57 (1957) pp. 107–44; Pogrebinski: 'Prodameta' in *Voprosi Istorii* 1958/10; Zalesski p. 106f.

[21]Tarnovski: *Formirovaniye* pp. 72, 88, 114f.

[22]G. Strumilin: *Izbranniye proizvedeniya* (5 vols. Moscow 1963f.) vol. 1 ('Statistika i ekonomiya'); cf. I. F. Gindin: 'Moskovskiye banki in *Istoricheskiye Zapiski* 58 (1957) pp. 38–106; Sidorov: *Ek. Pol.* p. 404f and *Fin. Pol.* p. 178ff.; L. Ya. Shepelev: *Aktsionerniye kompanii v Rossii* (Leningrad 1973) pp. 294–337; T. M. Kitanina: *Voyenno-inflyatsionniye kontserny* (Stakheyev) p. 95 shows how profits on cotton went to industrial investment.

[23]Strumilin op. cit. p. 186.

[24]Tarnovski p. 101.

[25]Shepelev: 'Fondovaya birzha' in *Istoricheskiye Zapiski* 84 (1969) pp. 121–63, esp. p. 127.

[26]Ibid. p. 162–3; cf. Strumilin op. cit. p. 360f.

[27]Ibid. pp. 349–51; Sidorov: *Ek. Pol.* p. 343.

[28]Ibid. p. 350.

[29]N. Ya. Vorobiev: *Vestnik Statistiki* vol. 14 (1923). The share taken by 'defence' rose, by 1916, to almost four-fifths of this output. It is curious that, none the less, the quantity, as distinct from the share, of this output which went to non-defence areas remained the same as before the war.

[30]Sidorov: Ek. Pol. p. 345; cf. Shigalin p. 144, using figures from the 1918 survey which, as Sidorov suggests, may well have under-stated output.

[31]Sidorov: *Ek. Pol.* p. 364.

[32]Mayevski p. 109 and 251–5.

[33]Litvinov-Falinski's memorandum: *prilozheniye* 2 in Manikovski vol. 3 pp. 243–52; cf. M.–L. Lavigne: 'Le Plan de M. Rjabušinskij' in *Cahiers du Monde Russe et Soviétique* V/I (1964) pp. 90–107 cf. *Dokumenty po istorii SSSR*. VI (1959) pp. 610–40.

[34]Sidorov: *Ek. Pol.* pp. 359f.

[35]N. Kozlov: *Ocherk snabzheniya russkoy armii voyenno-tekhnicheskim imuschestvom* (Moscow 1926) pp. 35f, 57f, 95f. By June 1916, 30,000 tons of barbed wire were produced, monthly—characteristically, with too few drums to wrap it round, so that it had to move by cart. S. V. Voronkova: 'Stroitelstvo avtomobilnikh zavodov' in *Istoricheskiye Zapiski* 78 (1965) pp. 147–69 recounts progress, with much scepticism; Ipatieff none the less reveals, at length, the great progress made in chemical matters; and a highly favourable impression of the whole war-economy is given in the official *Kratky otchet o deyatelnosti voyennogo ministerstva za 1916 god* (Archive of Grand Duke Nicholas, v. Golovin-Archive in the Hoover Institution, Stanford).

[36]Sidorov: *Ek. Pol.* p. 121ff, 313–4 and 316; Barsukov: *Russkaya artilleriya* vol. 1 p. 248–9 and 280, cf. 192–5, 198, 323f; Tarnovski p. 207f.

[37]Manikovski vol. 3 p. 170ff.; Langlois *Rapport* No. 8 (March 1917) Note 4 on Pyot's work; Tarnovski pp. 53, 232; N. A. Ivanova: 'Prinuditelniye obyedinyeniya' in Sidorov (ed.): *Ob osobennostyakh* pp. 234–49; Sidorov: *Ek. Pol.* p. 117f.; and the not wholly revealing official work, *Istoriya Organizatsii ... Vankova* discuss the Vankov organisation in detail. The organisation took 144,000 tons of steel and made 18 million shells from spring 1915 onwards. The bulk of production was in Moscow and the south, but half of Vankov's fuzes came from one factory in Petrograd—the highly-efficient 'Russki Renault', with a French management and a well-knit network of sub-contractors. The rôle of private entrepreneurs in war-work is shown in Kitanina op. cit. and Ipatiev: *Rabota khimicheskoy promyshlennosti na oboronu* (Petrograd 1920) and (with L. F. Fokin) *Khimicheski komitet pri GAU* (Petrograd 1921).

[38]These details come from Manikovski vol. 3 *prilozheniye* 6; cf. pp. 204–230 passim., and vol. 1 p. 34f. for output of rifles, which in 1916 covered 80% of demand. Langlois's *Rapport* No. 8 (March 1917) p. 8off., *tableaux* 1–3, and, with less conviction, Blair's despatch No. 4 of 28th July 1916 (WO. 106/1061) give good details.

CHAPTER TEN

[1]Lemke p. 161; Manikovski vol. 1 passim; *Sbornik* (Nastupleniye) p. 33ff.

[2]P. A. Zayonchkovski: *Voyenniye reformy* p. 66f. and Sidorov: *Fin. Pol.* p. 65.

[3]A. M. Anfimov: *Russkaya derevnya v gody pervoy mirovoy voyni* (Moscow 1962) p. 198.

[4]A. V. Fedorov: 'Vsesoslovnaya voinskaya povinnost' in *Istoricheskiye Zapiski* 46 (1954) pp. 182–97. cf. P. A. Zayonchkovski: *Samoderzhaviye i armiya* p. 114ff. 48% of those mustered were exempted by reason of "family-status", another 17% on physical grounds.

[5]Figures for losses and conscription may be obtained from the following: P. N. Simanski: *Razvitiye* (1938); Kersnovski vol. 4 p. 870ff.; *Rossiya v mirovoy voyne* (1925); various articles in *Voyennoye delo*, particularly 1918 No.17 pp. 19–20 ('kolichestvo russkikh soldat-uchastnikov voyni') and 1919 No. 15–16, where losses are discussed by N. Krzhivitski. Latterly, N. M. Gavrilov and V. V. Kutuzov have discussed 'Istoshcheniye lyudskikh rezervov russkoy armii v 1917 godu' in (ed.) A. L. Sidorov: *Pervaya mirovaya voyna* (Moscow 1968) pp. 145–67. Cf. their article on casualties in *Istoriya SSSR* 1964/2. A highly useful summary of the whole problem as to figures—where the ones used by previous writers come under severely damaging attack—is D. V. Verzhkhovski and

V. F. Lyakhov: 'Nekotoriye tsifry' in *Voyenno-istoricheski zhurnal* 1964/7. I have also used (a) a source of some value in the Golovin-Archive at the Hoover Institution, the *Kratky otchet o deyatelnosti voyennogo ministerstva za 1916* (where losses for 1916 are reckoned at 2,800,000 men, and for the whole war up till 1917 at 6,500,000); (b) despatches of Blair's, particularly No. 8 of 14th August 1916 (WO. 106.1014) where he reviewed possibilities of exploiting the *opolcheniye*, and his communication to Buchanan, sent on by Buchanan on 17th February 1915, in FO. 371.2447; (c) minutes of the Council of Ministers, where conscription was regularly discussed—SM. 1914 No. 398 (19th and 23rd December, with *ukaz* of 24th December calling up the class of 1915) and 1915 Nos. 50 (class of 1916, 26th January) 514 (class of 1917, 30th June) and 849 (class of 1918, 27th October). Educational deferments were discussed in 1914 No. 196 and 1915 Nos. 196, 443 and 913.

[6]C. J. Smith: *The Russian Struggle for Power* (New York 1952) and particularly A. Dallin and M. Abrash (ed.): *Russian Secret Diplomacy* (New York 1962).

[7]W. Winkler: *Die Einkommensverschiebungen in Oesterreich* (Vienna 1930) p. 122f.

[8]F. Fischer: *Griff nach der Weltmacht* (1967 ed. Düsseldorf) p. 482. A thorough, though inconclusive, review of the whole problem is J. Kocka: *Klassengesellschaft im Krieg* (Göttingen 1973).

[9]N. Valentinov: *Snosheniya* p. 80f. and his article: 'Russkiye voyska vo Frantsii i Salonikakh' in *Voyenno-istoricheski sbornik* (Moscow) No. 4 (1921) pp. 3–22 cf. Yu. A. Pisarev: 'Russkiye voyska na salonikskom fronte' in *Istoricheskiye Zapiski* 79 pp. 109–38. It was French politicians, rather than soldiers, who wanted to have Russian forces in France. There are some documents in *Sbornik* (Nastupleniye) on inter-allied relations at this time (Alexeyev: 'Worse than they now are, they cannot get': No. 1 p. 33ff. cf. Zhilinski's comment that 'Here there are no secrets, and you have to be thankful if things don't reach the newspaper-headlines').

[10]*Flot v mirovoy voyne* vol 2, passim; Lemke p. 192.

[11]Lemke p. 284–5.

[12]Lemke pp. 299ff. extensively covers this battle; there is not much in *Strategicheski ocherk* V (ed. Klembovski) and VI (ed. Zayonchkovski), but they have at least overall strategic material. There is a useful article on it by 'byvshi nashtayuz' (=Klembovski) in *Voyennoye delo* 1919/4 p. 192ff. and cf. *Oesterreich-Ungarns letzter Krieg* vol. 4, pp. 3–30.

[13]Lemke p. 509f., 644; Kersnovski vol. 4 pp. 770, 880.

[14]Laguiche's report of 6th June 1916, No. 8326, Carton 77 EMA.

[15]Neznamov: 'Dva proryva' in *Voyenno-istoricheski sbornik* 1921/4 pp. 105–31, cf. his work in *Voyennoye delo* 1918 Nos. 8 and 9, covering similar details.

[16]B. V. Kirey: *Artilleriya ataki i oborony* (ed. Burov, Moscow 1926) pp. 6f.

[17]On this subject, esp. Lemke pp. 152, 329, 666, 777; Blair's despatch No. 86 of 6th December 1915, WO. 106.1008 p. 1–3; Langlois's *rapports*, especially Nos. 6 and 7 (June and October 1916); Frantz: *Russland auf dem Weg*, especially the *Tagebuch des Grossfürsten Andrej Wladimirowitsch*, p. 141 (on Guliewicz and Bezobrazov); Kondzerovski pp. 38–9 and 53.

[18]Reichsarchiv: *Der Weltkrieg* vol. 10 pp. 424ff. covers this battle, and reckons that there were 11 infantry divisions in line, with nine in reserve, on the Russian side against five and three, respectively, on the German. The essential book on the Russian side is N. Podorozhny: *Narochskaya operatsiya* (Moscow 1938); French pressure appears in *Sbornik* (Nastupleniye) Nos. 2 and 4 of 18th and 22nd February 1916.

[19]Lemke p. 617.

[20]Ibid, pp. 685ff. quotes a long report in causes of failure, from which I take these details. Dug-outs were deliberately kept a full mile from the front.

[21]Lemke loc. cit. and Barsukov: *Russkaya artilleriya prilozheniye* 4 pp. 208–14, which is a *Stavka* document 'po povodu deystviy russkoy artillerii', showing that Pleshkov's group had 72 light and 156 medium or heavy guns, Masalski's group having 54 light and only 12 medium (48-line howitzers) of them.

[22]Lyakhov and Verzhkhovski: *Pervaya mirovaya voyna* (Moscow 1964) p. 178; cf. Alexeyev's account of the battle to Zhilinski, *Sbornik* (Nastupleniye) No. 12 of 29th April 1916.

CHAPTER ELEVEN

[1]Lemke p. 348ff. for literature on the Strypa offensive.

[2]Ibid. pp. 170, 187, 655, 685 and Rostunov: *Brusilov* p. 133.

[3]Lemke p. 636ff.; cf. Blair's despatch No. 2 of 1st June 1916 (WO. 106.1019) p. 10.

[4]Klembovski; *Strat. ocherk* vol. 5 p. 27; cf. Zayonchkovski: *Strat. ocherk* vol. 6 p. 20ff. and Rostunov p. 112. The essential work on Brusilov's offensive is RKKA: *Sbornik dokumentov mirovoy voyni na russkom fronte. Nastupleniye yugozapadnogo fronta* (Moscow 1940) which contains the documents of armies and front command for the offensive up to Baranovitchi. Beyond this, there is a considerable volume of literature, of which there is a list in the bibliography of Rostunov: *Brusilov*. Of these works, the most useful prove to be: A. Bazarevski: *Nastupatelnaya operatsiya 9. armii* (Moscow 1937); P. B. Cherkasov (ed.) *Mirovaya voyna. Lutski proryv* (Moscow 1924) which discusses the rôle of the other three armies. On the Central Powers' side, *Oesterreich-Ungarns letzter Krieg* vol. 4 and Reichsarchiv: *Der Weltkrieg* vol. 10 p. 450ff. are the main accounts. In English, there is nothing beyond a few remarks by Knox (*With the Russian Army* vol. 2 passim.) and Brusilov: *A Soldier's Notebook* (London 1929). For the meeting of commanders: *Sbornik* (Nastupleniye) Nos. 12 (Alexeyev's figures for Zhilinski, 29th April) 19–20 and 24 (Alexeyev's report to the Tsar); cf. appendices 3 and 5 of Klembovski: *Strategicheski ocherk* vol. 5.

[5]Zayonchkovski: *Strat. ocherk* vol. 6 p. 8; on methods: *Sbornik* (Nastupleniye) Nos. 29, 32, 36, 45, 48; Cherkasov p. 198ff. for XI Army; D. Nadezhny: *Boy 10. pekh. div. pod Lutskom* (Moscow 1925); A. Redkin-Rymashevski: *32. korpus* (Moscow 1926).

[6]Figures for strength: *Sbornik* (Nastupleniye) p. 19ff. and *prilozheniya* on supply and shell, cf. Cherkasov p. 16f.

[7]Zayonchkovski: *Strat. ocherk* vol. 6 p. 25.

[8]*Nachlass* Pflanzer-Baltin (B/50: *Tagebuch*, Mappe 13 for 5th June 1916) but cf. *Sbornik* (Nastupleniye) Nos. 73–4 pp. 165–9 for an exchange of 3rd May (old style) between Lechitski and Klembovski.

[9]E. v. Falkenhayn: *Die Oberste Heeresleitung* vol. 2 pp. 216f.; cf. Berndt's manuscript of 29th September 1929: 'Betrachtungen über die Schlacht von Olyka–Luck 1916' (*Kriegsarchiv*, manuscript collection) p. 8.

[10]The details following are taken from *Kriegsarchiv* documents: *Neue Feldakten, 4. Op. Armeekommando*, Fasz. 166 *Tagebücher* 10–11 (1916–17): No. 10 concerns this period, and I have quoted *Op. Nr.* 824 (14th April) p. 126, 887 (22nd April), p. 140, 888 (23rd April) pp. 141–2, 1013 (2nd May) p. 178, 1045–6 (12th and 13th May) pp. 190–1, 893 (15th May) p. 196–7, 1083 (16th May) p. 200 the *Oberkommando* order (No. 147) on p. 200, and Szúrmay's report of 2nd June on Russian desertions p. 238. The diary of 10.

Corps is also useful (4 *Tagebücher* 1916–17, of which No. 9 pp. 1094ff. and 1125–15th April and 15th May are pertinent, on losses from sickness etc.). On munitions: for IV. Army, Fasz. 154–6 and 199–200 (*Munitionsstände* 24th August 1915 to 2nd September 1916 and *Tagesrapporte der Munitionsfassungsstelle Luck*); for VII Army, 7. *Op. Armeekommando Art. Referat. Op. Sammelnummer 1200–1600.*

[11]*Nachlass* Berndt *Tagebücher* 6 and 7, especially 17th and 18th September, 4th October, 23rd December 1915 and 28th–29th February, 18th and 23rd April 1916. This diary, (*Kriegsarchiv* B/203) consists of 12 voluminous note-books, with a variety of interesting photographs and observations.

[12]Kundmann-*Tagebuch* 16th September 1915 and 23rd September 1915.

[13]Ibid. 27th May 1916; cf. Reichsarchiv: *Der Weltkrieg* X p. 451.

[14]*AOK. Op. B.* Fasz. 560 Nr. 19380 Tisza to Burián 30th December 1915 and Conrad to Tisza, 4th January 1916; A. v. Cramon: *Unser österreichisch-ungarischer Bundesgenosse* (Berlin 1921) pp. 118ff.

[15]AOK. Op. B. Fasz. 551, nos. 18076ff and 19181 of 11th December 1915, 19322 of 19th December; cf. Fasz. 560 Nr. 21317 of 6th February 1916. Conrad offered all German troops back to Falkenhayn; Falkenhayn, insultingly, refused the offer; and there was a complete breach at the turn of 1915–16.

[16]e.g. Kundmann-*Tagebuch* 2nd January, 3rd February, 4th and 21st May for quarrels over Verdun and the Trentino.

[17]*Sbornik* (Nastupleniye) Nos. 77ff. pp. 170–5.

[18]Klembovski: *Strat. ocherk* vol. 5 p. 32.

[19]*Sbornik* (Nastupleniye) No. 118ff. for the operation.

[20]Herberstein's report to the Emperor's *Militärkanzlei: AOK. OP. B.* Fasz. 450 Op. Geh. Nr. 3 of 19th June 1916.

[21]Rostunov p. 134f.

[22]Kundmann-*Tagebuch* 10th June 1916.

[23]Knox to Buchanan 24th June 1916, in FO. 371.2748 (Russia, War 1916).

[24]A. Bernhard: 'Okna' and E. Wisshaupt: '7. Armee' in the *Kriegsarchiv* manuscript collection.

[25]Minute by Macdonough (DMI) on WO. 106.1019, Blair's despatch No. 2 of 1st June 1916.

[26]Bazarevski's is the most thorough account of this: cf. M. Pitreich: *Okna* (1931) and the *Nachlass* of Pflanzer-Baltin, especially his *Tagebuch*, Mappe 13.

[27]Berhard pp. 11–16 and Wisshaupt p. 28.

[28]*Sbornik* (Nastupleniye) No. 553, p. 520.

[29]*AOK. Op. B.* Fasz. 460 Nos (Geh.) 14–15 of 25th and 29th June; the story is well-told in H. Meier-Welcker: *Seeckt* (Frankfurt 1967) cf. K. H. Janssen: *Kanzler.*

[30]Kundmann-*Tagebuch* 13th June.

[31]K. Korvin: 'Kostyukhnovka' in *Voyennoye delo* 11–12 (1919) p. 431f. and cf. Neilson's despatch of 24th October 1916 (WO. 106.1120).

[32]Klembovski pp. 48, 50–1; *Sbornik* (Nastupleniye) No. 322 p. 345 cf. No. 202 of p. 260 (Brusilov to Alexeyev, 18th and 10th June).

[33]Blair's despatch No. 3 of 8th July 1916 (WO. 106.1020).

[34]Reichsarchiv: *Der Weltkrieg* vol. 10 pp. 451f, 473–4. By 19th June, 8½ German divisions

had arrived, with two to come. Almost all were from the west or centre; Ludendorff did little, as Hoffmann recorded. (*Aufzeichnungen* ed. Nowak, Berlin 1929, vol. 2 p. 122).

[35]Kundmann-*Tagebuch* 8th June, cf. *AOK. Op. B.* Fasz. 450 Op. Geh. 2 of 19th June, and passim, in these documents, for the great confusion with reserves.

[36]Ibid. Geh. Nr. 3 (Tersztyánszky's message by Hughes apparatus of 19th June) and cf. Nos. 9 (30th June) and 19 (1st July).

[37]Kundmann-*Tagebuch* of 7th July 1916. He thought the way to Budapest was open.

[38]Kersnovski vol. 4 p. 700ff. and Zayonchkovski: *Strat. ocherk.* vol. 6 p. 60ff.

[39]Brusilov: *Notebook* pp. 259f.

[40]Blair's despatches nos. 6 and 9 of 8, 22nd August (WO. 106.1023,6); an exchange in *Voyennoye delo* 1919 Nos. 4, 9–10, 15–16 concerns 'Gvardiya na Stokhode' and supplies interesting details on the Kowel battles. Zay onchkovski: *Strat. ocherk* vol. 6 p. 44f. gives details of strength: III Army 86 batteries to 16, the Guard Army 96 to 28, each on less than ten kilometres of front: 'the battering-ram'.

CHAPTER TWELVE

[1]V. N. Vinogradov: *Ruminiya v gody pervoy mirovoy voyni* (Moscow 1969) is a convenient modern account and has a good bibliography. Older works: Kiritzesco: *La Roumanie dans la Guerre mondiale* (1935), Pétion: *Le drame roumain* (Paris 1928), Dabija: *România dîn războiul mondial* (4 v. Bucharest 1934–6) and the official two-volume work (1934–6) of the same title; some documents in Lemke pp. 839ff.

[2]Langlois: 8e *rapport* (8th March 1917) pp. 3–15 and throughout discusses the Romanian army.

[3]Vinogradov p. 229.

[4]*Oest. Ung. 1. K.* V p. 622 and Reichsarchiv: *Weltkrieg* X, p. 540.

[5]Hoffmann: *Aufzeichnungen* I, p. 165.

[6]F. Fischer: *Weltmacht* (3. ed. Düsseldorf 1964) and particularly K. H. Janssen: *Der Kanzler und der General* (Göttingen 1967) for these issues.

[7]Reichsarchiv: *Weltkrieg* X p. 523f. and *Oest. Ung. 1. K.* V p. 120f.

[8]Kersnovski vol. IV p. 800f. and A. M. Zayonchkovski: *Strategicheski ocherk voyni* (1923) vol. VI p. 57f. and V. Klembovski: *Strat. ocherk voyni* (1922) vol. V p. 94f.

[9]Hoffmann I p. 201.

[10]Kersnovski p. 800ff. and vols. V and VI of *strat. och. voyni* are the most convenient (but always inadequate) Russian accounts. Reichsarchiv X p. 540f. and *Oest. Ung. 1. K.* V 117–623 cover these battles from the other side.

[11]Kersnovski p. 844.

[12]v. his letter to Sazonov, 5th March 1916, in *Sbornik* (Nashipleniye) No. 15 p. 16f.

[13]On the military side: Zayonchkovski, *Strat. och. voyni* p. 57f. and F. I. Vasiliev: *Rumynski front* (vol. VII of *strat. och. voyni*, 1922) are the best Russian descriptions; cf. E. v. Falkenhayn: *Der Siegeszug der 9. Armee* (1924) and the Romanian works in Note 1.

[14]v. his report to Alexeyev in *Krasny Arkhiv* 58 (1934). The Dobrogea army had 124 battalions to 79 and 89 batteries to 62.

[15]v. *Flot v mirovoy voyne* (2 v. Moscow 1964) ed. Pavlovitch, vol. 2 p. 64.

[16]A. Bazarevski in *Les Alliés contre la Russie* ed. Shliapnikoff p. 210ff. for Russian diversions of strength at the Allies' request.

[17]Chaadaeva p. 19 and Pétion p. 139.

[18]v. Col. Constantini: 'La mission Berthelot' in *Revue historique de l'armée* 1967/4 and V. Fedorov: 'Russkaya voyennaya missiya v Rumynii' in *Voprosy istorii* 1947/8.

[19]V. Stupin: 'Mitavskaya operatsiya' in *voyenno–ist. sbornik* II (1919) pp. 31–93; Pukhov: *Mondzundskaya operatsiya* (Moscow 1957); *Flot v mirovoy voyne*; Reichsarchiv: XI and Kersnovski v. IV p. 840f.

CHAPTER THIRTEEN

[1]*Rabochi klass i rabocheye dvizheniye v Rossii v 1917 g.* ('Materialy', Moscow 1962) is a useful summary of this growth: v. especially A. S. Gaponenko's contribution (pp. 14–48): 'Rossiyski proletariat, ego chislennost. . .'; A. G. Rashin: *Formirovaniye rabochego klassa* (Moscow 1958); K. P. Leyberov and O. I. Shkataran: 'K voprosu o sostave petrogradskikh promyshlennikh rabochikh v 1917 g.' in *Voprosi istorii* 1967/1; K. P. Leyberov: 'O revolyutsionnikh vystupleniyakh petrogradskogo proletariata' in *Voprosi istorii* 1964/2 (with a good bibliography). The most useful survey of the interaction of economics and politics in 1917 is still P. B. Volobuyev: *Ekonomicheskaya politika Vremennogo pravitelstva* (Moscow 1962).

[2]A. M. Anfimov: *Rossiyskaya derevnya v gody pervoy mirovoy voyni* (Moscow, 1962) pp. 250, table 75 and 254 table 77 (for 44 provinces); cf. A. I. Khrashcheva: 'Krestyanstvo v voyne i revolyutsii' in *Vestnik Statistiki* 1920/Sept.–Dec. Nos. 9–12 pp. 4–47; esp. p. 29 (Tula, Tver and Penza).

[3]Sidorov: 'Zhelezno-dorozhny transport' in *Istoricheskiye Zapiski* 26 (1948) pp. 3–64, and the revised version in *Ek. Pol.* pp. 565ff. give good figures for the railway-problem generally.

[4]Sidorov: *Fin. Pol.* p. 247 and passim. Claus, *op. cit.* also reviews financial matters ably, and the work of M. N. Apostol: *Russian Public Finance* (New Haven 1932) is a convenient but often misleading account in English. The contemporary reports of G. D. Dementiev and P. L. Bark in *Krasny Arkhiv* 17 (1926) and 25 (1929) are useful mainly for the light they shed on contemporaries' failure to understand the heart of the problem, and much the same is true of P. B. Struve: *Price Control in Russia during the War* (New Haven 1932).

[5]Sidorov: *Fin. Pol.* p. 257.

[6]P. B. Volobuyev op. cit. p. 338ff.

[7]Ibid. p. 295ff. and cf. Sidorov; *Fin. Pol.* for similar discussion.

[8]J. Stamp: *Taxation during the War* (London 1932) p. 124.

[9]Ibid. p. 245.

[10]Volobuyev p. 340ff.

[11]R. Kahil: *Inflation and Economic Development in Brazil 1946–1963* (Oxford 1973), conclusion.

[12]Teodor Shanin: *The Awkward Class* (Oxford 1972) p. 10.

[13]Anfimov: *op. cit.* p. 63; cf. A. P. Minarik: 'Sistema pomeshchichego khozyaystva v Rakityanskom imenii Yusupovykh' in *Materialy po istorii selskogo khozyaystva i krestyanstva SSSR* Sb. 5 (Moscow 1962); for a rather traditional view of the agrarian revolt: Marc Ferro: 'La Révolution au village' in *Cahiers du Monde russe et soviétique* 14/1–2 (1974) pp. 33–53; army purchases: Anfimov p. 146f.

[14]Sidorov: *Ek. Pol.* p. 457 cf. Anfimov pp. 117f., 133.

[15]Anfimov p. 111.

[16]Ibid. p. 310. Kuban and Stavropol furnished 15 million poods in 1916, as against 103 million in 1915. Samara, Ufa and Orenburg together gave 22 million in 1916, as against 232 million in 1915.

[17]Anfimov p. 89 and table p. 142.

[18]T. Shanin; op. cit. passim.

[19]The census figures appear in English in Antsiferov: *Russian Agriculture during the War* (New Haven 1932), passim. They are criticized by V. S. Nemchinov: *Izbranniye proizvedeniya* (6 vols. Moscow 1967ff.) vol. 2 (1967) pp. 321ff. (sel.-khoz. statistika . . .') and vol. 4 ('Razmeshcheniye proizvoditelnikh sil') cf. Anfimov p. 119 on increases in sown land.

[20]Anfimov: table, p. 290 and cf. Sidorov: *Ek. Pol.* p. 573 for meat, butter.

[21]Quoted in Volobuyev p. 385–6.

[22]Volobuyev, table p. 464, cf. Sidorov: *Ek. Pol.* p. 488; effects generally, pp. 410–23 and particularly A. S. Gaponenko: *op. cit.* and 'Polozheniye rabochego klassa' in *Istoricheskiye Zapiski* 83 (1969) pp. 3–22.

[23]Volobuyev pp. 440ff. and cf. Struve: *op. cit.* for contemporary view of a liberal economist's; Volobuyev, Sidorov *Ek. Pol.* and Anfimov, passim, for figures.

[24]The railway-problem is discussed by Sidorov: *Ek. Pol.* pp. 545ff., which replaces his earlier article (1948). There are important figures in Strumilin: *op. cit.* vol. 3 pp. 398f. and 415. Claus *op. cit.* p. 114ff. is the only reliable account of the problem in a western language; Volobuyev p. 210 gives a figure of 15,500 for working locomotives in 1917, which is certainly more accurate than the figure, often found, of less than 10,000.

[25]The army has been subject of considerable literature, of which there is an excellent bibliography in Wettig: *Die Rolle der russischen Armee*. An important recent review of the subject is Marc Ferro: 'Le soldat russe' in *Annales ESC* 1971/1 pp. 14–39. The discovery that the Russian army did not really dissolve at all dates from: Gavrilov and Kutuzov: 'Perepis russkoy armii' in *Istoriya SSSR* 1964/2 pp. 87–91.

NOTE ON SOURCES

As general introductions to this subject, the most useful works are: Marc Ferro: *The Great War* (London 1973) and A. J. P. Taylor: *The First World War* (Paperback ed. London 1966). The best short Russian account is D. Verzhkhovski and V. Lyakhov: *Pervaya mirovaya voyna* (Moscow 1964). The problem of 1917, altogether, is discussed in all aspects by Marc Ferro: *The Russian Revolution of February 1917* (London 1972) The French and English editions, but not the American, contain a comprehensive-bibliography.

For the military side, the most convenient bibliographical work can be found, for Soviet sources, in Verzhkhovski and Lyakhov: 'Sovietskaya istoricheskaya literatura o pervoy mirovoy voyne' in *Voyenno-istoricheski zhurnal* 1964/12 pp. 86–92, which may still be supplemented by G. Khmelevski: *Mirovaya imperial. voyna . . . Sistematicheski ukazatel knizhnoy i stateynoy voyenno-istoricheskoy literaturi* (Moscow 1936) of which there is a photographic reissue by 'Oriental Research Partners, Cambridge'. A. Gering: *Materialy k bibliografii russkoy voyennoy pechati za rubezhom* (Paris, *Voyennaya byl* publications, 1968) is an essential addition for the émigré side. In western languages, M. Gunzenhauser: *Die Bibliographien zur Geschichte des Ersten Weltkrieges* (Frankfurt a. M. 1964) is extremely thorough, but has weak sections on the eastern European side. W. Lerat and A. Dumesnil (ed.): *Catalogue méthodique du fonds russe de la Bibliothèque de la Guerre* (Paris 1932) recites the works to be found in what is still the best collection for this subject in Europe, now re-named *Bibliothèque de documentation internationale contemporaine*. M. Lyons: *The Russian Imperial Army* (Stanford 1968) lists some regimental histories.

On the economic side, there is a useful bibliography of recent work in René Girault: *Emprunts russes et investissements français en Russie* (Paris 1973). The various works of A. L. Sidorov have proved essential to me throughout this book; a convenient list of them may be found in the volume of essays: *Ekonomicheskoye Polozheniye Rossii v gody pervoy mirovoy voyni* (ed. K. N. Tarnovski and others, Moscow 1973).

I have also used a number of archival sources. The Hoover Institution in Stanford, California, has some extremely valuable ones: for Russia, the minutes of the Council of Ministers (*Vysochayshe utverzhdenniye osobiye zhurnali sovieta ministrov i osobikh soveshchaniy*), the *Osnovniye direktivi i direktivniye ukazaniya Verkhovnogo Glavnokomand-uyushchego—Stavka* orders and conference minutes for 1914–15– and the *Kratky otchet o deyatelnosti Voyennogo Ministerstva za 1916 god.* The 'Golovin Archive' also contains numerous items of lesser value, but none the less of interest. The German archives have survived only very limitedly: v. *Militärgeschichtliche Mitteilungen* 1968/2 pp. 135–44 and R. Studanski: 'Die Bestände des deutschen Militärarchivs' in: *Zeitschrift für Militärgeschichte* Jg. 4 1965, which replace earlier articles. The finest collection of archives of the war still existing in Europe is probably the Vienna *Kriegsarchiv*, of which I have made extensive use, as indicated in the footnotes. British archives, in the Public Record Office, both Foreign Office and War Office, may be used with profit. The Index volume 178A shows the various military attachés' reports: those of Blair (985–1037) and Neilson (1119–1126) are the most valuable. Knox's were almost all printed in his *With the Russian Army*. The French observers were more reliable, on the whole, and the *Ministère de la Guerre: Archives historiques* (Château de Vincennes) 'Campagne contre l'Allemagne 1914–1918' Cartons 77–81 contain their reports. The essential ones here—and a source worth publishing—are the eight *Rapports du Colonel Langlois*, in Carton 79; the military attachés' reports in Carton 77 also contain important material.

Index

Index